Society Online

To the people who have given us a great context:
Alexandra, Elaine, Jodi, L. Z., and Ross

Society Online

The Internet in Context

Edited by

Philip N. Howard
University of Washington

Steve Jones
University of Illinois at Chicago

SAGE Publications
International Educational and Professional Publisher
Thousand Oaks ■ London ■ New Delhi

For information:

Sage Publications, Inc.
2455 Teller Road
Thousand Oaks, California 91320
E-mail: order@sagepub.com

Sage Publications Ltd.
6 Bonhill Street
London EC2A 4PU
United Kingdom

Sage Publications India Pvt. Ltd.
B-42, Panchsheel Enclave
Post Box 4109
New Delhi 110 017 India

Printed in the United States of America

Library of Congress Cataloging-in-Publication Data

Society online : the internet in context / edited by Philip N. Howard and Steve Jones.
    p. cm.
Includes bibliographical references and index.
ISBN 0-7619-2707-7 (Cloth) — ISBN 0-7619-2708-5 (Paper)
   1. Information society. 2. Internet. I. Howard, Philip N. II. Jones,
Steve, 1961-
HM851.S655 2004
303.48′33—dc21

                          2003008611

Printed on acid-free paper

03   04   05   06   07   08   09   10   9   8   7   6   5   4   3   2   1

Acquiring Editor:	Margaret H. Seawell
Editorial Assistant:	Alicia Carter
Production Editor:	Claudia A. Hoffman
Typesetter:	C&M Digitals (P) Ltd.
Copy Editor:	D. J. Peck
Indexer:	Molly Hall
Cover Designer:	Edgar Abarca

Contents

Acknowledgments

This book is the result of intense collaboration across the social sciences, and we are proud to have been humble nodes in an unusually creative network of sociologists, economists, political scientists, psychologists, historians, and legal, management, and communication scholars. Whether or not technology itself can cause collaborative constructive interaction, the contributors to this volume study technology with a collaborative constructive instinct.

The team at the Pew Internet and American Life Project, particularly Harrison "Lee" Rainie and Amanda Lenhart, helped to feed our research instinct with raw data and intelligent interpretation. Margaret Seawell and her colleagues at Sage Publications helped to keep us on track, on topic, and on time, for which we are very grateful.

Even though this volume is about society online, there is nothing about pornography in this collection. Quite deliberately, a couple of our authors chose to refer to a fake Web site—teensite.com—as a pseudonym for a fictional company they were analyzing. Unfortunately, a fellow who works as a real estate agent by day let us know that he believes he has copyright and trademarks for some business that will be using this URL shortly. Despite the legal precedents of academic "fair use," our contributors agreed to change their pseudonym. This volume still has nothing about pornography in it, and we wish that individual success with his venture.

Philip Howard thanks Eszter Hargittai, Alexis Cabrera, Tema Milstein, Christian Sandvig, David Silver, Jennifer Stromer-Galley, and Francisco de Zarate for the crucial support they gave him in this editing project. He gratefully acknowledges a fellowship with the Pew Internet and American Life Project during its first funding term, a fellowship that enabled him to play with numbers. Howard also acknowledges being too deeply embedded in cafés and libraries such as the following: Tryst in Washington, D.C., where he failed to look cool; Dos

Gringos in Adams Morgan, with a great view of a crazy street and where "Blelvis" (the black Elvis) would serenade him home after a long workday; Panini Panini in Roger's Park, a plain late night café with the best machiatto in Chicago; Ennui, where the friendly Kat badgered him about his Burningman pictures until he finally brought them in; Unicorn in Evanston, where he could actually do a little work; the Bourgeois Pig in Lincoln Park, where he was allowed to sleep; Intelligensia, where good coffee and Dave Grazian could often be found; and the unbeatable Future's on Bloor Street in Toronto. The Ryerson Library in the Art Institute of Chicago was a gloriously calm environment for real editing. Northwestern University should be deeply ashamed for reneging on its membership association with the library. Sonny's, in a hidden corner of the building next door, served lousy coffee in Styrofoam cups, but the ginger chicken certainly was a great staple lunch once a week for a year. Howard's real home context, with Alexandra, Elaine, and Ross, is now stretched across several time zones but is still a loving source of support. Aside from cafés and libraries, the best place to spend a summer editing a book is on a Spanish beach.

Steve Jones thanks the many students and colleagues at the University of Illinois at Chicago, particularly those in the Department of Communication, the Great Cities Institute, and the Electronic Visualization Lab, with whom and from whom he always learns much about media (new and old) and the world. Unlike Howard, Jones is monotonous in his choice of cafés (monocafeistic, one might even say), and he thanks Sun and Nick at Café Express on Main for sticking with it despite Star*ucks moving in across the street. He also thanks L. Z. and looks forward to many years together.

The contributors to this book deserve special thanks. They made our job as editors a pleasure, and their work and ideas were an inspiration to us.

—Philip N. Howard
Beaches of Tenerife, Spain

—Steve Jones
Office overlooking the Eisenhower Expressway, Illinois

Foreword

Harrison "Lee" Rainie
Pew Internet and American Life Project

nternet communication began with a computer crash and unmemorable twaddle. The first attempted transfer of information packets in 1969 was not launched with the same portentous thunder as was Samuel Morse's first telegraph message in 1844 ("What hath God wrought?"). Rather, Charley Kline, an engineer at the University of California, Los Angeles (UCLA), froze his computer in 1969 when he began typing "L-O-G" (on his way to "L-O-G-I-N") to start the file transfer program. Programmers fixed the glitch quickly, and the file sharing began.

E-mail did not come into being until 1971, and again there was no self-puffery in the inaugural text. Indeed, there was not even an effort to match the practical tone of Alexander Graham Bell's initial phone call in 1876 ("Mr. Watson, come here; I want you"). Instead, an engineer for a U.S. Defense Department contractor named Ray Tomlinson sent a test message from one computer to another that was sitting less than 5 feet away. He thinks the text was probably "QWERTYUIOP," although he cannot remember for certain. It was a milestone moment that was not self-evident. Tomlinson did not think much of his lovely little hack that allowed people using computers at remote sites to write electronic notes to each other. Indeed, the one thing for which Tomlinson is remembered is that he picked "@" as the locator symbol in electronic addresses.

Soon enough, however, the extreme humility that characterized the dawn of computer network communication was replaced by an orgy of extravagant claims about the revolutionary power of the internet. The predictions from technologists, government leaders, entrepreneurs, the business press, and investment carnival barkers were voluminous and unsparing. No aspect of people's social lives, business arrangements, workplace culture, media power, civic engagement, or learning environments would be immune from the internet's radical influence. The cultural gatekeepers were fond of asserting, "The internet changes everything."

The Pew Internet and American Life Project was born of the idea that these were testable propositions. Rebecca Rimel, president of the Pew Charitable Trusts, was struck by the fact that many of the debates about the impact of the internet were taking place without reference to data and basic social science research. She and the board of trustees of the foundation hoped that a research project could play a useful role in the disputes by providing nonpartisan facts and analysis about the social impact of people's internet use. The foundation provided generous support for a research agenda that would monitor Americans' use of the internet and focus on several aspects of internet use that were not major concerns of the many proprietary research firms that concentrated on e-commerce. Those areas of emphasis included how people's internet use affected their interactions with family, friends, and others; their involvement with various communities; their health care; their educational experiences; their civic and political lives; and their workplaces.

Much of the fruit of the Pew Internet and American Life Project's work is explored here, as are data from several other prominent research projects such as the General Social Survey (www.norc.uchicago.edu/projects/gensoc.asp), the HomeNet Study (http://homenet.hcii.cs.cmu.edu), the Survey2001 Project (http://survey2001.nationalgeographic.com), PoliticalWeb (http://politicalweb.info), and the UCLA Center for Communication Policy (www.ccp.ucla.edu). In the course of doing telephone interviews with more than 60,000 people during the past 30 months, the Pew project learned that internet use is helping Americans to share and acquire knowledge, make important health care decisions, deepen and extend their social networks, access cultural material, probe new corners of the planet, pursue their passions and hobbies, become more productive, gather up more consumer information, and entertain themselves more vividly. At the same time, we have learned that many users head in different "directions" online. Although Americans use online tools to connect to distant people and groups that share their interests, they also use those same tools to become more connected locally with the organizations and people in the places where they live. One overall message from respondents to our surveys was that the use of the internet is good for building new communities as well as for deepening existing relationships.

Of course, ties that bind can be helpful as well as harmful. For example, the same technology that helps those who suffer from rare cancers find each other and form life-enhancing support groups can just as easily be used by pedophiles to encourage each other and construct sophisticated rationales for their behavior. Not surprisingly, internet users have finessed the question of whether the internet is a good or bad thing. Their attitude can be summed up as follows: "I'm okay, they're not." Wired Americans believe that their own use of the internet benefits them and is socially enhancing, although they worry that others may be doing ugly, criminal, perverted, or self-destructive things online. Worse, wired Americans worry that all of the temptations of the virtual world can lure the impressionable—that is, everybody else—to the dark side. This is one of the many reasons why it is so hard to make policy that addresses the wide range of internet-spawned concerns. People do not want their own access to internet information and services curtailed, but they hope that *something* can be done to keep others from harming the innocent or even themselves.

To a degree, those who think in these "me or them" terms are right. It is easy to spot in the Pew Internet and American Life Project's data that context matters a great deal in the way in which people use the internet and how they feel about it. Various groups of people—by gender, age, race, income bracket, educational level, locale, or experience level—use the internet in different ways. People take to the online world the things that interest and motivate them in the offline world, so the variety and meaning of their experiences on the internet reflect that diversity. Moreover, patterns of use evolve over time. The longer people are online, the more likely they are to venture into new activities, explore new relationships, and rely on the internet to help them complete crucial tasks or make major decisions. This highlights one of the major continuing lines of research by the Pew project: Internet use and the impact of going online are highly contingent on the rationale for going online and circumstances of each cyberventure. We know that for most people, internet use enhances, extends, and supplements what they do offline. However, we still have much to learn about what internet use displaces in people's lives and what it motivates them to do.

We are delighted that some of the scholars who have written for this volume have found our work at the Pew Internet and American Life Project to be useful. We hope that they are not alone. Our data and reports are available free of charge through our Web site (www.pewinternet.org). This seems to be the least that a project like this can do to contribute to the open source spirit of the internet's most fevered partisans. We hope that others will find new insights in our data that we ourselves have missed or will feel free to challenge our interpretations of what we have seen. Maybe the collective intelligence of this network of researchers will eventually produce a reasoned and fact-buttressed judgment about the impact of a communications era that humbly began with a computer crash and a message that read as if a monkey had been banging on a keyboard.

—Harrison "Lee" Rainie
Washington, D.C.

Prologue:
The Case for
Multimethod Research

Large Sample Design
and the Study of Life Online

James Witte
Clemson University

S ocial scientists, particularly survey researchers, were slow on the uptake when it came to considering the impact of the internet on society. Once its significance crossed the academic radar screen, however, scrutiny has been intense and the debate has been loud and (at times) bitter. The discussion took on a particularly acerbic tone with Norman Nie's widely reported and cited statement (from *The New York Times* and *The Washington Post* to CNN and National Public Radio): "The internet could be the ultimate isolating technology that further reduces our participation in communities even more than television did before it" (Nie & Erbring, 2000b, p. 19). Perhaps Nie's strongest critic, sociologist Amitai Etzioni, flatly dismissed Nie's findings: "The internet, like other new technologies, changes our lives, and not all for the better. However, claims that it increases our social isolation are wholly unsupported, especially by this study" (Etzioni, 2000, p. 42). Nie and his collaborator, Lutz Erbring, began their response by referring to Etzioni as being "in the sunset of a distinguished career." Toward the end of their response, they concluded, "Professor Etzioni seems either more confused than we thought possible, or simply prepared to dispense with logic just so he can maul us coming and going, or both" (Nie & Erbring, 2000a, p. 45).

As the war of words raged, an important point was often overlooked: The study on which the debate turned was not only a study of the internet but also a study conducted using the internet. Nie and Erbring's negative assessment derived from their InterSurvey sample, a national "random sample" of 4,113 American adults in 2,689 households. Respondents were provided with free internet access and WebTV connections to participate in the survey. Their widely cited findings were based on those respondents who had internet access prior to the WebTV connection installed by InterSurvey (Nie & Erbring, 2000b). Indeed, throughout the discussion of their work, Nie and Erbring repeatedly drew on the quality of their sample as the feature that set their online research apart from others. Although the InterSurvey sample offered WebTV access to a random sample of individuals, there is no guarantee that those who actually participated in the survey constituted a random sample. As in the case of a telephone survey, a variety of unobserved selection processes may dramatically alter the random character of the sample. For example, an individual with established and regular patterns of internet use and online interaction would presumably be far less willing to adopt a new method of access than would a less committed user.

This point was amply illustrated by data from Survey2000, a Web-based convenience sample of visitors to the National Geographic Society (NGS) Web site (Witte & Howard, 2002). On the whole, this sample looked nothing like the anomic and isolated online world described by Nie and Erbring. As a group, these individuals had strong prosocial attitudes, were socially active, and were politically engaged. Because Survey2000 respondents used a variety of means to connect with the internet, it is possible to compare WebTV respondents with non-WebTV respondents within the Survey2000 group. Based on this comparison, the WebTV users in the Survey2000 sample closely resembled the inhabitants of the place Nie and Erbring described. Even controlling for gender, age, educational attainment, employment status, and household composition, significantly lower levels of social participation were found among WebTV respondents. Moreover, these differences were not small, outweighing the impact of many of the demographic control variables.

The point of this analysis is not to say that one author or pair of authors—Nie and Erbring or Etzioni—was more correct than another. Nor would one want to conclude that WebTV leads to social isolation. Indeed, it is far more plausible that a subtle selection bias came into play, leading less sociable individuals, regardless of demographics, to be WebTV users in the Survey2000 sample but also among the randomly selected individuals who were offered the WebTV as part of the InterSurvey sample. Instead, the aim here is to highlight the importance of sampling, particularly with a novel means of data collection such as a Web survey. For a number of reasons, the internet is likely to play an important role in the future of survey research. However, as survey research goes online, there are also a number of reasons to proceed with caution. This prologue begins with an overview of sampling issues particularly relevant to online surveys and studying life online. The empirical section of the prologue is organized around the 2000 General Social Survey (GSS) and Survey 2001, a follow-up study to the National Geographic's Survey 2000. After an introduction to the design, content, and data collection strategies associated with each of these surveys, the surveys are compared with an eye to several themes beginning with sample demographics. Subsequent sections consider the relationship between sampling and substantive results, specifically internet use and environmental issues.

Analysis of the Problem: Issues in Sampling

Web-based survey research represents the most recent addition to a growing repertoire of computer-assisted survey tools dating back to the early 1970s (Couper & Nicholls, 1998; Dillman, 2000). On the one hand, there are clear advantages to a Web-based approach. To begin with, as with all forms of computer-assisted survey research, a Web-based instrument allows for complicated skip patterns that tailor the survey to the respondent and eliminate redundant or irrelevant questions. Moreover, it does so with a degree of accuracy and transparency unmatched by computer-assisted telephone interviewing (Nicholls, Baker, & Martin, 1997). At the same time, computer-based systems, including Web-based surveys, may include detailed help functions to guide and assist the respondent to a degree that is not possible with paper-and-pencil, self-administered formats (Dillman, 2000; Jenkins & Dillman, 1997). Programming a Web-based survey can be costly, particularly if the instrument involves complex skip patterns or elaborate design elements. However, this cost is fixed. Unlike face-to-face or telephone surveys, increasing the sample size is not associated with added interviewer costs. As with other computer-assisted formats, a Web-based survey also eliminates the time and expense of data entry because this is performed by the respondent in the course of the survey (Baker, Bradburn, & Johnson, 1995). In addition, as with other self-administered formats, a Web-based survey potentially reduces interviewer effects and permits a degree of anonymity not found in survey modes that depend on respondent-interviewer interaction (Aquilino, 1994;

Aquilino & LoSciuto, 1990; Tourangeau & Smith, 1998; Turner, Forsyth, et al., 1998; Turner, Ku, et al., 1998). Finally, a Web-based survey may draw on the multimedia capabilities of the internet to yield instruments that collect data in an engaging and interactive manner.

On the other hand, many of these advantages are potential liabilities. Although interviewer effects may bias the data, a measure of social interaction as part of the survey process may prompt the respondent to complete the survey and to provide thoughtful and accurate data (Burton & Blair, 1991). Similarly, an engaging and interactive instrument may appear to be trivial or game-like, leading respondents to provide unreliable or incomplete data (Kiesler & Sproull, 1986). Moreover, even a well-developed "help" function might not respond as flexibly to respondent queries as would a trained interviewer. Most important, questions of sampling bias and unknown selection probabilities present real limits to inferential claims based on a Web-based survey sample.

The potential sample bias inherent in the use of the Web to collect data is generally identified as the critical methodological issue facing Web surveys. As a first reaction to a survey hosted by the NGS Web site, the reader may call to mind the famous *Literary Digest* election poll that predicted Alfred Landon's "victory" over Franklin Roosevelt in the 1936 U.S. presidential race. This poll had a sample size of more than 2 million but still came to the wrong conclusion (Dillman, 2000; Lohr, 1999). But the similarities run only skin deep. The *Literary Digest* poll made no effort to assess the representativeness of its sample, whereas Survey2001— like its predecessor, Survey2000—explicitly did so. Although one ought to be concerned about the limitations of a Web survey sample, one also should keep in mind that serious sample bias issues—whether associated with questions of coverage, questions of nonresponse, or a combination of factors—confront all forms of survey research (Witte & Howard, 2002). Little has changed since Smith (1983) reviewed various means to address nonresponse in the GSS and other surveys. Smith concluded, "There is no simple, general, accurate way of measuring nonresponse bias" (p. 402).

Methodologically, the goal of survey research is to collect data on a sample that represents a population. Randomness does not guarantee representativeness; rather, it provides the means to quantify the level of confidence with which one can say that the sample does not represent the population. Survey2001 did not yield a random sample, and we do not "know" the selection probabilities for sample members. However, this *does not mean that the survey cannot yield representative social science data*. Although we do not "know" the selection probabilities, our data allow us to "estimate" these probabilities. The survey collected data on standard demographic characteristics (e.g., gender, age, race, education), and combinations of these attributes for the sample can be compared with other data sources. The selection bias is also likely to be correlated with certain factors, such as attitudes and values toward community and culture, that cut across standard demographic variables. For this reason, a number of items used in Survey2001 were based on other studies, including the 2000 GSS and the widely used New Environmental Paradigm (NEP) instrument, that depend on traditional sampling and data collection methods. These items can also serve as external benchmarks to assess the representativeness of the sample despite its nonrandomness. Although the type of validity that one aspires to with traditional sampling methods remained beyond the reach of Survey2001, Donald Campbell's proximal similarities approach to validity suggests important ways in which data such as those collected by Survey2001 offer valuable social science information (Trochim, 2000). Although this approach uses quantitative techniques to consider differences between one's sample and the population, it ultimately relies on sociological insight rather than statistical rules to make judgments as to what one can say about the population based on the sample.[1]

Until internet access is as widespread as telephone access, survey researchers may need to use traditional survey modes to round out a Web-based sample (Schaefer & Dillman, 1998). To pursue this strategy efficiently, however, it is important to determine the characteristics of those who can be reached through Web-based methods. In cases such as Survey2001, where a sampling frame does not exist for the population, key informant sampling, targeted sampling, and snowball sampling are common techniques (Heckathorn, 1997). The Survey2001 project employed three specific strategies in an effort to address the limitations of the NGS convenience sample. First, outreach efforts invited respondents from locations other than the NGS Web site to participate in Survey2001. Banner and button graphics were distributed to hundreds of Web sites with a request to post these as links to Survey2001. Rather than directly linking to Survey2001 at http://survey2001.nationalgeographic.com/ngm, these links were set with a link such as http://survey2001.nationalgeographic.com/ngm/servlet/page1?sws= 9003, where "sws=" was set to a unique parameter for each participating site. This parameter was then captured as part of the referring link so that individual responses could be associated with the Web site that generated them.[2] Second, informal snowball sampling methods were employed. At the end of the survey, respondents were encouraged to send an e-mail invitation to three of their friends asking them to take the survey. Each of these invitations contained a link that included the anonymous survey identification number of the respondent who sent the e-mail. Third, a parallel phone survey was conducted to interview a random sample of 3,000 respondents nationwide. Although much shorter than the Web survey, these phone interviews provide a tool to assess the substantive impact of relying on Web data collection techniques.

Comparing Different Samples: Survey2001 and the 2000 GSS

DIFFERENT DESIGN, CONTENT, AND DATA COLLECTION

The Survey2001 project included two major data collection efforts: the Web survey hosted on the *National Geographic Magazine* (NGM) Web site and a parallel phone survey conducted using standard random digit dialing methods. The discussion here emphasizes the Web survey, although preliminary findings from the phone survey are discussed as well. The Survey2001 project was delivered using a database system that organized questions, possible answers, and responses in a single mySQL database. A Java servlet application managed communications between the server's database and the client's browser. This servlet not only guided the delivery and presentation of survey questions, including question layout and skip patterns, but also guided the recognition and collection of respondents' answers.

Survey2001 question content focused on several themes. Along with standard demographic items, questions addressed internet access and use, conservation attitudes and behavior, community participation, and cultural themes such as community orientation and activities, leisure time activities and preferences, reading behavior, political attitudes and participation, and belief in science and para-science. The basic Web survey instrument was designed to take 25 minutes to complete and included the demographic, internet, and conservation questions along with one randomly selected cultural theme. At the end of this basic questionnaire, respondents were thanked for their participation and asked whether they were willing to answer a set of further questions, those making up the other cultural themes. The Survey2001 telephone survey included considerably fewer questions than did the Web version, with the former emphasizing demographic characteristics, internet use and access, conservation, and musical taste. Individual items were selected to highlight similarities and differences in response patterns between the Web and telephone survey samples. Priority was given to those Web survey items that could best be adapted to a telephone survey format.

As noted previously, recruitment of Survey2001 respondents did not rely solely on the NGM Web page. Links to the survey were placed on more than 100 other Web sites, and survey respondents were encouraged to invite others to participate in the survey. Moreover, as each respondent started the survey, the referring link was captured, thereby identifying which avenue a respondent used to reach the survey. These data are summarized in Table P.1. Whereas 14,064 respondents (60.6%) linked to the survey from the NGS Web site, another 8,569 respondents (36.9%) came from the other sites that posted a link to Survey2001. Another 559 respondents (2.4%) were recruited through e-mail solicitation from other respondents. Table P.1 also indicates that these different avenues for participation drew in some respondents interested in taking the survey in languages other than English. Although the e-mail invitations to recruit other respondents were sent in all languages, this technique appeared to be particularly effective with English-language respondents, who made up 86.8% of the e-mail referral sample as compared with 75.0% of the total sample.

Looking further down Table P.1, it is also noteworthy that the relative share of complete surveys varied with language given that a greater proportion of English-language respondents (85.1% total) was found among complete surveys from each of the sources than was found among the surveys initiated. Here it is interesting to note that although the number of e-mail referrals leading to complete surveys was relatively small (267 or 3.4% of the total number of complete surveys), this represents a 42% increase in the relative share of survey respondents of this type. Therefore, this suggests that the use of e-mail referrals may be an effective means to obtain complete surveys.

In terms of sample design, the GSS is a very different type of study based on a traditional sampling of the U.S. noninstitutionalized adult population. The U.S. adult household population covers about 97.3% of the resident population of the United States; however, coverage varies greatly by age group. For example, just under 10% of the population ages 18 to 24 years lived outside of households (mostly in college dorms and military quarters) and are not represented by the sample. Thus, some of the heaviest users of the internet are systematically excluded from the GSS. GSS data collection began in 1972, with nationally representative samples of approximately 1,500 respondents typically being conducted every year—although at times every other year—until 1994, when the GSS moved to a regular 2-year cycle. The 2000 GSS was a face-to-face, 90-minute,

Table P.1   Origin and Language of Survey2001 Respondents

	Total	National Geographic Society Site	Other Site	E-mail Referral
Surveys initiated	23,192	14,064	8,569	559
Survey language (percentages)				
English	75.0	77.7	69.7	86.8
German	6.9	6.8	7.1	5.4
Italian	7.2	6.3	8.8	3.0
Spanish	11.0	9.2	14.1	4.8
Surveys completed: Adult demographics module	12,361	7,583	4,470	408
Surveys completed: Youth demographics module[a]	961	625	297	39
Surveys completed: All modules	7,767	4,831	2,669	267
Survey language (percentages)				
English	85.1	85.1	84.8	88.8
German	6.6	7.3	5.5	5.6
Italian	3.5	3.6	3.6	3.2
Spanish	4.7	4.0	6.1	3.4

a. A simpler, age-appropriate version of the survey was presented to all respondents under 18 years of age.

in-home interview conducted with 2,817 respondents between February and mid-June 2000. With funding from the National Science Foundation, the 2000 GSS focused on respondents' internet use and attitudes regarding the internet as well as on a variety of demographic and general attitudinal items. Extensive information regarding the GSS may be obtained through the National Opinion Research Center or from the GSS Web site (www.norc.org/projects/gensoc.asp).

During the first 3 years of data collection, the GSS employed a modified probability sampling technique, relying to a certain degree on filling quotas for particular subgroups. However, beginning in 1975, when higher funding levels became available, the GSS moved toward full probability sampling, which has been used exclusively since 1977. The sampling is conducted in two major stages. Primary sampling units, consisting of one or more counties, are selected in the first stage, and segments consisting of one or more blocks in each primary sampling unit are selected in the second stage. In a few cases, segments were subsampled, a procedure that constituted a third stage of sample selection.

For example, the 1990 sampling frame consisted of 100 primary sampling units, each of which was a metropolitan area or a nonmetropolitan county. Prior to selection, the United States was divided into 2,489 primary sampling units, which were sorted into strata according to region, state, percentage minority, and per capita income. This procedure ensured proportional representation according to the stratification criteria. Then 100 primary sampling units were selected, with the selection probability for each unit being proportional to the number of housing units. Of these primary sampling units, 19 were so large that they were automatically included in the first-stage sample. Then the selected units were subdivided and stratified, primarily according to geography and percentage minority, and second-stage sample segments were selected using systematic sampling with selection probability proportional to the number of housing units in the segment. Individual units were then randomly selected within each segment.

Once a sample was selected following these procedures, interviewers entered the field to conduct face-to-face interviews. For example, the original full-probability sample in 1996 consisted of 4,559 cases. After eliminating vacant dwellings, households where the interviewer experienced language difficulties, businesses, and other nondwelling addresses, the net sample came to 3,846 households. These households then yielded 2,904 completed surveys, with the bulk of the difference between eligible households and completed surveys being due to 757 respondent refusals, amounting to a refusal rate of 19.8%—quite low by industry standards. Nevertheless, despite the care used to determine the probability sample, there is no reason to assume that nonresponse is randomly distributed. Indeed, for more than two decades, it has been known that males are underrepresented in full-probability samples, including the GSS (Smith, 1979), and that this is primarily a function of nonresponse. It should also be pointed out that the full-probability GSS samples used since 1975 were designed to give each household an equal probability of inclusion in the samples. Thus, for household-level variables, the GSS sample is self-weighting. However, at the individual level, because only one individual per household is interviewed, individuals living in large households are underrepresented. Individual weights to correct for these factors are distributed with the GSS and should be used—as they are in the GSS results presented here—when the individual is the unit of analysis.

SAMPLING AND DIFFERENT DEMOGRAPHICS

It comes as no surprise that the very different sampling strategies employed by the 2000 GSS and Survey2001 lead to obvious and predictable differences in the

Table P.2 Demographics of 2000 GSS and Survey2001: U.S. Respondents

	2000 GSS[a]	Survey2001[b]
Average age (years)	43	35
Gender (percentages)		
Male	48.0	47.8
Female	52.0	52.7
Region (percentages)		
New England	5.1	5.7
Middle Atlantic	15.8	12.1
East North Central	16.6	14.9
West North Central	6.9	6.2
South Atlantic	18.0	25.9
East South Central	6.6	3.5
West South Central	10.7	6.8
Mountain	6.3	7.6
Pacific	14.1	17.2
Educational attainment (percentages)		
Less than high school	15.8	1.5
High school	53.9	34.9
Junior college	7.4	7.0
Bachelor's degree	15.2	33.7
Graduate degree	7.7	23.0
Employment status (percentages)		
Working full-time	55.2	57.3
Working part-time	11.4	17.3
Temporarily not working or unemployed	4.5	6.1
Keeping house	11.5	3.2
Retired	12.1	6.8
Other	5.4	9.4
N	2,817	6,966

a. Weighted using GSS weights.
b. Unweighted U.S. respondents age 18 years or over.

sample according to demographics. These differences are readily apparent in Table P.2. The demographic characteristics of the 2000 GSS roughly parallel the conventional picture of the U.S. population.

For example, the U.S. Department of Education reports that 15.9% of Americans age 25 years or over have not obtained a high school degree (National Center for Education Statistics, 2001, Table 8). Looking at Table P.2, the GSS results are nearly identical at 15.8%. The full GSS sample is intended to represent adults age 18 years or over. Filtering out the 18- to 24-year-olds, however, has a little effect, leaving 14.9% of the 2000 GSS respondents age 25 years or over without a high school degree.

As noted previously in the sampling discussion, weights should be used with GSS individual-level data. Their impact is most obvious when one considers gender directly; males make up 43.6% of the unweighted sample as compared with 48.0% after weighting. However, considering other demographic characteristics, the effects are minimal even when there is some correlation with gender. For example, weighting has almost no effect on education; compared with the distribution presented in Table P.2, the percentages at each level of education change by no more than 0.3% when weights are not used.

Having said this, however, there is no guarantee that weighting by demographic characteristics will yield proportional response patterns for other variables. This would be the case only if the lower response rate among men were randomly distributed across all men. More realistically, one should assume that nonresponse is concentrated among certain types of men and that, more specifically, it is these types of men who are underrepresented in the sample. This requires a more sophisticated model of weighting that takes into account the social processes that account for the disproportional representation of particular demographic groups in the unweighted sample in the first place.

The Survey2001 sample, on the other hand, is younger, differently distributed regionally (with heavier concentrations in the South Atlantic and Pacific regions), more highly educated, and more likely to be employed (especially part-time) than the population-at-large. Indeed, the characteristics of the Survey2001 sample better approximate popular conceptions of the online population than they do the general U.S. population.

SAMPLING AND DIFFERENT SUBSTANTIVE RESULTS: INTERNET USE AND STUDY DESIGN

Clearly, one would expect to find differences in incidence of computer use and internet access between the 2000 GSS and Survey2001 respondents. The 2000 GSS found that approximately 60.0% of Americans had access to a computer at home, at work, or somewhere else. Among this group, 79.8% reported that they had access at home, whereas 65.7% of all employed individuals reported having access to a computer at work. An overwhelming majority of persons with a computer at home (85.9%) also reported having internet access at home. Another

Table P.3   Online Activities of 2000 GSS and Survey2001 Internet Users: Visits to Types of Web Sites During the Past 30 Days

	All Respondents		Respondents With a College Degree	
	2000 GSS[a]	Survey2001[b]	2000 GSS[a]	Survey2001[b]
News and current events (percentages)				
Never	24.7	9.4	13.9	8.6
1 to 2 times	26.9	17.2	25.7	16.7
3 to 5 times	17.8	17.5	18.0	17.6
More than 5 times	30.6	55.9	42.4	57.1
Television and movies (percentages)				
Never	63.7	33.7	62.5	30.9
1 to 2 times	24.6	24.8	26.8	25.6
3 to 5 times	6.9	18.9	4.9	19.3
More than 5 times	4.8	22.7	5.7	24.2
Health and fitness (percentages)				
Never	50.3	34.4	47.1	32.9
1 to 2 times	28.3	26.9	29.5	25.4
3 to 5 times	13.6	21.4	15.3	22.3
More than 5 times	7.8	17.3	8.0	19.3
N	691	2,345	266	1,639

a. Weighted using GSS weights.
b. Unweighted U.S. respondents age 18 years or over.

3.0% of those without a computer at home reported having internet access via WebTV. Not surprisingly, greater rates of access were recorded among Survey2001 respondents; indeed, they needed some means of internet access simply to participate in the survey. Nearly all Survey2001 respondents (94.0%) said that they had access to a computer at home. Among employed persons, 86.1% reported computer access at work.

Given these obvious differences in access, it is nonetheless interesting to consider the type and level of internet activity among those respondents who reported that they use the internet in each sample. The results presented in Table P.3 summarize the frequency with which individuals visited specific types of Web sites during the past 30 days. The findings consider visits to three types of sites: news and current event sites, television and movie sites, and health and fitness sites. Simply comparing all respondents, the differences are extremely large, with far less frequent visits to Web sites reported by GSS respondents than by Survey2001 respondents. For example, 24.7% of GSS respondents had not visited a news or current event Web site during the past 30 days as compared with only 9.4% of Survey2001 respondents. Considering television and movie sites, the difference between the two samples was larger still in that as 63.7% of the GSS respondents had never visited such a site as compared with 33.7% of the Survey2001 respondents. The GSS respondents were somewhat less likely (50.3%) to have not visited such a site during the past 30 days. This number was still notably higher than that found among the Survey2001 respondents, of whom only 34.4% had not been to such a site during the past 30 days.

Certainly, some measure of this difference is rooted in the much higher level of educational attainment of the Survey2001 sample, as noted earlier in the discussion of Table P.2. To get a handle on the importance of this difference, the final two columns of Table P.3 consider visits to sites of these types only among those respondents in each sample who reported that they had a 4-year college degree. As one would expect, focusing on the better educated members of these samples decreases the proportion of those who reported that they had not visited a Web site of each of these types during the past 30 days. Not surprisingly, the change was relatively minor among the Survey2001 respondents given that more than two thirds of this sample reported having a college degree. Yet even among the GSS sample, the magnitude of change tended to be modest, particularly when it comes to visiting television and movie sites as well as health and fitness sites.

Faced with this conflicting evidence regarding the frequency of specific online activities, one's first inclination may be to deem the GSS findings as more accurate and attribute the Survey2001 results to that survey's unconventional and obviously nonrandom sampling strategy. To do so, however, would be to ignore other sources that suggest levels of use closer to Survey2001 data than to GSS data. For example, using random digit dialing techniques, the Pew Internet and American Life Project found that 64% of all internet users reported that they had obtained health information online in 2001, with a similar percentage indicating that they had used the internet as a news source (Horrigan & Rainie, 2002). Furthermore, the Pew data indicate that the use of the internet for such purposes varies with individuals' internet experience, as nearly three quarters of long-time internet users reported that they had used the internet for health information.

SAMPLING AND DIFFERENT
SUBSTANTIVE RESULTS: ENVIRONMENTAL ISSUES

Table P.4, which compares Survey2001 subsample responses with a subset of eight NEP items, hints at the value of this approach. The first three rows of data for each item compare three Web subsamples: respondents coming directly from the NGS site, respondents coming from the Sierra Club site, and respondents from all other sites. Focusing on the extreme "pro-environmental" responses for each item,[3] the NGS respondents stand out as holding stronger environmental views than those of respondents coming from the mixed category of other sites. Sierra Club respondents, however, are seen as even more pro-environmental than NGS respondents. It is also noteworthy that a much smaller percentage of Sierra Club respondents selected "don't know" than did either the NGS respondents or those from other sites. At first glance, finding clearer preferences and pro-environmental attitudes among visitors to an avowedly environmental club Web site is hardly surprising. However, it raises an important point. These predictable and highly plausible findings are the product of a nonrandom online survey. The results are from a nonrandom sample, but they are from a representative sample.

Results from the Survey2001 phone survey provide useful data regarding the impact of the data collection mode.[4] In this instance, our phone sample is limited to a targeted subset of upper middle class urban respondents who are demographically quite similar. Despite their demographic similarities, when we look at their responses to the conservation items in Table P.4, two clear differences emerge between the phone samples (the fourth row for each item) and the Web samples (the first three rows for each item). Most generally, we see that both the NGS and Sierra Club samples tended to articulate stronger environmental concerns than did the phone samples drawn from these two highly educated, relatively affluent areas. Moreover, for the most part, the results from this phone sample (albeit preliminary data with a small sample size) are relatively similar to those provided by respondents from a heterogeneous mix of Web sites.

Although it is plausible to conclude that the stronger environmental views found among these two groups of Web respondents (as compared with the phone respondents despite similar demographics) may be attributed to selection bias, a second pattern found in Table P.4 does not lend itself to a similar interpretation. For seven of the eight items in this table, the proportion of individuals who selected "don't know" for their response was greater in the NGS and other Web samples than in the phone sample—often by a large margin. Among the Sierra

Table P.4 Survey2001 Respondents' Attitudes Regarding Conservation and the Environment (percentages)

Respondent Source[a]	Strongly Disagree	Disagree	Agree	Strongly Agree	Don't Know
We are approaching the limit of the number of people the Earth can support.					
National Geographic Society	5.1	18.6	35.1	25.0	16.2
Environmental group	4.0	5.5	36.2	46.0	8.3
Other Survey2001 source	7.5	25.0	32.9	13.9	20.6
Telephone	3.6	22.0	40.8	26.9	6.7
Humans have the right to modify the natural environment to suit their needs.					
National Geographic Society	23.2	41.1	20.8	3.0	11.8
Environmental group	34.7	37.7	14.1	4.0	9.5
Other Survey2001 source	12.5	40.7	29.4	3.8	13.5
Telephone	14.3	40.8	32.3	4.9	7.6
When humans interfere with nature, it often produces disastrous consequences.					
National Geographic Society	3.0	10.6	44.6	34.4	7.4
Environmental group	4.5	5.8	36.7	48.0	5.0
Other Survey2001 source	3.3	15.4	48.0	22.6	10.5
Telephone	3.1	11.2	52.9	26.5	6.2
Plants and animals have as much right to exist as do humans.					
National Geographic Society	1.8	6.5	36.2	51.1	4.3
Environmental group	2.0	4.0	27.7	64.0	2.3
Other Survey2001 source	2.9	11.2	45.5	33.7	6.7
Telephone	3.1	17.9	50.7	22.0	6.2

(Continued)

Table P4 Continued

Respondent Source[a]	Strongly Disagree	Disagree	Agree	Strongly Agree	Don't Know
The so-called "ecological crisis" facing humankind has been greatly exaggerated.					
National Geographic Society	32.2	38.0	9.1	4.4	13.4
Environmental group	61.7	27.5	1.8	4.8	3.0
Other Survey2001 source	20.1	37.2	14.4	5.6	20.5
Telephone	33.6	42.2	17.0	3.1	4.0
The Earth is like a spaceship with very limited room and resources.					
National Geographic Society	2.5	17.0	47.0	22.7	10.8
Environmental group	3.3	10.2	41.2	39.4	5.9
Other Survey2001 source	3.0	25.0	45.2	12.7	14.1
Telephone	0.4	19.3	57.0	20.2	3.1
Humans were meant to rule over the rest of nature.					
National Geographic Society	36.1	34.2	13.4	4.4	11.9
Environmental group	54.6	28.8	5.6	3.6	7.4
Other Survey2001 source	21.1	35.8	22.4	6.1	14.6
Telephone	23.8	49.8	15.7	3.6	7.2
If things continue on their present course, we will soon experience a major ecological catastrophe.					
National Geographic Society	3.8	10.5	37.2	25.9	22.6
Environmental group	4.3	3.1	36.0	45.4	11.2
Other Survey2001 source	5.2	17.8	35.1	14.4	27.4
Telephone	1.8	17.0	51.1	20.6	9.3

a. The four sources of respondents are the Web-based sample of U.S. National Geographic Society respondents age 18 years or over ($n = 3,964$), the Web-based sample of U.S. national environmental group respondents age 18 years or over ($n = 531$), the remaining sample of all other U.S. respondents age 18 years or over in the Survey2001 sample ($n = 2,360$), and the telephone sample of 269 U.S. respondents in urban areas.

Club respondents, it is plausible to see low levels of "don't know" responses as being associated with higher levels of knowledge and concern. However, such an interpretation is not compelling for the phone sample, which did not set itself apart through its environmental positions. In this case, the greater decisiveness of the phone respondents may have resulted from their answering to a human interviewer in contrast to the Web respondents, who answered only to a server.

Conclusion

The primary aim of this prologue has been to show that sampling matters when studying life online. Indeed, this statement is true for all research, regardless of the topic. The goal of this prologue has also been to show that this truism holds for face-to-face interviews and phone surveys as well as for the emerging field of Web surveys. The results presented here demonstrate that the Survey2001 sampling strategy presented a picture of a society that is far more wired than the population-at-large. This is readily conceded. However, the analyses presented here also show that more traditional sampling methods have their own limitations as well. The effects of nonresponse are rarely given the attention they are due in traditional survey techniques. Furthermore, in the case of the 2000 GSS, coverage restrictions simply excluded a small but particularly wired segment of the population—young people living in institutional settings, especially college dorms and the military. On the other hand, Survey2001, as a Web-based survey of online life, was better positioned to capture a large sample of individuals who were particularly plugged into life online. This is readily evident in the findings presented here showing that the Survey2001 respondents were more frequent users of various types of Web sites than were the 2000 GSS respondents, even after restricting the comparison to college-educated respondents.

Quite simply, one should not let the sampling weaknesses of Web-based surveys fully obscure the strengths of such surveys. Preliminary results with the Survey2001 data also permit comparisons between the Web samples and phone samples regarding online activities. Focusing on the urban, well-educated phone subsample most like the Web sample, particular types of online activities— mailing list participation, online education, and surfing the Web for recreational purposes—were far more common among the Web respondents. Further analysis with these data may show that these patterns are Web survey specific; however, they also raise an important rival interpretation. Telephone surveys, with their own patterns of nonresponse and selection, may give an inaccurate picture of Web users. The virtues of multimethod studies may extend to covering the blind spots of telephone surveys as well as those of Web surveys.

In addition, one should take care that a preoccupation with sampling issues in Web surveys does not obscure other critical issues associated with such a new form of survey research. The large increase in "don't know" responses to Web surveys, as compared with phone surveys, calls attention to the significance of "interviewer effects" even when an interviewer is not physically present. Similarly, preliminary analyses of experimental use of photo prompts in Survey2001 strongly suggest that the instrument effects of Web surveys are myriad and subtle. Thanks to the careful methodological research of individuals working with face-to-face, mail, and phone surveys, we have a pretty good understanding of how important such influences may be. However, all bets are off when one simply assumes that such effects will operate in the same fashion online. Nevertheless, this uncertainty should not discourage survey researchers from taking to the Web and conducting online surveys. After an initial period of neglect, debates such as those between Nie and Erbring (2000a) and Etzioni (2000) focused the attention of social scientists on the internet. Their disparate conclusions have alerted social scientists to a variety of complex methodological issues related to the study of the internet. As a result, we find ourselves in a new phase of internet research. Now is the time for "the tradition-bound activity of normal science" (Kuhn, 1962, p. 6). In fact, it is only through such efforts that survey research will acquire the experience and data needed to make the most of the internet as a new and exciting data collection tool.

Notes

1. An often overlooked fact in discussions of the *Literary Digest* polls is that in the previous four presidential elections, they correctly predicted the winner. Beyond the 1936 truth that a large sample does not guarantee accurate results, it ought to be emphasized that a nonrandom sample does not amount to a recipe for invalid results.

2. Using results from the first 12 weeks of Survey2001 data collection, 22 sites contributed at least 30 observations. Most important in this group were the Sierra Club (1,051 respondents) and Science News Online (539 respondents).

3. These are "strongly agree" for the first, third, fourth, sixth, and eighth items in Table P.4 and "strongly disagree" for the second, fifth, and seventh items.

4. The phone sample includes two targeted subsamples: 1,400 randomly selected respondents from rural Maine and rural California and 269 randomly selected urban respondents from Cambridge, Massachusetts, and Santa Monica, California. This latter group was sampled to pretest the instrument on a group of respondents likely to demographically resemble NGS Web site visitors, particularly with regard to education and income.

References

Aquilino, W. (1994). Interview mode effects in surveys of drug and alcohol use. *Public Opinion Quarterly, 58,* 910–940.

Aquilino, W., & LoSciuto, L. (1990). Effect of interview mode on self-reported drug use. *Public Opinion Quarterly, 54,* 362–395.

Baker, R. P., Bradburn, N. M., & Johnson, R. (1995). Computer-assisted personal interviewing: An experimental evaluation of data quality and survey costs. *Journal of Official Statistics, 11,* 415–449.

Burton, S., & Blair, E. (1991). Task conditions, response formulation processes, and response accuracy for behavioral frequency questions in surveys. *Public Opinion Quarterly, 55,* 50–79.

Couper, M., & Nicholls, W., II. (1998). The history and development of computer assisted survey information. In M. Couper, J. Bethlehem, C. Clark, J. Martin, W. Nicholls, & J. O'Reilly (Eds.), *Computer-assisted survey information collection.* New York: John Wiley.

Dillman, D. A. (2000). *Mail and internet surveys: The tailored design method.* New York: John Wiley.

Etzioni, A. (2000, May–June). Debating the societal effects of the internet: Connecting with the world. *Public Perspective,* pp. 42–43.

Heckathorn, D. A. (1997). Respondent-driven sampling: A new approach to the study of hidden populations. *Social Problems, 44,* 174–199.

Horrigan, J. B., & Rainie, L. (2002). *Getting serious online.* Working paper, Pew Internet and American Life Project.

Jenkins, C. R., & Dillman, D. A. (1997). Towards a theory of self-administered questionnaire design. In L. Lyberg, P. Biemer, M. Collins, E. DeLeeuw, C. Dippo, N. Schwarz, & D. Trewin (Eds.), *Survey measurement and process quality.* New York: John Wiley.

Kiesler, S., & Sproull, E. (1986). Response effects in the electronic survey. *Public Opinion Quarterly, 50,* 402–413.

Kuhn, T. S. (1962). *The structure of scientific revolutions.* Chicago: University of Chicago Press.

Lohr, S. L. (1999). *Sampling: Design and analysis.* Pacific Grove, CA: Duxbury.

National Center for Education Statistics. (2001). *Digest of education statistics, 2001.* Washington, DC: U.S. Department of Education.

Nicholls, W., Baker, R., & Martin, J. (1997). The effect of new data collection technologies on survey data quality. In L. Lyberg, P. Biemer, M. Collins, E. DeLeeuw, C. Dippo, N. Schwarz, & D. Trewin (Eds.), *Survey measurement and process quality* (pp. 221–248). New York: John Wiley.

Nie, N., & Erbring, L. (2000a, May–June). Debating the societal effects of the internet: Our shrinking social universe. *Public Perspective,* pp. 44–45.

Nie, N., & Erbring, L. (2000b). *Internet and society.* Unpublished manuscript, Stanford Institute for the Quantitative Study of Society.

Schaefer, D. R., & Dillman, D. A. (1998). Development of a standard e-mail methodology: Results of an experiment. *Public Opinion Quarterly, 62,* 378–397.

Smith, T. W. (1983). The hidden 25 percent: An analysis of nonresponse on the 1980 General Social Survey. *Public Opinion Quarterly, 47,* 386–404.

Smith, T. W. (1979). *Sex and the GSS: Nonresponse differences.* General Social Survey Methodological Report No. 9.

Tourangeau, R., & Smith, T. (1998). Collecting sensitive information with different modes of data collection. In M. Couper, J. Bethlehem, C. Clark, J. Martin, W. Nicholls, & J. O'Reilly (Eds.), *Computer-assisted survey information collection.* New York: John Wiley.

Trochim, W. M. K. (2000). *The research methods knowledge base.* Cincinnati, OH: Atomic Dog Publishing.

Turner, C. F., Forsyth, B. H., O'Reilly, J. M., Cooley, P. C., Smith, T. K., Rogers, S. M., & Miller, H. G. (1998). Automated self-interviewing and the survey measurement of sensitive behaviors. In M. Couper, J. Bethlehem, C. Clark, J. Martin, W. Nicholls, & J. O'Reilly (Eds.), *Computer-assisted survey information collection.* New York: John Wiley.

Turner, C. F., Ku, L., Rogers, S. M., Lindberg, L. D., Pleck, J. H., & Sonensteh, F. L. (1998). Adolescent sexual behavior, drug use, and violence: Increased reporting with computer survey technology. *Science, 280,* 867–873.

Witte, J., & Howard, P. N. (2002). Technological and methodological innovation in survey instruments: The future of polling. In F. Cook & J. Manza (Eds.), *Navigating public opinion* (pp. 272–289). Oxford, UK: Oxford University Press.

1

Embedded Media

Who We Know,
What We Know, and Society Online

Philip N. Howard
University of Washington

Within the developed world, members of the current generation are experiencing political, economic, and cultural life through a set of communication technologies barely older then they are. This collection of research about society online is unique. Rather than trying to cover every possible topic relating to new communication technologies in society, we have organized a series of arguments about how these new technologies mediate the various spheres of our social lives. First, the collection is not devoted exclusively to a particular technology or to the internet specifically; rather, it is devoted to a range of technologies and technological possibilities labeled *new media* (Manovich, 2000). Obviously, the label *new media* cannot last forever, but many observers use the term to describe a range of communication technologies very different from the media that were prominent a decade ago. Second, this collection does not mark the importance of new media in everyday life with indications that the technology is a banal ordinary part of our daily activities. Different people have different kinds of access to new media, and those with access use new media in

AUTHOR'S NOTE: The author thanks Alexi Cabrera, Mark Donovan, Mark Farrelly, Tema Milstein, Rhian Salmon, David Silver, and Francisco Zarate for their helpful comments.

different ways. The technology itself and how it is used evolve daily, so it makes sense to focus on the general properties of new media and their application in both daily and unusual circumstances. Third, this collection has an overarching argument. Communication technologies became deeply embedded in personal lives very quickly, mediating our interactions with other people and the way in which we learn about our world. Understanding society online requires that we study media embeddedness—how new communication tools are embedded in our lives and how our lives are embedded in new media.

New media technologies have not simply diffused across society; rather, they were rapidly and deeply embedded in our organizations and institutions (Howard, Jones, & Rainie, 2001). The content of new media tends to more closely reflect the actual interests of the population, which plays the role of producer and consumer of content, software, and hardware. For example, some people use new media to produce music at home, others use commercial software to organize and store purchased music, and still others use software to make their music collections available to their networks of family and friends. The technology itself is deeply embedded in that its software and hardware can be controlled by, and often developed by, users of the new media. In contrast, a relatively small social elite owns, manages, produces, and channels information through media such as television, radio, and newspapers.

Studying Society Online

RESEARCH METHOD

Several of the chapters in this collection are good examples of how methodological diversity can lead to better understanding about the role of new media in our lives. Two kinds of lessons about how to research the relationship between technology and society emerge. First, we must better evaluate the ways in which communication tools constrain and empower research. Witte does this in the prologue in describing how sample design constrains research when it is part of the explanation for findings, and Bainbridge (Chapter 19) takes advantage of the new media as a powerful research tool in his experiment with online survey instruments. Second, we must better evaluate the way in which conceptual tools—metaphors and categories—help and hinder our explanations of what we find when we present our research. Both Shade (Chapter 4) and Nakamura (Chapter 5) illustrate how the survey instruments can give an incomplete rendering of gender online. The same may be said for race, class, and the other forms of social inequality that get replicated online when some people have better access to new media tools than do other people, when some people know how to use new media better than do other people, and when some people find more affinity with the cultural content of new media than do other people. As Shade argues, researchers not only must study the way in which social inequalities are replicated online but also must build projects to redress these inequalities. Content creation, education, civic engagement, policymaking, and governance are the key ways in which to do this.

Witte argues that researchers should not confine themselves to telephone-based survey samples given that many people use a variety of communication technologies for their daily tasks. Because the sampling error of traditional random digit dial surveys is growing, and because the chance that someone will not be invited to participate is not randomly distributed across the population, the social sciences need to surrender the unquestioned goal of randomness for the more meaningful and achievable goal of representativeness and purposive sampling. If the distribution of people who do not respond to a survey is the same as the distribution of people who do respond, then all is well. However, nearly 5% of the adult U.S. population is simply inaccessible to most telephone surveyors: people in prisons, health care facilities, soup kitchens, college dormitories, and the military as well as people who can pay for technology that protects them from computer-assisted telephone interview (CATI) systems. Witte's piece is an important introduction to this volume because he cogently makes the case for multimethod studies:

> Telephone surveys with their own patterns of nonresponse and selection may give an inaccurate picture of Web users. The virtues of multimethod studies may extend to covering the blind spots of telephone surveys as well as those of Web surveys.

New media permit researchers to experiment with a range of respondent stimuli and the survey instrument itself. By extension, the process of triangulating on answers necessarily partners qualitative, comparative, and quantitative methods (Howard, 2002).

As editors, we have deliberately sought out examples of the diverse methods that scholars are using to study society online. Silver and Garland (Chapter 10) conduct a systematic content analysis of magazine advertisements, and Rice and Katz (Chapter 7) use the comparative method to contrast data about politics online in 1996 and 2000. Hargittai (Chapter 16) uses quasi-experimental methods and does probit analysis of her results. Norris (Chapter 2) and Robinson, Neustadtl, and Kestnbaum (Chapter 15) use ordinary least squares regression techniques. Stromer-Galley (Chapter 6) does logistic regression. Griswold and Wright (Chapter 13) hold small focus groups. Larsen (Chapter 3), Schneider and Foot (Chapter 9), and Bainbridge (Chapter 19) work with means and cross-tabs, having developed unique archiving methods for analyzing large volumes of Web site content. Shade and Nakamura analyze survey results. Dessauer (Chapter 8), Neff and Stark (Chapter 11), and Kotamraju (Chapter 12) report the findings of their ethnographic and autoethnographic work. Peterson and Ryan (Chapter 14) use historical methods in their study of evolving music technologies. Starke-Meyerring, Burk, and Gurak (Chapter 17) do a comparative analysis of policy traditions. Witte and Bainbridge treat new media themselves as a research tool.

These core arguments and challenging questions are grouped by the community, political, economic, cultural, personal, and global spheres of life in which we all participate:

- Social capital, community, and content
- Wired news and politics online
- Economic life online
- Culture and socialization online
- Personal and global context of life online

Data from many prominent social science projects studying new media are represented in this collection: the General Social Survey, the HomeNet Study, the National Telecommunications and Information Administration, the Pew Internet and American Life Project, the Stanford Institute for the Quantitative Study of Society, the Survey2001 Project, the UCLA Center for Communication Policy, the Webarchivist.org, and the World Values Survey. The core arguments in this volume are strengthened by the fact that the contributors use their various disciplinary interests and methods to triangulate on answers to some of the most challenging questions about the role of new media in society.

SOCIAL CAPITAL, COMMUNITY, AND CONTENT

Norris (Chapter 2) starts off Part I of this volume by testing out the role of various kinds of online community groups if one can predict how such groups bridge and bond people from other backgrounds. Bridging and bonding are the two key components of Putnam's (2000) formulation of social capital, and Norris finds that most Americans feel that their membership in online communities both widens and deepens their social relationships. As one might expect, Norris finds that different kinds of groups have different bridging and bonding roles and that such roles can be socially constructive or dysfunctional. She takes us beyond simple propositions that internet-based communities are good for those who find camaraderie or are bad for those who isolate themselves in narrowly defined interest groups. Her cogent analysis allows us to compare the relative effects of various kinds of groups. For example, Norris finds that religious groups seem to have a modest bonding function but a low bridging function.

The role of new media in our spiritual lives is understudied, so Larsen (Chapter 3) gives us a closer look at religious communities online, investigating both the organization of religion and individual spiritual conduct online. The internet, she notes, "is a space at once both solitary and social." Some new media technologies such as the internet have been criticized for encouraging small groups with narrow specialized interests to form and flourish. Her findings suggest that the internet has provided a fertile ground for spiritual exploration and that having a place for religious artwork, debates about canonical law, and devotional support has enriched the lives of many people deliberately looking for guidance and like-minded spiritual communities. The internet has helped these spiritual communities to organize themselves, extend their services, and expand their memberships. In a nice convergence with Norris, Larsen finds that although people recommend their favorite Web sites to friends, *reinforcing* social networks, people rarely go online to *extend* their social networks of devout friends.

People with different demographics backgrounds look for different kinds of content online (Howard et al., 2001). For example, African American internet users more frequently seek spiritual information online. Although the proportion of male and female users reflects that of the total population, the different genders do different things with new media. Women are twice as likely to search for health information than are men, and they tend to spend more time communicating with friends and family through e-mail. They are less likely to get news, visit government Web sites, or use the internet for work. Controlling for other variables, women are less likely to research or buy products online. Shade (Chapter 4) explores the implications of the recent surge of female internet users. To what degree has the content—or the technology itself—been feminized by the surge of female users that occurred as the technology became popular? Shade suggests that a balanced analysis must look at both corporate interests in supplying gendered content and user demand for such content. We can safely say that all content is political. Nakamura (Chapter 5) discusses both how racial categories are represented by the content of new media and how racial minorities are excluded from the use of the technology. Many internet users may be able to extend their social capital by bridging or bonding with new communities and ideas. However, the content of new media is not free of cues about race, gender, or class or about forms of social inequality we find in life offline.

WIRED NEWS AND POLITICS ONLINE

Although many pundits have lauded new media technologies for their potential roles in democratic deliberation, there is quite a difference between imagining how a technology might play such a role, building such applications, and getting the public to use them as desired. To open Part II, Stromer-Galley's (Chapter 6) analysis of what people think of voting online offers insight into the complexities of the transition between technological dreams and political applications. She finds that an internet voting system, as currently imagined, would probably not draw new voters into participating. She charts a careful route between being technologically overdetermined and being sociologically overdetermined. On the one hand, she learns that internet use is a strong predictor of preferences for voting online; we might expect that because as more people are using the internet, the number of people who would like to vote online is increasing. On the other hand, familiarity with a technology bears little relationship to a person's sense of duty or interest in politics. With her research, we can now make a measured distinction between the degree to which a technology may enable more efficient voting participation and the degree to which people must be motivated to vote. Overall, being familiar with new media appears to have a greater effect on the likelihood of voting online then on having a strong sense of duty to do so.

Whereas Stromer-Galley investigates people's perception of internet voting tools and finds marked enthusiasm for their use, Rice and Katz (Chapter 7) conduct a comparative study of the role of the internet during the 1996 and 2000 elections. They report that a growing number of people use the internet to enrich their political lives—participating in online discussion groups, researching candidates and policy options, and following political news. They also make the important point that it is too early to expect any rise in voter sophistication, and they offer reasons as to why the internet may have only a limited role in making people smarter citizens. In weighing the question of whether the internet has had a negative impact, no impact, or a positive impact, Rice and Katz crunch the numbers and arrive at a mildly positive ruling. Dessauer (Chapter 8) writes about the evolution of the production and consumption of news: "With the evolution of internet news, the traditional news product has become either the basis for a story that is 'repurposed' or repackaged for new media." The habit of news production has changed radically; journalists conduct more research online than many are willing to admit in professional circumstances, television news has adapted interactive techniques to engage television viewers, and some internet users treat personal Web logs (or "blogs") as alternative news sources. Moreover, there is a growing industry of alternative media production that relies on the efforts of solitary individuals equipped with handheld computers, digital cameras, and wireless technologies to bear witness to political violence that established media consider too controversial for their prime-time viewers. Whereas Dessauer describes changing patterns in the production and consumption of news in the United States, Schneider and Foot (Chapter 9) take a close look at a specific case of how the internet was used in a moment of social crisis. They make one of the first systematic studies of internet use following the terrorist attacks of September 11, 2001, covering its use as an emergency response tool for getting and providing information, assistance, and support; as a means of sharing personal expression; and as a forum for political advocacy.

ECONOMIC LIFE ONLINE

Even though themes of gender and race are introduced in the section on community and content, they are not sequestered there. To begin Part III, Silver and Garland (Chapter 10) investigate how advertisers tried to influence the technology choices of young women. Whereas advertisers wanted teenage girls to see the internet as an easy way in which to shop, teenage girls were interested in chatting with instant messaging (IM) tools. Silver and Garland's piece is interesting for the way in which it describes the tension between individual agency and social construction—girls who want to IM and an advertising industry that wants them to shop.

But advertisers have not been the only ones *doing* the "social construction" of new media. In fact, such work just became defined as a valuable skill set during the past decade, and Kotamraju's (Chapter 12) project is to trace the evolution of Web design skills. Focusing on the San Francisco Bay area, her story of professionalization and rationalization brings perspective to the dot-com boom and bust that involved, and often preoccupied, a generation of young people and an international economy of billion-dollar technology businesses. Although Kotamraju's case study teaches us that the meaning of the professional Web designer has changed over time, Neff and Stark (Chapter 11) suggest that the designers of new media technology have had lasting organizational influences. As a complement to Kotamraju's case of micro-level changes in professional definition, Neff and Stark describe how software and hardware choices influence organizational behavior. They find that "the values embedded in widely used information technologies have become encoded into the routines of the market and into organizational forms." The stock *value* of many dot-coms inflated and deflated over several short years, but the *values* embedded in new organizational forms seem to be long lasting.

CULTURE AND SOCIALIZATION ONLINE

Griswold and Wright (Chapter 13) and Peterson and Ryan (Chapter 14), in the opening chapters to Part IV, wrestle with two general hypotheses about patterns of cultural consumption and production over new media. The first is a kind of *more-more* hypothesis: The more time people spend with technologies such as the internet, the more they will learn about culture—reading literature and listening to music, either online or offline. The second is a kind of *zero-sum* hypothesis often associated with studies of reading behavior, playing video games, and watching television: The more time people spend watching television, the less time they spend reading or listening to music. Does this apply to new media use? Griswold and Wright take a close look at reading behavior and internet use and make some modest claims about positive reinforcement—not just association—between the use of internet technologies and the consumption of literary culture offline. Peterson and Ryan examine how musical tastes may be changing with the exposure offered to various cultures. They provide a significant amount of historical and archival depth that is important for their probe into the role of new media in shaping the way in which we produce and consume music. Their thesis is that with the advent of new technologies, from notational innovations to recording and distributing technologies, music has been *disembodied* from its creators.

But in terms of socialization and cultural sophistication, do people really meet new people and learn new things online, or do they merely extend and reify their existing social networks and personal interests? Robinson, Neustadtl, and Kestnbaum (Chapter 15) find that, independent of education, age, and other demographic factors, internet users *are* more open and tolerant folk. The first internet users tended to be wealthy, educated, and more conservative, but Robinson finds something of a demographic and ideational transition happening online. One cannot use standard labels, such as liberal and conservative, to describe many internet users; instead, Robinson and his colleagues plumb the subtle variations in the issues on which internet users seem to be increasingly tolerant.

PERSONAL AND GLOBAL CONTEXTS OF LIFE ONLINE

Whereas the previous sections focus on social phenomena within the United States, contemporary life online also has a personal and global context. The personal context of life online consists of not only the hardware and software to which we have access individually but also our personal skills with new media. Some of the best contemporary data on the digital divide appear in the contributions from Rice and Katz (Chapter 7) and Robinson, Neustadtl, and Kestnbaum (Chapter 15), but Hargittai (Chapter 16) digs into a kind of *second-order* learning divide. In the opener to Part V, she finds that personal skills with new media vary widely but that a significant portion of the variation in how long it takes people to complete a search online can be explained by the type of information being sought, their schooling, and the presence of children in the household. We rely heavily on our social network both for learning new skills and for getting suggestions on the kinds of content to explore. As Starke-Meyerring, Burk, and Gurak (Chapter 17) add, not only do skills vary widely, but so do privacy norms. To be more accurate, individuals seem to have strict privacy norms but little knowledge of how to protect their privacy online. Conversely, many corporations have less regard for our privacy expectations because transparent markets—and competitive edge—require knowledge about our preferences as consumers. Starke-Meyerring and her colleagues identify three approaches to the management of individual privacy and compare and contrast the European model of state-led protections, the American model of corporate self-regulation, and a model of citizen management.

This is one example of how the personal context of life online, our individual research skills and privacy expectations, has a difficult fit with the global context of life online, a world of competing corporations and nation-states vying for our business and trying to protect our interests. Sassen (Chapter 18) writes about other ways in which personal and global contexts connect in her piece on how sited digital materials move. She wrestles with the conceptual challenge of studying communication technologies that both construct new social dynamics and reproduce old ones, constraining some human activities while providing capacity for others. Part of the solution, she argues, lies in making sure that the study of life online includes the territorial context in which users actually live.

Whereas Stromer-Galley (Chaper 6) investigates social expectations for polling technologies, Bainbridge (Chapter 19) takes a much broader look at expectations for the future through scenarios about how new media will *stay* new. However, he does so in an interesting way. Rather than presenting many people with short, mutually exclusive statements about the future, he takes one respondent and offers many different scenarios. He takes advantage of new media, turning the internet itself into a research tool, and presents more than 2,000 scenarios to a *single* respondent, asking for careful distinctions between what the respondent *expects* and *wants* from the communications technologies to come. Bainbridge presents the results of the Question Factory, a unique project that turns traditional survey research on its head. Rather than asking a large number of people to choose from a small range of responses to questions limited by survey designers, the Question Factory asks one person to generate the widest possible range of responses to the questions deemed important.

Cross-Cutting Themes

Even though this collection has been explicitly organized around these different spheres of life—community, political, economic, cultural, personal, and global— there are two implicit themes that cut through the collection. The first has to do with the commercialization of life online. The second has to do with what I call the demographic transition online.

CONSUMERISM, COMMERCIALIZATION, AND COMMODIFICATION ONLINE

For those who study new media and society, one of the most pernicious claims is that the content of new media has been spoiled by consumerism, commercialization, and commodification. One question more frequently asked of internet users is whether they feel that the technology has improved their ability to shop. The statistics tell us that being older predicts a negative response and that even though being female is a slightly positive predictor, it is not statistically significant, so we cannot generalize about whether women feel like better shoppers because of new media (Howard et al., 2001). When Silver and Garland (Chapter 10) do their analysis of the relationship between the interests of young teen women and the goals of the teen advertising industry, they find that female teens have been intent on using IM and have resisted advertisers' efforts to construct new media as a shopping tool. Women tend to look for information about health care and dealing with other kinds of life problems. But does having more content about health and welfare on the internet represent some kind of feminization? Shade (Chapter 4) tackles that question. One of the most pronounced negative effects is racial categories, such that people who self-describe as being part of a racial minority clearly do not feel empowered by new media technologies. Such tools do not make African Americans, Asian Americans, or other minorities feel as though they are smarter shoppers, more equipped in the workplace, or better able to pursue hobbies or interests. However, other research suggests that minorities are more likely to use the internet for political activism and spiritual information (Howard et al., 2001). Both Shade and Nakamura (Chapter 5) wrestle with the question of whether engendering content and making it racially reflective is or should be a commercial enterprise. Kotamraju (Chapter 12) writes about the commodification of skills, a process that promotes raw coding and systems administration skills over artistic design skills among Web site creators.

Even though this is a collection of chapters from social scientists leading research into the role of new media in society, there are a number of points of disagreement. For example, whereas Shade and Nakamura comment on signs of the commercialization of racial identities and gendered content, Silver and Garland find that advertisers failed to lure teen girls into treating the Web as a shopping tool. Similarly, Neff and Stark (Chapter 11) report on a minor revolt when the teen users of an online magazine asserted the right to participate in the editing and design of the Web site. Thus, researchers find consumerism, commercialization, commodification, and powerful acts of resistance in society online. Two of the most forward-looking pieces may have contradictory implications. Whereas Bainbridge's (Chapter 19) respondent predicts that voting online will happen by 2100, Stromer-Galley (Chaper 6) makes a number of cautionary notes about the important social context in which online voting would be socially acceptable and logistically practicable. These points of disagreement signal that although we are learning much about society online, crucial questions about the political, economic, cultural, personal, and global contexts of new media inspire vibrant debate and require innovative research.

DEMOGRAPHIC TRANSITION ONLINE

One of the key hypotheses of demography is called the demographic transition—that all societies go from a stage of growth in which they are made up mostly of young people to a stage in which they are made up mostly of old people. We observe a similar demographic transition online. There are many people who do not use the internet and other new media tools, but their numbers are dwindling. Of the group of people who are not online, some are eager and just waiting for costs to drop. Many of the rest are reluctant to come online or say that they never will, but this group gets older and smaller every year (Lenhart, 2000). In this sense, the proportion of people familiar with new media is ever growing. Not only are most college students now quite familiar with the internet, but the number of people who must use the internet as part of their job profiles is also increasing (Jones, 2002). Yet even those who do claim familiarity with new media tools such as the internet might not always have regular access, as Rice and Katz (Chapter 7) and Robinson, Neustadtl, and Krestnbaum (Chapter 15) remind us; might not have the best research skills, as Hargittai (Chapter 16) finds; and may participate in the consumption of cultural content but not in its production, as Nakamura (Chapter 5) illustrates.

But it is not enough to state that the older folks who are unfamiliar with technology are diminishing in numbers. It is more useful to estimate trajectory—to figure out the direction of social currents. The principle of generational turnover has important implications for our study of the internet and society. For Peterson and Ryan (Chapter 14), the next generation of internet users will have diverse musical tastes. For Shade (Chapter 4) and Nakamura, the internet may be feminized and racially representative. Rice and Katz find a modest political role for new media during the 1996 and 2000 elections, Stromer-Galley (Chapter 6) analyzes survey data about voting habits and find that a growing number of people would prefer to vote online, and Bainbridge's (Chapter 19) in-depth study finds an interesting set of expectations about new media and politics:

> The general public will have ready access to government information and services over their computers. The internet will be an agent for democracy, as each community will have an electronic town hall. Voting will be done online via personal computer. Internet-based voting will dramatically strengthen democracy. The selection of leaders will be done via electronic media, without paper ballots or voting booths. Citizens will vote from home

by computer on daily and weekly issues which are raised by their elected representatives.

It is not simply that expectations for new media are high but that the social context of technology development only partly explains patterns of use. Stromer-Galley finds that internet use is the strongest predictor of a person's interest in voting online. She is one of the first to measure these effects in a comparable way. However, the effect of being a savvy internet user is greater than one's sense of duty or political interests, suggesting that the popular expectation for being able to conduct our political business online will grow only as the technology diffuses. Robinson and his colleagues confirm that as people get more and more experience with new media technologies, they seem to be more tolerant of other ideas. This is very different from the claim that has been made for some time—that the people online are also the more educated, richer, and more tolerant elites of the country. This is a tentative claim about causality—that internet exposure seems to make people more tolerant. The importance of these advancements cannot be understated. For a long time, scholars were cautious about discussing internet effects, and it was assumed that the golden age of "netizenship" passed when the masses started signing up for America Online. But several of these contributors are making nuanced, albeit bold, claims: People manage their social networks, learn about various cultures, and become more tolerant *as they spend more time online.* We used to be able to say that internet users had more social and cultural capital before they came online (e.g., more income, more education) and that was why internet users seemed like such sophisticated and tolerant people. It turns out that there are some observable threshold effects in the relationship between technology and tolerance: Controlling for things such as education and income, people who use new media seem to become a more sophisticated and tolerant bunch.

To what degree do the people who use the internet become more tolerant, giving sensitive responses to questions of social controversy? The degree of tolerance appears to be a simple function of exposure to new media technologies. In this volume, we learn that people who use the internet read more; tend to discover new literature, music, and other forms of culture; tend to work in interesting organizational patterns that take advantage of knowledge networks; tend to find community online, building their social capital by bridging and bonding various kinds of community; and query political and news content as it interests them. To what degree are these changes causally related?

Who We Know and What We Know

The literature on new media and society has often tried to explain internet users' political, economic, or cultural sophistication by the year they began using new media technologies. For survey researchers, the question "When did you come online?" was the best proxy for technological savvy. The assumption was that the early users were in sophisticated military, scientific, or economically elite circles and were more likely to have extensive social networks, altruistic motives, and technological savvy. In contrast, our contemporary contributors explore the connection between all of these positive attributes and how much time is spent online during an average day—a much better proxy for user sophistication. We already know that the people who started using new media were the wealthier and more educated people in the country—cultural omnivores, in Peterson and Kern's (1996) words. Because it appears that the interesting relationship is between the average number of hours spent online in a week and all of these positive attributes, we can hypothesize that the benefits of familiarity with new media accrue to those who are, well, familiar with new media. In other words, someone who came online only recently and invests a significant amount of time taking advantage of new media tools may enjoy the benefits as much as does the tech-savvy "old guard" who started using bulletin board systems during the late 1980s. Confirming this relationship with panel studies and time series should be next on the research agenda. For now, we have good data about how we ourselves perceive the role of new media in our lives. These data let us control for the effects of experience online—either how many years ago people started using the internet or how much time people spend online during an average day.

People seem to think that new media technology improves their social and cultural capital. Social capital can be defined as *who we know,* and cultural capital can be defined as *what we know.* People report feeling that new media technology has allowed them to solidify and extend their social networks and to expand their understanding of cultural, political, and economic matters. The contributors to this collection offer a number of important caveats and cautionary notes, and they use a variety of methods and data sources to flesh out their arguments. But a unique data series from the Pew Internet and American Life Project sheds some light on how many people felt about the role of new communication tools in their lives at the turn of the 21st century. In this panel, a sample of people were first interviewed in March 2000 and then again a year later.[1] Tables 1.1 and 1.2 present

Table 1.1 New Media and Who We Know: Odds (e^B) of Responding Positively to Questions About Relationships to Family and Friends, Modeled With Demographics, Status, and Experience Online

	All Respondents					Internet Users		
	Yesterday, did you:		When you need help, would you say that you can turn to:			How much, if at all, has the internet improved your:		
	Call a friend or relative just to talk?	Visit with family or friends?	Many people?	Just a few people?	Hardly any people?	Connections to your friends?	Connections to your family?	Your ability to meet new people?[a]
Constant	1.158	3.086***	0.898	0.703**	0.119**	0.119**	0.068**	0.044**
Age	0.993**	0.988***	0.990**	1.003	1.010	0.972***	0.938***	0.980**
Gender (female)	2.491**	1.544***	1.719***	0.766***	0.578***	1.364***	1.372***	1.088
College degree or more	0.892	0.881	1.118	1.068	0.587***	1.836***	1.464***	1.245
$50,000 or more	1.102	1.104	1.139	1.003	0.729*	1.217*	1.357**	1.064
Hispanic	1.070	0.703**	0.606**	1.150	1.803**	0.937	0.724	1.030
Race (white as reference category)								
African American	1.547**	0.572**	0.476**	1.279*	2.448*	0.794	0.796	0.725
Asian American	0.777	0.365**	0.406***	1.897***	1.035	0.935	1.057	0.384
Other	1.012	1.139	0.989	0.801	1.416	0.827	0.681	0.494
Revisited in 2001	0.977	0.894	1.063	1.036	0.893	7.924**	7.026**	—

(Continued)

Table 1.1 Continued

| | All Respondents | | | | | Internet Users | | |
| | Yesterday, did you: | | When you need help, would you say that you can turn to: | | | How much, if at all, has the internet improved your: | | |
	Call a friend or relative just to talk?	Visit with family or friends?	Many people?	Just a few people?	Hardly any people?	Connections to your friends?	Connections to your family?	Your ability to meet new people?[a]
When came online (nonuser as reference category)						(new user as reference category)		
During the past 6 months	1.040	1.080	1.002	1.244	0.675	—	—	—
1 year ago	1.087	1.136	1.109	1.114	0.563**	3.100**	2.965**	2.611**
2 or 3 years ago	1.106	1.192	1.154	0.965	0.705*	3.242**	3.425**	2.029**
More than 3 years ago	1.407**	1.106	1.304**	0.866	0.790	4.107**	3.607**	1.485
Nagelkerke R^2	0.077	0.044	0.059	0.013	0.074	0.339	0.296	0.048
n	71	502	1,736	1,649	397	702	814	111

SOURCE: Data from Pew Internet and American Life Project (www.pewinternet.org).

NOTE: Overall, there were 5,036 completed surveys, 1,501 of which were collected in the callback survey. In most models, the amount of explained variation is less than 30%, although the models still make statistically significant improvements to the predictive power of baseline odds alone.

a. This question was asked only in the callback survey.

*Significant at 0.05 level; **Significant at 0.01 level.

the results of logistic regressions for several dependent variables modeled with the following independent variables: age, gender, educational background, income, time of interview, ethnicity, race, and when they came online. Although it is common to report the coefficients from the logistic regression of independent variables onto dependent variables, the exponentiated coefficients are the more intuitive "odds ratios." An odds ratio is the probability that one variable, controlling for all of the other factors in a model, will predict a person's positive response to a question. For example, all other things being equal, the odds that a female respondent called a friend or relative just to talk are 149.1% greater [(2.491 − 1) * 100] than the odds that a man would have called a friend or relative. Moreover, it is possible to predict particular responses to questions such as "Yesterday, did you call a friend or relative just to talk?" For example, a 30-year-old woman with a B.A. degree who does not use the internet, earns less than $50,000 a year, and self-identifies as African American but not Hispanic would probably have responded positively (the odds are 118.6 to 1 in this sample). In contrast, if this respondent had reported using the internet for more than 3 years, she would very likely have responded positively (the odds would increase to 166.8 to 1 in this sample).[2]

NEW MEDIA AND WHO WE THINK WE KNOW

Overall, people who join society online believe that they know more people as a result. Table 1.1 illustrates some of the ways in which people have extended their social networks. These models predict a person's positive responses to a number of questions while controlling for several demographic factors. The table shows some of the questions that were asked of all respondents and some that were asked of internet users specifically. Of the statistically significant variables, being younger decreases the likelihood that someone telephoned a friend or relative to talk (because the odds are less than 1:1 [i.e., 0.993:1]), whereas being female, being African American, or having come online more than 3 years ago greatly increases that likelihood (because the odds are 2.491:1, 1.547:1, and 1.407:1, respectively). Of the statistically significant variables, being younger, Hispanic, African, or Asian American decreases the likelihood that someone visited family or friends, whereas being female increases that likelihood. Even though most of the categories about when someone came online are not statistically significant, their positive direction suggests that people who use the internet are probably in greater contact with their family and friends than are nonusers. Because the question about how many people a respondent can turn to can be modeled three ways with the three different response options, we have a more nuanced picture of how people who use the internet *feel* more connected. The older a person is, the fewer people that person feels he or she can turn to for social support. However, being female significantly increases the likelihood that a person feels he or she can turn to many people. Having a college degree or an annual family income of at least $50,000 decreases the chance that a person feels he or she can turn to hardly any people. In contrast, being Hispanic, African, or Asian American increases the odds that a person feels he or she can turn to only a few people or hardly anyone. Most interesting for our purposes, people who have more experience online were less likely to choose the *hardly any people* option, and more likely to report feeling they can turn to *many people,* than were nonusers.

But several questions about social life were put specifically to internet users. Of the statistically significant variables, being older decreases the likelihood that a person will feel that the internet has improved his or her connections to friends and family or improved his or her ability to meet new people. In contrast, being female, having a college degree, and having an annual income of at least $50,000 increases the odds that a person will feel more connected to friends and family because of the internet. However, the single largest effect lies with the fact of being reinterviewed a year later. In other words, after a year of using the technology, people were seven times more likely to say that connections to their friends and family had improved as a result of using the internet since their first interview in March 2000.[3] Statistically, the enthusiasm increases the longer a person has been using the technology. Compared with new users who had just started using the technology during the past 6 months, those who had been using it for more than a year were at least three times more likely to say that the internet had improved their social connections. Similarly, more experienced users were twice as likely to report that the internet had improved their ability to meet new people.

NEW MEDIA AND WHAT WE THINK WE KNOW

Overall, people who join in society online think that they know more things as a result. Table 1.2 illustrates some of the ways in which people garner information. Many people watch television news or read newspapers on a daily basis. Being older, having at least a college degree, having an annual household income of at least $50,000, being part of the sample that was resurveyed in 2001, or having experience with the internet increases the odds that a respondent either watched television news or read newspapers on a daily basis. In contrast, being female or a racial minority other than African American or Asian American decreases these odds. Being African American increases the odds of having watched television news on a daily basis, but as with being Hispanic, it decreases the odds of having read newspapers on a daily basis. Internet users with more experience seem to spend more time staying connected to daily news through notably non-internet media than do nonusers.

For those who use the internet regularly, Table 1.2 illustrates that the strongest predictors of how a person feels about new media technology is the amount of time he or she has had to grow familiar with the technology, either during the year since the person was last surveyed or over the course of several years of regular use. These odds ratios are useful in allowing us to compare effects. For example, they tell us that whether respondents feel that the internet has improved their ability to do their jobs depends much more on whether they have a college degree than on whether they have an annual household income of at least $50,000. This suggests that what we get out of new media technology depends more on our education than on our income level. Furthermore, having a college degree or a high family income may double the odds that a person feels that the internet has improved his or her ability to manage personal finances, but the effect of having come online more than 3 years ago is four times as great. In other words, having more than 3 years experience is a better predictor of how someone feels about managing his or her finances online than is whether that person is well educated or has much money to manage.

Conclusion: The Embedded Media Perspective

Some scholars debate whether new media such as the internet are mass media. The internet is increasingly commercialized, just like other mass media, and 55% of households in the United States were online at the turn of the 21st century. Others frame new media technologies as personalized, tailored, user-driven media. But a more useful analytical frame emerges across contributors in this volume—an embedded media perspective. This collection has an overall argument about how people actually perceive the relationship between new media technology and their quality of life. Millions of people who use new media find them deeply embedded in their lives, whether the uses involve encoding new organizational forms in the market, building new kinds of activism in the

Table 1.2 New Media and What We Know: Odds (e^B) of Responding Positively to Questions About Managing Information, Modeled With Demographics, Status, and Experience Online

	All Respondents				Internet Users				
	Yesterday, did you:				How much, if at all, has the internet improved your ability to:				
	Watch a news program on television?	Read a daily newspaper?	Shop?	Get information about health care?	Manage your personal finances?	Learn about new things?	Do your job?[a]	Deal with problems in your life?[a]	Pursue your hobbies or interests?[a]
Constant	0.416**	0.142**	0.099	0.032**	0.046**	0.217**	0.060**	0.033**	0.074**
Age	1.025**	1.032***	0.960**	0.985**	0.972***	0.964***	0.985***	0.984***	0.993
Gender (female)	0.947	0.782***	1.104	1.565***	0.783	0.978	1.220	1.559***	0.953
College degree or more	1.072	1.647***	1.607***	1.519***	1.892***	1.809***	2.595***	1.827***	1.384***
$50,000 or more	1.076	1.551**	1.931***	1.244	2.279***	1.481**	2.275***	1.526**	1.617***
Hispanic	1.083	0.728*	0.973	1.291	0.892	0.924	0.599	0.878	0.600
Race (white as reference category)									
African American	1.451**	0.604**	0.681	1.139	0.904	0.927	0.508*	0.610	0.504**
Asian American	0.902	0.768	1.786	0.967	1.441	1.104	0.120*	0.248	0.379
Other	0.737*	0.680*	0.492*	0.947	0.679	0.874	0.790*	0.489	1.004
Revisited in 2001	1.275**	1.164*	8.230**	6.830**	5.225**	8.705**	—	—	—

| | All Respondents | | Internet Users | | | | | | | |
| | Yesterday, did you: | | How much, if at all, has the internet improved your ability to: | | | | | | | |
	Watch a news program on television?	Read a daily newspaper?	Shop?	Get information about health care?[a]	Manage your personal finances?[a]	Learn about new things?[a]	Do your job?[a]	Deal with problems in your life?[a]	Pursue your hobbies or interests?[a]
When came online (nonuser as reference category)			(new user as reference category)						
During the past									
6 months	1.107	1.100	—	—	—	—	—	—	—
1 year ago	1.332*	1.160	2.267**	2.805**	1.967**	3.418**	1.354	1.678*	1.917**
2 or 3 years ago	0.940	1.261*	2.128**	2.597**	1.551**	3.509**	1.442*	1.615*	2.140**
More than									
3 years ago	1.229*	1.165	4.242**	3.316**	4.243**	3.114**	1.305	1.827**	1.522**
Nagelkerke R^2	0.061	0.14	0.308	0.230	0.238	0.365	0.118	0.069	0.072
n	359	849	493	444	313	501	301	152	340

SOURCE: Data from Pew Internet and American Life Project (www.pewinternet.org).

NOTE: Overall, there were 5,036 completed surveys, 1,501 of which were collected in the callback survey. In most models, the amount of explained variation is less than 30%, although the models still make statistically significant improvements to the predictive power of baseline odds alone.

a. These questions were asked only in the callback survey.

*Significant at .05 level; **Significant at .01 level.

political landscape, or experimenting with culture in ways that are exciting and new yet deeply ingrained in both the biases and beauties of social life offline. New media are more socially embedded than traditional mass communication technologies because users often produce and consume content *and* can design the software and hardware technology itself. Traditional media do not permit this fast dynamic production, consumption, and redesign.

In economic sociology, the term *embeddedness* has been used to describe the important ways in which market mechanisms are grounded in social contexts, not behaving as idealized rational, transparent, bias-free tools for exchange (Granovetter, 1985; Uzzi, 1996). In this volume, many contributors take what we suggest is an *embedded media perspective* by researching how new media mechanisms are also culturally laden tools for communication grounded in social contexts.[4] The embeddedness theme emerges from Larsen's (Chapter 3) piece. She finds that traditional media do not present the full spectrum of spiritual life, whereas new media create homes for this rich variation because they are embedded in the rich variety of ideas and aspirations of our communities. New media are not greedy as television is, according to Griswold and Wright (Chapter 13). New media are not exclusive media demanding all of our attention and are more deeply embedded in our day—coexisting with other technologies that save and consume our time in the day. In this sense, new media are embedded in the context of both traditional media and traditional technologies. For example, contemporary news programming frequently references Web site content, and Web sites increasingly archive full video news actualities. Dessauer (Chapter 8) finds that new media content is embedded in both internet and television technologies, such that distinctions are difficult if not meaningless. However, she does suggest that, as a society, we may be sacrificing local and network television news for online news. Dessauer and Schneider and Foot (Chapter 9) discuss blogging, through which some people document their personal experiences while other people treat them as reference sources. Embedded media link each other. Hargittai's (Chapter 16) focus groups reveal that one's ability to use new media technology is deeply embedded in the context of his or her family's information-gathering skills. For Neff and Stark (Chapter 11), the interesting story of the new economy is not so much the crash of the overvalued dot-com businesses as the more lasting and deeply embedded effects on organizational structures and logistics. They discuss several cases in which users play the role of both producers and consumers of content, a kind of distributed construction that occurs across communities of users. Similarly, Kotamraju (Chapter 12) writes about the embedding of a profession—from a loosely defined category of artsy Web site development skills to a well-codified set of programming skills. Sassen (Chapter 18) writes about the conceptual challenges of writing about digital materials that are territorially embedded.

The process of embedding new media in our social relations, and of embedding social relations in the media, need not be speedy or automatic. Stromer-Galley (Chapter 6) and Rice and Katz (Chapter 7) note that new media such as the internet have no direct or exclusive role in shaping political outcomes, so it is difficult to find how our individual or group behavior may be changing. Stromer-Galley suggests that the growing proportion of people comfortable with the new media, those for whom new media are ubiquitous technologies, are most likely to see them as useful tools for exercising franchise. In fact, the process of embedding media is a competitive one, as Silver and Garland (Chapter 10) illustrate with their example of teens who want to use IM and advertisers that want teens to shop. But ultimately, new media are also embedded in our economic and cultural lives because many of our economic transactions, and much of our daily work and cultural consumption, occur online. Shade (Chapter 4) and Nakamura (Chapter 5) note that minority and feminine cultures are weakly embedded online and that the champions of this process are looking for ways in which to profit by bringing offline cultures online. Starke-Meyerring, Burk, and Gurak (Chapter 17) remind us that privacy issues, and the privacy technologies available for our use, are embedded in legal institutions in *multiple* jurisdictions. They, like Sassen, develop stories about the way in which our technologies and the digital materials we compose both are locally sited and have global span. In this way, Sassen adds to the argument that digital technologies are embedded in global politics, but we posit that many digital technologies are more deeply embedded in our lives than are traditional media. Traditional media did not faithfully display Zapatista grievances to the world; it was left to new media to play that role (Garrido & Halavais, 2003). Whereas television stood alone, sometimes providing background noise to the day with static content, it competed with books and music for our attention. Embedded media are networked, deliver dynamic content, and allow us to produce our own, holding multiple forms of textual, aural, and visual cultural content. As Griswold and Wright (Chapter 13) and Peterson and Ryan (Chapter 14) frame them, the zero-sum arguments about competing media might not apply precisely because the technology is deeply embedded in our lives. We develop personalities online, and our personalities develop online. Cyberspace becomes a powerful cultural icon of its own, and prominent social organizations become dependent on new media for day-to-day operations.

FIT, STATUS, AND LINK

An embedded media perspective is a powerful analytical frame for describing the way in which new media are deeply set in our social and personal lives. The embedded media perspective assesses the capacities and constraints of social life online by three measures: fit, status, and link (Table 1.3). First, in terms of *fit*, embedded media suit our daily routines without requiring our exclusive attention or demanding new habits. They are immersed in the background of our lives, and in engineering jargon, the applications and tools of new media are extremely *sticky*. Media that fit well with existing social habits become deeply entrenched, difficult for us to give up, and fixed mediators of our social interaction. Moreover, we seem quick to give up communication technologies that are ill fitting and not easily embedded in our daily lives. Second, in terms of *status*, embedded media situate us as both producers and consumers of political, economic, and cultural information. New information technologies often tax our skill set, but we use media to the best of our ability to improve our social status and quality of life. Our ability to integrate digital media in our lives may be partly explained by race, gender, education, income, and other attributes, and the attributes of larger communities may explain how digital media are integrated in community life. By design, embedded media can help us form (or hinder us from forming) our own political opinions, become smarter consumers, or learn about other cultures. Third, in terms of *link*, these technologies connect different spheres of our lives more efficiently and effectively than do traditional media. We work at our home computer and do our personal business over the workplace internet. We can quickly learn about the global consequences of personal actions. Data about our policy preferences and shopping habits equally influence political positioning and commercial advertising campaigns. We use these technologies to manage our strong and weak links to other members of society.

For researchers, the analytical frame of an embedded media perspective offers several advantages. First, the embedded media perspective requires that the level of analysis we choose to take is local and immediate. We must examine how people use technology in their immediate social contexts. Taking a rational actor approach with general surveys will reveal something about *users*, but other methods are needed to dig deeply into the context of life online. Moreover, people have much more control over embedded media than they do over traditional

Table 1.3   The Embedded Media Perspective: Investigating the Individual and Social
Contexts of Life Online

		The Social Context of Embedded Media	
		Capacity	*Constraint*
	Fit	What capacity do technologies have for fitting into the daily routines of our social lives?	How do less ubiquitous, ill-fitting technologies restrict the daily routines of our social lives?
The Individual Context of Embedded Media	*Status*	What production or consumption capacity do technologies have for enriching our political, economic, and cultural lives?	What constraints do technologies place on our production or consumption of information about politics, economics, and culture?
	Link	How do technologies enable us to link to who or what we want to know?	What constraints do technologies place on our ability to link to who or what we want to know?

media. New media users act deliberately when they choose to produce and consume tools and content, but their choices may structure the constraints and capacities of new media later on. The embedded media perspective explains why trust is so prevalent online. We trust the information we find ourselves, we trust online news sources and companies with good reputations offline, and we trust new organizational forms that use new media. Despite the wide-ranging access that new media communication tools provide, people still prefer to interact with the people they know and trust.

Second, the embedded media perspective takes the position that communication tools provide both capacities and constraints for human action and that individual users are responsible for taking advantage of capacities and overcoming constraints in daily use. Thus, people are not simply solitary rational actors or extensions of their terminals as Castells (1996) or Nie and Erbing (2000) might suggest, nor are they exclusively social beings unencumbered by the limits of technology as Barlow (1996) might suggest. There is mutual structuration; technological use patterns conform to relations in a personal network, but the habits of personal networking adjust to the communication tools available. Witte (prologue) and Bainbridge (Chapter 19) take advantage of new media embeddedness by building a more nuanced survey instrument. Whereas traditional media force respondents to choose from a range of options preselected by researchers, embedded new media can offer multiple cues and allow respondents to reveal genuine preferences (Zaller & Feldman, 1992).

We argue here that these new technologies have been deeply embedded in multiple spheres of life—cultural, political, and economic—such that the global and personal contexts of our lives are fitted together and tightly linked. The central project of this collection is to assess the life of society online. Arguing that people *feel* more connected and *think* they know more things is different from trying to establish that people are more connected and do know more things. However, establishing how society feels about its online interaction is an important introduction to research by some of the world's leading social scientists exploring the role of new media in society in terms of how people feel, think, and act.

Notes

1. The survey was conducted using a rolling daily sample, with a target of completing 75 to 80 interviews each day of a survey period. For results based on the total sample, one can say with 95% confidence that the error attributable to sampling and other random effects is ±2.5 percentage points. For more on survey methodology, go to www.pewinternet.org or see Howard et al. (2001).

2. In the first example, the odds = 1.158 × 0.993(Age) × 2.491(Female) × 0.892(B.A.) × 1.102(Income) × 1.070(Hispanic) × 1.547(African American) × 0.777(Asian American) × 1.012(Other) × 0.977(Revisited in 2001) × 1.040(During past 6 months) × 1.087(1 year ago) × 1.106(2 or 3 years ago) × 1.407(More than 3 years ago), and because $e^{(0)} = 1$, the odds = 1.158 × 0.993(30) × 2.491(1) × 0.892(1) × 1 × 1 × 1.547(1) × 1 × 1 × 1 × 1 × 1 = 118.6. In the second example, the only difference is that the respondent reports having used the internet more than 3 years ago, so the odds = 1.158 × 0.993(30) × 2.491(1) × 0.892(1) × 1 × 1 × 1 × 1.547(1) × 1 × 1 × 1 × 1 × 1 × 1.407(1) = 166.8.

3. It is possible that some of this can be attributed to an instrument effect in that people were flattered at being revisited or eager to sound positive about the internet for the Internet and American Life Project.

4. At the time of this writing, news agencies began referring to the placement of journalists within mobile military units in Iraq as "embedded journalism." This label—and this phenomenon—fits with the notion of media embeddedness in that the journalists could do their fieldwork only if they were equipped with the latest satellite video phones. Technologies such as these allowed journalists to be entrenched in the immediate context of soldiers at war, allowing audiences to "experience" life on the front lines.

References

Barlow, J. P. (1996). *A declaration of the independence of cyberspace.* [Online]. Retrieved April 28, 2003, from www.eff.org/~barlow/declaration-final.html

Castells, M. (1996). *The rise of the network society.* Cambridge, MA: Blackwell.

Garrido, M., & Halavais, A. (2003). Mapping networks of support for the Zapatista movement: Applying social networks analysis to study contemporary social movements. In M. McCaughey & M. Ayers (Eds.), *Cyberactivism: Critical practices and theories of online activism*. London: Routledge.

Granovetter, M. (1985). Economic-action and social-structure: The problem of embeddedness. *American Journal of Sociology, 91*, 481–510.

Howard, P. N. (2002). Network ethnography and the hypermedia organization: New media, new organizations, new methods. *New Media & Society, 4*, 550–574.

Howard, P. N., Jones, S., & Rainie, H. (2001). Days and nights on the internet: The impact of a diffusing technology. *American Behavioral Scientist, 45*, 382–404.

Jones, S. (2002). *The internet goes to college: How students are living in the future with today's technology*. Washington, DC: Pew Internet and American Life Project.

Lenhart, A. (2000). *Who's not online*. Washington, DC: Pew Internet and American Life Project.

Manovich, L. (2000). *The language of new media*. Cambridge, MA: MIT Press.

Nie, N., & Erbing, L. (2000). *Internet and society: A preliminary report*. Palo Alto, CA: Stanford Institute for the Quantitative Study of Society.

Peterson, R., & Kern, R. (1996). Changing highbrow taste: From snob to omnivore. *American Sociological Review, 61*, 900–907.

Putnam, R. D. (2000). *Bowling alone: The collapse and revival of American community*. New York: Simon & Schuster.

Uzzi, B. (1996). The sources and consequences of embeddedness for the economic performance of organizations: The network effect. *American Sociological Review, 61*, 674–698.

Zaller, J., & Feldman, S. (1992). A simple theory of the survey response: Answering questions versus revealing preferences. *American Journal of Political Science 36*, 579–616.

Part I

Social Capital,
Community, and Content

2

The Bridging and Bonding
Role of Online Communities

Pippa Norris

Harvard University

A long tradition in sociological theory among writers such as Durkheim, Marx, Weber, Tonnïes, and Simmel has been concerned about the loss of community and the weakening of the face-to-face relations of *Gemeinschaft*, a theme revived recently in the work of Putnam (2000). The role of new communication technologies, especially the internet, has often been regarded as important for this phenomenon either by exacerbating social isolation or by reviving communities ties virtually. Contemporary debates about social capital have noted that many local networks and associations strengthen social cohesion, but another darker downside exists in community life (Edwards & Foley, 1998; Portess & Landholt, 1996). To understand this phenomenon, Putnam (2000, 2002) has drawn an important distinction between "bridging" groups that function to bring together disparate members of the community, exemplified by mixed-race youth sports clubs in South Africa and the Civic Forum in Northern Ireland, and "bonding" groups that reinforce close-knit networks among people sharing similar backgrounds and beliefs. In Putnam's (2002) words,

> Bridging social capital refers to social networks that bring together people of different sorts, and bonding social capital brings together people of a similar sort. This is an important distinction because the externalities of groups that are bridging are likely to be positive, while networks that are

bonding (limited within particular social niches) are at greater risk of producing externalities that are negative.

This conceptual distinction should be seen as a continuum rather than a dichotomy because in practice many groups serve both bridging and bonding functions, but networks can be classified as falling closer to one end of this spectrum or the other. Heterogeneous local associations (e.g., Parent-Teacher Associations, the Red Cross) are believed to have beneficial consequences for building social capital, generating interpersonal trust, and reinforcing community ties. Homogeneous bonding organizations can serve these positive functions as well, but the danger is that they can also exacerbate and widen existing social cleavages, especially in pluralistic societies splintered by deep-rooted ethnonational, ethnoreligious, or racial conflict. The dysfunctional types of bonding networks are exemplified by the Ku Klux Klan in Mississippi, La Cosa Nostra in Sicily, and the Irish Republican Army in Belfast.

This distinction raises important questions about how best to promote inclusive networks to foster crosscutting cleavages in divided societies. One problem is that if cities such as Belfast, Johannesburg, and Los Angeles are deeply divided but local neighborhoods are socially homogeneous, associations within each area are likely to reflect the background, beliefs, and interests of the predominant group within each community. Fragmented pluralism exacerbates the challenges facing aggregating institutions. Many believe that one important way in which to overcome these limitations could be through the transition from territorial communities of place toward online communities of identity. The growth of the internet population generated a substantial literature theorizing about the potential consequences of virtual communities for exacerbating or overcoming the "tragedy of the commons" (Bimber, 1998; Jones, 1998; Rheingold, 1993; Schuler 1996; Tsagarousianou, Tambini, & Bryan, 1998). Empirical research has examined many dimensions of online communities, including in-depth ethnographic studies of particular groups such as *The Well*, content analyses of participants in internet listservs and chat rooms, and studies of the most effective features of community organization Web sites (Davis, 1999; Gaines & Shaw, 2001; Hafner, 2001; Hill & Hughes, 1998; Holmes, 1997; Jones, 1998; Kim, 2000; Norris, 2001; Preece, 2001). Yet many questions remain. How do territorial and online communities overlap and interact? Were participatory online groups an early phase among internet enthusiasts that may be dying with the "normalization" of the more passive internet population? And the particular the focus of this study: *Do online groups serve a bridging or bonding function for society as a whole?*

Theoretically, there are intriguing possibilities. On the one hand, certain features of the digital world, especially its fragmented hyperpluralism, should encourage interaction and exchange within social groups having similar beliefs and values. The internet is a medium where users have nearly unlimited choices and minimal constraints about where to go and what to do. Commitments to any particular online group can often be shallow and transient when another group is but a mouse click away. Most purely online communities without any physical basis are usually low-cost, "easy-entry, easy-exit" groups. To avoid cognitive dissonance, it is simpler to "exit" than to try to work through any messy bargaining and conflictual disagreements within the group. Like adherents to particular left-wing or right-wing talk radio shows or readers of highly partisan newspapers, the result of participating in online communities could be expected to reinforce like-minded beliefs, similar interests, and *ideological* homogeneity among members. So many interest groups, organizations, and associations are available on the internet that it is exceptionally easy to find the niche Web site or specific discussion group that reflects one's particular beliefs and interests, avoiding exposure to alternative points of view. Thousands of networks are devoted to bringing together like-minded souls ranging from anarchists and hippies to skinheads and survivalists. A cornucopia of discussion groups span everything from the issues of abortion and Afrocentrism to those of welfare reform and xenotransplantation. One can monitor human rights with Amnesty International, the environment with Greenpeace, or the state of democracy with the National Democracy Institute. Or, one can visit hundreds of policy "think tanks" in the nation's capital ranging from the Heritage Foundation and Cato Institute to the Brookings Institution and Twentieth Century Fund. Hyperpluralism and over-specialization among marginalized groups can be expected to encourage bonding among regular members.

Yet this is far from the whole story because, on the other hand, certain features of the internet could be expected to bridge traditional social divides. Textual communication via the internet strips away the standard visual and aural cues of social identity—including those of gender, race, age, and socioeconomic status—plausibly promoting heterogeneity, where "no one knows that you are a dog on the Internet" (Holmes, 1997). Social psychologists suggest that this anonymity could be most important for marginalized populations that are otherwise isolated from cultural interactions outside of their groups such as single

	Social Homogeneity	Social Heterogeneity
Ideological Homogeneity	Bonding	Mixed
Ideological Heterogeneity	Mixed	Bridging

Figure 2.1   Typology of Groups

mothers working at home, gay men, and rural poor populations (McKenna & Bargh, 1998). The digital divide during the early years of adoption hinders social diversity, but the normalization of the internet population in the United States, as access spreads more widely, should also promote greater inclusiveness for poorer and less educated sectors as well as for women and ethnic minorities. The lack of barriers to entry means that once social groups are online, most virtual communities are fairly permeable to new members.

These considerations lead us to the typology of the societal function of online communities outlined schematically in Figure 2.1. The classification assumes that pure bonding groups are most likely to occur online where social homogeneity and ideological homogeneity overlap, deepening networks among people sharing similar backgrounds and beliefs. In contrast, where the internet draws together those from diverse social backgrounds and beliefs and thereby widens contacts, the typology suggests that this generates pure bridging groups. Nevertheless, this pattern can be expected to vary systematically (a) by the type and depth of the social cleavage (e.g., by gender, race, or class) and (b) by the type of online group (e.g., by religious, union, or local community group). Just as the social background and ideological beliefs of members in nonvirtual communities typically vary in predictable ways (e.g., more men usually join sports clubs, trade unions, and political associations, whereas more women often belong to religious organizations), online communities can be expected to reflect these differences as well.

Survey Evidence

To explore these propositions further, we can turn to the Pew Internet and American Life Project, which has developed perhaps the more detailed series of daily tracking surveys investigating the practices and habits of internet users in the United States (for details, see Horrigan, Rainie, & Fox, 2001). From January 17

Table 2.1   Factor Analysis of the Bridging and Bonding Functions of the Internet

How Much Has the Internet Helped You at:	Bonding	Bridging
Becoming more involved with groups and organizations you already belong to?	.802	
Connecting with groups and organizations that are based in your local community?	.754	
Finding people or groups who share your interests?	.745	
Finding people or groups who share your beliefs?	.655	
Connecting with people from different racial or ethnic backgrounds?		.860
Connecting with people from different economic backgrounds?		.806
Connecting with people of different ages or generations?		.732
Total variance explained (percentage)	33.8	30.8

SOURCE: Data from Pew Internet and American Life Project. (www.pewinternet.org).

NOTE: Extraction method used: principal components analysis. Rotation method used: varimax with Kaiser normalization.

to February 11, 2001, Pew conducted a special survey on Communities and the Internet, including multiple items monitoring internet use, behavior and attitudes toward both online and local communities, and the standard sociodemographic factors.[1] To learn about people's experiences with the internet, the Pew survey asked whether the internet had helped people to do seven different things such as "becoming more involved with groups and organizations you already belong to," "finding people or groups who share your interests," and "connecting with people of different ages or generations."

Factor analysis showed that these items fell into two principal dimensions, representing the extent to which people believed that their internet experience helped them in (a) bridging social divisions of generation, race, and class or (b) bonding with people with similar interests and beliefs (Table 2.1). These items were recoded and summed to create separate bridging and bonding scales, standardized to 100 points for ease of interpretation.

What types of online groups promote experience of bridging and bonding? The first issue is how far various types of groups, such as unions, community associations, and sports clubs, proved to be stronger at promoting the experience of the bridging and bonding functions of the internet. The Pew survey asked the extent to which people used the internet to have any contact with, or to get any information from, a range of 13 different types of online groups. Respondents were also asked to indicate which of these groups they were in contact with most

Table 2.2   The Bridging and Bonding Functions of Various Online Groups

Percentage Ever[a]	Percentage Most[b]		Mean Bridging Scale	Mean Bonding Scale
50	24	A trade or professional association	46	53
50	21	A group for people who share a hobby, an interest, or an activity	51	56
31	7	A fan group for a particular television show, entertainer, or musical group	54	55
29	7	A support group for a particular sports team	49	54
29	3	A local community group	50	57
28	4	A group of people who share your personal beliefs	58	62
28	5	A support group (e.g., for a medical condition)	49	55
24	6	A group of people who share your lifestyle	56	63
22	3	A political group or organization	51	57
21	5	A religious group or organization	48	56
20	5	A sports team or league in which you participate	49	54
15	2	An ethnic or cultural group	59	61
6	1	A labor union	52	59

SOURCE: Data from Pew Internet and American Life Project (www. pewinternet.org).

a. Percentage ever: "Have you ever used the internet to be in contact with or get information from …"

b. Percentage most: "Which of these groups are you in contact with most often through the internet?"

NOTE: The 100-point bridging and bonding scale is based on the distribution of factor analyses between 0.00 and 1.00 in Table 2.1. The scales were estimated for those who had *ever* used the internet to contact these groups. The differences between the mean scores on the bridging and bonding scales for those who had ever used the internet to contact these groups and those who had not all were significant at the .01 level, as measured by analysis of variance.

often. Table 2.2 and Figure 2.2 show the mean scores on the perceived bridging and bonding functions of the internet as experienced by users of various types of online groups. Overall contact with online groups was believed to serve both functions, but the experience was slightly stronger for reinforcing bonding (deepening contact with people having similar beliefs or interests) than for bridging (widening contact with people from diverse social backgrounds). There were variations by type of group, as expected, with the experience of contact with

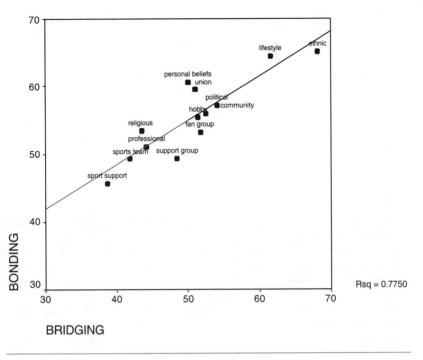

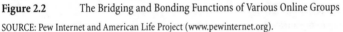

Figure 2.2   The Bridging and Bonding Functions of Various Online Groups
SOURCE: Pew Internet and American Life Project (www.pewinternet.org).

ethnic/cultural groups and groups sharing similar lifestyles rated highest in both functions. Many groups clustered in the middle of the distribution. Contact with sports groups, as either a supporter or a participant, was perceived to generate the least social benefits. Overall, there was a strong relationship between these two functions ($R^2 = .77$). To see whether these differences among groups remained significant, ordinary least squares regression models were run predicting the impact of contact with various types of groups on experience of the bridging and bonding functions of the internet, including the standard social controls for age, sex, education, income, and race. The models in Table 2.3 show that even after controls were introduced, contact with most groups remained a significant predictor of evaluations of the bridging and bonding functions of the internet. The pattern suggests that online contact does bring together like-minded souls who share particular beliefs, hobbies, or interests, probably due to the hyperpluralism and ideological diversity widely evident on the internet as well as widening social diversity.

Table 2.3   Ordinary Least Squares Regression Model Predicting Bonding and Bridging

	Model 1:		Model 2:	
	Bonding Function (deepening interests)	Standard Error	Bridging Function (widening contacts)	Standard Error
Constant	124.11***	3.66	119.52***	4.27
Demographics				
Age	0.10***	0.02	0.14***	0.03
Gender (female)	1.39**	0.70	0.32	0.81
Education (last grade completed)	−0.68***	0.23	1.03***	0.27
Income (household)	0.28*	0.15	0.52***	0.18
Race (white)	1.80**	0.89	4.28***	1.04
Type of online group contact:				
Group sharing your personal beliefs	5.98***	0.58	6.22***	0.67
Hobby, interest, or activity	4.61***	0.56	2.26***	0.65
Local community group or association	3.82***	0.61	2.08***	0.71
Political group or organization	5.30***	0.88	4.73***	1.03
Entertainment fan club	4.08***	0.80	7.33***	0.93
Share your lifestyle	2.58***	0.52	2.49***	0.61
Personal support group	3.32***	0.75	3.14***	0.87
Trade or professional association	2.66***	0.62	0.75	0.73
Religious group or organization	2.86***	0.83	0.77	0.84
Play on sports team	1.85**	0.86	1.17	1.00
Ethnic or cultural group	1.47**	0.72	4.42***	1.43
Labor union	1.40	1.23	−0.20	0.86
Sport supporter club	0.95	0.74	−0.40	0.97
Adjusted R^2	0.253		0.182	
N	3,002		3,002	

SOURCE: Pew Internet and American Life Project (www.pewinternet.org).

$*p < 0.10$, $**p < 0.05$, $***p < 0.01$.

These results can be broken down by type of social diversity by comparing responses to the specific item that the internet helped to "find people who share my beliefs" with responses to the three items monitoring whether the internet helped to connect people from various racial/ethnic, economic, or generational backgrounds. Figure 2.3 shows that participation in most online groups did little to bridge racial divides in the United States other than aiding in contact with specific ethnic/cultural organizations. Group contact was also fairly ineffective at bridging the socioeconomic or class divide. But online communities did seem to

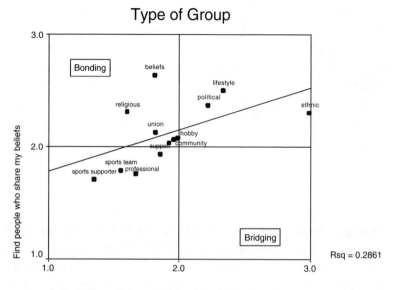

Connect with people from different racial backgrounds

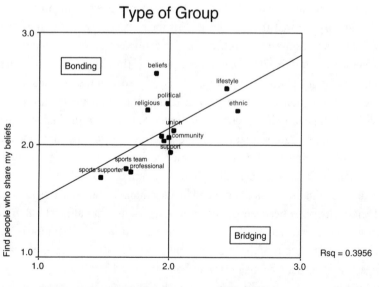

Contact with people from different economic backgrounds

Figure 2.3   Group Types by Race, Class, and Generational Bridging

SOURCE: Data from Pew Internet and American Life Project (www.pewinternet.org).

have greater capacity to cut across generational lines; those engaged in the online groups organized around lifestyles, ethnicity, community, hobbies/interests, and political associations found that the internet helped to connect people of various age groups. More groups fell into the mixed category (generating experience of ideological homogeneity and social heterogeneity) by age group than by class or race. The reasons for this could be the younger age profile of the internet population and the tendency for more middle-aged memberships in many traditional organizations, resulting in online groups becoming a generational meeting place.

Conclusions

Many believe that any erosion in the traditional face-to-face sociability and personal communications or Gemeinschaft in modern societies represents a threat to the quality of civic life, collaborative social exchanges, and the community spirit. Whether the internet has the capacity to supplement, restore, or even replace these social contacts remains to be seen. As an evolving medium that is still diffusing through the population, it is still too early to predict the full consequences of this technology. Nevertheless, the Pew survey evidence among existing users allows us to explore whether those Americans who are most active in online groups feel that the internet *widens* their experience of community (by helping them to connect with others who have different beliefs or backgrounds) or whether they feel that it *deepens* their experience (by reinforcing and strengthening existing social networks). The analysis suggests that the internet generally serves both functions, although the strength of this effect varies in important ways by the type of online group in the United States. To go further, we need to explore more ethnographic studies of the inner lives of communities, including those both functional and dysfunctional for society as a whole. It is hoped that online communities could perhaps help to overcome traditional divisions among territorial communities, as exemplified by the ethnoreligious enclaves in Belfast, the sharp divisions between the poor inner cities and the affluent suburbs in Detroit, and the racial divides in Johannesburg. If we can extrapolate more broadly from this study of the internet population in the United States, the results suggest that these hopes may prove to be exaggerated, but online participation has the capacity to deepen linkages among those having similar beliefs as well as to serve as a virtual community that cuts across at least some traditional social divisions.

Note

1. Princeton Survey Research contacted a sample of 3,002 respondents using a random-digit sample of telephone numbers designed to be representative of the U.S. adult population and then identified a subsample of internet users ($n = 1,697$). The sample data are weighted in the analysis to be representative of the population.

References

Bimber, B. (1998). The internet and political transformation: Populism, community, and accelerated pluralism. *Polity, 31*(1), 133–160.

Davis, R. (1999). *The web of politics.* Oxford, UK: Oxford University Press.

Edwards, B., & Foley, M. W. (1998). Civil society and social capital beyond Putnam. *American Behavioral Scientist, 42,* 124–139.

Gaines, B. R., & Shaw, M. L. G. (2001). Human-computer interaction in online communities. *Journal of Research and Practice in Information Technology, 33*(1), 3–15.

Hafner, K. (2001). *The Well: A story of love, death, and real life in the seminal online community.* New York: Carroll & Graf.

Horrigan, J., Rainie, L., & Fox, S. (2001). *Online communities: Networks that nurture long-distance relationships and local ties* (Pew Internet and American Life Project). [Online]. Retrieved April 15, 2003, from www.pewinternet.org

Hill, K. A., & Hughes, J. E. (1998). *Cyberpolitics: Citizen activism in the age of the internet.* Lanham, MD: Rowan & Littlefield.

Holmes, D. (1997). *Virtual politics: Identity and community in cyberspace.* London: Sage.

Jones, S. (Ed.). (1998). *Cybersociety 2.0: Revisiting computer-mediated communication and community.* Thousand Oaks, CA: Sage.

Kim, A. J. (2000). *Community building on the Web.* Berkeley, CA: Peachpit Press.

McKenna, K. Y. A., & Bargh, J. A. (1998). Coming out in the age of the internet: Identity "demarginalization" through virtual group participation. *Journal of Personality and Social Psychology, 75,* 681–694.

Norris, P. (2001). *Digital divide.* Cambridge, UK: Cambridge University Press.

Portess, A., & Landholt, P. (1996). The downside of social capital. *The American Prospect, 26,* 18–21.

Preece, J. (2001). Sociability and usability in online communities: Determining and measuring success. *Behaviour & Information Technology, 20,* 347–356.

Putnam, R. D. (2000). *Bowling alone.* New York: Free Press.

Putnam, R. D. (2002). Introduction. In R. D. Putnam (Ed.), *The dynamics of social capital.* Oxford, UK: Oxford University Press.

Rheingold, H. (1993). *The virtual community: Homesteading on the electronic frontier.* Reading, MA: Addison-Wesley.

Schuler, D. (1996). *New community networks: Wired for change.* Reading, MA: Addison-Wesley.

Tsagarousianou, R., Tambini, D., & Bryan, C. (1998). *Cyberdemocracy.* London: Routledge.

3

Deeper Understanding, Deeper Ties

Taking Faith Online

Elena Larsen

Pew Internet and American Life Project

R eligion leads followers through the deepest questions, sorrows, and joys of
their lives. It provides a framework for finding elusive understanding, and
its practice requires engaging all aspects mind, body, and spirit. Followers study
the texts of their faith but know that words are often insufficient to convey the
meaning they seek. So they pray, they contemplate, and they fast. They create
music and art. They engage in physical, emotional, and fiscal disciplines to gain
another step on the path to understanding and fulfillment.

The internet is a natural place for the faithful to take their questions and
practices. It is a space at once both solitary and social. It provides unprecedented
access to information, to artwork, and to others of like minds. Whether individuals need advice on fine points of canonical law, special music for a service, ideas
for devotional study, material for a religious class, support in prayer, or simply a
spirited debate that they cannot introduce in their own circle of friends, they can
find it all in the glow of a connected monitor. The Web allows the faithful wide
access to resources and links, and it offers the doubtful or curious a safe place to
explore. It is a favored venue for those rejecting mainstream religions to revive
ancient faiths. It allows for Luther-esque defiance of the hierarchical powers, as
demonstrated by exiled Roman Catholic bishop Jacques Gaillot's online "diocese

without borders" (www.partenia.org/eng). The richness of the landscape is explored here in a survey of how online Americans use cyberspace in the course of their religious and spiritual lives.

The religious Web has attracted academic, evangelical, and spiritual interest. Brasher (2001) documented the religious internet as a space as timeless and boundless as religious thought itself. Accessing the internet is comparable to accessing the infinite; thus, it is natural not only for seeking religious resources but also for creating new religious rituals and thought. Barna Research Online (1998) warned churches too bound up in tradition that they would lose their younger members to the freedom, convenience, and culture of online religious space.

This chapter provides a general overview of online religious activity among Americans. It is based on the results of two studies conducted by the Pew Internet and American Life Project concerning the internet and religion. One is a telephone survey of people who had identified themselves as having sought religious content online. It asked a series of questions about what types of activities people carry out in religious Web space and how such activities affect their lives. The other is an online survey of congregations in the United States that asked how they used their own Web sites.

Although the survey instruments were developed with some analytical goals in mind, they are primarily exploratory. The surveys approached individuals as content consumers and approached congregations primarily as content creators, a rough distinction that tells only part of the online religion story. The studies seek to answer basic questions about the religious use of the internet in the United States and to provide primary data that can serve as groundwork for future studies. This chapter seeks to provide a demographic portrait of Americans who use the internet for religious purposes so as to ascertain what types of religious material are most popularly sought out online, what services "religion surfers" attempt to provide over the internet, and what effects (if any) the internet has on religious practice among Americans.

Methodology

PHONE SURVEY

These findings are based on several surveys of Americans about their use of the internet. The overall figures about the size of the religion surfer population comes from a survey of 2,247 American adults (age 18 years or over) between August 13 and September 10, 2001. A more in-depth survey was given to 500 persons who have told survey takers at Princeton Survey Research Associates (PSRA) that they had ever gone online for religious or spiritual information. The telephone interviews among those age 18 years or over were conducted by PSRA between July 24 and August 15, 2001. For results based on the total sample, one can say with 95% confidence that the error attributable to sample and other random effects is plus or minus 4 percentage points. In addition to sample error, question wording and practical difficulties in conducting telephone surveys may introduce some error or bias into the findings of opinion polls.

At least 10 attempts were made to complete an interview at every household in the sample. The calls were staggered over times of the day and days of the week to maximize the chances of making contact with potential respondents. Interview refusals were recontacted at least once to try again to complete an interview. The final response rate for the callback portion of the survey was 66%.

CONGREGATIONAL SURVEY

These findings are derived from an online survey of 1,309 congregations. Roughly 12,000 congregations with Web sites and e-mail addresses were invited to participate in the survey, which ran from November 21 to December 8, 2000. Congregations received one invitation and one follow-up reminder and were offered individualized summaries of their own Web site use compared with that of other congregations of their size or denomination as an incentive to participate. As with many studies that require sampling internet pages, the results of this survey must be considered descriptive rather than scientifically generalizable. A scientifically valid survey requires that a sample of respondents be drawn from the entire population. There is no single comprehensive listing of congregational Web sites in the United States. Some surveys of internet sites have used random page generators to mimic a random sample of pages. But such generators cannot limit the pages it produces to any specific type of page, so that method was not suitable for this study.

The framework for identifying Christian congregation Web sites was drawn from the Web sites of Christian denominations with more than 1 million members, as reported in the 2000 edition of the *Yearbook of American and Canadian Churches*. Many, but not all, of these sites provided links to the sites of member congregations. Sites of nondenominational congregations, as well as sites of congregations whose denominations did not provide congregational links, were drawn from the generic portal Yahoo! and the Christian portal Goshen. Jewish congregations were drawn from umbrella sites for Conservative, Reform, and Reconstructionist Judaism; attempts to correspond with a Web site for Orthodox Judaism were not successful. Neither were there sufficient numbers of Islamic and Buddhist congregational sites to include in this study. But all in all, 19 congregations in various religions, denominations, and branches were solicited.[1]

WHO ARE THE RELIGION SURFERS?

One in four adult internet users in the United States has sought religious material on the internet at one point or another. These religion surfers are present in all segments of society. They are fairly evenly spread out among men and women, blacks and whites, age groups, and economic and educational attainment levels. Unlike many other online activities, the act of getting religious or spiritual information online is not strongly related to an internet user's level of experience. In many other activities, additional years of online experience correlate with greater participation in online activities such as getting news online, purchasing goods online, and doing work-related research online. Religion surfing, however, is conducted by internet novices and masters alike. The religion surfers surveyed parallel the religious profile of the American population at large. Christianity predominates among American religion surfers, but the group also includes a mix of religious minorities such as Unitarians, Baha'i, Taoists, Pagans, and yoga practitioners.

However, the intensity of religious devotion of religion surfers distinguishes them from the general population. Some 81% of online religion surfers described their commitment to faith as "very strong." In contrast, the 1998 General Social Survey found that only 19% of the American population described themselves as "very religious."[2] Furthermore, religion surfers back up these claims in practice; nearly three fourths (74%) of them reported that they attend religious services at least once a week, compared with estimates ranging from 26% to 39% for the general population.[3] And 86% of religion surfers pray or meditate at least once a day, compared with 54% of all Americans. More than one in three religion surfers (36%) has converted to a faith or practice other than the one in which he or she was raised. Approximately 12% of religion surfers consider themselves outsiders who feel isolated or discriminated against due to their religious beliefs.

Similarly, congregations that publish Web sites do not fall neatly into any single category. It would be reasonable to expect that Web sites are the bailiwick of wealthier congregations with highly connected members. But responding congregations were fairly evenly spread across annual budget levels. Of course, the higher the budget, the more likely a congregation was to own Web space. But many others could get free space through their denominations (15%), donations of space from members (15%), advertisement-funded groups (8%), or groups such as ForMinistry.com that provide free space and site templates for faith groups (7%). Nearly half of responding congregations (41%) reported an average weekly attendance of between 50 and 150, indicating that even smaller churches are going online.

WHAT ARE RELIGION SURFERS LOOKING FOR ONLINE?

Reference and Study. Religion surfers enjoy perusing religious topics, and the internet remains a browser's dream. The top uses by religion surfers are simply to find information on their own faith or another one. Fully 67% of Christians have used the internet for this purpose (Table 3.1). In contrast, nearly all non-Christians (96%) reported looking up information on their own faiths. In this predominantly Christian country, the internet may well be the most fruitful and convenient source of information on other religious traditions.

Social Activities. Old-fashioned, face-to-face socializing is much more appealing to religion surfers than are tech-aided interactions related to faith. Among the five least-used activities among religion surfers, three are largely social: engaging in online chat, playing faith-oriented computer games,[4] and using faith-oriented matchmaking services. Things are different within a congregational setting, however. More than 90% of online congregations reported that their members e-mail each other for fellowship purposes, and one in three reported that this is done "a great deal" of the time. In a different sense, however, the very nature of seeking religious material online appears to be a social one. Half of religion surfers have recommended a site to a friend or relative, and these recommendations are primary sources of favored sites. Some 44% of those who have a single favorite site learned of it from a friend or relative rather than through their own searching. And 63% of religion surfers with a single favorite site pass along the URL to friends or relatives. However, although favorite sites may bounce around existing social networks, they do not serve to

Table 3.1   Activities of Online Religion Surfers (percentages)

Look for information about own faith	67
Look for information about another faith	50
E-mail a prayer request	38
Download religious music	38
Give guidance over e-mail	37
Buy religious items online	34
Plan religious activities over e-mail	29
Get ideas for ceremonies	28
Subscribe to a listserv	27
Download sermons	25
Get ideas for holidays	22
Seek guidance over e-mail	21
Find a new church	14
Chat	10
Play religious computer games	5
Participate in online worship	4
Take an online religion course	3
Use a faith-oriented matchmaking service	3
N	500

SOURCE: Data from Pew Internet and American Life Project, *Religion Surfers Survey* (www.pewinternet.org)

create new ones. Only 15% of those with a single favorite site reported using the site to meet new people.

Advice and Support. Those intrepid souls willing to admit a need for advice or assistance need never fear that help is far away. Religion surfers are quite generous. When asked about the support capabilities of the Web, they were far more likely to report giving faith-oriented advice (37%) than to report asking for it (21%). Women are more active than men in both seeking and giving advice. Approximately 38% of religion surfers have used e-mail to request prayer assistance. Online, one can put out prayer requests to close friends within one's own congregation, to total strangers who volunteer their prayer time at Web sites, or to strangers who come together in online prayer circles to request prayers from, and to post them for, each other. Congregation members are more than three times as likely (42% vs. 12%) to have e-mailed prayer requests, suggesting that this intimate kind of interaction might be practiced mostly within existing communities. In fact, 86% of congregations reported that members use e-mail to share concerns and to support each other spiritually, with 33% saying that this happens a great deal of the time.

Fresh Content. Advice manuals for creating successful Web sites repeatedly stress the need to keep content fresh and interesting. One means of providing regular fresh content is to provide a listserv. Religion surfers can sign up for daily devotional material or updates from religious news services. Nearly one in three religion surfers (27%) is signed up with some sort of listserv, but listservs are particularly popular among those who seek religious material most often. Nearly half (46%) of those who seek religious content online several days per week are also on a faith-oriented listserv. Fresh content is a particular challenge to congregations, many of which rely on volunteers to create and maintain their sites. Many respondents commented that they would like to do more with their sites but simply did not have the necessary resources.

Membership. Although only 14% of religion surfers have gone online to look for a new church, temple, or other congregation to join, fully 83% of the responding congregations included features intent on attracting new visitors. This was a feature important to all groups regardless of faith, budget, number of people within the congregation with internet access, or whether membership was steady, growing, or declining. Many reported that new visitors had come into their midst after learning of the churches or synagogues through their Web sites, and one noted that *all* of its new members first learned of the church through its Web page. One synagogue noted that its site has prompted calls from people asking whether they could visit even if they are not Jewish.

WHAT ARE THEY GIVING?

Prayer and Support. Some 37% of religion surfers reported that they have given prayer or spiritual support online—significantly more than the 21% who reported having sought such support. At the same time, 18% of congregations that participated in our survey reported that they offered a place on their Web sites where people could post prayer requests. Another 22% reported that they would like to offer such a service in the future. Churches that do accept prayer requests have encountered unanticipated opportunities for outreach and ministry. One noted that it had linked with prayer sites from other churches so that it could now pray for "thousands of hurting people." Such opportunities also appear when churches receive prayer requests from nonmembers, and one church noted that most of its prayer requests came from non-Christian countries.

Information and Links. Congregational Web sites are in tune with religion surfers' desire to learn more about their faiths. Three in four sites provided some sort of faith-related text on their Web pages. Among Unitarians, the proportion climbed to approximately 90%. Similarly, 60% of congregations surveyed tried to serve the 85% of religion surfers who lay great importance on meditation and prayer by providing links to devotional or study material. Comments submitted by respondents show that these resources are used both for the personal benefit of individuals who use them and for the preparation of worship services and religious-school activities.

Opportunities for Service. Fully 71% of religion surfers reported that volunteering their services to others is "very important" to their spiritual lives, making service second only to prayer in the eyes of this group. Only 15% of congregations actively solicit volunteers for service projects in their communities, although another 14% may do so in the future.

WHAT IS THE INTERNET EFFECT?

Just as there were concerns that e-commerce would sound the death knell for brick-and-mortar stores, some have wondered whether the internet would not also draw people out of their churches and temples to worship in private and at convenient times (Barna Research Online, 1998). Many of the congregations in our survey admitted that they did not have the time or expertise to maintain quality, up-to-date sites. Still, many voiced the fear that they would be unable to attract new members, particularly young people and families, without these sites.

Studies in all areas have tried to get at the issue of whether the internet technology has powers that can change people. Concerns have arisen (and been challenged) as to whether internet use fosters social isolation. The Southern Poverty Law Center (SPLC), a group that defends victims of hate crimes, watched with alarm as the number of hate sites on the Web seemed to skyrocket. SPLC later determined that Web sites themselves were relatively ineffective in actually drawing young people into violent groups ("Hate Online," 2001). This leaves a very slippery question: To what extent can use of the internet significantly affect a person's religious life?

Neither of the two religion studies attempted to operationalize any individual's or group's religiosity or spirituality. Rather, both relied on respondents' reports of the role of faith, faith practices, and the internet in their own lives. When one congregation reports that the use of e-mail has improved the spiritual life of the community and another reports that it has not, there is no basis to conclude that the first community is now more "spiritual" than the other. Rather, the two studies assessed the claims of individuals and congregations as to what difference the internet has made in their faith lives.

A Devotional Aid But Not a Replacement. The internet leads people to examine their religious traditions more closely and to aid in personal devotion. It does not, however, replace current practices. Our findings show that people take to religious life on the internet to augment lives that are already devout. They use the internet to increase their understanding of their own faith and find it to be an unexcelled resource for doing so. Nearly two thirds of religion surfers (64%) reported that it is easier to find study materials online than to find them anywhere else. Nearly half (44%) said the same about finding prayer and devotional resources. Given that more than 80% of religion surfers attributed importance to study and prayer, the internet is providing unprecedented opportunity for observers to examine and practice their beliefs more deeply.

Meanwhile, there is little evidence to suggest that these alluring features are so compelling as to draw people out of their congregations. Fully 84% of religion surfers do belong to a congregation. And those who seek religious material most often (at least three times per week) are more likely to attend church weekly than are less frequent religion surfers (86% vs. 70%). Whatever activity religion surfing is replacing, it is not communal worship. In fact, religion surfers who do not currently belong to a church are most likely to have used the internet to look for one. Similarly, few people are looking to the internet as a space to rival a church or temple for group worship. Only 4% of religion surfers have participated in online worship. Less than 5% of even the wealthiest, most wired congregations offer online worship, although 12% hope to do so at some time in the future. It remains to be seen whether increased broadband capabilities will make online worship more popular in the future.

The Third-Person Effect. However, the internet is seen to have a more positive effect on the lives of others than on oneself. Television researchers have observed what they call the "third-person effect"; that is, the belief that although the technology does not have an effect on oneself, it is bound to affect others much more profoundly and negatively (Atwood, 1994). Religion surfers appear to have a more optimistic spin on their assessment of what the internet can accomplish in the faith realm. Although they enjoy their online excursions into the faith world, few recognize significant effects on their faith lives. Only 2% reported that internet surfing is a major aspect of their faith lives, 15% reported that online resources have contributed to their own faith commitment, and 27% reported that online resources have improved their spiritual lives to at least a modest degree.

In contrast, religion surfers are surprisingly optimistic that the internet can have a beneficial effect on the lives of others. More than one in three (35%) believe that the internet has had a "mostly positive" effect on the religious lives of others. Fully 62% believe that the availability of material on the internet "encourages religious tolerance." Those who see themselves as outsiders in their communities are less likely to share this rosy outlook, but nearly half of them (47%) agree. And 86% of all religion surfers believe that the internet helps people to find others who share their religious beliefs.

More traditional third-person effect worries also appear. Christians, in particular, worry about the effects of undesirable material on the Web. Nearly two thirds (64%) indicated that there is too much material on the internet that is sacrilegious, but only 27% of non-Christians shared this fear. By the same token, 55% of Christian religion surfers agreed that "it is too easy for fringe religious groups to use the internet to hurt people," but only 35% of surfers from other faiths agreed with this comment. The belief that internet content alone can lead to harm or benefits for viewers appears to exist in religion surfers but might not be limited to them. It echoes long-running debates in this country over sex, violence, and commercialism in television programming.

Support for Solitary Worship. Among the one in six religion surfers who does not belong to any formal religious community, the internet provides some particular benefits. Nonmembers are less likely than members to describe themselves as having a "somewhat strong" or "very strong" commitment to their faiths (81% vs. 99%), but nonmembers are by no means less interested in tending to their spiritual lives. The internet appears to provide for them many of the benefits of a congregation. Nonmembers are nearly twice as likely as members to find it easier to meet people of the same faith online than within their own social and community circles. Nonmembers are also more likely to rely on the internet than on offline resources for reference materials, faith-oriented conversations, prayer resources, worship, speaking with clergy, or finding volunteer opportunities. And nonmembers are more likely to have sought out a new congregation (24% vs. 12%), even if they have not yet found one. The internet provides a library, a gathering space, and a meditation space that has no parallel for those who have no religious community.

Consolidator, Rather Than Creator, of Groups. In addition to religious Web sites, religious listservs and chat rooms offer surfers the opportunity to discuss issues of faith with those of like (and unlike) minds all over the world. These groups offer opportunities for surfers to expand their faith communities. However, religion surfers as a whole tend not to use the internet for this purpose. Only 10% have taken part in religious chat rooms, and only one in four subscribes to a faith-oriented listserv. Asked whether it is easier to engage in discussions on spiritual matters online or offline, a whopping 85% responded that it is easier to initiate such discussions in their personal circles rather than online. Of those who have a favorite religious site, only 15% reported that they use it to create or maintain personal relationships with other site users. And of this 15%, only one in three said that these relationships were the most important reason for visiting the site.

Given that most religion surfers already belong to a congregation, it is not surprising that online communities compare poorly with long-established connections in the community. Another study by the Pew Internet and American Life Project found that among surfers who became interested in the online workings of a local organization to which they already belonged, one third were tuning in to congregational Web sites.[5] Although many of these individuals may participate passionately in online discussion groups and communities, they already have well-established personal connections in their congregations and the internet is too new to compete.

An interesting contrast to cement this point is the history of neo-pagan groups in the United States. According to NightMare (2001), paganism has long been practiced in the United States but has been kept under wraps due to community hostility and the far-flung dispersion of practitioners. NightMare credited much of the renewed interest in paganism to the internet. It has provided uncensored publishing space providing information about the practice and a safe space for people to meet, talk, and build community (NightMare, 2001).

Congregations, on the other hand, have enthusiastically endorsed internet tools for improving connections and communications among their members. In contrast to the 27% of individuals who claimed that their spiritual lives have been improved through the workings of cyberspace, 83% of congregations that participated in our study in 2000 reported that their Web sites and use of e-mail had helped the spiritual lives of the congregations either "some" or "a lot." By creating better ties within a preexisting community, by creating a Web presence, and by facilitating discussions that can be difficult to hold in other settings, congregations tightened bonds within their groups, reestablished connections with former members, and (in some cases) expanded their missions on a global scale.

Of course, not all congregational sites are created equal in this regard. The best-funded churches and synagogues with the most-wired congregations were the most likely to report that their Web sites had helped promote their communal spiritual lives. Fully 91% of the churches with budgets of more than $500,000 reported that their Web sites had helped, compared with 78% of the churches with budgets of less than $150,000. Similarly, 90% of the high-access congregations reported that their Web sites had helped their spiritual lives, compared with 67% of the low-access congregations. Finally, congregations with well-established Web sites—those in operation for more than 2 years—were more likely to report that the sites had aided the congregations' spiritual lives than were those with newer Web sites.

When it comes to the impact of e-mail on the life of the faith community, one surprising finding is that congregations in flux—those whose membership has been increasing or decreasing over the past 3 years—are equally impressed with what e-mail does for their faith communities. Improved communications between congregational staff and members due to e-mail is more noted among congregations that have grown (94%) or decreased (92%) in size than among congregations whose membership has remained stable (79%). Perhaps those congregations undergoing change were more motivated to use internet and e-mail tools to meet their changing needs.

Finally, the internet allows congregations to reassess the bodies of people they serve. A few congregations make strategic use of their sites to serve people who live beyond their communities. As noted earlier, one congregation has been able to use its site to create a prayer ministry that extends to non-Christian countries. Some sites serve dispersed groups such as gays/lesbians and the deaf. New Life Gypsy Ministries (www.newlifeforthegypsies.org) was created by a Lutheran pastor of Gypsy origin to serve Gypsies worldwide.

Conclusion

This chapter has sought to present a general portrait of online religious life in the United States. The survey methodologies used are useful for presenting general findings, but they also raise many interesting questions for more in-depth study. Given the religious makeup of the United States, any broad-based study is going to necessarily reflect a Christian bias. Fully 91% of the respondents to our phone survey identified themselves as Christians. This mirrors the 89% of religiously affiliated Americans who say the same (American Religious Identification Survey, 2001). Of course, American Christians are a varied lot, with widely differing beliefs about the nature of scripture, worship, and spirituality. But the current survey methodologies do not capture enough non-Christian respondents to assess cross-faith comparisons.

Congregations uniformly gave positive assessments of their Web sites. While understanding the limitations they had in producing sophisticated sites, respondents—most of whom were webmasters or clergy—did not hesitate to attribute to them improvements in congregational life. Determining whether the congregations as a whole agree with these assessments, and the extent of the improvements realized, requires more in-depth research than our survey could provide. In-depth interviews, and perhaps ethnographic study, could shed further light on these findings.

Notes

1. The following types of groups were solicited: Jewish–Conservative, Jewish–Reform, Jewish–Reconstructionist, Unitarian Universalist, Roman Catholic, Southern Baptist, United Methodist, the Church of God in Christ, Evangelical Lutheran Church in America, Presbyterian U.S.A., Lutheran Church Missouri Synod, Assemblies of God, African Methodist Episcopalian (AME), Episcopal, Greek Orthodox, American Baptist Churches U.S.A., Pentecostal Assembly of the World, United Church of Christ, and AME Zion.

2. The 19% figure is taken from the 1998 General Social Survey in response to the question "To what extent to you consider yourself a religious person?" (www.icpsr.umich.edu:8080/gss/rnd1998/merged/cdbk/relpersn.htm).

3. Figures are taken from the 1998 General Social Survey (www.icpsr.umich.edu:8080/gss/rnd1998/merged/cdbk/attend.htm) and the 2000 National Election Study (www.umich.edu/~nes).

4. Many online faith-oriented games are multiplayer role-playing games; thus, they constitute social rather than individual activity.

5. See *Online Communities* (www.pewinternet.org/reports/toc.asp?report=47).

References

American Religious Identification Survey. (2001). [Online]. Retrieved April 17, 2003, from www.gc. cuny.edu/studies/key_findings.htm

Atwood, L. E. (1994). Illusions of media power: The third-person effect. *Journalism Quarterly, 71,* 269–281.

Barna Research Online. (1998, April 20). *The cyberchurch is coming.* [Online]. Retrieved April 17, 2003, from www.barna.org/cgi-bin/pagecategory.asp?categoryid=14

Brasher, B. E. (2001). *Give me that online religion.* San Francisco: Jossey-Bass.

Hate online: Reevaluating the Net. (2001, Summer). *Intelligence Report,* pp. 54–55.

NightMare, M. M. (2001). *Witchcraft and the Web: Weaving pagan traditions online.* Quebec: ECW Press.

4

Bending Gender Into the Net

Feminizing Content, Corporate Interests, and Research Strategy

Leslie Regan Shade
Concordia University, Montreal

During the mid-1990s, feminists, policymakers, and educators expressed concern about ensuring equal access to the internet for women. Various studies assessed why women were online in such low numbers. Factors included technological temerity, socioeconomic reasons, a paucity of content to attract women, and time constraints. In 2000, statistics indicated that, at least in the United States, there was no longer a gender gap in access to the internet. As various Pew Internet and American Life reports also established, women are using the internet for activities that reinforce and correspond to their everyday lives such as e-mailing friends and relatives, searching for health information online, and for engaging in leisure time activities. In a sense, then, the internet has become domesticated, similar to other communication technologies in the household such as the television and the telephone.

This chapter examines some of the facets of gender online. First, however, it grounds the discussion by focusing on the gender-technology dynamic. A significant body of contemporary research has looked at how communication technologies have been gendered, both via their social uses and through design. Some of this research, particularly on the telephone, shows similarities to the current adoption of the internet by women. Data from various Pew reports describing how American women use the internet, and the gendered nature of how men and women use the internet, are then discussed. Given that men and women seek different kinds of information online, the chapter then looks at online content designed for women, particularly some of the mechanisms by which corporate interests are attempting to attract the "feminine audience."

There is a sense of optimism that the internet, despite the still-present "digital divide," has reached a level of gender parity for the American population. But is access to the internet the only determinant of gender equity? Is the internet really a level playing field for men and women? What other considerations should we consider in terms of equity? Even though women might be on an equal par with men in terms of internet use (despite the differences in information-seeking behavior), is there equity in terms of design, administration, ownership, and governance of this infrastructure? The chapter concludes by considering issues that affect women, including the digital divide, education, and employment.

Research on the Gender-Technology Relation

Before describing some of the research on gender and the internet, it is helpful to situate it within a significant body of research that has examined how communication technologies have been gendered, both through their social uses—which have often been unintended—and their design. The telephone, the radio, and the television have been the focus of much of this research. The use of these technologies to both forge new communities and nurture existing place-based communities has been a recurrent theme (Shade, 2002).

The telephone is particularly illustrative here. As Rakow (1992) and Moyal (1992) showed, women have used the telephone as a tool of community bonding and family "kin keeping." Rakow's 1985 ethnographic study on women's use of the telephone in a small community in the midwestern United States revealed how the telephone is a gendered technology:

> The telephone is a site on which the meanings of gender are expressed and practiced. Use of the telephone by women is both gendered work—work delegated to women—and gender work—work that confirms the community's beliefs about what are women's natural tendencies and abilities. (Rakow, 1992, p. 33)

Moyal's (1992) research for the Australian federal government on the prospective impact of timed local calls on women concluded that there was a distinctive feminine use of the telephone. Women's use of the telephone was primarily for keeping in touch with family: "The study has revealed a pervasive, deeply rooted, dynamic feminine culture of the telephone in which kin-keeping, caring, mutual support, friendship, [and] volunteer and community activity play a central part" (p. 67).

However, as Martin (1991) demonstrated in a historical study of the rollout of telephone services in Canada, the original purpose of the telephone, envisioned by Bell Canada, was as a tool for businessmen. The feminization of the telephone became apparent first when women were hired as operators and then later when a viable culture of the telephone developed for socialization. Telephone technology and design has since changed considerably so as to appeal to the female consumer, reflecting its status as an indispensable domestic artifact through stylistic trends, including colors (from plain black to pale hues), design (from the Princess telephone to the cartoon-licensed telephones), and technological innovations (from push-button telephones to portables) (Lupton, 1993).

Gender, consumption, and technology relations have also been documented by scholars (Cockburn & Furst-Dilic, 1994; Cowan, 1985; Horowitz & Mohun, 1998; Oldenziel, 1999). They have pointed out how technologies that exist in the women's sphere (e.g., domestic technologies) are often not considered "real" technologies. It is assumed that these "technologies of consumption" (Lubar, 1998) are to be consumed by women in a passive fashion. Technological designers and promoters rarely consider that technologies can be used or resisted in unforeseen ways.

When the internet first burst onto the public screen during the mid-1990s, popular culture and the media tended to reflect women as cyber-phobic, victims of harassment, or potential online pickup material. Early academic research on gender online examined the participation of women in computer science and computer networking, noting the paucity of women in the educational and industrial sectors and paying particular attention to access issues, social interactions, and pornography (Balka, 1993; Herring, 1993; Shade, 1994). Thus, questions of access and equity were seen as a major issue, with the goal to ensure gender parity.

Other academic studies have since examined the interpersonal dynamics of online gender/computer-mediated language use such as conversational analysis in internet relay chat (IRC) and listservs (Herring, 1999) and gender negotiation in a multi-user domain (Kendall, 2002). Identity and issues of "gender bending" in virtual environments have also been a recurrent theme (Roberts & Parks,

2001). The intersection between feminist theory and cyberculture has also created a significant corpus of work (Flanagan & Booth, 2002; Kirkup, Janes, Woodward, & Hovenden, 2000).

What Do the Pew Data Tell Us?

More than 9 million women have gone online for the first time during the past 6 months, and this surge has led to gender parity in the internet population. It has also reshaped America's social landscape because women have used e-mail to enrich their important relationships and enlarge their networks. The internet has the opposite of an isolating effect on these users. Women report that e-mail has helped them to improve connections to their relatives and friends. More women than men say that they are attached to e-mail and pleased with how it helps them (*Tracking Online Life,* 2000, p. 7).

ACCESS

Examining several Pew reports that touch on the demographics of gender and the gendered use of the internet, we might conclude that gender parity has been reached.[1] Data reinforce the view that the internet has become domesticated; it is now woven into the daily lives of Americans. For many women, information and communication technologies (ICTs) have become a routine part of the mundane (Green & Keeble, 2001).

Tracking Online Life (2000) revealed that gender parity had been reached; women make up half of internet users, with older women getting online at a slightly higher rate than other users (*Wired Seniors,* 2001). Women are characterized as "Instant Acolytes" because they are the fastest growing group of people getting online; three of five women (58%) were Instant Acolytes in 2000, compared with 50% of the entire internet population (*New Internet Users,* 2000). Instant Acolytes were further characterized as "more female, less wealthy, and less educated than the overall internet population" in March 2000 (p. 6). In particular, the percentage of women ages 18 to 24 years who became Instant Acolytes grew from 44% in 1998 to 59% in 2000. Women between 30 and 45 years of age were 61% of internet Acolytes in 2000, compared with 57% in 1998. Furthermore, more women today are "Net Joiners" (i.e., people who join various online groups after being on the internet for a while), particularly those who are younger, are non-white, have a lower household income and less education, and are relatively new to the internet (*Online Communities,* 2001).

Gender differences in access are revealed, however, when ethnicity is taken into account. Among African Americans, women are more likely to be online than are men (56% vs. 44%), with women comprising 61% of internet newcomers (*African Americans and the Internet,* 2000). African Americans online tend to have lower incomes and lower educational levels than their white counterparts, and 56% of African American users are under 34 years of age, compared with 40% of white users.

Among Asian Americans, more men are online than are women (58% vs. 42%), with Asian Americans who speak English the largest and most experienced group of people online (*Asian Americans and the Internet,* 2001). Asian Americans are the most experienced racial and ethnic group on the internet, with more veteran users (55% of them came online more than 3 years ago). Of those, 40% of Asian American women are veterans, with nearly three quarters of them having 2 or more years of experience; this is contrasted with white women (29%), African American women (23%), and Hispanic women (25%). New Asian American women users (i.e., those who have been on the internet less than 6 months) comprise less than 10%; this is contrasted with white women (15%), African American women (23%), and Hispanic women (20%).

APPLICATIONS AND PATTERNS OF USE

Despite the gender parity in internet access, Pew reports revealed differences in the various Web activities of men and women. The most popular use of the internet for women was e-mail, which was used to keep up with distant family and friends and served as an "isolation antidote." Popular Web activities for women included looking for health or medical information, checking out job information, playing games online, and hunting for religious or spiritual information. Men, on the other hand, listed as their favorite Web activities looking for news and financial information online, selling and buying stocks online, looking for information about products or services, participating in online auctions, looking for information about hobbies or interests, seeking political information, and checking sports information.

Both men and women use the internet as a tool for sociability. Men are drawn to online groups whose subject matter is politics, sports, or professional activities, whereas women are drawn to online groups whose subject matter is health information (e.g., medical support groups), local community associations that are online, or entertainment sites (*Online Communities,* 2001).

More women than men use e-mail on a daily basis (19% vs. 5%) (*Getting Serious Online,* 2002). More than half of women (57%) find e-mail to be a useful way in which to keep in touch with family, compared with 44% of men (*Tracking Online Life,* 2000). More than half of African American women (56%) say that using e-mail has helped them to strengthen intrafamily connections and 37% say that e-mail has strengthened family connections, compared with 43% and 20% of African American men, respectively (*African Americans and the Internet,* 2000). Nearly two of three women (65%) say that they use e-mail to keep in touch with family and friends because it is efficient, compared with 59% of men. More than half of women (53%) use e-mail to reach out to geographically dispersed relatives, compared with 43% of men. And more women than men are apt to use e-mail to communicate a variety of messages (*Tracking Online Life,* 2000). Women are more likely to go online from home rather than from work (*New Internet Users,* 2000), and they spend more time online than do men (33% vs. 25%) (*Time Spent Online,* 2001).

Pew reports revealed differences in how ethnic groups use the internet for entertainment and leisure activities. For instance, Asian American women are big consumers and users of financial information, with nearly half of them (44%) accessing this information at least one time, including 15% accessing it on a regular basis. Approximately 16% of Asian American women have sold stock, and 4% have done so on a typical day. This is twice the rate for Hispanic American women and four times the rate for white and African American women (*Asian Americans and the Internet,* 2001).

Pew reports also revealed differences in how men and women seek news as well as government and civic information. Two thirds of men (66%) have received news online, compared with 53% of women (*Tracking Online Life,* 2000). This rate increases as socioeconomic factors are increased. More Asian American men (72%) have gone online for news than have other men, with 42% going online on a typical day, compared with only 24% of Asian American women (*Online Communities,* 2001).

However, more women than men seek out health-related information on the internet, particularly information related to a specific illness, material related to symptoms, or after visiting a doctor (63% vs. 46%). Two thirds of women between 30 and 49 years of age have gone online for health-related information. Women are twice as likely as men to look for material related to the health needs of their children (16% vs. 7%), but both men and women seek out health information related to parents or other relatives. Women are more concerned than men about the reliability of the health information they find online. More women than men are "very concerned" that Web sites will give out personal information about the women (73% vs. 65%). Men are slightly more privacy conscious in that they tend to read the privacy policies of Web sites more often than do women. Because of the anonymous nature of the Web, more men than women search for sensitive information online (*The Online Health Care Revolution*, 2000).

Content: Toward the Feminization of the Net?

In many traditional ways, women's and men's behavior on the Web mirrors their behavior in consuming other forms of media, in performing everyday chores, and in enjoying leisure time. Just as women and men tend to watch different television shows, read different sections of the newspaper, and purchase different types of magazines and books, they also gravitate to the online activities that resemble the media products they like (*Tracking Online Life*, 2000).

What do the Pew data tell us? First, they reveal that gender parity, at least in terms of access to the internet, has been achieved (although a digital divide in access for lower income women is cause for concern). This is reason for optimism. However, more disconcerting is what the Pew data tell us about how women and men differ in their use of the internet. There are tensions in gender differences, whereby women are using the internet to reinforce their private lives and men are using the internet more for engaging in the public sphere. Women are avid users of e-mail, often for the purpose of connecting with family and friends. This use is similar to how women adapted the telephone as a social and domestic utility, and this also replicates what other studies have told us (see Boneva, Kraut, & Frohlich, 2001). When men use e-mail, they are less inveterate users, at least so far as informal and familial sociability is concerned.

Women's information-seeking behavior tends toward health or medical information; again casting women's internet use into a caregiving mode. Women tend to go online for religious or spiritual information (again possibly falling into the "warmer and fuzzier" role of mothers/caregivers). In contrast, the favorite

Web activities of men include seeking news and financial information, selling and buying stocks, looking for information on their hobbies, seeking political information, and checking out sports information. Thus, men's internet use falls into activities that tend to reside in the public sphere.

Although these data are based on telephone surveys and subtleties in internet use (e.g., multitasking while using the Web in the home might not be revealed), the premise of gendered use is disturbing. Women are not using the internet for the purpose of civic participation. The internet has been promoted as a way in which to increase social capital (for optimistic and pessimistic scenarios of internet use for increased political participation and community involvement, see Rice, 2002), but women apparently are not using it for this purpose.

However, this void could be merely a limitation of the Pew studies. Acknowledging that gender is a complex and contested concept, one must ask whether the quantitatively driven Pew data provide an accurate portrayal of gender online. Van Zoonen (2002) argued for a mutual shaping of gender and technology where "social meanings of the internet will emerge from particular contexts and practices of usage" (p. 20). Because Pew data are reliant on telephone surveys, there is no way in which to ascertain the gendered nuances of the internet in everyday domestic life. Thus, ethnographic studies examining the use and negotiation of the internet in domestic spaces could yield some rich and surprising aspects of gender use and negotiation (Bakardjieva & Smith, 2001).

One must also be cautious of generalizing and essentializing the category of "women." Many women and women's groups have been actively using the internet as a way in which to produce and consume feminist communication. Use of the internet by the global women's movement as a method of facilitating policy-oriented activism is quite vital (Shade, 2002), and this is particularly the case with initiatives to ameliorate the digital divide for women in developing countries. One such example is provided by the International Research and Training Institute for the Advancement of Women (INSTRAW), which has hosted a virtual seminar exploring the use of ICTs for women in terms of empowerment and disempowerment, the "neutrality" of ICTs, the digital divide, and social capabilities.

What is clear is how the internet has been increasingly feminized. Web content has been designed and created for a particular audience of women—middle to upper class white women. This includes portals adapting a magazine-type format featuring health, beauty, cooking, parenting, and shopping tips; "interactive" discussion forums; quizzes; and e-commerce ventures (e.g., clothes, makeup, toys). An example of this is iVillage.com, whose partners include America Online,

Clairol, Milano Cookies, Dewey Color System, and Maternity Mall. Other examples abound; Handbag.com, Oxygen.com, and Women.com are just a few of these types of portal sites. The internet is also becoming feminized via the design of multimedia products where ideas about the female gender are incorporated into the process (Spilker & Sorenson, 2000) as well as through the design of internet appliances that feature e-mail and calendaring devices that have been developed and marketed as a specific female consumer item.[2]

Pew data also reveal that American women are ethnically diverse and that their Web use differs. One example is Asian American women. Pew data reveal that they are more likely than other women to go online to listen to music and to seek out sports information and financial information. But are the various interests of these women being met (or courted) by portals? Or, is there an erasure of race? One can argue that there is. As Nakamura (2002) contends, "Gender and race can just as easily be co-opted by the e-marketplace. Commercial sites such as these tend to view women and minorities primarily as potential markets for advertisers and merchants rather than as 'coalitions'" (p. 328). "Cybertyping," Nakamura also argued, is apparent in the deployment of internet services such as broadband, resulting in the redlining of neighborhoods not considered affluent enough for micro- and psychodemographic marketing.

Conclusion: Real Equity?

So, is there really gender equity online? If we consider issues of women using the internet for civic participation (a rich research question to tackle), factor in the demographics of the digital divide, examine the entry of women into computer science programs, and look at how women are designing information technologies and participating in governance issues, the answer is less optimistic than a resounding *yes.*

DIGITAL DIVIDE ISSUES

The internet population looks increasingly like the overall population in the United States, but there are notable exceptions; income and age determine who is online. Fully 82% of those in households with incomes of at least $75,000 are online, compared with only 38% of households with incomes less than $30,000. Those in the lower economic range, however, are getting online quickly (*More Online, Doing More,* 2001).

Pew studies reported that half of adults (age 18 years or over) in the United States are not online (49% of men and 54% of women). This corresponds to lower socioeconomic and educational levels, and age plays a factor as well:

> Part of the reason more women do not have Internet access is that women make up a large proportion of the elderly in the United States and that is also the group most likely to be outside the Internet population. Thus, 55% of those not online for any reason are women, and 45% are men. (*Who's Not Online*, 2000)

Race and ethnicity are also factors both in terms of access to the internet itself and in terms of internet use itself.

EDUCATION AND EMPLOYMENT

Women are underrepresented in the networking field (concerned with the design, development, and production of hardware and software), and fewer young women are entering into computer science programs. De Palma (2001), citing research from the American Association of University Women (AAUW), reported that a mere 17% of female high school students take advanced placement examinations in computer science and that they receive only 28% of the undergraduate degrees. Ascertaining why these numbers are so low and designing a more inclusive computer science curriculum was the goal of Jane Margolis and Allan Fisher at Carnegie Mellon University. They reported on a program to "unlock the clubhouse" through the creation of specific policy changes that resulted in an increase of women computer science majors from 7% in 1995 to 42% in 1999. These initiatives included more flexible admission requirements and curriculum changes (Margolis & Fisher, 2001). Kramarae (2001), in another report for the AAUW, examined barriers to women partaking in distance education and other online programs and found that a veritable "third shift" existed for working mothers who were pursuing higher education in this fashion. Juggling the demands of family and other domestic responsibilities, coupled with work outside of the home and heavy course loads, proved to be onerous for many women. Thus, the touted benefit of flexible, just-in-time lifelong learning facilitated by networking technologies has proved to be a bust for many women.

Even though young women and girls are using computers and the internet on a par with young men and boys, females are not majoring in computer science or engineering at the same rate as are males and so are not represented on an equal basis in the workplace. One such consequence is that consumer products tend to be designed with the needs and desires of men in mind. This is not to say that the needs of women are dismissed; quite often, the unintended consequences of women's use and appropriation of a technology changes its consumer trajectory. One merely needs to remember the early development of the telephone and when it switched from being a male business prerogative to one that encompassed female sociability. Indeed, this is the case with broadband internet development. A recent press release from AT&T Broadband reported on "anthropological research" that revealed a pattern dubbed by AT&T as "Web snacking," an activity whereby household members leave their broadband access on all of the time but frequently and sporadically log on to cruise the Web or send and receive e-mail. Mothers are the main "snackers," and according to Cheryl Persinger, an AT&T Broadband applied mathematician and mother of three, access to "high-speed internet connection has made many mothers more efficient and is revolutionizing the way they connect with the world." Mothers "nibble" at internet services throughout the day, multitasking at various chores and most frequently "checking news, reference sources, banking, e-mailing, and communicating with other parents in an online community" (AT&T, 2002).

GOVERNANCE

Who is responsible for the administration and policy coordination of the internet? The Internet Corporation for Assigned Names and Numbers (ICANN), which acts as the internet's central coordinating committee, has been embroiled in debates about representation of countries (currently the United States dominates) and organizations (commercial vs. nonprofit). But gender plays a role here as well. Few women have registered as voting members of ICANN. According to Emerson Tiller, a professor of business law at the University of Texas at Austin, in North America, women represent 9.9% of ICANN registrants, whereas men represent 78.2% (11.8% did not report their gender).[3]

Diffusion of the internet into the daily lives of Americans has proceeded at a quicker pace than have other communications technologies. During the past decade, we have seen women go from a paltry 10% of internet users to more than half of the users in the United States. Is this equity? Yes, there is reason for optimism about these numbers, but it is even more optimistic to envision the next

10 years as an era of truer equity for women online—in content creation, education, civic engagement, policymaking, and governance.

Notes

1.   Pew reports consulted included *New Internet Users: What They Do Online, What They Don't, and Implications for the Net's Future* (2000); *Tracking Online Life: How Woman Are Using the Internet to Cultivate Relationships With Family and Friends* (2000); *Who's Not Online: 57% of Those Without Internet Access Say They Do Not Plan to Log On* (2000); *African Americans and the Internet* (2000); *Asian Americans and the Internet: The Young and the Connected* (2001); *More Online, Doing More: 16 Million Newcomers Gain Internet Access in the Last Half of 2000 as Women, Minorities, and Families With Modest Incomes Continue to Surge Online* (2001); *Online Communities: Networks That Nurture Long-Distance Relationships and Local Ties* (2001); *Getting Serious Online* (2002); *The Online Health Care Revolution: How the Web Helps Americans Take Better Care of Themselves* (2000); *Hispanics and the Internet* (2001); *Women Surpass Men as e-Shoppers During the Holidays* (2002); *Music Downloading Deluge: 37 Million American Adults and Youths Have Retrieved Music Files On the Internet* (2001); *Time Spent Online: Why Some People Use the Internet More Than Before and Why Some Use It Less* (2001); *Trust and Privacy Online: Why Americans Want to Rewrite the Rules* (2001); and *Wired Seniors* (2001).

2.   Examples of these new domestic technologies include the now defunct Audrey, released with great fanfare by 3Com in 2000 but shelved a mere 5 months later, and the cordless MailStation.

3.   The press release reporting Tiller's finding can be found at www.bus.utexas.edu/news/pressreleases/disparity/asp.

References

African Americans and the internet. (2000). [Online]. Retrieved April 22, 2003, from www.pewinternet.org/reports/toc.asp?report=25

Asian Americans and the internet: The young and the connected. (2001). [Online]. Retrieved April 22, 2003, from www.pewinternet.org/reports/toc.asp?report=52

AT&T. (2002, April 28). *Metroplex women find Internet "snacking" feeds needs.* [Online]. Retrieved April 22, 2003, from www.att.com/news/item/0,1847,10375,00.html

Bakardjieva, M., & Smith, R. (2001). The internet in everyday life. *New Media & Society, 3,* 67–83.

Balka, E. (1993). Women's access to online discussions about feminism. *Electronic Journal of Communication, 3*(1).

Boneva, B., Kraut, R., & Frohlich, D. (2001). Using e-mail for personal relationships: The difference gender makes. *American Behavioral Scientist, 45,* 530–549.

Cockburn, C., & Furst-Dilic, R. (Eds.). (1994). *Bringing technology home: Gender and technology in a changing Europe.* Buckingham, UK: Open University Press.

Cowan, R. S. (1985). *More work for mother: The ironies of household technology from the open hearth to the microwave.* New York: Basic Books.

De Palma, P. (2001). Why women avoid computer science. *Communications of the ACM, 44*(6), 27–29.

Flanagan, M., & Booth, A. (Eds.). (2002). *Reload: Rethinking women + cyberculture.* Cambridge, MA: MIT Press.

Getting serious online. (2002). [Online]. Retrieved April 22, 2003, from www.pewinternet.org/reports/toc.asp?report=55

Green, E., & Keeble, L. (2001). The technological story of a women's centre. In L. Keeble & B. D. Loader (Eds.), *Community informatics: Shaping computer-mediated social relations* (pp. 53–70). London: Routledge.

Herring, S. (1993). Gender and democracy in computer-mediated communication. *Electronic Journal of Communication, 3*(2).

Herring, S. (1999). The rhetorical features of gender harassment online. *The Information Society, 15,* 151–167.

Hispanics and the internet. (2001). [Online]. Retrieved April 22, 2003, from www.pewinternet.org/reports/toc.asp?report=38

Horowitz, R., & Mohun, A. (Eds.). (1998). *His and hers: Gender, consumption, and technology.* Charlottesville: University Press of Virginia.

Kendall, L. (2002). *Hanging out in the virtual pub: Masculinities and relationships online.* Berkeley: University of California Press.

Kirkup, G., Janes, L., Woodward, K., & Hovenden, F. (2000). *The gendered cyborg: A reader.* London: Routledge.

Kramarae, C. (2001). *The third shift: Women learning online.* Washington, DC: Association for American University Women.

Lubar, S. (1998). Men/Women/Production/Consumption. In R. Horowitz & A. Mohun (Eds.), *His and hers: Gender, consumption, and technology* (pp. 7–37). Charlottesville: University Press of Virginia.

Lupton, E. (1993). *Mechanical brides: Women and machines from home to office.* New York: Cooper-Hewitt National Museum of Design, Smithsonian Institute, and Princeton Architectural Press.

Margolis, J., & Fisher, A. (2001). *Unlocking the clubhouse: Women in computing.* Cambridge, MA: MIT Press.

Martin, M. (1991). *Hello central? Gender, culture, and technology in the formation of telephone systems.* Montreal: McGill-Queen's University Press.

More online, doing more: 16 million newcomers gain internet access in the last half of 2000 as women, minorities, and families with modest incomes continue to surge online. (2001). [Online]. Retrieved April 22, 2003, from www.pewinternet.org/reports/toc.asp?report=30

Moyal, A. (1992). The gendered use of the telephone: An Australian case study. *Media, Culture, and Society, 14,* 51–72.

Nakamura, L. (2002). After/Images of identity: Gender, technology, and identity politics. In M. Flanagan & A. Booth (Eds.), *Reload: Rethinking women + cyberculture* (pp. 321–331). Cambridge, MA: MIT Press.

New internet users: What they do online, what they don't, and implications for the net's future. (2000). [Online]. Retrieved April 22, 2003, from www.pewinternet.org/reports/toc.asp?report=22

Oldenziel, R. (1999). *Making technology masculine: Men, women, and modern machines in America, 1870–1945.* Amsterdam: Amsterdam University Press.

Online communities: Networks that nurture long-distance relationships and local ties. (2001). [Online]. Retrieved April 22, 2003, from www.pewinternet.org/reports/toc.asp?report=47

Rakow, L. (1992). *Gender on the line: Women, the telephone, and community life.* Champaign: University of Illinois Press.

Rice, R. E. (2002). Primary issues in internet use: Access, civic and community involvement, and social interaction and expression. In L. Lievrouw & S. Livingstone (Eds.), *The handbook of new media* (pp. 105–129). Thousand Oaks, CA: Sage.

Roberts, L. D., & Parks, M. R. (2001). The social geography of gender-switching in virtual environments on the internet. In E. Green & A. Adam (Eds.), *Virtual gender: Technology, consumption, and identity* (pp. 265–285). London: Routledge.

Shade, L. R. (1994). Gender issues in computer networking. In A. Adam et al. (Eds.), *Women, work, computerization: Breaking old boundaries, building new forms* (pp. 91–105). Amsterdam: Elsevier.

Shade, L. R. (2002). *Gender and community in the social construction of the internet.* New York: Peter Lang.

Spilker, H., & Sorenson, K. H. (2000). A rom of one's own or a home for sharing? *New Media & Society, 2,* 268–285.

The music downloading deluge: 37 million American adults and youths have retrieved music files on the internet. (2001). [Online]. Retrieved April 22, 2003, from www.pewinternet.org/reports/toc.asp?report=33

The online health care revolution: How the Web helps Americans take better care of themselves. (2000). [Online]. Retrieved April 22, 2003, from www.pewinternet.org/reports/toc.asp?report=26

Time spent online: Why some people use the internet more than before and why some use it less. (2001). [Online]. Retrieved April 22, 2003, from www.pewinternet.org/reports/index.asp

Tracking online life: How women use the internet to cultivate relationships with families and friends. (2000). [Online]. Retrieved on April 22, 2003, from www.pewinternet.org/reports/toc.asp?report=11

Trust and privacy online: Why Americans want to rewrite the rules. (2000). Retrieved April 22, 2003, from www.pewinternet.org/reports/toc.asp?report=19

van Zoonen, L. (2002). Gendering the internet: Claims, controversies, and cultures. *European Journal of Communication, 17*(1), 5–23.

Who's not online: 57% of those without internet access say they do not plan to log on. (2000). [Online]. Retrieved April 22, 2003, from www.pewinternet.org/reports/toc.asp?report=21

Wired seniors: A fervent few, inspired by family ties. (2001). [Online]. Retrieved April 22, 2003, from www.pewinternet.org/reports/toc.asp?report=40

Women surpass men as e-shoppers during the holidays. (2002). [Online]. Retrieved April 22, 2003, from www.pewinternet.org/reports/toc.asp?report=54

5

Interrogating the Digital Divide

The Political Economy of Race and Commerce in New Media

Lisa Nakamura

University of Wisconsin–Madison

"Kill your television" bumper stickers are very popular in many American cities, and we all have come across people who deliberately abstain from television. They are not framed as backward or on the wrong side of a technological divide. If anything, they are considered to know more about media than do most people. Their position usually garners respect because it represents a critique of television's oppressive mass media qualities such as manipulative commercials, ethnic and racial stereotyping, and sexualized violence. Those who do not watch television are often perceived as intelligent, savvy, and discriminating consumers who have a critical perspective on media. And it follows that members of oppressed and marginalized groups are clearly those who lose the least by killing their televisions given that theirs are the images most frequently exploited, commodified, and misrepresented by that medium.[1]

The assumption in much discourse regarding the digital divide is that the internet is somehow exempt from the critiques that we make of television and that it is de facto "enriching." In addition, and paradoxically, the internet is thought to have more in common with "popular" media forms than with mass ones because of its supposed openness and interactivity; theoretically, any user can post his or her own content to it. In practice, however,

The most striking change to occur in the late 1990s has been the quick fade
of euphoria of those who saw the Internet as providing a qualitatively different and egalitarian type of journalism, politics, media, and culture. The
indications are that the substantive content of this commercial media in the
Internet, or any subsequent digital communication system, will look much
like what currently exists. (McChesney, 1998, p. 24)

Despite the internet's vaunted interactivity, during recent years it has shifted
from "being a participatory medium that serves the interests of the public to
being a broadcast medium where corporations deliver consumer-oriented information. Interactivity would be reduced to little more than sales transactions and
e-mail" (Beacham, as quoted in McChesney, 1998, p. 24).

Despite this state of affairs, in the popular imagination, the internet gets to
have it both ways; unlike television, film, and other mass media, it is still perceived as inherently educational (perhaps because it is both a new medium and
one that involves computer use). Thus, it is perceived as a contributor to democracy and equality even though it is not accessible to nearly as many users as are
other mass media. Most interestingly, it is people of color, a newly expanding and
overwhelmingly young group of new internet users, who most highly value the
internet for its educational properties and are most enthusiastic about it for the
sake of their children if they have them:

About 53% of online blacks have a child under the age of 18 at home, while
42% of online whites are parents of children that age. Users often perceive
gaining access to the Internet as an investment in the future, and this seems
especially true in African-American families. (Spooner & Rainie, 2000, p. A7)

This is also the case for Hispanic families, 49% of whom have a child at
home. "Hispanic parents, like other parents, often see the purchase of a computer
and internet access as an investment in their children's future" (Spooner &
Rainie, 2001, p. B8). I would venture that few Americans of any race would frame
television access as an "investment in their children's future"; the language of
progress, class mobility, and education is generally lacking in discussions of that
medium. Yet as McChesney (1998) noted, the differences between the internet
and other popular noninteractive media, such as television, are eroding if not
already functionally gone. Thus, families of color are putting their faith in an
internet that is coming to resemble less of an "information superhighway" and

more of a sprawling suburban shopping mall. It is becoming increasingly clear that people of color missed the "golden age of cyberculture."

Despite these critiques, the internet does still retain at least the potential for interactivity that television lacks. Because "the people" are able to add content to the internet, this would seem to qualify it as a form that is popular—or "of the people," to use Fiske's (1989) formulation—and thus as a possible site of resistance to the majority culture and the mass media that support and promulgate it. Yet this question of "the people" is a vexed one; *which* people are at issue here, and what is their relation to the medium in actual practice as opposed to theory? Until now, questions of race have not much entered the picture when scholars speculate about internet interactivity and its meanings.[2] One of the great contributions that the Pew Foundation has made to the scholarship on race and the internet is its groundbreaking study of Asian Americans, whites, African Americans, and Hispanics that tracks their use of this new medium in more detail than ever before. This allows a more nuanced discussion of who the people online are, what their presence consists of, and the areas in which they are present or absent in specific areas of cyberspace. It also allows for an examination, in more complex terms, of how race matters online.

This chapter examines some differences among racial groups in terms of how they use the internet and briefly examines it as a "popular" medium.[3] The chapter also makes a case for how minority expressive cultures in cyberspace, particularly those produced and consumed by youth of color, may provide sites of resistance to offline racial hegemonies that call for serious consideration.[4]

Race has long been a vexed issue on the internet. In 1996, John Perry Barlow wrote *A Declaration of the Independence of Cyberspace* in which he explained,

Ours is a world that is both everywhere and nowhere, but it is not where bodies live. We are creating a world that all may enter without privilege or prejudice accorded by race, economic power, military force, or station of birth. We are creating a world where anyone, anywhere may express his or her beliefs, no matter how singular, without fear of being coerced into silence or conformity.

Race is the very first thing that Barlow (1996) claimed would be eradicated in cyberspace. This implies that of all the body handicaps recognized as oppressive, race is somehow the most oppressive. Barlow's statement was part of the first wave of utopian thinking on the internet; thus, critiquing it is like shooting fish in a barrel.[5] Few people really believe these lyrical claims anymore.[6] However, unlike the original *Declaration of Independence,* Barlow's statement did highlight an intense awareness of race as a problem of access that needs to be overcome. And Barlow was correct in stressing it; data gathered by the Pew Foundation do indicate that there are still significant disparities in access to the internet based on race, with African Americans and Hispanics being *much less likely* to be online than are whites. More than half (58%) of whites have used the internet, compared with 43% of African Americans and 50% of Hispanics (Spooner & Rainie, 2001). Only Asian Americans are more likely to have access; fully 75% of them have used the internet, making them "one of the most wired groups in America" (Spooner, 2001). Furthermore, although the gap in access between people of color and whites is closing, African Americans with access to the internet do not go online as often in a typical day as do whites; only 36% of African Americans go online in a typical day, compared with 56% of whites (Spooner & Rainie, 2000).

Past digital divide discourse has tended to perpetuate the "gap" metaphor, stressing the absence of people of color online and implying that this is a state of things that needs to be remedied.[7] The Pew Foundation's study of internet use and race, which tracks minority participation in four major categories (fun, information seeking, major life activities, and transactions), examines the ways in which all three minority groups studied participate proportionally *more* in several activities. For example, 54% of the African Americans online listened to music online, whereas only 32% of whites online did so. Hispanics and Asian Americans online also listened to music proportionally more than did whites online; nearly half (48%) of Hispanics did so, compared with 46% of Asian Americans. This represents quite a significant digital divide in terms of use of the internet as a means to get access to music, with whites on the "wrong" side despite their superior numbers in terms of general access to the internet. This divide extends into several different types of activities. The Pew data indicate that when racial minorities get online, more of them spend their time online chatting, sending and reading instant messages, looking for sports information, and downloading music than do whites online. This held true for all three racial non-white racial groups. (This is even more interesting considering how different Asian Americans look in this study in comparison with other racial minority groups; as noted earlier, they are the only non-white group whose members present online in greater numbers than do whites, yet when it comes to "fun" activities, their patterns of internet use resemble those of other minorities across the board much more than they do those of whites.) It seems clear that their investments in the medium are different from those of white users and that they are far more engaged with the internet as a source of expressive or popular culture than as a way to buy or sell stocks, get weather reports, or get hobby information—all activities in which whites online participate proportionally more than do Hispanics, African Americans, or Asian Americans online.

Indeed, the relative absence of people of color in these informational and retail spaces can be read as a healthy divide given the "massification" of the internet by corporations that envision the medium as primarily a way in which to sell products or services.[8] This is not to say that popular culture is not itself a commodity; of course it is—and a very important one in the global economy. However, popular music, movies, and sports all have the distinction of featuring Americans of color on a fairly regular basis, as performers and players if not as owners and producers. Popular musical forms (e.g., hip-hop, rap) and sports (e.g., basketball, football, baseball) provide images of American ethnic minorities as creative, innovative, and powerful.

Significantly, using the internet to access music, movies, sports information, and social functions such as chatting and instant messaging is categorized by the Pew study under the heading of "fun." The titles of the remaining three categories—information seeking, major life activities, and transactions—rhetorically imply that participating in popular culture is not a "major life activity" or a way in which to get important "information." On the contrary, rather than devaluing those online spaces where the small but growing cadre of American minorities are spending their time and energy, a reenvisioning of what constitutes a "major life activity" or salient "information" may be in order. In the case of people of color, popular culture practices constitute a discursive domain where they are more likely to see cultural producers who resemble them. This is important information in the context of the internet and their lived realities. Thus, manifestations of expressive cultures on the internet may provide an online oasis or refuge for users of color, most of whom are relatively young and new to the medium.

In any event, these data confirm the contention of the "Afro-futurists" that, contrary to popular opinion, there is a sizable and culturally significant African diasporic investment in information technologies, including the internet. This would seem to fly in the face of much digital divide discourse. Instead, it appears that users of color are quite selective in their use of the internet and tend to favor activities related to expressive culture, such as music, movies, chatting, and using multimedia sources, over other activities. However, the data do enable a new perspective on what people of color actually do when they are online as opposed to the old focus on the digital divide and information "haves" and "have-nots." Thus, the project is very much in the spirit of the Afro-futurist group that, in a special issue of *Social Text* (Nelson, 2002) and in the collection *Technicolor* (Nelson, 2001), brought to light neglected examples of "African diasporic technophilia" and its long history, debunking the "underlying assumption of much digital divide rhetoric . . . that people of color, and African Americans in particular, cannot keep pace with our high-tech society" (Nelson, 2002, p. 6).

As stated previously, there are several areas of online life in which people of color participate more fully, in proportion to their numbers, than do whites. African Americans, Hispanics, and Asian Americans generally participate more often in activities coded as "fun" by the Pew study. These activities are as follows:

- Browse just for fun
- Get hobby information
- Send an instant message
- Chat online
- Use video/audio clip
- Play a game
- Look for sports information
- Look for information about music, books, or other leisure activities
- Listen to music
- Download music

As the report noted, this is partly explained by the relative youth of minority groups in comparison with whites. This is especially true of Asian Americans and Hispanics. "The online Hispanic population is very young. . . . About 61% of online Hispanics are 34 [years old] or under. In comparison, about 37% of white internet users and 54% of African American users are in that cohort" (Spooner & Rainie, 2001). In addition, "The Asian American internet population is also one of the most youthful on the Web. Almost two-thirds (63%) of Asian American users are between the ages of 18 and 34 [years]" (Spooner, 2001). More than half of all people of color who use the internet are young. This has a tremendous bearing on their relation to popular culture because "youth culture" and expressive cultures tend to cross and overlap in numerous ways.

But we must also consider the relation between expressive or popular culture and racial identity and being in the world. Expressive culture practices such as music have always been media spaces where people of color are visible as producers and performers, although of course this should not be read as an unalloyed good. As Gray (1995) wrote,

> Marginalized and subordinated communities have creatively transformed and used popular cultural artifacts such as music, costumes, parades, traditions, and festivals to transgress their particular locations, to express their visions, and [to] invent themselves. What characterizes black youth culture in the 1990s and therefore warrants careful attention is the central role of the commercial culture industry and mass media in the process. (p. 151)

If indeed the internet has become a mass medium and has lost some of its potential as a space for transgression, expression, and reinvention of mass images of race, gender, and identity, this is alarming—but perhaps less so than it seems. Black youth culture is already closely engaged with the commercial culture industry. As Kelley (1997) wrote, "In a nation with few employment opportunities for African Americans and a white consumer market eager to be entertained by the Other, blacks have historically occupied a central place in the popular culture industry" (p. 46).

This partial empowerment in people of color over their own self-representations and imagery in the popular commercial sphere is enacted in multiple media, and the internet is becoming the most recent addition to this process. In some cases, the internet has enabled young people of color to critically intervene in particular aspects of the culture industry such as fashion, another commodified expressive culture with its own set of politics and investments in youth culture. In April 2002, Abercrombie & Fitch, a popular mall retailer that markets its casual clothing to the high school and college set, produced a series of graphic T-shirts that depicted images of Asians with "slanty eyes [and] rice paddy straw hats" along with slogans such as "you love long time" and "two Wongs can make it white." The latter slogan was paired with an image of two Asian laundry workers. The response to these T-shirts was immediate, and the internet was instrumental in the process. An e-mail campaign was organized both informally (my brother, David K. Nakamura, circulated the protest e-mail to Abercrombie & Fitch that he posted to the *San Jose Mercury News* to a list of more than a dozen recipients that included me—in fact, that was how I learned about the incident) and formally through two Web sites. The first was initiated for the sole purpose of organizing this protest and can be found at www.Boycott-af.com. The other can be found at www.PetitionOnline.com/bcaf/petition.html. Each provides an area where a user can sign a petition on the Web as well as links to Abercrombie & Fitch's e-mail address and a link that enables a user can send the petition to a friend. Ultimately, this internet organizing resulted in several rallies in front of Abercrombie & Fitch bricks-and-mortar stores, and the Organization of Chinese Americans attributed this to angry complaints, phone calls, and e-mail campaigns that spread quickly among Asian/Pacific Islander students, community members, and leaders nationwide. The Web petition gathered more than 6,500 signatures, and it is impossible to track how many Asian Americans used private e-mail to circulate this information. The T-shirts were withdrawn shortly afterward, and Abercrombie & Fitch delivered an apology to the Asian American community. Here, the internet's ability to spread information "like wildfire" provided a politicized space that allowed Asian Americans, a minority that struggles against popular images of themselves as hookers and laundry workers, to intervene in the commercial culture industry. In this case, Asian Americans used their status as "the young and the connected" to register their determination not to be represented as slanty-eyed stereotypes. This successful struggle over popular racist imagery by young people of color is notable because of the integral role played by the internet. However, it is yet to be seen whether this protest hurt Abercrombie & Fitch's bottom line.

In addition, although the e-mail campaign against Abercrombie & Fitch's racist T-shirts is encouraging, it is one in which users of color are still constructed as "angry customers" in relation to online commerce. The language of boycott is still that of dissatisfied consumers who use their clout as a "market" to influence retailers' policies. In effect, this is just more of the same; business as usual ported to the internet is only likely to duplicate existing power relations in terms of race and racism. Rigorous scholarship into the distinctions between internet users as consuming audiences and producers of online discourse is crucial to guard against the further reduction of people of color to markets.

I begin to wind things up now by returning to my starting part, that is, the novel idea that it might not be an unmitigated ill for people of color to be absent from the internet. During recent years, only a few cultural critics have been brave enough to buck the trend of internet boosterism, with Fusco (2001) and Hester-Williams (2001) being the most perceptive of these. Their critiques cannot be ignored.[9] Neither espoused a Luddite anti-technological stance; rather, both examined "the price that is exacted for participating in corporate-mediated cyberspaces that take advantage of our search for 'beloved community' on the net by reifying and subjecting our identities to the law of the market" (Hester-Williams, 2001). The question, "Does the internet really offer spaces of representation and resistance constructed 'for us' and 'by us'?," was answered in the negative by Hester-Williams. Fusco's (2001) critique was similar; she noted that the alliance between globalization and the commodification of cyberspace has enabled the "techno-elite's search for a more efficient work-force, which at this point means better trained at the top, less trained at the bottom, and more readily positioned for increased consumption of commodified leisure" (p. 192). Unlike other critics who see any deployment of minority expressive culture in *any* medium as a form of resistance,[10] Fusco stressed the distinction between commodified leisure and noncommodified leisure.[11] And she was correct in noting that noncommodified spaces are becoming increasingly difficult to find on the internet's particular iteration of hypercapitalism.

Thus, it is crucial that future demographic studies of the internet and race track *production* as well. How many people of color are putting up Web sites; posting their music, images, and videos; managing and contributing to listservs; or adding content to other textual sites? The Pew category "using e-mail" conflates passive e-mail activities, such as reading and deleting porn spam and "tribally marketed" hypercapitalistic advertising, with more active ones, such as writing or even forwarding politically oriented messages on racial identity issues (e.g., Abercrombie & Fitch's "two Wongs can make it white" T-shirts), sending pictures of grandchildren to relatives, and distributing family newsletters.

This is why future studies of internet use in the United States must ask questions regarding people of color as *producers* of internet content, not just as consumers of such content. Tracking the extent to which racial minorities are availing themselves of the internet's interactivity will tell us how much they are adding to the discourse rather than only describing which images, texts, and products they are consuming online—whether they are *being constructed* as markets and credit card holders as opposed to *constructing themselves* as authors, artists, community members, experts, interlocutors, and everyday online people. It is imperative that we devise some rigorous methodologies that help us to understand what constitutes meaningful participation online, that is, participation that opens and broadens the kinds of discourse that can be articulated online. It is not enough to merely "be there"; the figure from old-time online culture of the "lurker" reminds us of the passivity and ghostliness of those who watch from the sidelines of online life.

It may be helpful to envision various *categories* of online citizens rather than thinking in terms of gaps and divides. Just as on airplanes, there are vast tracts of economy-class users on the internet who surf the Web at work and buy quotidian objects online; smaller numbers of business-class users who make Web logs, send e-mail, and purchase more abstract things (e.g., stocks and bonds) from home; and the exclusive few first-class users who put up fully featured Web pages, know how to avoid spam, and may even work in information technologies. This metaphor of the internet as an airline may be useful because it dodges the problematics of the binary digital divide by envisioning internet use as subject to several gradations and because it also places the medium within a matrix that more closely resembles the global capitalistic environment of which the internet is both a symptom and an initiating force. These "classes" of service cut across race in interesting ways. Latinos and African Americans are overwhelmingly in economy class but, unfortunately, have the most faith in the airline. And although Asian Americans are in all classes and occupy more of the seats proportionally given their numbers, it is not possible to tell from the data provided by the Pew study whether they are content producers.

New media at their best have always challenged the distinction between producers and consumers, hence their appeal to postmodernist theorists, who proposed several decades ago that the right kinds of literature accomplished the same thing.[12] The hope for Hester-Williams's (2001) ideal "beloved communities" of color on the internet is just beginning to take hold in the vital, lively, and diverse expressive popular cultures and playspaces of chatting, gaming, and music that are *already* drawing users of color. It may also be significant in this context that African Americans are much more likely to use the internet to "seek religious information," an activity that the Pew study characterized as "information seeking." This difference is quite striking; fully one third (33%) of African Americans use the internet as a spiritual medium, whereas only 20% of whites do so. Perhaps the internet is functioning as a potential space for *religious* beloved community in a way that might be compared to African American churches, which have long been a nexus of ethnic community and human connection.

In any event, it seems that the current story of race online is more complex than had been thought. Simplistic notions of the digital divide do not obtain when we examine the decisive role of popular and expressive cultures in the growing minority presence online. The challenge now is to ensure that these new members of online culture are upgraded to higher classes of service and that they not remain in the steerage class of online lurkers and consumers. The internet's increasingly corporate culture works incessantly to turn us all into markets, and the greatest challenge of race in cyberspace is to resist this downgrading of what we are and what we can become.

Notes

1. See the extensive literature on the topic of racial stereotyping and media, particularly television, such as Gray's (1995) *Watching "Race,"* Hamamoto's (1994) *Monitored Peril,* Morrison's (1993) *Playing in the Dark,* Noriega's (2000) *Shot in America.*

2. See in particular works by Nelson (2001, 2002), Hester-Williams (2001), Fusco (2001), and Foster (1999, 2000) for some exceptions to this rule.

3. This needs to be addressed more fully in cyberculture scholarship. See McLaine's (2003) essay, "Ethnic Online Communities."

4. See Poster's (2001) *What's the Matter With the Internet?* for a nuanced critical theory approach that identifies and analyzes sites of resistance on the internet.

5. See Silver's (2000) formulation of the three stages of internet scholarship in his essay published in *Web.Studies.* He described these stages as "popular cyberculture" (characterized by a journalist bent and utopian tone), "cyberculture studies," and "critical cyberculture studies." Barlow's (1996) proclamation belongs to the first group.

6. See the extensive literature recently published on the digital divide, including Compaine's (2001) collection from MIT Press titled *The Digital Divide: Facing a Crisis or Creating a Myth?* This collection contains two of the most widely influential social science studies of the digital divide: Hoffman and Novak's "The Evolution of the Digital Divide: Examining the Relationship of Race to Internet Access and Usage Over Time" and the National Telecommunications and Information Administration's study titled "Falling Through the Net: Defining the Digital Divide." For cultural and media studies approaches to digital divide issues, see also *Race in Cyberspace* (Kolko, Nakamura, & Rodman, 2000), *Technicolor* (Nelson, 2001), *Cybertypes* (Nakamura, 2002), and Foster's work on cyberculture, in particular "The Souls of Cyber-folk" (Foster, 1999) and "Trapped by the Body?" (Foster, 2000).

7. See Warschauer's (n.d.) "Reconceptualizing the Digital Divide" for a further critique of this concept. Warschauer's article argues, "The concept provides a poor framework for either analysis or policy and suggests an alternate concept of technology for social inclusion."

8. In *Dark Fiber,* Internet critic Geert Lovink identified three "phases" of the internet: the first one dominated by military and scientific uses of the network; the second one, or the "golden age of cyberculture," with its "mixture of yuppies and hippies, characterized by an individualistic anti-state attitude"; and the third and current one, defined by "the coming of the online masses" or massification (Lovink, 2002, p. 137).

9. Alkalimat (2001) presented an entirely different perspective. He is the founder and promoter of "eBlack," described in his article of the same name as the technological successor to black studies. Its manifesto reads that "eBlack, the virtualization of the Black experience, is the basis for the next stage of our academic discipline," and that "eBlack depends upon everyone having access to and becoming active users of cybertechnology." But Alkalimat is not at all interested in black expressive culture on the internet despite the fact that this is how most people of color online are using it. He affirmed that the internet must be used for educational purposes and that that is where its value lies. In this way, Alkalimat is a classic digital dividist, meaning that he has an unreflectively positive opinion of the internet's "educational" value to people of color.

10. See Kelley (1997) and Rose (1994) on hip-hop music for a discussion of this dynamic. See also Gilroy's (2000) *Against Race.*

11. Needless to say, this is the holy grail of cultural studies scholars, from Dick Hebdige onward. See Hebdige's (1981) *Subculture* for an illustration of this. Kelley (1997) provided a brilliant discussion of the complicated relation between the popular culture and its commodification in *Yo Mama's DysFUNKtional!*

12. See Barthes's (1991) *S/Z* for a definition of the readerly (or passive text) and the writerly (or active text). The postmodern is characterized by the latter, but his point is that any text can be read in a writerly or active fashion. See Landow's (1997) *Hypertext 2.0* for a postmodern affirmation of hypertext's potential as a revolutionary medium.

References

Alkalimat, A. (2001, October). eBlack: A 21st century challenge. *Mots Pluriels,* No. 19. [Online]. Retrieved on April 21, 2003, from www.arts.uwa.edu.au/jmc/motspluriels/mp1901aa.html (Original work published 2000)

Barlow, J. P. (1996). A declaration of the independence of cyberspace. [Online]. Retrieved April 21, 2003, from www.eff.org/publications/john_perry_barlow/barlow_0296.declaration

Barthes, R. (1991). *S/Z.* New York: Noonday Press.

Compaine, B. (2001). *The digital divide: Facing a crisis or creating a myth?* Cambridge, MA: MIT Press.

Fiske, J. (1989). *Reading the popular.* New York: Routledge.

Foster, T. (1999). The souls of cyber-folk: Performativity, virtual embodiment, and racial histories. In M-L. Ryan (Ed.), *Cyberspace textuality: Computer technology and literary theory* (pp. 137–163). Bloomington: Indiana University Press.

Foster, T. (2000). "Trapped by the body?" Telepresence technologies and transgender performance in feminist and lesbian rewritings of cyberpunk fiction. In D. Bell (Ed.), *The cybercultures reader* (pp. 439–459). New York: Routledge.

Fusco, C. (2001). *The bodies that were not ours.* New York: Routledge.

Gilroy, P. (2000). *Against race.* Cambridge, MA: Harvard University Press.

Gray, H. (1995). *Watching "race": Television and the struggle for blackness.* Minneapolis: University of Minnesota Press.

Hamamoto, D. (1994). *Monitored peril: Asian Americans and television.* Minneapolis: University of Minnesota Press.

Hebdige, D. (1981). *Subculture: The meaning of style.* London: Routledge.

Hester-Williams, K. (2001, October). The reification of race in cyberspace: African American expressive culture, FUBU, and a search for beloved community on the Net. *Mots Pluriels,* No. 19. [Online]. Retrieved April 21, 2003, from www.arts.uwa.edu.au/motspluriels/mp1901khw.html

Kelley, R. (1997). *Yo' mama's disFUNKtional! Fighting the culture wars in urban America.* Boston: Beacon.

Kolko, B., Nakamura, L., & Rodman, G. (2000). *Race in cyberspace.* New York: Routledge.

Landow, G. (1997). *Hypertext 2.0.* Baltimore, MD: Johns Hopkins University Press.

Lovink, G. (2002). *Dark fiber: Tracking critical internet studies.* Cambridge, MA: MIT Press.

McChesney, R. W., with Wood, E. M., & Foster, J. B. (Eds.). (1998). *Capitalism and the information age: The political economy of the global communication revolution.* New York: Monthly Review Press.

McLaine, S. (2003). Ethnic online communities: Between profit and purpose. In M. McCaughey & M. Ayers (Eds.), *Cyberactivism: Critical theories and practices of online activism* (pp. 233–254). New York: Routledge.

Morrison, T. (1993). *Playing in the dark*. New York: Vintage.

Nakamura, L. (2002). *Cybertypes: Race, ethnicity, and identity on the internet*. New York: Routledge.

Nelson, A., with Tu, T., & Hines, A. (2001). *Technicolor: Race, technology, and everyday life*. New York: New York University Press.

Nelson, A. (2002). Introduction: Future texts. *Social Text, 20,* 1–15.

Noriega, C. (2000). Shot in America: Television, the state, and the rise of Chicano cinema. Minneapolis: University of Minnesota Press.

Poster, M. (2001). *What's the matter with the internet?* Minneapolis: University of Minnesota Press.

Rose, T. (1994). *Black noise: Rap music and black culture in contemporary America*. Hanover, MA: Wesleyan University Press.

Silver, D. (2000). Looking backwards, looking forwards: Cyberculture studies 1990–2000. In D. Gauntlett (Ed.), *Web.studies: Rewiring media studies for the digital age* (pp. 19–30). London: Arnold.

Spooner, T. (2001). Asian Americans and the internet: The young and the connected (Pew Internet and American Life Project). [Online]. Retrieved April 21, 2003, from www.pewinternet.org/reports/toc.asp?report=52

Spooner, T., & Rainie, L. (2000). *African Americans and the internet* (Pew Internet and American Life Project). [Online]. Retrieved April 21, 2003, from www.pewinternet.org/reports/toc.asp?report=25

Spooner, T., & Rainie, L. (2001). Hispanics and the internet (Pew Internet and American Life Project). [Online]. Retrieved April 21, 2003, from www.pewinternet.org/reports/toc.asp?report=38

Warschauer, M. (n.d.). Reconceptualizing the digital divide. *First Monday.* [Online]. Retrieved April 21, 2003, from www.firstmonday.dk/issues/issue7_7/warschauer

Part II

*Wired News
and Politics Online*

6

Will Internet
Voting Increase Turnout?

An Analysis of Voter Preference

Jennifer Stromer-Galley
University at Albany, State University of New York

The U.S. presidential election of 2000 served as a stark reminder of the importance of the way in which Americans vote. Not only is it important for people to vote in a democratic republic, but it is also important *how* they cast their votes. Much energy is spent on efforts to increase voter turnout, particularly during a time when voting turnouts are at 60-year lows. Some of that energy has focused on considering how people vote and finding methods that might increase turnout. Over the past 10 years, some states have experimented with alternative methods to voting at a polling place. Liberalized absentee voting laws in 21 states and early voting options in 14 states have been crafted with the explicit intention of increasing voter turnout. By making voting more convenient and flexible, the thinking goes, more people will cast ballots (Dubin & Kalsow, 1996).

With the expansion of the internet into a mass medium,[1] people also look to it as another avenue for voting. Internet voting was put to the test in March 1999, when the Arizona Democratic party held the first statewide binding vote using both traditional polling places and internet access. In the general election of 2000, the U.S. military experimented with internet voting for overseas service men and women. In Arizona, voter turnout increased, but voting occurred over a 3-day period (rather than the normal 1-day period) and there was a highly publicized "get out the vote" effort, making it difficult to compare the turnout with those in prior elections (for an assessment of that election, see Gibson, 2001). The U.S. military experiment did not yield a high turnout. Of the 250 volunteer, overseas military voters in the test case, only 84 participated (Dunbar, 2001).

Nonetheless, in both cases, the systems were established so that not only did people vote using a computer, but their votes were sent over the internet, across telephone lines and fiber-optic cables, to a server that recorded the votes. A useful definition of internet voting comes from the California internet Voting Task Force, composed of government officials, computer and security experts, and nonpartisan voter organizations, that was established to determine the feasibility of internet voting. The task force defined it as a secure and secret electronic ballot that is transmitted over the internet. The proponents of internet voting make arguments similar to those made by proponents of early voting and liberalized absentee voting. In particular, proponents argue that internet voting would accommodate the busy lifestyle of the average American, thereby increasing voter turnout (Mohen & Glidden, 2001).

Whether these new voting procedures actually increase voter turnout is still an unanswered question. Although the states have not yet had an election or series of elections from which researchers can determine whether internet voting increases turnout, some educated guesses can be attempted. Conducting a comparison of people who have a preference for internet voting with prior studies of absentee and early voting may provide some indication of the likelihood of an increase in turnout, based on the similarities or differences between the kinds of people who prefer internet voting and the kinds of people who use liberalized voting methods (i.e., voting early or by alternative methods) or who are likely to vote at a polling place on Election Day. It is predicted that people who prefer internet voting share similar demographic and political characteristics with those who vote by absentee ballot or who vote early. As a result, it may be the case that the same people who vote on Election Day take advantage of early and alternative voting options, suggesting neither an increase in turnout nor a broadening of the franchise to people who would otherwise not vote.

Alternative Voting Methods: Measuring Success

The United States has experienced a decline in voter turnout over the past 60 years. In an effort to increase turnout, several states have adopted new methods for voting such as allowing people to vote early in convenient locations (e.g., shopping malls) (Center for the Study of the American Electorate, 2001) and liberalizing absentee voting beyond the standard qualifying excuse (e.g., disability, religious holiday conflict). Absentee or remote voting is on the rise, with approximately 50% of Washington State voters and 25% of California voters using mail-in ballots (Kantor, 1999). In Oregon, place-based voting has been abolished, with the mail-in ballot taking its place.

Internet voting continues the trajectory of liberalizing and changing the process of voting. Internet voting is a particular process of voting—the kind experimented with in the 2000 Arizona Democratic primary and in the 2000 U.S. presidential election experiment by the military. To vote over the internet is to cast a vote from a home-, work-, or library-placed personal computer, or at a computer established at a traditional polling center, that is sent through the internet to a centralized server. The mechanics work something like this. A person uses a computer to go to a particular Web site and enters a secure password or other identifying code word. The person then selects for whom he or she is voting. This information is sent across the internet to a centralized server, which may be housed at the county or state level of government or by a private firm that then passes the information to the county responsible for the vote tabulation. All votes are dissociated from information that might allow for tracing back to the voters, and then the votes are tabulated.

One of the key assumptions behind this push toward alternative methods to voting at a polling place on Election Day is that voting at a polling place is thought to be inconvenient, particularly for those who live in two-income households with children, who commute, or who are elderly, disabled, or in the military. In most states, polling places open at 8 a.m. and close at 8 p.m., and voting is always on a workday. If a person wants to vote, she or he has to juggle jobs, children, and/or the commute to cast a ballot. Long lines during the evenings when people try to vote after work may discourage some from going to a polling place. Trying to get out of work for a few hours and commute back home to vote might not seem to be worth the hassle. If one is elderly, has a disability, or is in the military, it is difficult if not impossible to get to a polling place on Election Day. The solution then becomes early voting and relaxed absentee voting, which allow people to vote when they choose to vote—during the weekends, during the evenings, or whenever they have a little spare time.

Studies of the effects of liberalized absentee and early voting laws often focus on particular states and local races, making them hard to generalize to the larger

American population. The few national studies that do exist offer a mixed picture of the effect of liberalized voting laws on voter turnout. Nonetheless, these studies begin to draw a picture of the kinds of people who are likely to take advantage of these new opportunities to vote, and they begin to offer a sense as to whether these liberalized laws are enabling more people and different people to vote.

Two studies of particular states' voting turnouts suggest that the kinds of people who prefer and take advantage of early voting and liberalized absentee voting laws tend to be those who also would be likely to vote on Election Day. Southwell and Burchett (1997) studied Oregon voters in a 1996 senate election. They found that people who vote by mail were more likely to be older, better educated, interested in politics, and politically knowledgeable. Vote-by-mail voters were also more likely to be political independents. The authors concluded that the long-term effect of mail-in ballots on voter turnout is "likely to be slight" (p. 57). Stein (1998) studied early voters and regular voters in a Texas gubernatorial election in 1994 and found that early voters were older, strongly partisan, more politically interested, more conservative, and slightly poorer and that men were more likely to vote early than were women.

Two additional state election studies came to the opposite conclusion, that is, that liberalized absentee voting and mail-in voting enabled voting by people who might not have done so otherwise. Dubin and Kalsow (1996) studied a 30-year period of absentee voting in California. They found that African Americans vote absentee less often, whereas people over 64 years of age, people with children, people who work full-time, and poorer people were more likely to vote absentee. They did not find differences between urban and rural dwellers, but they did discover that renters were more likely to vote absentee than were home owners. Southwell and Burchett (2000) again studied Oregon, this time the 1996 special senate election, which was the first federal election conducted entirely with mail-in ballots. They found that mail-in voters—people who voted in the 1996 special election but who had not voted in 1992 or who had stated that they rarely voted—were older, better educated, more knowledgeable, and more likely to care about the outcome of the election than were nonvoters. In comparing the traditional voters (those who voted in 1992 and 1996 or who stated that they vote frequently) to the mail-in voters, the authors found that these two types of voters are quite similar. They explained, "This all-mail election facilitated the participation of the 'cream of the crop' of previous nonvoters by facilitating the participation of those previous nonvoters who were, in general, more involved in the political process" (p. 841), a possibility that they had also identified in their 1997 study. Their conclusion in the more recent study was more positive on the question of increasing voter turnout, stating that mail-in voters, alongside traditional voters, will continue to vote in future elections, contributing to a "surge in turnout without any substantial shift in relative two-party strength or overall information level of the electorate" (p. 844).

Two studies that assessed the effects of multiple states' liberalized voting laws on voter turnout came to opposite conclusions. Oliver (1996) found that students, senior citizens, singles, and renters were more likely to vote absentee. Higher income, increased levels of education, and suburban dwelling were also positively related to absentee voting. He argued that electoral turnout did appear to be stimulated by liberalized absentee voting laws but that such an increase was observed as occurring in conjunction with strong "get out the vote" efforts by political parties. Kenski (2001) compared states that used early voting with those that used standard voting and found that early voters were more likely to be older, to have fewer children, to not be full-time workers, and to be Republican. She also found that early voters were more likely to be politically interested in the campaign and generally paid more attention to government and public affairs. Kenski concluded that the kinds of people who use early voting were the same kinds of people who are likely to vote on Election Day.

These six studies split along different lines in their interpretations of the effect of early voting, mail-in voting, and liberalized absentee voting on voter turnout.[2] What is shared across all six studies is that people who are older, are more educated, have higher incomes, are conservative, and are politically interested are more likely to cast their ballots using one of the liberalized voting means. Although there is some dispute in the studies regarding income, partisan strength, employment status, and whether the voters have children, on the whole, the findings suggest that the people who vote by standard means on Election Day are the same people who are likely to cast absentee ballots. Studies by Wolfinger and Rosenstone (1980), Blais (2000), and Verba, Schlozman, and Kim (1978) suggested that education, income, political interest, and age are key predictors in whether someone will vote or not. Older, better educated, politically interested people with higher incomes are likely to come to the polls on Election Day. As the liberalized voting studies also identified, older, politically interested, and more educated people are the ones who capitalize on the new voting options. The argument that the kinds of people who vote early, through the mail, or with absentee ballots are likely to be different from the kinds of people who vote at the polls does not seem to hold up based on the evidence from these studies. Although the 30-year California study did find that people with children and people who worked full-time were more likely to vote absentee, suggesting that these new voting methods are capitalized on by busy people, the other studies did not concur with that finding.[3]

Measuring Internet Voting Success

internet voting as a method has not been measured systematically to determine whether it increases turnout, particularly among groups of people who would otherwise not vote such as young people and those who are less educated or less interested in politics. An analysis conducted of people's preference for internet voting, as compared with people's preference for mail-in voting and voting at a polling booth, can provide a glimpse into what kinds of people would at least prefer to vote over the internet. Such an analysis cannot speak to whether people *will in fact* vote over the internet because the United States has not experienced a wide-scale internet voting option. Thus, survey questions must be based on a person's perceived preference for voting online. In doing this analysis, the intention is to shed light on whether there is some likelihood that certain kinds of people, and perhaps more people, might prefer to vote over the internet than go to a polling place on Election Day.

The data for this analysis come from the Pew Center for the People and the Press, which conducted a survey of a nationwide sample of 2,174 adults during the period from June 14 to 28, 2000. This survey's demographic characteristics are comparable to other national telephone surveys using the random digit dial technique.[4] The majority of the survey asked questions about the 2000 presidential candidates and the presidential campaign. It also included questions about political party preference, past voting behavior, interest in the election and politics, the existence or absence of a sense of duty to vote, and standard demographics. Of particular interest for this study was a question about voting preference: "If you had the choice of voting in a booth at a polling place on Election Day, or over the internet, or through the mail during the weeks leading up to Election Day, which would you prefer?" That question served as the basis for this analysis.

Findings

The majority of the respondents preferred voting at a traditional polling place over voting by mail or voting over the internet (Table 6.1). Only 22% preferred

Table 6.1   Voting Method Preferences (percentages)

Voting booth/Polling place	51
Mail-in ballot	26
Voting over the internet	22
None/Either	1

$N = 2,135$

voting over the internet, whereas 26% preferred voting by mail and 51% preferred voting at a polling place. At least in terms of overall preference, people preferred what they have done before, that is, voting at a polling place. Americans have been voting at a polling place for more than two centuries and are aware of the process, its strengths, and its pitfalls. Voting by mail, too, has grown to become a common way of voting for many Americans, particularly on the West Coast. It is perhaps not surprising, then, that voting over the internet is selected by the smallest number of people given that internet voting has been experienced by few Americans. Many do not know how internet voting would work and may be concerned that their votes would be compromised through fraud or attack by hackers (Gibson, 2001).

Setting aside, for the moment, the issue of a minority of Americans indicating a desire to vote over the internet, there is still the question of the obstacles that appear to exist that prevent people from voting at a polling place. Perhaps the people who see place-based voting as an obstacle are more inclined to look to the internet as a solution. The Pew survey asked people to identify which obstacles they experienced in trying to vote. Three of the options dealt with knowledge and likeability of the candidates and a desire to be involved in politics, two of the questions tackled the obstacle of registration and getting to the polling place, and one question identified a desire to be politically involved in ways other than voting.

In general, people identified both the candidates themselves and their knowledge of the candidates to be greater obstacles than registration or getting to the polling place (Table 6.2). Nearly 75% of the respondents indicated that one reason why they do not vote is that they do not like the candidates. In contrast, only 25% indicated that they find it difficult to get to the polling place.

This pattern is mirrored in examining people who indicate that they prefer voting at a traditional polling place, those who prefer mail-in balloting, and those who prefer internet voting. Given that liberalized voting laws are designed to

Table 6.2   Obstacles to Voting Cited by People (percentages)

Obstacle	Agree	Disagree
I sometimes feel that I don't know enough about the candidates to vote.	65	35
I sometimes don't like any of the candidates.	74	26
I don't want to involve myself with politics.	35	65
It's complicated to register to vote where I live.	13	87
It's difficult for me to get out to the polls to vote.	25	75
I can make more of a difference by getting involved in my community than by voting in elections.	47	53
N	1,131	

SOURCE: Adapted from Pew Internet and America Life data.

NOTE: "Agree" and "Disagree" categories are compiled; "Agree" is the total of "agree" and "strongly agree" responses, and "Disagree" is the total of "disagree" and "strongly disagree" responses.

Table 6.3   Cross-Tabulation of Voting Procedure Preferences and Perceived Difficulties in Getting to the Polls

"It's difficult for me to get out to the polls to vote"	Voting Preference			
	Polling Place	Internet	Mail	All Respondents
Completely agree	7	8	12	9
Mostly agree	12	18	18	16
Mostly disagree	34	25	26	29
Completely disagree	47	49	44	47
N	426	371	282	1,079

Source: Adapted from Pew Internet and America Life data.

NOTE: Pearson chi-square = 21.10, $df = 9$, $p < 0.01$.

remedy the difficulty of getting to a polling place, it is of particular interest to determine which voting method is preferred by people who also find it difficult to get to the polls. In examining people's voting method preferences and comparing them with people's perceived difficulty in getting to the polling place to vote, it is clear that there is a difference (Table 6.3). People who find it difficult to go to the polls are more likely to prefer internet voting or voting by mail. Of those who prefer internet voting, 26% reported that they find it difficult to go to the polls. Of those who prefer voting by mail, 30% reported that they find it difficult to go to the polls. In contrast, of those who prefer voting at a polling place, 19% reported that they find it difficult to go to the polls. Does this suggest, then, that people who find it difficult to get to the polls will be more likely to select voting over the internet? The data indicate that such people prefer voting by mail (chi-square = 5.89, $df = 1$, $p < .02$) and do not prefer voting at a polling place (chi-square = 11.24, $df = 1$, $p < .01$) but are no more or less likely to select voting over the internet (chi-square = 0.58, $df = 1$). This suggests that those who find getting to a polling place difficult are likely to pick voting by mail as their preferred method of voting rather than voting over the internet.

So far, a rather negative picture has emerged of the likelihood that people would select the internet as their preferred method for voting if it were available. People do not identify it as their first choice of voting method, and those people who find voting at a polling place to be an obstacle are likely to select voting by mail as their preferred remedy. The final analysis focuses on whether the people who would prefer to vote online have the same characteristics as those who prefer to vote by mail. In particular, are they likely to be Republican, older, more politically interested, and more educated, as studies of absentee and liberalized voting have found?

Using three logistic regressions, each preferred voting method was used as a dependent variable, and a model was built incorporating the variables included in prior studies of absentee and liberalized voting: gender, age, marital status, children, education, race, income, employment, and whether the person owns a home.[5] Political party, political interest,[6] and one's perceived duty to vote[7] were also included. Because the question at hand is about internet voting, a variable of internet use was also included. This question asked people whether they did or did not use the internet for e-mail or surfing the Web. Finally, because of the argument that people who are disabled might be drawn to alternative methods of voting, a variable of physical disability was included, that is, whether the person is blind, is deaf, and/or has a physical disability (Table 6.4).

The first model predicted a respondent's preference for voting at a polling place, controlling for other variables. Of the statistically significant variables, being female, having many years of education, and using the internet decreases the likelihood that a respondent will prefer voting at a polling place. Being older, having a heightened interest in politics, and feeling a duty to vote increases the likelihood that a person will prefer voting at a polling place. The second model predicted a respondent's preference for using a mail-in ballot, controlling for other variables. Of the statistically significant variables, being Republican increases the likelihood that a respondent will prefer using a mail-in ballot. Being an internet user decreases the probability that a person will prefer using a mail-in ballot. The third model predicts a respondent's preference for voting online, controlling for other variables. Being older, owning a home, being politically

Table 6.4   Logistic Regression of Voting Preferences and Independent Variables

	Model 1: Prefer Voting Booth/ Polling Place	Model 2: Prefer Mail-In Ballot	Model 3: Prefer Internet Voting
Constant	−2.16***	−0.38	−0.90
Demographics			
Gender (female)	−0.25*	0.25	0.08*
Age	0.03***	−0.01	−0.04***
Years of education	−0.10***	−0.01	0.12***
Income	−0.07*	−0.01	0.09**
Race (white)	−0.29*	0.01	0.29
Married	−0.00	−0.12	0.20
Children	−0.01	0.27	−0.11
Employed full-time	−0.06	0.03	0.12
Own a home	0.20	0.13	−0.31*
Possible reasons for voting mechanism preferences			
Political party (Republican)	−0.01	0.07*	−0.03
Political interest	0.46***	−0.16	−0.40***
Duty to vote	0.46***	−0.12	−0.18**
Ever go online	−0.51***	−0.67***	1.77***
Physical disability	−0.39*	0.32	0.16
Chi-square	172.57	38.56	206.54
Pseudo R^2	0.19	0.05	0.23
n	497	219	389

NOTE: $N = 1,105$. "Go Online" is a dichotomous variable. The question: Do you ever go online to access the Internet or World Wide Web or to send and receive e-mail?

$*p < 0.10, **p < 0.05, ***p < 0.01.$

knowledgeable, and feeling a duty to vote are statistically significant variables that decrease a respondent's likelihood to prefer internet voting. Variables that predict a person's likelihood to prefer internet voting include having more years of education, having a higher income, and being an internet user. Of all the variables predicting how a person would prefer to vote, being an internet user is the largest and most significant.

Discussion

Is it possible that internet voting, if it were made available, would increase voter turnout? Do people who feel that voting at a polling place is difficult see the internet as a solution to that problem, and do the people who prefer voting by mail share similar demographic and other characteristics with those who say that they prefer internet voting? It is clear that internet voting is not at the top of the list of methods for voting currently given that people prefer the standard voting booth or voting by mail over internet voting. It is also clear that people who find getting to a polling place difficult do not necessarily see the internet as a solution to that obstacle. It is not clear, however, whether the kinds of people who prefer voting over the internet are the same kinds of people who would prefer voting by mail.

The model for discerning which demographic and other variables predict a preference for using mail-in ballots is not strong. It is possible that mail-in balloting competes with internet voting as a preference. As a result, no clear patterns can be seen among particular demographic groups for a preference to vote by mail. What becomes interesting in light of this, then, is the comparison of the particular groups of people who prefer voting at a polling place with those who prefer voting over the internet.

The people who prefer voting over the internet appear to be strikingly different from the people who prefer voting at a traditional polling place. First, older people prefer voting at a polling place and younger people prefer voting over the internet. This is not surprising given that younger people are more likely to use the internet than are older people (Howard, Rainie, & Jones, 2001). It is also clear that people who prefer internet voting—mostly these younger people—are also quite likely to use the internet at least occasionally. Thus, they are familiar with the technology, they use it in their daily lives, and perhaps they see internet voting as a natural extension of the capacity of the internet. Second, people with more education are more likely to prefer internet voting than are people with less education. This may result from more highly educated people being more likely to use the internet and understanding how internet voting might work. People who prefer internet voting are also more likely to be renters and to have a higher income. As other studies suggest, income and education are often correlated (Wolfinger & Rosenstone, 1980), so it is not surprising that those who prefer internet voting have both higher education and higher income. Also, the fact that young people are more likely to rent than are older people may help to explain this finding. It is noteworthy that internet use is a variable predicting vote preference. Internet users are more likely to indicate that the internet would be their preferred voting method. This can be explained, at least in part, by the fact that they are familiar and perhaps more comfortable with the technology. They might not have apprehensions about the internet as a voting medium as a result of their daily encounters with it. Finally, the common assumption that people who are busy—people who work full-time and who have children—are likely to prefer internet voting does not appear to be true. They are not any more likely to choose the internet for voting than to choose a polling place for voting. Thus, although the internet may be an easy way in which to vote, for any number of reasons, busy people do not yet see it as preferable to voting by other means.

If one stopped at this point, this analysis might suggest that the kinds of people who prefer internet voting are different from the kinds of people who prefer voting at a polling place. Internet voting might bring into the voting process a whole segment of the American population that so far does not turn out in large numbers—young people. Wolfinger and Rosenstone (1980) explained that voter turnout is low during young adulthood and gradually increases until men are in their 80s and women are in their 70s, at which point there is a marked decline in turnout due to physical ailments and other reasons. Based on the analysis, it would appear that internet voting might change that pattern, starting young people off voting at a much higher rate than is currently seen.

It would be a mistake, however, to stop at this point or draw such a conclusion. Two other critical variables, political interest and a sense of duty to vote, fill out more of the picture and signal that internet voting might not contribute to an increase in voter turnout among young people. People who prefer voting at a polling place are highly likely to be politically interested; for example, they follow politics generally, they followed the news of the 2000 U.S. presidential election, and they gave some thought to it. Political interest, as measured and reported in the six studies discussed earlier, was a key factor in all of these studies. It makes logical sense that people who are interested in an election and are following news stories about it are likely to vote on Election Day. Those who are not interested and are not following such news might not feel knowledgeable enough about the candidates to cast their votes. This conclusion is backed by the finding that people identify not knowing about the candidates as a major obstacle to voting.

People who prefer voting at a polling place are also likely to feel a sense of duty to vote. In contrast, people who prefer internet voting generally do not have a similar interest in politics and do not feel a sense of duty to vote. It is true that people are more likely to view voting as a duty as they get older (Blais, 2000), and this might help explain, in part, the stark difference between those who prefer voting at a polling place and those who prefer voting online. More important, however, Blais (2000) found that a sense of duty is strongly correlated with actual voting behavior. Using a computer simulation of voting behavior, he found that if people had no sense of duty to vote, turnout was markedly depressed. In additional studies that Blais conducted, he found that a sense of duty to vote "is an important consideration for most voters" (p. 104). There is no clear reason to assume that internet voting is going to increase a person's interest in a political election or increase a person's sense of duty to vote. Young people generally are less likely to vote, and if people who prefer internet voting do not have an interest in politics or a sense of duty to vote, they are not likely to be induced to vote even if internet voting were made available. Although Wolfinger and Rosenstone (1980) identified education as the most important predictor of voting, the studies on liberalized and early voting (except those of Oliver, 1996, and Southwell & Burchett, 2000) suggest that education is not a factor, lending more weight to other factors, particularly political interest and a sense of duty to vote.

The final complicating part of this picture is that internet use is the strongest independent predictor of internet vote preference—stronger than either a person's level of political interest or his or her sense of duty to vote. However, internet voting as an option probably does not alter a person's sense of duty to vote or his or her political interest. As people's internet use increases, their familiarity and comfort with the technology should also increase. As a result, people may grow more open to the idea of internet voting as an option or even a preference. This again raises the possibility that those who find it difficult to get to a polling place or who face other obstacles to voting at the polls, but who have a sense of duty to vote and an interest in politics, may turn to the internet as an easier way in which to vote.

Conclusions

The findings from this study may be proven wrong if internet voting becomes an option in the United States and the number and kinds of people who exercise the franchise increases. The findings from this study suggest that even though people are aware of online voting as an option, voter turnout is a complex phenomenon that is driven simultaneously by political interests, a sense of duty to vote, and the mechanism of voting. Currently, people do not prefer internet voting as a mechanism over traditional voting methods. Even those who find it difficult to get to a polling place do not view the internet as a good alternative. More important, those people who currently say that they would prefer internet voting over place-based voting might not be people with much interest in politics or a strong feeling of duty to vote. The internet may be a remarkable technology, but it cannot in and of itself generate these necessary elements that draw people to cast ballots. That inspiration comes from the political world offline.

Notes

1. The Pew internet and American Life Project has reported that 55% of households had Web access in 2001.

2. Part of the cause of the variability may have to do with the differences in each state. Oregon, Texas, and California have distinct populations that make it difficult to generalize to a larger American population. The ways in which the studies were conducted also cause problems in making concrete conclusions about voter turnout. The two studies that suggest a possible increase in voter turnout have methodological problems. The Dubin and Kalsow (1996) study used data gathered at the county level; thus, these authors' conclusions are based on an aggregate of counties rather than on individual-level data. The Southwell and Burchett (2000) study of the 1996 special senate election was conducted using telephone interviews of people. Their analysis relied on self-reported voting patterns, raising some question about the validity of the data. Moreover, their study interpreted the data as indicating a likelihood of a general increase in voter turnout based on an assumption that people who voted in the 1996 special election, but who did not vote in the 1992 election, would not have voted in 1996 if mail-in ballots were not an option and will continue to vote in future elections. It is not clear whether the people who did not vote in 1992, but who voted in 1996, will continue to vote in future elections. There is no clear evidence to suggest that once people commit to voting by mail in one election, they will continue to do so in future elections.

3. The reason why the California study findings are contradictory to the other studies may be due, in part, to the longitudinal nature of the California study. It may be that the other cross-section studies captured a current moment in which people were simply too busy to contemplate voting early and so used Election Day as their deadline for voting. Another reason for the different findings may be due to the nature of the data. The California study looked at aggregate data at the county level rather than at individual-level data used in the other studies. It could be that the aggregate data masked phenomena that become evident when looking at individuals.

4. Comparing the Pew survey respondents to Annenberg Public Policy Center (APPC) national telephone survey respondents indicates that the Pew sample is slightly younger, better educated, and more likely to be white than the APPC survey respondents.

5. Dummy variables were created for all demographic variables except income and education. Rural- and urban-dwelling variables were included in an initial regression model but were found to be nonsignificant predictors and contributed very little to the overall percentage of variance explained by the model. They were removed from further analysis.

6. Political interest is an index created by combining three questions: how closely a person has followed the news about candidates for the 2000 U.S. presidential election, how frequently a person follows what is going on in government and public affairs generally, and whether a person has given much thought to the coming presidential election (Cronbach's alpha $= .74$, $M = 2.17$, $SD = 1.04$).

7. Duty to vote is an index created by combining two questions: how strongly a person feels it is his or her duty to vote and how frequently a person votes (Cronbach's alpha $= .63$, $M = 1.78$,

$SD = 1.31$). I wanted to have a measure of duty to vote that is both a person's self-report that he or she has a sense of duty to vote and a measure of recollection of behavior to vote. I felt that including the behavior component would make the measure more reliable given that most people view voting as a duty (Dennis, 1970).

References

Blais, A. (2000). *To vote or not to vote: The merits and limits of rational choice theory.* Pittsburgh, PA: University of Pittsburgh Press.

Center for the Study of the American Electorate. (2001, January 9). *Two pro-participation reforms actually harm voter turnout; other reforms suggested* [press release]. Washington, DC: Author.

Dennis, J. (1970). Support for the institution of elections by the mass public. *American Political Science Review, 64,* 819–835.

Dubin, J. A., & Kalsow, G. A. (1996). Comparing absentee and precinct voters: A view over time. *Political Behavior, 18,* 369–392.

Dunbar, J. (2001). Internet voting project cost Pentagon $73,809 per vote. *The Public i.* [Online]. Retrieved April 25, 2003, from www.public-i.org/story_01_080901.htm

Gibson, R. (2001). Elections online: Assessing internet voting in light of the Arizona Democratic primary. *Political Science Quarterly, 116,* 561–583.

Howard, P. N., Rainie, L., & Jones, S. (2001). Days and nights on the internet: The impact of a diffusing technology. *American Behavioral Scientist, 45,* 382–404.

Kantor, J. (1999, November 2). Obstacles to e-voting. *Slate.* [Online]. Retrieved April 23, 2003, from http://slate.msn.com/netelection/entries/99-11-02_44394.asp

Kenski, K. (2001, August). *Evaluating absentee and early voters in the 2000 general election: Are individuals who vote on Election Day different from those who vote early?* Paper presented at the meeting of the American Political Science Association, San Francisco.

Mohen, J., & Glidden, J. (2001). The case for internet voting. *Communications of the ACM, 44*(1), 72–85.

Oliver, J. E. (1996). The effects of eligibility restrictions and party activity on absentee voting and overall turnout. *American Journal of Political Science, 40,* 498–513.

Southwell, P. L., & Burchett, J. (1997). Survey of vote-by-mail senate election in the state of Oregon. *PS: Political Science & Politics, 30*(1), 53–57.

Southwell, P., & Burchett, J. (2000). Does changing the rules change the players? The effect of all-mail elections on the composition of the electorate. *Social Science Quarterly, 81,* 837–845.

Stein, R. M. (1998). Introduction: Early voting. *Public Opinion Quarterly, 62,* 57–69.

Verba, S., Schlozman, K. L., & Kim, J-O. (1978). *Participation and political equality: A seven nation comparison.* Cambridge, UK: Cambridge University Press.

Wolfinger, R. E., & Rosenstone, S. J. (1980). *Who votes?* New Haven, CT: Yale University Press.

7

The Internet and Political
Involvement in 1996 and 2000

Ronald E. Rice
Rutgers, the State University of New Jersey

James E. Katz
Rutgers, the State University of New Jersey

The internet promises to transform the nature of political participation and expression. Some say that the internet has or will become enormously beneficial for democratic processes in particular and for society in general. Others argue that the internet will be either harmful or ruinous. Another possibility—seldom considered—is that the internet will have only minimal impact (Katz & Rice, 2002). The stakes riding on the political impact of the internet are enormous. The technology could potentially affect the democratic nature of American society, the global human and natural condition, and the ability of special interests to capture billions of taxpayer dollars.

Despite this, until recently, few investigators have provided substantial empirical information about the internet's nascent political consequences (Bimber, 2002). Prior to the 2000 election cycle, there appears to have been only one national random survey of political participation comparing users with nonusers (Katz, Aspden, & Reich, 1997).

The situation was markedly different in 2000. Many pundits proclaimed that 2000 would be "the year of the internet." Millions of dollars of governmental and private foundation-sponsored research was being conducted, and tens of millions of dollars of venture capital was being pumped into making the prophecy of the pundits come true (although, of course, that was not the reason for the investments). For example, in terms of the national party conventions, online portal services that were freely available included live streaming video, moment-by-moment and in-depth online reporting, and reams of retrievable documents, position papers, speeches, and statements.

The current study is in the unique position of being able to report analyses of historically relevant internet use data from the 1996 and 2000 national elections. This research is part of the Syntopia Project (2002). The project's aim has been to create, through random digit dialing phone surveys as well as case studies, in-depth observations, focus groups, and Web site analyses, a multiyear program charting social aspects of Americans' mediated communication behavior on the internet and Web and through mobile telephones.

Sources of Data

The Syntopia data come from a series of national representative telephone surveys in 1995, 1996, 1997, and 2000 designed by the chapter authors but administered by commercial survey firms. The sample sizes were 2,500 for October 1995, 557 plus a supplemental sample of 450 users for November 1996, 2,148 plus a supplemental sample of 153 users for November 1997, and 1,305 for March 2000. For 1996 and 1997, the analyses reported population estimates of internet use from the initial unaugmented samples but used the combined (regular and augmented) samples for comparing relative distributions of variables. The percentage of respondents who indicated that they were using the internet rose from 8.1% in 1995 to 18.8% in 1996, to 30.1% in 1997, to 59.7% in 2000.

This study also analyzes some data from the Pew Internet and American Life Project election survey in 2000, which included all cases of completed surveys (from adults over 18 years of age) by Princeton Survey Research Associates from October 1 to November 26, 2000.

Both sets of surveys followed rigorous sampling protocols and used random digit dialing to produce statistically representative samples of the adult U.S. population. The following analyses of the Syntopia and Pew data do not use weighted responses. Of course, all of the standard disclaimers about survey and opinion research apply to this research as well (Fisher & Katz, 2000).

Summary of Digital Divide
Trends and Influences: 1992 to 2000

Before delving into the detailed results of the political aspects, this section briefly summarizes results concerning the "digital divide" (America Online, 2000; Katz & Aspden, 1997a, 1997b, 1997c; Katz & Rice, 2002; Katz, Rice, & Aspden, 2001; McConnaughey, 2001; "Net Users," 2001; Norris, 2001; Walsh, Gazala, & Ham, 2001; Wresch, 2002).

DEMOGRAPHIC DIFFERENCES BY
SURVEY YEAR AND BY USER COHORT

The percentage of users who were female went from 46.4% in 1996 to 45.0% in 1997 to 50.6% in 2000 (the 1995 percentage was 62.5%, clearly an example of high variability in small samples). The percentage of users age 40 years or over increased from 34.8% in 1995, to 37.7% in 1996, to 42.2% in 1997, to 44.4% in 2000. The percentages of users with an income of more than $35,000 were 69.3% in 1995, 62.8% in 1996, 78.8% in 1997, and 77.0% in 2000. The percentages of users without a college degree were 48.0% in 1995, 52.4% in 1996, 51.2% in 1997, and 56.0% in 2000. And the percentages of African American users were 6.0% in 1995, 5.1% in 1996, 7.5% in 1997, and 9.1% in 2000. (Census figures for 1998 or 2000 for each demographic category were as follows: female, 51%; at least 40 years old, 55%; less than $35,000 income, 44.6%; less than a college education, 71.9%; African American, 12.7% [U.S. Bureau of the Census, 2001].)

Each of the Syntopia national surveys also asked users the year in which they started using the internet (referred to as "the internet, also known as the Information or Electronic Superhighway"). This allows analysis of cohorts of users—those starting in 1992 or before and those starting in each subsequent year. Across the cohorts of users, the proportion of female users increased, new internet users were proportionally more female, and new users were more likely to be female overall. The proportion of users age 40 years or over increased, and new internet users in a given year were older than the average age of all users in that survey year, but they were still well below the proportion age 40 years or over in the general population (approximately 55%) (and this disproportion is extreme for respondents over 65 years of age). The proportion of new internet users with a household income less than $35,000 increased slowly, although those with a lower income were more likely to stop being internet users. The proportion of non-college graduates was 28% for those users who started in 1992 or before and rose to 67% for the 1999–2000 cohort. The proportion of African Americans using the internet rose and then declined a bit over both of the cohort years.

INTERNET DROPOUTS

The Syntopia analyses identified a second digital divide, that is, dropouts (i.e., those who used the internet at one time but no longer did so as of the survey year). The percentages of dropouts were 7.8% in 1995, 11% in 1996, 10% in 1997, and 11.5% in 2000. Dropouts were significantly younger, less affluent, and less well educated than were users, but they were not more likely to be female or African American. Details on reasons that dropouts gave for no longer using the internet were reported elsewhere (Katz & Aspden, 1998; Katz & Rice, 2002).

AWARENESS OF THE INTERNET

This research identified a third digital divide, that is, relating to awareness of the existence of the internet (defined by the question "Have you heard of the internet or the Information Superhighway?"). The percentage of the samples who were not even aware of the internet dropped from 15.2% in 1995, to 10.1% in 1996, to 9.9% in 1997, to 8.3% in 2000. The percentage of respondents who were aware of the internet but who still were not users dropped from 69.1% in 1995, to 59.8% in 1996, to 50.2% in 1997, to 21.4% in 2000. Of those who were aware of the internet, the percentage of women rose from 45.5% in 1995 to 53.3% in 2000, the percentage of those age 40 years or over rose from 47.9% in 1995 to 50.2% in 2000, the percentage of those earning less than $35,000 per year fell from 52.1% in 1995 to 33.5% in 2000, the percentage of those with less than a college education dropped from 70.6% in 1995 to 64.9% in 2000, and the percentage of those who were African Americans rose from 7.2% in 1995 to 10.5% in 2000. Thus, the awareness divide seems to have largely disappeared according to gender, age, and race but seems to be increasing by income and education, implying a persistent and troubling problem with reaching the most disadvantaged.

COMBINED INFLUENCES ON INTERNET USE

In 1995, significant regression predictors of being an internet user were as follows: male, young, greater income, and higher education (16% variance explained, $n = 1,676$). In 2000, significant regression predictors of internet use were as follows: young, greater income, and higher education (45% variance explained, $n = 924$). Once awareness was achieved, there was no digital divide in 2000 based on gender or race.

Issues of Internet and Political Involvement

A central issue, also discussed elsewhere (e.g., Katz & Rice, 2002; Wellman & Haythornthwaite, 2002), is whether internet involvement decreases community involvement, political participation, social interaction, and integration (Katz & Aspden, 1997c; Kraut et al., 1998; Putnam, 2000; Rice, 2001; Selnow, 1994) and destroys "authentic" social interaction (Turkle, 1996; Wynn & Katz, 1997) and meaningful interpersonal social networks. Even before the internet was invented, voter participation was a hotly contested issue in terms of its meaning both as a collective action and as a summary statistic of social involvement (Winders, 1999).

Social scientists exploring this topic have formulated strong opinions about the nature of these changes (Browning, 2002; Davis, 1999; Gronlund, 2002; Grossman, 1995; Hague & Loder, 1999; Norris, 2001; Rash, 1997; Wresch, 2002), although they remain sharply divided as to the direction and magnitude of these changes (Rice, 2002). Some argue that lack of access to internet resources by various groups in society, relative to traditional outlets such as newspapers, radio, and television and the self-reinforcing use of the internet by small, "net-savvy," special interest communities, would translate into a narrowing of the basis of political participation and legitimacy of government (Starobin, 1996; White, 1997). Some theorists have argued that the internet is destroying community groups and voluntary associations, or is diverting the citizenry away from traditional political processes, that are necessary for the democratic process to succeed (Carpini, 1996; Putnam, 2000; Rash, 1997; Turkle, 1996). On the other hand, some argue that involvement can create alternative communities that are as valuable and useful as our familiar, physically located communities and perhaps more involved in democratic debate and diversity (Baym, 1995; de Sola Poole, 1983; Kapor, 1993; Katz & Rice, 2002; Rice, 1987a, 1987b, 2002).

Internet Use and Offline and Online Political Activity: 1996 Syntopia Survey

OFFLINE POLITICAL ACTIVITIES

Table 7.1 provides the percentages of the 1996 Syntopia survey respondents indicating that they participated in a variety of offline and online political

Table 7.1   Questions About Offline and Online Political Activity, and Political Importance of Media: 1996 Syntopia Survey (percentages)

	Yes
I am going to ask you about some political activities and whether you did any of them in the past year: ($n = 1,008$)	
Attend any political rallies	10
Make phone calls on behalf of candidates	5
Write or fax any letters to elected officials	13
Give money to a political cause, committee, or campaign	14
Have any face-to-face or phone discussions with friends/ family about the 1996 political campaign and election	69
Watch the Republican convention on television	55
Watch the Democratic convention on television	54
Vote in the November general election earlier this month	73
Thinking back to the period since the beginning of October, in terms of your online activities and the 1996 election campaign, did you: ($n = 549$)	
Have any e-mail exchanges or chat room discussions or postings with friends or family about the 1996 political campaign and election?	17
Read any bulletin board or discussion group postings about the campaign or election?	22
Receive any e-mail about the campaign or election?	15
Send or receive any e-mail to or from a government official, candidate for office, or political campaign committee?	8
Send any e-mail to others about the campaign or election?	10
Visit any Web sites with campaign-related information?	23
Follow any part of the election by reading the news online?	24
Follow the voting on Election Day from your computer?	10
View information online about the election after it was over?	21

activities. In terms of offline political activities, only about 1 in 10 respondents engaged in overt political activity, ranging from making phone calls on behalf of candidates (5%) to giving money to a political cause, committee, or campaign (14%). However, more than two thirds did discuss the political campaign and election either by phone or face-to-face (69%), and more than half watched the Republican or Democratic convention on television. Nearly three quarters of the respondents said, within a few weeks of the 1996 general election, that they had voted. (The actual percentage of eligible citizens who voted was 49.1% in 1996 and 50.7% in 2000 [U.S. Bureau of the Census, 2001]. There is a perennial bias in surveys toward reporting socially approved behaviors, such as going to church, contributing to charities, and voting [Fisher & Katz, 2000].) The respondents tended to rate various media as of either medium or high importance, from national and local television shows (86%), to newspapers (81%), to television (79%), to campaign commercials or leaflets (38%).

There seems to be one dimension of *offline political activity* consisting of whether the respondents attended any political rallies, wrote or faxed letters to elected officials, made phone calls on behalf of candidates, and/or gave money to a political cause (18% variance explained, scale alpha = .59). There are two dimensions of the importance of traditional forms of *political media activity.* "Reading" consisted of the importance of leaflets and magazines, news/opinion magazines, and newspapers in the 1996 campaign (16.6% variance explained, scale alpha = .57). "Television" consisted of the importance of national and local television shows, television, and television interview shows in the 1996 campaign (15.0% variance explained, scale alpha = .46).

Table 7.2 shows cross-tabulations among respondents' political activity, demographic measures, and internet use. Those who reported that they were registered to vote and did vote in the 1996 presidential election were more likely to be married, have a lower income, and be older (only for being registered). Internet use alone, or even the extent of internet use (e.g., times per month, recency), was not associated with registration or voting during this early period of internet use.

Regression analyses included two dependent variables—*voting* and *offline political activity*—with income, education, marital status, gender, age, race, and whether one was a current internet user or not (and, if the respondent was a user, number of hours of internet use during the past week) used as predictors. (For this analysis, all respondents under 18 years of age were deleted because they could not vote, and internet dropouts were not included.)

Concerning both users and nonusers, those reporting having *voted* in the 1996 election and those reporting having engaged in more *offline political activity* were more likely to be married (2% and 1% variance explained, standardized betas = .47 and .11, $p < .05$ for both regressions, n's = 672 and 647, respectively).

Concerning users only, *offline political activity* was only slightly more likely for males than for females (3% variance explained, beta = .05, $p < .01$, $n = 405$) but was not otherwise explained by demographics or level of internet use. The importance of *print media* for political concerns was slightly predicted by being single, but again no other factors were influential. The political importance of *television* was unexplained by the demographics and internet use variables. Put differently, for the 1996 election, being registered to vote, voting, and the

Table 7.2   Political Activity by Demographic and Internet Variables: 1996 Syntopia Survey
(percentages, except figures in "total" columns)

| | Internet Users Only | | | | Users vs. Nonusers | |
| | Registered to Vote | | Voted | | | |
Question	Yes	Total	Yes	Total	Users	Total
Overall, how satisfied are you with the way your life is going?						
Satisfied	86.4	25	77.3	25	17.5	126
Dissatisfied	72.0	22	64.0	22	10.1	248
Chi-square		1.4		1.0		4.1*
Gender						
Male	75.0	32	68.8	32 8	5.0	376
Female	84.6	52	75.0	52	16.0	326
Chi-square		1.2		0.4		9.2***
Do you have any children under 18 years of age now living in your household?						
Yes	72.2	36	63.9	48	12.2	295
No	87.5	48	79.2	36	11.8	407
Chi-square		3.1		2.4		0.0
Marriage status						
Not married	66.7	33	54.5	33	10.3	320
Married/Cohabiting	90.2	51	84.3	51	13.4	382
Chi-square		7.2**		8.9**		1.5
Work						
Full-time	86.7	45	80.0	45	11.7	383/
Other	73.7	38	63.2	38	12.2	311
Chi-square		2.2		2.9		0.0
Income						
< $35,000/year	100.0	20	90.0	20	6.9	290
> $35,000/year	76.4	55	67.3	55	17.7	310
Chi-square		5.7*		3.9*		16.1***
Age						
18–39 years	72.9	48	68.8	48	14.5	331
40–65+ years	91.7	36	77.8	36	9.7	371
Chi-square		4.7*		0.8		3.8*
Education						
Less than college	75.0	36	69.4	36 7	5.0	477
College or more	85.4	48	75.0	48	21.3	225
Chi-square		1.4		0.3		27.6***

(Continued)

Table 7.2, Continued

| | Internet Users Only | | | | | |
| | Registered to Vote | | Voted | | Users vs. Nonusers | |
Question	Yes	Total	Yes	Total	Users	Total
Race						
White	80.0	70	70.0	70	11.8	591
Black	100.0	6	100.0	6	10.0	60
Chi-square		1.5		2.5		0.2
Internet user						
Yes	81.0	84	72.6	84		
No	80.4	618	71.2	618		
Chi-square		0.01		0.07		
Internet users only:						
How often do you go online?						
20 times/month	76.9	52	67.3	52		
20 times/month	85.2	27	81.5	27		
Chi-square		0.8		1.8		
When did you first start going online?						
Within past year	86.0	43	74.4	43		
More than a year ago	75.6	41	70.7	41		
Chi-square		1.5		0.1		
Interactive online political activities						
None	84.2	38	78.9	38		
Any	42.9	7	42.9	7		
Chi-square		5.8**		3.9*		
Browsing online political activities						
None	86.5	29	79.3	29		
Any	62.5	16	62.5	16		
Chi-square		3.4		1.5		

NOTE: Total ns in columns are the sums of "yes" and "no" or "user" and "nonuser" responses. Percentages reported are only those for "yes" or "user." Analyses exclude respondents under 18 years of age and internet nonusers.

$*p < 0.05, **p < 0.01, ***p < 0.001.$

importance of print and television for political information were equally likely for internet users as for internet nonusers. Being a more extensive internet user was not associated with offline political activity (although being female was slightly associated).

ONLINE POLITICAL ACTIVITIES

As Table 7.2 also shows, up to one quarter of internet users engaged in some kind of online political activity, ranging from sending or receiving e-mail to or from a government official, candidate for office, or political campaign committee (8%), to reading election news online (24%), to visiting campaign-related Web sites (23%), to reading bulletin board or discussion list postings about the campaign or election (22%).

There were two dimensions of *online political activity*. Online political *browsing* included reading bulletin boards or discussion groups, visiting Web sites with political information, following the election online, following the Election Day online, and viewing information online after the election (26% variance explained, alpha = .72). Online political *interaction* consisted of participating in electronic discussions; receiving e-mail concerning the election; sending or receiving e-mail to or from a government official, candidate for office, or political campaign committee; and sending e-mail to others concerning the election (24% variance explained, alpha = .70). Nearly half (46%) of internet users engaged in some kind of browsing, whereas just over a quarter (28%) of internet users participated in at least one of four online political activities. All scales were computed as the means of the sets of variables.

Internet Use and Online Political Activities. As Table 7.2 shows, those respondents engaged in interactive online political activities were less likely to be registered to vote or to actually vote. The sample sizes are extremely small, however. Summary results from logistic regressions show that, concerning users only, online political browsing and online political interaction both were predicted by more hours spent using the internet during the prior week (3% and 5% variance explained, standardized betas = .15 and .20, respectively, $p < .001$ and $n = 405$ for both regressions). So, whereas during the early years of internet use, those who engaged in online interactive political discussions may have participated less in offline political activities, those who have used the internet more recently engage a bit more in online political activity. This runs counter to the critique that internet use reduces political interest and participation.

PERCEIVED IMPACT OF INTERNET USE

Respondents were asked to indicate how strongly they agreed with a variety of statements about the ways in which their online activities affected them. The following percentages of respondents either strongly agreed or somewhat agreed (as opposed to somewhat disagreed or strongly disagreed) that they can follow subjects that interest them in great depth (84%), they can participate in issues with people around the world (72%), their quality of life has improved (62%), their personal privacy is at risk when they go online (56%), their online activities made them more aware of issues in the world (55%), their online participation has been important to their personal growth (51%), they have learned useful information about politics online (35%), their sources of information about the world have narrowed (23%), it is easy for the government or businesses to monitor the activities of people online (17%), and information they have found or received online has changed their political opinions (17%) ($ns = 484$ to 531). Two items in particular related to political information: "learned useful information about politics online" and "information I have found or received online has changed my political opinions." A scale derived from these two measures was associated in a regression with more online political browsing, more online political interaction, less offline political activities, and greater importance placed on political reading but not number of hours of internet use during the prior week (13% variance explained).

Related Results From the 2000 Pew Survey

This section summarizes some results of a Pew report (Pew Internet and American Life Project, 2000) that compared measures from Pew's 1996 and 2000 election surveys. The section also provides new cross-tabulation and regression analyses of the 2000 data that compare internet nonusers to internet users, and across internet use levels, with respect to political and demographic measures. The 1996 Syntopia survey and the 2000 Pew survey did not include all of the same variables. However, the 2000 Pew data, when comparable, were recoded and dichotomized to match the Syntopia 1996 data.

USE OF THE INTERNET FOR ELECTION NEWS

The percentage of Americans reporting they went online for any news about the presidential campaign (from less than weekly to several times a day) rose from about 10% in 1996 to 25% in 2000. In 2000, 12% of Americans used the internet for political news on Election Day and 18% used it the day after. Fully 79% of election news consumers sought information about the candidates' positions on the issues, and 38% sought background on candidates' voting records. Comparing Pew 1996 and 2000 results, the reasons why users went online for election news included the fact that information is more convenient (45% vs. 56%, respectively), other media do not provide enough news (53% vs. 29%), they can get information that is not available elsewhere (26% vs. 12%), and internet news sources reflect their personal interests (24% vs. 6%). For those who advocate the internet as a way in which to foster political activism, it is interesting to note that 45% of all internet users (but more of experienced internet users) said that they encountered election news inadvertently, that is, when they had gone online for other purposes.

SOURCES, BROWSING, AND INTERACTION

A small subsample of internet users were asked whether they ever went to specific sites to get election news (similar to the online browsing political activity noted previously), ranging from Web sites of broadcast television networks (23.0%), to national newspapers (19.3%), to MSNBC.com (28.0%) or CNN.com (28.4%), to special interest groups (11.9%), to a specific candidate or campaign (15.8%). Summing these browsing online activities, 43.4% visited up to three of them, whereas 56.7% went to at least four of them.

Again, a small subsample of users were asked whether, when they went online to get information about the election, they did a variety of what could be considered more interactive online political activities: participated in online discussions or chat groups (9.9%), registered their opinions in an online poll (38.2%), got information about a candidate's voting record (38.5%), got information about when and where to vote (15.7%), received or sent e-mail supporting or opposing a candidate for office (29.8%), contributed money through a candidate's Web site (7.9%), or looked for more information about candidates' positions (79.2%). Summing these interactive online activities, 60.1% participated in one or two of them, whereas 39.9% participated in at least three of them.

OFFLINE POLITICAL ACTIVITY

Table 7.3 shows cross-tabulations of media use, offline political activity, demographics, and levels of internet use. The minimal measures of political activity used here were (a) being registered to vote in the 2000 election (81.6% said that they were) and (b) planning to vote in the 2000 presidential election (71.1% indicated that they were absolutely certain they would vote, 15.7% were

Table 7.3   Political Activity by Demographic and Internet Variables: 2000 Pew Survey (percentages, except figures in "total" columns)

| | Internet Users Only | | | | | |
| | Registered to Vote | | Plan to Vote | | Users vs. Nonusers | |
Question	Yes	Total	Yes	Total	Users	Total
Overall, are you satisfied or dissatisfied with the way things are going in this country today?						
Satisfied	83.9	454	73.5	456	59.3	777
Dissatisfied	84.1	271	77.4	270	51.1	534
Chi-square		0.0		1.2		8.3**
Just thinking about *yesterday,* did you get a chance to read a daily newspaper or not?						
Yes	89.0	327	81.8	329	56.9	580
No	79.1	446	69.0	445	53.7	843
Chi-square		12.4**		15.5**		1.3
Did you watch the news or a news program on television yesterday or not?						
Yes	86.0	456	80.2	459	54.9	841
No	79.5	317	66.0	315	55.3	580
Chi-square		5.2*		18.9**		0.0
Gender						
Male	81.4	387	72.9	388	58.1	465
Female	85.3	387	76.0	387	52.1	750
Chi-square		1.8		0.8		4.9*
Are you the parent or guardian of any children under 18 years of age now living in your household?						
Yes	89.1	331	78.8	330	64.8	512
No	79.2	442	71.3	442	49.3	908
Chi-square		12.8**		5.2*		31.2**
Marriage status						
Not married	75.5	306	65.4	306	50.2	621
Married/ Cohabiting	88.4	464	80.4	464	49.3	791
Chi-square		20.9**		21.2**		10.2**
Work						
Full-time	84.7	511	76.0	508	65.4	784
other	80.5	261	71.5	263	42.3	629
Chi-square		1.9		1.6		74.6**
Income						
< $40,000/year	76.3	228	65.0	226	44.6	514
$40,000/year or more	87.9	396	79.5	396	71.8	554
Chi-square		13.3**		15.1**		80.8%
Age						
18–44 years	77.6	517	67.1	517	69.2	756
45–65 + years	95.2	249	89.5	248	39.2	638
Chi-square		36.2**		42.9**		124.8**

(Continued)

Table 7.3 Continued

	Internet Users Only				Users vs. Nonusers	
	Registered to Vote		Plan to Vote			
Question	Yes	Total	Yes	Total	Users	Total
Education						
Less than college	76.5	439	66.7	439	46.0	969
College or more	92.2	333	84.4	333	75.5	441
Chi-square		32.3**		29.9**		105.0**
Race						
White	85.3	618	75.8	619	55.7	1,120
Black	81.8	77	80.3	76	45.8	168
Chi-square		10.8**		15.5**		5.4*
Internet user						
Yes	83.3	774	74.5	775		
No	79.4	631	66.9	628		
Chi-square		3.6*		9.7**		
Internet users only:						
How often do you go online?						
Less than once a day	83.1	267	71.4	269		
At least once a day	84.2	467	76.6	465		
Chi-square		0.1		2.2		
When did you first start going online?						
Within past year	76.0	221	65.8	225		
More than a year ago	86.3	548	78.0	545		
Chi-square		11.3**		11.8**		
General online activities						
1–2 activities	82.7	196	77.8	198		
3–5 activities	74.0	100	62.6	99		
Chi-square		2.6		6.9**		
Interactive online political activities						
1–2 interactive	90.0	100	83.0	100		
3–7 interactive	91.0	67	89.4	66		
Chi-square		0.0		0.9		
Browsing online political activities						
1–3 browsing	90.1	121	80.8	120		
4–14 browsing	87.3	142	83.1	142		
Chi-square		0.3		0.1		

NOTE: Total *ns* in columns are the sums of "yes" and "no" or "user" and "nonuser" responses. Percentages reported are only those for "yes" or "user." Analyses exclude respondents under 18 years of age and Internet nonusers.

$*p < .05, **p < .01, ***p$ .001.

fairly certain or not certain, and 13.3% were not planning to vote [these last two categories were combined]).

Being registered to vote in the 2000 election and being absolutely certain about planning to vote were positively associated with reading a daily newspaper or watching television news the day before, beginning to use the internet more than a year ago, having children in the house, being married, having a household income greater than $40,000, being age 45 years or over, having a college degree, and being white.

Internet users were more likely to be satisfied with the way things were going in the country, be registered to vote, plan to vote in the November election, be more liberal, be male, have children in the household, not be currently married, work full-time, earn more than $40,000 per year, be under 40 years of age, have graduated from college, and be white. Recent internet adopters were more likely to be registered to vote and plan to vote in the November election, and those engaged in fewer general online activities were more likely to plan to vote in the November election.

A first set of two summary logistic regressions identified the significant predictors of being registered to vote as being an internet user (standardized beta = .4), having children in the household (.79), being over 45 years of age (1.4), and having a college degree (1.1) (14% variance explained, $p < .01$, $n = 1,369$). The same variables predicted planning to vote (11% variance explained, $p < .01$, $n = 1,366$).

The second set of logistic regressions included only users. Significant unique predictors of being registered to vote and planning to vote in the November election were first going online more than a year earlier (standardized beta = .71), having children in the household (1.03), being over 45 years of age (1.8), and having a college degree (1.0) (21% and 16% variance explained, $p < .01$ for both regressions, n's = 758 and 768, respectively). So, internet users and long-term internet users were more likely to register to vote or to intend to vote in the November election, controlling for major demographic variables.

PERCEIVED IMPACT OF INTERNET USE

The Pew survey indicated that online election information had a substantial impact in 2000 in that nearly half (47.1%) of a small subsample ($n = 187$) of election news consumers reported that it affected their voting decisions ("made you want to vote for or against a particular candidate"). This compares with 31% reported in the 1996 Pew survey.

Conclusion

Based on these analyses, it seems that the internet had a mild positive impact on political activity during the 1996 and 2000 elections. Neither internet use/nonuse nor frequency of internet use was associated with many online or offline political activities or with perceptions of the importance of print media or television for political issues. However, a large percentage of internet users did participate in some kind of online political activity. Moreover, some reported a considerable effect on their voting decisions in the 2000 election. And both users and long-term users were more likely to register to vote and to plan to vote in the November elections in 1996 and 2000. Thus, rather than the internet diminishing traditional forms of political activity, it is associated with somewhat greater traditional as well as new political activities.

The internet appears, at least based on the Syntopia 1996 survey and the Pew 1996 and 2000 presidential election surveys, to be a way in which to expand political involvement without sacrificing current modes of political activity. Contrary to the oft-repeated fears of some, the data showed no support for the notion that there would be mass political defections or that the internet would lead people to "tune out" politics. If anything, the opposite was the case. There were some modest associations of internet use with political activity, especially in 2000, and there were some respondents who reported that their opinions had changed due to their online involvement. On the other hand, the data do not suggest that the internet was a source of radical change in people's political activities and access to political information. The unique significant predictors are still age, education, and income. The situation is likely to change only incrementally as the Syntopian integration of various communication technologies with facets of real life continues.

References

America Online. (2000). *American Online/Roper Starch Cyberstudy 2000* (Roper No. CNT375). Dulles, VA: Author.

Baym, N. K. (1995). The emergence of community in computer-mediated communication. In S. G. Jones (Ed.), *Cybersociety: Computer-mediated communication and community* (pp. 138–163). Thousand Oaks, CA: Sage.

Bimber, B. (2002). *Information technology and the "new" politics*. [Online]. Retrieved April 11, 2002, from www.itas.fzk.de/e-society/preprints/egovernance/bimber.pdf

Browning, G. (2002). *Electronic democracy: Using the internet to transform American politics*. Medford, NJ: CyberAge Books.

Carpini, M. X. D. (1996). Voters, candidates, and campaigns in the new information age: An overview and assessment. *Harvard International Journal of Press/Politics, 1,* 36–56.

Davis, R. (1999). *The web of politics: The internet's impact on the American political system.* New York: Oxford University Press.

de Sola Poole, I. (1983). *Technologies of freedom.* Cambridge, MA: Belknap.

Fisher, R. J., & Katz, J. E. (2000). Social desirability bias of the validity of self-reported values. *Psychology and Marketing, 17*(2), 105–120.

Gronlund, A. (Ed.). (2002). *Electronic government: Design, applications, and management.* Hershey, PA: Idea Group Publishing.

Grossman, L. K. (1995). *The electronic republic: Reshaping democracy in the information age.* New York: Viking/Penguin.

Hague, B., & Loader. B. (Eds.). (1999). *Digital democracy: Discourse and decision making in the information age.* New York: Routledge.

Kapor, M. (1993, July–August). Where is the digital highway really heading? *Wired,* pp. 53–59, 94.

Katz, J., & Aspden, P. (1997a). Motivations for and barriers to internet usage: Results of a national public opinion survey. *Internet Research: Electronic Networking Applications and Policy, 7*(3), 170–188.

Katz, J., & Aspden, P. (1997b). Motives, hurdles, and dropouts: Who is on and off the internet and why. *Communications of the ACM, 40*(4), 97–102.

Katz, J., & Aspden, P. (1997c). A nation of strangers. *Communications of the ACM, 40*(12), 81–86.

Katz, J., & Aspden, P. (1998). Internet dropouts in the USA: The invisible group. *Telecommunications Policy, 22,* 327–339.

Katz, J., Aspden, P., & Reich, W. (1997, September). *Elections and electrons: A national public opinion survey on the role of cyberspace and mass media in political opinion formation during the 1996 election.* Paper presented at the 25th annual Telecommunications Policy Research Conference, Arlington, VA.

Katz, J. E., & Rice, R. E. (2002). *Social consequences of internet use: Access, involvement, and interaction.* Cambridge, MA: MIT Press.

Katz, J. E., Rice, R. E., & Aspden, P. (2001). The internet, 1995–2000: Access, civic involvement, and social interaction. *American Behavioral Scientist, 45,* 404–419.

Kraut, R., Lundmark, V., Patterson, M., Kiesler, S., Mukopadhyay, T., & Scherlis, W. (1998). Internet paradox: A social technology that reduces social involvement and psychological well-being? *American Psychologist, 53,* 1017–1031.

McConnaughey, J. (2001, June). *Taking the measure of the digital divide: Net effects of research and policy* (summary of results of the U.S. Department of Commerce in 2000). Paper presented to Web workshop, Department of Sociology, University of Maryland.

Norris, P. (2001). *Digital divide: Civic engagement, information poverty, and the internet worldwide.* New York: Cambridge University Press.

Pew Internet and American Life Project. (2000). *Internet election news audience seeks convenience, familiar names.* [Online]. Retrieved April 22, 2003, from www.pewinternet.org/reports/pdfs/prc_politics_report.pdf

Putnam, R. D. (2000). *Bowling alone.* New York: Simon & Schuster.

Rash, W. (1997). *Politics on the nets: Wiring the political process.* New York: Freeman.

Rice, R. E. (1987a). Computer-mediated communication and organizational innovation. *Journal of Communication, 37,* 65–94.

Rice, R. E. (1987b). New patterns of social structure in an information society. In J. Schement & L. Lievrouw (Eds.), *Competing visions, complex realities: Social aspects of the information society* (pp. 107–120). Norwood, NJ: Ablex.

Rice, R. E. (2001). The internet and health communication: A framework of experiences. In R. E. Rice & J. E. Katz (Eds.), *The internet and health communication: Experiences and expectations* (pp. 5–46). Thousand Oaks, CA: Sage.

Rice, R. E. (2002). Primary issues in internet use: Access, civic and community involvement, and social interaction and expression. In L. Lievrouw & S. Livingstone (Eds.), *Handbook of new media* (pp. 105–129). London: Sage.

Selnow, G. W. (1994). *High-tech campaigns: Computer technology in political communication.* New York: Praeger.

Starobin, P. (1996, June 25). On the square. *National Journal*, pp. 1145–1149.

Syntopia Project. (2002). [Online]. Retrieved April 22, 2003, from www.scils.rutgers.edu/~rrice/syntopia.htm

Turkle, S. (1996). Virtuality and its discontents: Searching for community in cyberspace. *The American Prospect, 24,* 50–57.

U.S. Bureau of the Census. (2001). *Table A-2: Reported voting and registration by region.* [Online]. Retrieved April 21, 2002, from www.census.gov/population/socdemo/voting

Walsh, E., Gazala, M., & Ham, C. (2001). The truth about the digital divide. In B. Compaine (Ed.), *The digital divide: Facing a crisis or creating a myth?* (pp. 279–284). Cambridge, MA: MIT Press.

Wellman, B., & Haythornthwaite, C. (Eds.). (2002). *The internet in everyday life.* Oxford, UK: Blackwell.

White, C. S. (1997). Citizen participation and the internet: Prospects for civic deliberation in the information age. *Social Studies, 88,* 23–28.

Winders, W. (1999). The roller coaster of class conflict: Class segments, mass mobilization, and voter turnout in the U.S., 1840–1996. *Social Forces, 77,* 833–862.

Wresch, W. (2002). *Disconnected: Haves and have-nots in the information age.* New Brunswick, NJ: Rutgers University Press.

Wynn, E., & Katz, J. (1997). Hyperbole over cyberspace: Self-presentation and social boundaries in internet home pages and discourse. *The Information Society, 13,* 297–329.

8

New Media, Internet
News, and the News Habit

Carin Dessauer
American Press Institute

I t may have sounded like a science fiction movie during the 1980s. Millions of Americans going online to get news, using mobile devices to obtain breaking news alerts, and sending and receiving news-related e-mail by cell phone—all made the 1960s cartoon *The Jetsons,* about a family living in the space age, not so futuristic. The internet's growth since the 1990s has proven the power of the Information Age. Enabling news consumers to access another news source besides print, television, and radio, the internet has transformed the media landscape. This chapter examines the state of internet news in American life by providing (a) a brief history of its rise, (b) a detailed definition of internet news, (c) an examination of its growth and the evolution of journalism, and (d) an analysis of the positive and negative aspects of the news medium.

Media History and Internet News Development

To truly understand the rise and growth of internet news, it is important to put into perspective how quickly the medium has grown. Consider the number of years that transpired between the initial mass communication developments. The first major development arguably occurred in 1456 (Rodman, 2001) when Johannes Guttenberg published the Bible, making the mass distribution of books available for the first time. That technology did not change much until some

400 years later when the linotype, a machine that automatically set type, was invented. Newspapers began during the 1600s, and magazines began during the 18th century. But not until the Industrial Revolution, during the early 19th century, did mass communication technological advances develop at a more rapid pace. First came the telegraph, followed by telephone transmission, the phonograph, and the motion picture projector. Radio ushered in the change from "wired" to "wireless" technology during the 1890s (Rodman, 2001). The first commercial radio station began operating in 1920, paving the way for President Franklin D. Roosevelt to communicate directly to the American people in his famous radio "fireside chats" during the 1930s.

Television, invented in 1927, was first demonstrated at the 1939 World's Fair, but its popularity, known as the "golden age," did not arrive until the 1950s. Cable television came onto the scene during the late 1970s and 1980s. Alternative channels such as TBS, CNN, ESPN, and MTV started to challenge the traditional broadcast television networks. But the overall power of cable was not felt until the 1990s, when the growing number of cable programming outlets and 24-hour breaking news venues combined to create real competition for broadcast television.

Some media analysts have argued that the internet took less time to become a mass medium than did any other technology in the past. It took electricity 50 years to reach 50 million users in the United States, whereas it took radio 38 years, it took personal computers 16 years, it took television 13 years, and it took the internet just 4 years (J. Warner, presentation during panel discussion at University of Texas, April 5, 2002).

In 1993, when the World Wide Web and the first internet browser were made public, the internet had only started becoming a household word (Rodman, 2001). The next year, commercial sites (e.g., Yahoo!) started to appear, companies such as America Online (AOL) allowed users to send and receive e-mail, and the White House went online. The internet as we know it began in earnest in 1995, when it was turned over from the military to the public (Margolis & Resnick, 2000). That same year, internet news got started in full force when national news organizations such as CNN started to develop Web sites. In 1996, coverage of the Olympics and the presidential election made people notice internet news. For example, by the end of 1996, CNN.com saw its traffic increase by 700% in 1 year (S. Woelfel, presentation to class at George Washington University, October 4, 2001).

The growth of information online took off rapidly. According to the *Hobbes' Internet Timeline*, there were fewer than 150 Web sites during the period prior to 1993, pre-internet as we know it (Zakon, n.d.). By the end of 1994, there were slightly more than 10,000 sites. By mid-1995, that number had more than doubled to approximately 23,500. By early 1996, there were some 100,000 sites. And later that same year, there were 299,403 sites. The growth continued, and by 2000 there were more than 20 million Web sites. Two years later, that number had edged toward 100 million (Zakon, n.d.). In comparison, it took the Library of Congress 195 years to collect 14 million books (Rodman, 2001).

Media historians have argued that a mass media revolution takes roughly 30 years. Paul Saffo has called this the "30-year rule" (Fidler, 1997). Some media analysts believe that the internet truly became an essential medium in 1998, when the "Starr Report," the official legal document that detailed the affair between President Bill Clinton and White House intern Monica Lewinsky, was released. This was the first time that such an important document was made available online, even before most news outlets had it. More than 20 million users logged onto the Web to read the Starr Report (Rodman, 2001). The story first appeared on online gossip sites such as *The Drudge Report.* The Starr Report release day remained the top story day for numerous national news sites until the 2000 presidential election.

Early on, the internet was viewed as "new" and was treated as distinctly different from other media such as television, print, and radio. However, those within the industry quickly realized that the internet, at its core, was about convergence (bringing other media together) and integration and synergy (working together). To be successful, the news Web sites that would eventually develop the largest followings combined both old media (e.g., text, images, graphics, audio, video) with the new capabilities unique to the internet, making them multimedia.

What Is Internet News?

What has made internet news distinctive? First, let us define the difference between new media and internet news. When the internet began, *new media* was the label given to the then "new" medium, but the term has since come to refer to the broad medium, including all of the related wireless and portable technologies. Whereas internet news has been defined as the practice of journalism online, there are seven characteristics that, taken together, have made internet news unique.

First, internet news has offered dynamic content, reported in real time and updated often. Nearly all of the major news sites have offered immediate breaking news and a breaking news e-mail option. As the first minutes and hours of the September 11, 2001, terrorism attacks on the World Trade Center and Pentagon unfolded, the top news sites constantly updated images and information and e-mailed breaking news alerts.

Second, users have been able to control their information choices—both *what* and *when*. For example, the financial news sites have offered the option to research a particular stock. Other sites, such as USAToday.com, have had a zip code feature to check local weather. Users have been able to obtain internet news whenever they want, 24 hours a day.

Third, internet news has used so-called hyperlinks. News sites have presented live links to other related information, including past stories, multimedia features, and links to other Web sites that offer primary source information. For example, as part of CNN.com's in-depth coverage of the Middle East conflict and peace discussions between the Israelis and Palestinians, the Web site offered numerous links such as maps, a historic time line, key players, relevant documents, a virtual 360-degree tour of the region, video and audio, and related Web sites.

Fourth, nearly all of the major news sites have showcased multimedia offerings, and many sought out partnerships just so that they could provide this content. For example, WashingtonPost.com and MSNBC.com established a relationship whereby MSNBC.com added *Washington Post* stories to its site and *The Washington Post* offered video from MSNBC and NBC—content that the newspaper did not have originally. Other times, news sites have taken content that the main news organizations already gathered and have showcased that material online. For example, *USA Today* has become known for its graphics. The newspaper's site, USAToday.com, has featured graphics and, at times, has brought them alive by making them interactive.

Fifth, internet news has showcased the "interactivity"—user participation—unique to the internet. Consider the "chat" on ABCNews.com or the "quick votes" on CNN.com. Whereas television and radio have allowed for call-in questions from viewers and listeners, the internet has allowed for more participation both live and in advance of an event. When President Clinton granted the first ever presidential online news interview to CNN.com in February 2000, more than 10,000 people were in the live chat room submitting questions for the president. Although these were record numbers at the time for CNN, they paled in comparison with the chat numbers that AOL has produced over the years. According to an AOL spokesperson, the record chat day for AOL to date was on September 11,

2001, when a record 2.5 million "chatters" collectively participated in chats throughout the course of the day (personal communication, May 2003).

Sixth, internet news has offered customization, that is, the selection of personal preferences to "customize" a version of a particular site. For example, WashingtonPost.com has allowed users to customize the site for news headlines, weather, traffic, and columnists, among others.

Finally, internet news has used "layered journalism," that is, journalism that offers many in-depth, multimedia, and interactive layers. These layers have included the entire mix of unique characteristics just referenced. This characteristic was on full display on all of the top news sites in 2003 during the war in Iraq.

It is important to note that the nature of internet news has somewhat expanded the definition of a news provider. Besides the emergence of new news entities that were originally devoted exclusively to online coverage, such as MotleyFool.com, organizations that were not considered media entered the business simply by providing news. Sites such as Yahoo!, AOL, and MSN have not covered news themselves. Still, they all have developed robust "news" sections that feature coverage from their respective news "partners," either internal or external to their companies. Microsoft's MSN.com main page has featured news from Microsoft's various news entities such as MSNBC and its online publication, *Slate*. AOL has featured content from other parts of the AOL Time Warner media family, such as CNN and Time Inc., as well as from "partners" outside of the company, such as *The New York Times* and CBS. Yahoo!, AOL, and MSN are also examples of portals, that is, sites where people have first gained access to the internet. In addition, other sites, such as *The Drudge Report,* also present news, linking to coverage by bona fide news organizations. Such sites have been part of a public publishing cottage industry of "weblogs" or "blogs," that is, sites that update lists of links and provide commentary. In 2002, there were roughly 500,000 blogs ("The Trees Fight Back," n.d.).

The Rise of the Use of Internet News and the Resulting Changes in Journalism

During the mid-1990s, analysts questioned how soon new media would compete with other media and whether they would eventually supplant traditional media, becoming *the* news provider. Clearly, internet news has begun to compete with other media. But although the use and power of the internet have grown very quickly, it is not yet the dominant news source.

To put internet use and growth into better perspective, consider that over a short time period the number of U.S. adults who have gone online has grown dramatically. According to CNN internal data provided to the author, in 1996, when internet use was starting to take off, an estimated 28.9 million adults were online in this country. By 2000, that number had increased 149% to 72 million. By the end of 2001, there were 138 million people online in the United States. Estimates have projected that by the end of 2005, 194 million people would be online in this country. This would represent a 41 percent increase from 2001 and account for 68 percent of the population, roughly equivalent to the American cable television audience (S. Woelfel, presentation to class at George Washington University, October 4, 2001). By the end of 2001, 62% of Americans had some type of online access (Nielsen/Net Ratings, 2001).

At the same time, use of individual news sites has grown significantly, recording thousands of unique users during the early days and now recording millions of users. For example, in just the month of March 2003 alone, an estimated 26 million unique users visited CNN.com, according to a CNN spokesperson (personal communication, May 2003).

Early polling data showed the internet to be "exploding," but respondents were "uncertain" as to where the technology was headed. The Pew Research Center for the People and the Press (1995) was one of the first to conduct comprehensive and (later) regular polls on the topic. The center's October 1995 survey found that the number of Americans going online had more than doubled during the previous year. At that point, the only internet habit that Americans had developed was the use of e-mail. There was no growing trend that Americans had started to develop the internet news habit (Pew Research Center for the People and the Press, 1995).

By December 1996, the same pollsters found that the internet was beginning to "play a role in the news habits" of Americans (Pew Research Center for the People and the Press, 1996). More than 1 in 5 Americans went online. Furthermore, 1 in 10 Americans used the internet to get information about the 1996 election, and 3% of voters on Election Day indicated that internet sites or online services were their principal election news sources. Still, the survey found that there was "little indication" that online news was supplanting traditional media. In fact, the data showed a fair amount of crossover between old media and new media. And the pollsters identified the growing habit of people coming across news rather than searching for it. The survey found that those online were beginning to use the internet because of the impression that information on the

Web was not available elsewhere and because of the convenience factor. In addition, the pollsters saw a trend that internet news users went to the sites of the "major news organizations." Moreover, the number of people using the Web had grown dramatically during the previous year—from 21% to 73% (Pew Research Center for the People and the Press, 1996).

A June 1998 Pew survey revealed that although Americans were listening, watching, and reading news as often as they were in 1996, the number of those getting their news online was "growing at an astonishing rate" (Pew Research Center for the People and the Press, 1998). Specifically, the numbers had tripled from those of just 2 years earlier. In addition, the survey found that the internet was "quickly becoming a part of American daily life" in that nearly as many people went online as read magazines. This was occurring at the same time that pollsters were finding that watching cable television news was becoming as common as viewing network television news, partly because of the decline of viewership of network nightly newscasts. Still, there was no substantial evidence at that point that the increased internet news habit was at the expense of traditional news (Pew Research Center for the People and the Press, 1998).

By the time the Starr Report was released in September 1998, there was no denying the power of the internet. The next month, Web monitor Media Metrix found that "news content sites" had "overtaken search engines as the most popular port of call for internet users" (NUA Internet Surveys, 1998b). A December 1998 survey by Jupiter identified that although the majority of U.S. consumers went to television first for breaking news, a growing number were turning to the internet (NUA Internet Surveys, 1998a).

As the internet news audience was growing, it was also becoming more "mainstream" (Pew Research Center for the People and the Press, 1999). A January 1999 Pew survey found that in comparison with 2 years earlier, when stories about technology were of top interest to online users, the popularity of "general interest" news subjects, from entertainment to the weather, was growing. The overall growth in the use of internet news continued as the number of Americans who went online had nearly tripled from 1995 (Pew Research Center for the People and the Press, 1998).

As 2000 approached, and certainly during the year of the presidential election, the evidence was clear that internet news had arrived. One of the Republican presidential contenders, Steve Forbes, announced his presidential candidacy on the internet. The presidential candidates granted online news interviews. President Clinton, as noted earlier, granted his first online news interview. And

"Internet Alley" and "Internet Avenue," the online media working areas, were established for the first time at the political party conventions during the summer.

As internet news was growing, Americans were losing the "news habit" (Pew Research Center for the People and the Press, 2000) and internet news was "sapping" the broadcast news audience, according to a June 2000 Pew survey. The poll found that while the use of internet news had more than doubled during the previous 2 years, regular viewership of network news and local television news had fallen. Specifically, internet news users were spending less time watching network television news. Just 2 years earlier, there had been no difference between internet news users' and nonusers' television news habits (Pew Research Center for the People and the Press, 2000).

In 2001, the confidence in the growth of internet news was somewhat eclipsed by the so-called "dot-com bust," as many technology companies ran into financial troubles and/or went out of business, some news organizations were cutting their online staff, and a number of internet ventures (including some in news) closed. A *Washington Post* story headline in February of that year read, "Is Online Journalism On Its Way Out?" (Kurtz, 2001). When the economic realities had set in, with the once robust American economy taking a downward turn, internet news faced the same financial challenges as did traditional news. The difference was that expectations had been set that internet news would generate more money at a faster pace than would traditional news organizations. Still, internet use continued to grow.

Then came the September 11 news and its aftermath. Would the internet eclipse traditional news sources? Not for this story. Americans relied mostly on television for their news (given that the story was primarily visual) and on the telephone for their communication, according to a September 2001 Pew survey (Pew Internet and American Life Project, 2001). Some internet users encountered problems getting on some of the major news sites on the day of the attacks due to technical challenges that some sites faced when record number of users tried to access them. Still, the top news sites received record traffic. At the time of this writing, CNN.com's biggest single-day audience to date remained September 12, 2001, when a record 337 million page impressions were recorded (personal communication, May 2003).

In June 2002, the Pew biennial survey examining Americans' news habits had some startling news for internet enthusiasts (Table 8.1). After years of dramatic growth for internet news, the number of Americans who went online for

Table 8.1   Trends in Regular News Consumption (percentages)

	May, 1993	April, 1996	April, 1998	April, 2000	April, 2002
Local TV news	77[2]	65	64	56	57
Cable TV news	—	—	—	—	33
Nightly network news	60[2]	42	38	30	32
Network TV magazines	52[2]	36	37	31	24
Network morning news	—	—	23	20	22
Radio[1]	47[3]	44	49	43	41
Call-in radio shows	23[4]	13	15	14	17
National Public Radio	15[2]	13	15	15	16
Newspaper[1]	58[3]	50	48	47	41
Online news[5]	—	25	13	23	25

NOTES: 1) Newspaper and Radio figures based on use "yesterday." All responses collected in April of each year except 2) collected May 1993, 3) from February 1994, 4) from April 1993, and 5) from June 1995. 6) Online news at least 3 days per week

Source: The Pew Center for the People & the Press, June 9, 2002 survey.

news at least once a week had increased only slightly, up 2% from 2 years earlier (Pew Research Center for the People and the Press, 2002). Still, the survey found that among those under 30 years of age, online news had a larger following than did other news except local television news. Although earlier polls had suggested that the rise of internet news was hurting television news, 73% of those surveyed said that going online did not affect their use of other media, compared with 58% who had said this just 2 years earlier. The survey showed that the number of Americans who watched television network evening news, which had been decreasing for years, actually increased slightly (2%) from 2 years earlier. At the same time, newspaper reading, which had also been gradually declining over the years, continued to slide another 7%. Finally, the survey showed that roughly half of those surveyed identified themselves as "news grazers," that is, people who check news from time to time over the course of the day. They tended to be younger and less interested in serious news, using media less often except for the internet and cable television (Pew Research Center for the People and the Press, 2002).

The war in Iraq confirmed that Americans were relying on television as their principal news source, but according to a March 2003 Pew survey, the online news audience had "jumped to record levels." The survey showed that 17% of Americans online indicated that the internet was their main source for news about the war, compared with just 3% after the September 11 terrorist attacks on the United States (Pew Internet and American Life Project, 2003).

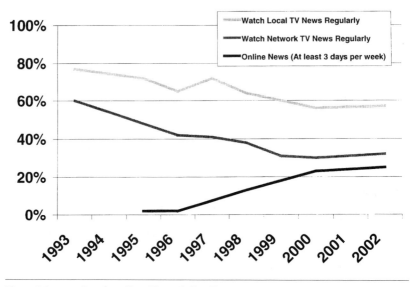

Figure 8.1   Broadcast News Versus Online News, 1993–2002

SOURCES: Pew Research Center for the People and the Press (2000, 2002).

As news consumption has changed as a result of the growth of the internet, the practice of journalism and the newsroom organization have also evolved, particularly within news organizations that have both traditional and internet news operations (Figure 8.1). The core of journalism or "Journalism 101," defined as the basic components that go into the craft of obtaining and disseminating news, has not changed. These include researching, reporting, and writing. The goals have remained the same: to gather the facts as well as to be accurate, thorough, and timely. However, the art of how these components and goals are achieved has changed. Prior to new media, the art was almost entirely linear, revolving around one goal and one medium. With the evolution of internet news, the traditional news product has become either the basis for a story that is "repurposed" or repackaged for new media—what some within this arena have called "shovel-ware"—or new pieces have been generated. What this has meant specifically for writing and editing has produced what Mark Stencel, the editorial liaison between *The Washington Post* and WashingtonPost.com, labeled "back to the future elements" (personal communication, July 2002). This has meant that journalists either have had to develop skills or relearn old ones. "It is a bit like the return of the practices of afternoon newspapers," Stencel argued. Writing has not changed; the internet has just allowed for more styles, lengths, and formats to be showcased. The future part of the equation has meant that no matter what deadline—morning, evening, or weekly—a news organization was operating under, its internet news division had to become more timely, presenting breaking news immediately. In 1995, mostly the 24-hour news operations' news sites took this approach, but soon other sites realized that they had to present breaking news if they wanted to compete.

Given the nature of the internet, journalists had to start thinking "outside of the box" of traditional journalism and provide even more perspective. Jeff Webber, publisher of USAToday.com, explained it this way: "The internet opens up the potential for enormous depth," putting more pressure on what his team has labeled the "enterprise side" (personal communication, July 2002). Journalists have always strived to answer the *what, where, when, why,* and *how* questions, but the depth of the internet has called for even more "added value," as Webber described it. Journalists have also expanded their arsenal of basic tools such as the telephone to include video and satellite phones, among others, and actually using the internet to conduct research. In addition, even sites that just showcased their core news product—whether print, television, or radio—moved to start offering multimedia features. This evolution to journalism has resulted in changes to newsroom operations.

When individual news entities started their own Web sites, most established separate divisions to produce the sites and did not account for much cross-polli-nation between the traditional newsroom and the new newsroom. Coordination was present but at times tenuous, depending on the individual news organiza-tion. Many traditional news outlets looked at their Web sites as simply a market-ing tool for the traditional product and as a way in which to highlight those news organizations' ability to break news. The old approach was one task per person. When an assignment was given, a reporter reported the story, an editor edited, and a producer produced. Once each person accomplished his or her task, the job was done. The new media approach has evolved into journalists wearing many hats, multitasking, and contributing cross-platform. An example might be a reporter writing for a newspaper and calling in an analysis story directly to the site or a Web reporter being used as an on-air analyst.

Coverage of the release of the Starr Report in 1998 was a key turning point in greater cooperation between old and new newsrooms, as traditional journal-ists realized the reach and depth of the internet, allowing their material to be showcased on a broader scale. *Convergence* and *integration* became the buzzwords, and internet news gained broader acceptance. Traditional journalists, some of whom were slow to warm up to the Web, started to change their outlook, and newsrooms demanded greater cooperation. Despite the dot-com challenges during the early 2000s, the September 11 story and its aftermath became what some have referred to as a watershed. "The medium showed what it could do," observed USAToday.com's Webber, who argued that it was analogous to what World War II did for radio, what the assassination of President John F. Kennedy did for television, and what the Gulf War did for cable, with each putting that respective medium on the map. Still, real convergence was just getting started and there were still challenges. A poll released in 2002 by the Online News Association showed that although the public had confidence in internet news, rank-and-file traditional journalists were slower to accept the medium (Online News Association, 2002).

What Does All of This Mean for Journalism, and Why Does It Matter?

So, has internet news been good or bad for journalism in American life? The answer is mixed. On the positive front, internet news has added a news option for users, one that has provided combined features—instant accessibility, convenience, greater depth, and multimedia—unavailable in any other individual medium.

During a time when people are leading busier lives, convenience has become more critical. Traditional news habits have changed with additional "24/7" options and news outlets. As a result, the audience members have taken more control in deciding when they want their news and in what format. The medium has been able to hold the news interest of news grazers.

The "portability" of the medium has been another positive. Internet news has been accessible not just on personal computers or laptops but also on numerous high-tech devices such as cell phones, pagers, and palm pilots. And the options will become greater as the technology continues to grow.

Although other media have offered interactive capabilities, no other media have allowed for interactivity as internet news has done. Users have been able to get more involved in the news process—posting on message boards, asking newsmakers questions, and so forth. And as the technology continues to develop, such as the convergence of television and the internet, more options will be possible.

Internet news has also been able to broaden the American news audience beyond its borders. Although other media can be distributed throughout the world, it has not been without great costs. Only internet news producers have been able to publish content and reach the whole world for the same costs as reaching their own country's users—making country boundaries meaningless. Thus, international online users have been able to access internet news and participate in online chats at the same time as have American news consumers.

Still, there are negatives to internet news. First, its rise has helped, in part, to develop a fragmented news audience because people have been given more options as to where to get their news. The negative consequences relate to the greater challenges created for each individual medium in holding and growing its audience.

Despite the convenience it has provided, even internet news has not been able to force-feed news consumers into choosing news. For example, months after the September 11 terrorist strikes, Americans had not increased their international news appetite, according to a Pew survey in June 2002. So, although internet news has made getting news more convenient, news users ultimately decide how they consume news.

The definition of "news" has been broadened even more due to internet news. Traditional journalists have not viewed these other sites as pure media, but certain Web sites, such as journalist Andrew Sullivan's site, have drawn regular traffic and been referenced by traditional media (Eakin, 2002). And even some portals have joined major national news sites in becoming the top news online news destinations (Web Site News Total Visitors Chart, 2002).

Finally, although it arguably has not hindered the initial rise of internet news, the economics of internet news has hurt its credibility somewhat among others in the media and the public as a whole (Online News Association, 2002). As discussed earlier, because the growth of the internet took off at a more rapid pace than that of other mass media, expectations were raised as well—expectations that included the medium becoming economically viable in a more condensed time period. The bar was raised. So, although many internet news divisions and companies had become economically viable, others had not, and the downward turn in the economy made this even more challenging. Analysts and practitioners forgot that it took years for other media, similar to other businesses, to work out their financial models.

So, where are the media during the age of the internet headed? Clearly, the internet has become a part of normal life, resulting in more news choices and control for news consumers. Users have had to sort out the main media brands versus the growing nontraditional media sources such as portals and blogs. Overall, internet news has been a positive addition to media. Still, there are challenges ahead given that true convergence has just begun and the economic obstacles are still being surmounted. This is an evolving process, so internet news in 2005 and 2015 may be similar or very different.

Conclusion

Internet news has been defined as the art of practicing journalism online, an extension of new media. Internet news offers seven distinctive features: dynamic content, user control, hyperlinks, multimedia, interactivity, customization, and layered journalism.

Cable television news created the 24/7 news concept, but internet news put the consumer in control of choosing news—the *who, what, when,* and *where.* "The 24-hour news cycle has changed the news landscape forever," maintained Merrill Brown, editor in chief of MSNBC.com (personal communication). As Americans lead busier lives, the internet has provided a useful news product and, as a result, a real public service. Even a longtime traditional journalist such as *Washington Post* Executive Editor Leonard Downie Jr., author of *The News About the News,* acknowledged the power of the internet for all journalists when he said that if it were not for the internet and its resulting technology—satellite and video phones—American journalists could not have covered the September 11 story and its aftermath in the same way. "It demonstrated the power of the internet in providing the audience news at anytime, 24 hours a day" (personal communication, July 2002).

Yet the changes to media overall have just begun. "We do not understand the full potential of the power of the internet and internet news," argued Scott Woelfel, one of the cofounders and former president of CNN Interactive/CNN.com (personal communication, June 2002). "It is clear that when it comes to news, the internet will have as much of an impact, if not more, than the introduction of any mass communication medium introduced in the last 100 years." Clearly, the internet is still very much in its infancy. The outcomes of the internet revolution and how internet news will ultimately evolve are for future users to determine. Although it seems difficult to believe, at the time of this writing, the internet as we know it is approaching only its 10th anniversary. Accordingly, it is probably too soon to predict another "mass media revolution." As noted earlier in the chapter, such revolutions historically take approximately 30 years. Stay tuned.

References

Eakin, E. (2002, August 10). The ancient art of haranguing has moved to the internet, belligerent as ever. *The New York Times*, p. A15.

Fidler, R. (1997). *MediaMorphosis: Understanding new media*. Thousand Oaks, CA: Pine Forge.

Kurtz, H. (2001, February 21). Is online journalism on its way out? *The Washington Post*, pp. C1.

Margolis, M., & Resnick, D. (2000). *Politics as usual: The cyberspace "revolution."* Thousand Oaks, CA: Sage.

Nielsen/Net Ratings. (2001, November). *Internet usage climbs to record high in October, with 115 million Americans online.* [Online]. Retrieved April 24, 2003, from www.nielsen-netratings.com/pr/pr_011113.pdf

NUA Internet Surveys. (1998a). *Internet a growing news provider.* [Online]. Retrieved April 24, 2003, from http://www.nua.com/surveys

NUA Internet Surveys. (1998b). *Web users visit news sites first.* [Online]. Retrieved April 24, 2003, from http://www.nua.com/surveys

Online News Association. (2002). *Digital Journalism Credibility Study.* [Online]. Retrieved April 24, 2003, from www.onlinenewsassociation.org/programs/credibility_study.pdf

Pew Internet and American Life Project. (2001). *How Americans used the internet after the terrorist attack.* [Online]. Retrieved April 24, 2003, from www.pewinternet.org/reports/pdfs/pip_terror_report.pdf

Pew Internet and American Life Project. (2003). *The internet and the Iraq War.* [Online]. Retrieved May 3, 2003, from www.pewinternet.org/reports/pdfs/pip_iraq_war_report.pdf

Pew Research Center for the People and the Press. (1995). *Americans going online: Explosive growth, uncertain destinations.* [Online]. Retrieved April 24, 2003, from http://people-press.org/reports/display.php3?reportid=136

Pew Research Center for the People and the Press. (1996). *News attracts more internet users.* [Online]. Retrieved April 24, 2003, from http://people-press.org/reports/display.php3?reportid=117

Pew Research Center for the People and the Press. (1998). *Internet news takes off.* [Online]. Retrieved April 24, 2003, from http://people-press.org/reports/display.php3?reportid=88

Pew Research Center for the People and the Press. (1999). *The internet news audience goes ordinary.* [Online]. Retrieved April 24, 2003, from http://people-press.org/reports/display.php3?reportid=72

Pew Research Center for the People and the Press. (2000). *Internet sapping broadcast news audience.* [Online]. Retrieved April 24, 2003, from http://people-press.org/reports/display.php3?reportid=36

Pew Research Center for the People and the Press. (2002). *Public's news habits little changed by September 11.* [Online]. Retrieved April 24, 2003, from http://people-press.org/reports/display.php3?reportid=156

Rodman, G. (2001). *Making sense of media: An introduction to mass communication.* Needham Heights, MA: Allyn & Bacon.

The trees fight back: Should old media embrace blogging? (n.d.). *The Economist.* [Online]. Retrieved August 2002 from http://economist.com/research/articlesbysubject/displaystory. cfm?story_id=1218702&subjectid=348963

Web site news total visitors chart. (2002, July 8). *The New York Times,* p. C7.

Zakon, R. (n.d.). *Hobbes' internet timeline* [Online]. Retrieved April 2002, from http://zakon. org/robert/internet/timeline

9

Crisis Communication and New Media

The Web After September 11

Steven M. Schneider
State University of New York Institute of Technology

Kirsten A. Foot
University of Washington

The terrorist attacks in the United States on September 11, 2001, stimulated intense and widespread reactions by many around the world. Both the online and offline press carried stories about Web activity during the hours, days, and weeks after the attacks. Hu and Sandoval (2001) were among the first to report on the increased traffic and resultant slowdowns in access to some Web sites produced by news organizations, government entities (e.g., Federal Bureau of Investigation, Pentagon), and airlines on September 11. However, the increased traffic to these high-profile sites was only the tip of the proverbial iceberg of Web activity in the aftermath of the attacks. In an article posted on News.com the afternoon of September 11, Olsen (2001) noted that within hours of the attacks, individual New Yorkers and others around the world created personal Web sites and also used e-mail and chat applications to check in with each other. She also reported on the immediate use of corporate Web sites by several New York businesses affected by the attacks—including Marriott Hotels, Morgan Stanley, and the law firm of Sidley Austin Brown & Wood—to report on the status of employees and visitors. McCormick (2001), in a commentary on the efforts by information and communication technology companies to assist those affected most by the attacks, cited Prodigy Communications' National "I'm Okay" Message Center (http://okay.prodigy.net), launched shortly after the attacks and designed to help people locate friends and family with whom they had lost contact during the attacks, as an example of Web features/sites created or adapted by corporations in response to the attacks to assist the affected.

The increased use of the Web for a range of purposes during the weeks following the attacks was noticed and commented on by many, including the U.S. president and other federal officials. Guglielmo (2001), in an *Interactive Week* editorial published September 24, 2001, noted that although government sites initially offered scanty information about the attacks, President George W. Bush urged Americans to use the Web to offer support and assistance after the attacks. She also quoted Federal Bureau of Investigation (FBI) chief Robert Mueller as having announced that the FBI received more than 47,000 leads through its "tips" Web site during the first 10 days after the attacks.

Although Goldsborough (2001) argued that television "trumped" the internet in delivering breaking news in the immediate aftermath of the attacks, he noted that the Web provided several distinct advantages: more depth, a greater number of perspectives (including international ones), archives of visual images, and more firsthand accounts through personal Web sites or "blogs" and online discussion groups. "Perhaps what's most valuable about the personal nature of the internet [in a crisis] is its capacity for community-building. During a disaster, it's a natural human impulse to reach out to others, and the internet is nonpareil in bridging the distance that often separates us" (p. 19).

Fisher and Porter (2001), writing a week after the attacks, cataloged some of the ways in which Web producers responded to the events. Their list of producer actions included the creation by hackers of mirrors of news sites to help Web users gain quicker access to breaking news, the posting by producers of professional psychology associations of guidance on handling emotional distress and talking with children about the attacks, and the blacking out of Web sites around the world by many kinds of producers, temporarily replacing their sites' regular content with "a picture, a message, or a list of other sites doing the same." Some site producers, especially news organizations such as CNN.com and MSNBC.com, turned to content delivery networks such as Akamai to handle the dramatically increased demand for content (Mears, 2001). Major search engines and portals reworked their approaches to serving Web users. Google, for example, transformed itself from a pure search tool to something closer to a destination or portal site, a significant departure from its carefully cultivated strategic positioning (Wiggins, 2001).

The reports just cited can be read as field notes from those who were observing activity on the Web in near real time. This chapter analyzes Web activity in the aftermath of the terrorist attacks. The primary aim is to examine concomitant trends in the rapid emergence of online structure created by Web producers and the online actions engaged in by Web users during the days and weeks following September 11. The features of archived Web sites that were produced by a variety of entities and that carried content relevant to the attacks, as well as survey data on Web use patterns during the month following the attacks, are analyzed. Finally, substantive and methodological implications of the findings from this study are suggested.

The Web as a Medium for Crisis Communication

One aim of this chapter is to contribute to the nascent literature on the role of the Web as a crisis communication medium as well as to understandings of the Web as a surface for producer and user actions. Although most of the literature in the field of crisis communication is based on case studies of how individuals or organizations respond to crises, some more general insights can contribute to a conceptual framework for interpreting September 11-related Web activity. Fishman (1999) offered a useful set of five characteristics common to crisis communication situations, four of which are relevant to the September 11 attacks. First, an unpredictable event occurs. Second, important values for an individual or institution are threatened. Third, the situation is time sensitive; that is, actors do not have an infinite amount of time in which to respond. Fourth, a crisis communication situation entails "a dynamic or multi-dimensional set of relationships within a rapidly-changing environment" (p. 5). The events of September 11 clearly constitute a crisis according to these characteristics; thus, the chapter authors suggest that Web activity oriented around the events can be analyzed as crisis communication.

Observations on the pre-Web functions of traditional print and broadcast news producers in crisis communication situations help to provide context for interpreting September 11-related Web activity. In this vein, Sood, Stockdale, and Rogers's (1987) analysis of how news organizations operate in response to natural disasters is useful. This article is a comparative case study of five separate natural disasters and the response by local and national press organizations, along with their relationship with emergency organizations (both governmental and nongovernmental), collected from 1979 to 1984. The authors explored how the press, whose normal (offline) channels of communication are likely to be affected, diffuse news rapidly during natural disasters. Their findings include the following. First, news content can be a "mirror of reality" (p. 30), that is, focused on accuracy. Second, the "gatekeeping" role of the press is often suspended. Third, news, as a social construction of the event, affects public understanding of the disaster event. Fourth, in reaction to an initial shortage of information, the press offers extensive or "blanket" coverage of the disaster that may include as yet unverified information. The perceived need for a constant flow of information leads news producers to reassign employees to the disaster, but when the expanded need cannot be met by press personnel, news emanating directly from members of the public is employed (p. 32). Sood and colleagues noted that press and governmental officials often have conflicting goals during an emergency; thus, the news producers are usually regarded as the only credible information source for the public during a disaster event. The emerging evidence regarding press coverage of the September 11 events on the Web and offline appear to confirm these observations.

As the population of internet users in the United States grows, and as the Web itself continues to expand, recent studies suggest that the Web is an increasingly important source of news and information for those with access to it. However, there are few recent systematic studies of media preference in crisis situations. Piotrowski and Armstrong (1998) provided an analysis of which information or media modalities the public relied on in anticipation of and during Hurricane Danny in 1997. Their findings show a strong preference for "local" sources of information over national ones and for television over FM news radio and print newspaper media. They noted that a sizable minority tuned into the internet for information, and their recommendations for future research included the suggestion that internet use during disasters should be studied rigorously.

Constance (1996) reported on one of the earliest experiments of the Web's utility as a medium for crisis communication—a demonstration by National Science Foundation (NSF) technicians on the utility of the Web, as employed by governmental officials and other selected experts, for coordinating crisis response. The 1996 exercise involved representatives of 27 Eastern and Western European nations. According to Don Bennett, then deputy director of emergency planning in the U.S. Office of the Under Secretary of Defense for Planning, the purpose of the demonstration was to "show governments in the former Soviet Union how they can enhance collaboration with their neighbors to quickly assess disasters, identify resources, and ask the right questions'" (p. 2). NSF technicians demonstrated that "it soon may be possible to provide much of the communications and information needed to support emergency relief coordination via an ordinary, public-access Web server" (p. 2). This report on the demonstration gives no indication as to whether Web activity by producers other than the designated governmental officials and industry representatives was anticipated or accounted for in this early exercise in using the Web as a medium for managing crisis communication. The findings of this study demonstrate that the crisis communication situation caused by the September 11 attacks precipitated Web-based attempts at relief coordination by a wide range of actors.

As already illustrated, there are a number of ways in which to think about crisis communication. This chapter links concepts from crisis communication with ideas about social mobilization and builds on earlier work (Schneider & Foot, 2002) in which the notion of "online structure" is introduced. This conceptualization of online structure is derived from the literature on social movements and attempts to build on the work distinguishing between "structure" and "action" (Klandermans, Kriesi, & Tarrow, 1988). Much theoretical work in the social movements literature focuses on the relationship among political mobilization, formal organizations, external political processes, and internal organizational features (Johnston & Klandermans, 1995; Mueller, 1992). The so-called new social movement theorists have tended to emphasize what they call "micromobilization" features related to the structures or contexts within which individuals enact political behaviors. Toward this end, McAdam, McCarthy, and Zald (1996) provided a comparative analysis of various theoretical approaches to using the structure of mobilization processes as an analytical tool. This literature suggests the utility of distinguishing between the structure for action and the action itself and draws attention to the characteristics of the "micromobilization contexts" (McAdam, 1988), "free spaces" (Evans & Boyte, 1986), and other associational forms (Cohen & Rogers, 1995; Oldenburg, 1989, 2001) that facilitate political action. Thus, "online structure" is conceptualized as an electronic space composed of various HTML pages, features, links, and texts within which an individual is given an opportunity to act. In this study, the online structure produced within and between sites through hyperlinks, the actions enabled by this online structure in the post-September 11 Web sphere, and the actions taken by Web users in response to the attacks are analyzed.

Methods

This chapter is based on two independently collected data streams: an archive of Web sites related to September 11 and a series of daily telephone surveys of individuals about their online behavior during the days and weeks following the terrorist attacks.

Understanding about the behavior of site producers, and about the structures they created to enable online actions, is gleaned from an analysis of Web sites archived between September 11 and December 1, 2001. During this time period, the chapter authors worked with the Pew Internet and American Life Project, the U.S. Library of Congress, the Internet Archive, and volunteers from around the world to identify and archive URLs that were likely to be relevant to the question of how Web site producers were reacting to the events of September 11.[1] Twelve basic categories of site producers that were expected to be responding to the attacks on the Web were identified. The analysis presented here is based on an examination of Web sites produced by nine of these: news organizations such as CNN, *The New York Times,* and Salon.com; federal, state, and local government entities; corporations and other commercial organizations; advocacy groups; religious groups (including denominations and congregations); individuals acting on their own behalf; educational institutions; portals; and charity and relief organizations.

Systematic searches were conducted for URLs produced by these sets of actors, and links to other URLs were followed to find more sites with relevant content. In most cases, the salient feature of these sites was content referring to the attacks and/or their aftermath. In some cases, the absence or removal of such content was salient. These collection efforts identified nearly 29,000 different "sites." Each site was archived on a daily basis from initial identification to the end of the collection period. The objective of the archiving activity was to preserve not only the bits and content but also the experiential dimensions of this rapidly emerging Web sphere (Arms, Adkins, Ammen, & Hayes, 2001). By capturing pages and sites in their hyperlinked context, the archiving tools preserved not just the collection of Web pages but also an interlinked Web sphere, characterized and bounded by a shared object orientation or reference point, in this case, the September 11 attacks (Schneider, Foot, & Harnett, 2001). For this study, a sample of 247 sites was generated for analysis. The sampling strategy, designed to include a broad representation of site producers and to focus on those sites that were captured closest to September 11, yielded a sample of three "impressions" or site captures of the various Web sites. A preliminary analysis of the site pages had eliminated those without content relevant to the September 11 events as well as those not captured in a readable format by the archiving tools. The refined sample of Web sites were then closely examined by trained observers for the range of online actions made possible by site producers.

Estimates of the Web behavior and attitudes of post September 11 internet users are based on analyses of daily surveys taken by the Pew Internet and American Life Project during the 6 weeks following September 11. The surveys employed random digit dialing to reach adults across the continental United States. The data were then weighted according to a special analysis of the Census Bureau's March 2002 Current Population Survey to account for nonresponse bias in telephone surveys.

Online Structure for Online Action

An analysis of the online structure created by Web producers that facilitated online action during the days and weeks following September 11 is the focus of this section. Assessment of the Web sphere produced during this period suggests that September 11-relevent site features facilitated seven online actions: (a) getting information, (b) providing information, (c) getting assistance/support, (d) providing assistance/support, (e) allowing for personal expression, (f) accessing others' expression, and (g) engaging in political advocacy.

Getting Information. This was the action most immediately and most commonly enabled by most types of Web sites. Examples of getting information actions include obtaining news and information about the terrorist attacks and the subsequent rescue and recovery operations, civic response, criminal investigations, military response, and terrorism in historic and political context. Content associated with this kind of action includes news, information, photographs, and the like produced by professional (for-profit) organizations, nonprofit organizations, and individuals (amateurs).

Providing Information. This was made possible as Web sites enabled visitors to contribute newsworthy information to the public. For example, individuals were able to provide "tips" to authorities related to the investigation of the terrorist investigation and (later) the anthrax investigation. Other sites enabled individuals to post information about the attacks and the rescue/recovery operations that were under way.

Getting Assistance/Support. This was facilitated by structures, which emerged soon after the attacks, to serve victims as well as the families and friends of victims. Some of the Web-based services provided information *for* those in the immediate vicinity of the attacks, and others provided or sought information *about* individuals who were in the immediate vicinity. Examples of these services include registries of victims, lists of those missing in the attacks, lists of survivors ("I'm okay" sites), and resource and referral directories.

Providing Assistance/Support. These emerging Web structures also enabled a number of different online actions in support of various public and private activities such as rescue and recovery efforts, counseling, education, criminal investigations, community organizing, and solidarity-building efforts. Some examples of this kind of action include contributing money to relief efforts; obtaining the information, direction, and support needed by community organizers, service providers, and educators; providing information to law enforcement agencies; and obtaining symbolic merchandise (e.g., flags, shirts) and content (e.g., images, songs, texts) facilitating participation in solidarity-building efforts.

Allowing for Personal Expression. Some Web features provided opportunities for individuals to express views and perspectives about the terrorist attacks as well as about the subsequent rescue and recovery operations and governmental and civic response. In addition to personal emotional and/or spiritual expression, this kind of action includes joining in communal expression of grief and mourning. Existing sites accommodated some expressive actions, whereas other actions required the emergence of new services. Furthermore, some producers who did not previously support these types of actions became involved in providing some of the expressive structure that emerged.

Accessing Others' Expression. Opportunities for Web users to enter into the experiences and responses of others were provided on some sites. These sites, including memorial and grief sites, allowed visitors to examine a range of expression contributed by other Web users.

Engaging in Political Advocacy. Finally, Web producers developed forms of online structure that allowed individuals to engage in political advocacy. For example, individuals could sign online petitions, send e-mail to government representatives, read or post views in online discussion groups, and contribute money to interest and advocacy groups.

Not surprisingly, the type of site producer was strongly related to the type of action for which online structure was provided. Getting information was the most common action facilitated by the Web sites examined; it was possible on 63% of these sites. Press and government sites were considerably more likely than the overall group of sites to facilitate this action; charity and religious sites were much less likely to do so. The second most common action, accessing others' expression, was possible on 55% of the sites examined, most commonly on personal and educational sites and least often on government and portal sites. In general, personal sites were much more likely than the overall group of sites to allow Web site visitors to post their own personal expression, provide assistance/support, provide information, and engage in political advocacy. Press, business, advocacy, and portal sites were considerably less likely to provide structure for many of the kinds of actions examined than were the set of sites in general. However, the finding that 50% of press sites allowed visitors to provide expression was counterintuitive considering that the traditional user action enabled by the press via any medium is that of getting information.

This analysis also took note of the type of online structure provided by the Web sites examined. Two types of online structures were identified: labeled on-site and coproduced. An *on-site structure* is one in which the site producer provides the content directly, whereas a *coproduced structure* is created when a site producer links to another site to facilitate the particular action. Many sites combined these types of online structure, providing some of the content themselves and linking to other sites for additional content or functionality. Linking is a form of coproduction in that both site producers—the producer providing the link and the producer of the Web site that is voluntarily or involuntary linked—jointly enable the action in question (Foot & Schneider, 2002). Structure for providing assistance was most likely to be coproduced; features that enabled getting expression and providing expression were most likely to be provided on-site. Approximately 70% of the sites that facilitated providing assistance/support did so using coproduction, whereas 80% of the sites that allowed visitors to access others' expression and 75% of the sites that allowed visitors to provide personal expression did so on-site. The tendency for various types of site producers to enable actions on-site versus coproducing actions through links is presented in Table 9.1. Personal sites were much more likely to coproduce online structure than were any

Table 9.1   Mean Number of Actions Possible on Web Sites Relating to September 11
                Terrorist Attacks, by Type of Web Site Content and Structure

| | Web Site Structure | | | | | |
| Content of Web Site | Content Produced On-Site | | Content Coproduced | | Total | |
	Mean Number of Actions	Number of Actions	Mean Number of Actions	Number of Actions	Mean Number of Actions	Number of Actions
Educational	1.82	17	1.88	17	3.23	17
Personal	2.00	57	1.83	58	2.98	58
News	2.20	24	0.63	24	2.50	24
Government	1.71	38	1.03	36	2.31	36
Advocacy	1.73	22	0.95	22	2.23	22
Portal	1.52	19	0.74	19	1.95	19
Charity	1.52	17	0.89	18	1.94	18
Religious	1.26	19	0.74	19	1.84	19
Business	1.17	29	0.43	30	1.46	30
Total	1.71	242	1.09	243	2.34	244

other types of site producer. Business and advocacy producers were much less likely to do so. Advocacy, religious, educational, and business producers were most likely to produce on-site structure to facilitate online action by their site visitors.

Online Actions by Internet Users

In examining online actions engaged in by internet users, it is useful to first set the context of reaction to the events of September 11 by reviewing patterns of behavior in the offline world. As reported by Rainie and Kalsnes (2001), the online response among the American people to the September 11 attacks was part of a larger collective experience. The Pew survey asked respondents whether they had engaged in any of five offline activities related to September 11: attended a religious service, tried to donate blood, attended a meeting to discuss the attacks, flown an American flag outside their home, or given money to relief efforts. By September 19, the first day for which a representative sample is available, the mean participation rate in offline September 11-related activities had climbed to 1.36; by September 25, the mean had reached 1.99 activities.[2] Among those respondents surveyed between September 12 and October 7, nearly 30%

Table 9.2   Number of Sites Visited Prior to and as a Result of September 11 Terrorist Attacks (percentage)

Number of Educational, Personal, News, Government, Advocacy, Portal, Charity, Religious, or Business Web Sites Visited	Percentage Americans Reporting Visits to These Types of Web Sites, Prior to September 11	Percentage Americans Reporting Visits to These Types of Web Sites During the 6 Weeks Following September 11
0	11	64
1	20	23
2 or 3	42	10
4 or more	26	2
Unsure	1	1
N	673	

Data from Pew Internet and American Life Project.

had participated in three or more activities, 56% in one or two activities, and 15% in no activities. In the discussion that follows, the online behaviors among respondents are compared with their level of participation in offline activities.

The online actions engaged in by those using the Web during the days and weeks following September 11 were analyzed using survey data collected by the Pew Internet and American Life Project. More specifically, the level of Web use reported, the types of sites that Web users reported visiting, and the types of action in which Web users reported engaging are discussed in what follows. Differences among users based on the level of Web use, as well as the amount of reported offline activity related to September 11, are reported.

Rainie and Kalsnes (2001) reported that the overall number of people using the internet during the 2 weeks following the attacks declined by about 5% to 8% before returning to established levels by the beginning of October. This decline in overall internet use was noted among all types of Web users, including the most frequent and most experienced groups. However, although overall internet use declined, those reporting using the Web for news increased considerably. The percentage of internet users reporting getting news from the Web on a typical day rose more than 25%—from 22% during the 4 weeks prior to the attacks to 28% after the attacks.

Survey respondents were asked about their visits to eight different types of Web sites corresponding to the producer types examined in the site analysis discussed in the previous section. As presented in Table 9.2, all but 11% of the respondents reported visiting at least one of the eight types of Web sites prior to September 11, and 26% reported visiting four or more types. In addition, 35% of the respondents reported visiting at least one of the types of Web sites during the 6-week period following September 11 as a result of the events of that day. However, most Web users focused their efforts on relatively few types of sites; fully one third of those respondents who visited any of the types of sites examined as a result of September 11 reported visiting only one, two, or three of them. At the same time, more frequent users of the internet reported visiting a somewhat wider variety of sites as a result of September 11. Of those who went online several times a day, 26% visited one type of site, 17% visited two or three types, and 4% visited four or more types.

Most Web users visited press sites. Nearly one quarter of all internet users reported visiting a press site as a result of September 11. None of the other types of site producers was visited by more than 10% of the internet users as a result of the terrorist attacks. This suggests that although the Web enables virtually anyone to be an information provider, during times of crisis, press organizations still dominate. More frequent Web users were more likely to visit every type of site than were less frequent Web users. However, there was little relationship between participation in offline activities related to September 11 and visiting sites produced by most types of site producers.

With an understanding of the types of sites visited by Web users following September 11, we now turn to an assessment, presented in Table 9.3, of the specific online actions in which internet users engaged. Nearly half of all internet users reported using the Web to find news about the terrorist attacks. More than one third of the internet users reported using the Web to find information about the reaction of the financial markets to the attacks. About a quarter of those online sought out information about Osama bin Laden or Afghanistan. More than a quarter of those online used the Web to post or read the opinions of other individuals. About one fifth of the internet users downloaded a picture of the American flag or sought information about victims or survivors. Not surprisingly, more frequent internet users were more likely to engage in every single action examined than were less frequent users. However, engagement in offline activities related to September 11 was related only to online actions associated with expression; online actions related to information, advocacy, or assistance were not associated with offline activities.

The final set of analyses presented here assesses the extent to which internet users found the Web to be helpful. Respondents were asked whether they believed that the Web helped them to "learn what was going on" or to "connect with people." As summarized at the bottom of Table 9.3, nearly one fifth of all

Table 9.3   Frequency of Internet Use and Engagement in Offline Actions Related to September 11

	Internet Use Not Every Day (percentage)		Internet Use at Least Once a Day (percentage)		All Online Respondents	
	Unengaged Offline	Engaged Offline	Unengaged Offline	Engaged Offline	Percentage	Number
Get information						
General news	25	34	54	63	48	2,857
Information about reaction of financial markets	10	20	41	49	36	1,599
Information about Afghanistan	7	16	28	34	26	1,599
Information about Osama bin Laden	5	15	28	35	26	1,597
Information about Islam	2	10	13	21	15	1,599
Political advocacy						
Signed petition online	3	3	6	7	6	682
Contacted elected official by e-mail	0	2	5	8	5	684
Participated in online polls	1	6	8	16	11	929
Information about local rallies or demonstrations	0	4	6	9	7	682
Information about getting involved politically	0	2	4	8	5	684
Expression						
Post or read others' thoughts about attacks	17	25	24	35	28	1,598
Visited commemorative site	11	10	11	18	14	1,597
Downloaded picture of flag	8	14	12	27	20	915
Obtain assistance						
Information about victims or survivors	8	10	17	22	17	1,599
Check flight information	12	5	6	22	14	914
Perceived value of internet after September 11						
Helped a lot to learn what was going on	11	10	22	26	18	1,254
Helped a lot to connect with people	10	10	22	23	17	1,251
Played major role in shaping views about U.S. response to attack	0	15	10	17	14	271
Played major role in shaping views about cause of attack	13	20	28	24	23	272
Played major role in shaping views about preventing future attacks	0	13	19	27	21	273

respondents said that the Web helped them "a lot." Respondents were also asked to assess the extent to which information gathered from the Web played a "major role" in shaping their views about the cause of and response to the attacks or about preventing future attacks. Similarly, about one fifth of the respondents indicated that the Web played a major role in shaping their views. Frequency of Web use was not associated with believing that the Web played a major role in shaping respondents' views.

Implications

Online actions engaged in by internet users are, in part, a function of online structures provided by producers. This analysis illustrates some of the synergies between these two types of data. Although the data presented in this analysis do not account for the frequency with which users visited sites offering different online structures and so do not allow a full analysis of the relationship between online action and online structure, some preliminary estimates can be made. For example, the percentage of internet users who reported getting information from the Web during the days and weeks following September 11 may have been a function of the number of sites that facilitated this action. Similarly, the relative paucity of sites facilitating advocacy or enabling the provision of information would have accurately predicted the relatively few users who reported engaging in this action. Although the provision of structure does not guarantee action, it is clear that online action is not possible without online structure.

Although a sample of 247 Web sites is substantial for this kind of study, the number of sites per each type of site producer included in this analysis is relatively small; thus, these findings should not be presumed to be fully representative of any one category of producer type. Further research should be conducted using a larger sample stratified by producer type to verify and extend the findings presented here. Even so, the findings presented here are significant for the following reasons.

First, these findings provide additional evidence of the emergence and development of online structure for action. Conceptually, this study extends previous work on online structure and online action in two ways: by distinguishing between structure produced on a single site and structure produced through links and by identifying a set of actions that were manifested on the Web in response to a crisis. Both of these may be useful for future analyses of other

Web spheres. The differences among site producer types with regard to the coproduction of online structure are intriguing and invite further investigation and analysis.

Second, the findings from this study illustrate the importance of the internet, and particularly the Web, as a significant component of the public sphere, enabling coordination, information sharing, assistance, expression, and advocacy in a crisis situation. In addition, they demonstrate the value of the latent capacity of the Web production community as a resource to be deployed during a time of crisis. Hundt (2002) observed that one lesson to be drawn from the events of September 11 is that to maintain an effective communications system in the face of any calamity, the internet should be protected and promoted as a primary network, encouraging the private sector and using the resources of the public sector to make it faster, more robust, ubiquitous, and better integrated with other media. This policy would be consistent with the internet's original development as an aspect of national security.

Finally, the methodological, technological, and legal challenges entailed in this study are worth noting. Conceptualizing the Web in terms of online structures that enable and/or constrain social and political action required innovative operationalizations. Retrospective analysis of online structure and action required a high-quality and accessible Web archive consisting of retrievable page- and site-level records with which human-generated meta-data could be associated electronically. In addition, the processes of creating such an archive and securing scholarly access to it had to be managed with respect to evolving interpretations of intellectual property law. Scholars must identify and meet these challenges to complete the robust analyses necessary to fully examine the role of the Web, both as a crisis communication medium and as a surface for producer and user action.

Notes

1. See the September 11 Web Archive (http://september11.archive.org).

2. Because the data are from a rolling cross-sectional survey, we calculate each day's mean by pooling the respondents from that day and the previous 6 days. In other words, a mean reported for September 18, 2001, is calculated with respondents surveyed between September 12 and September 18 inclusive. In this case, as more and more people participate in September 11-related offline activities, we would expect to see the mean number of activities ever done to climb rapidly as the days pass.

References

Arms, W., Adkins, R., Ammen, C., & Hayes, A. (2001). Collecting and preserving the Web: The Minerva prototype. *RLG DigiNews, 5.* [Online] Retrieved April 26, 2003, from www.rlg.org/preserv/diginews/diginews5-2.html

Cohen, J., & Rogers, J. (1995). *Associations and democracy.* London: Verso.

Constance, P. (1996, November 4). Disaster relief is on the way—in the form of Web communications. *Government Computer News,* pp. 47–48.

Evans, S. M., & Boyte, H. C. (1986). *Free spaces: The sources of democratic change in America.* New York: Harper & Row.

Fisher, L., & Porter, H. (2001, September 24). The online community stands together. *Time,* p. 22.

Fishman, D. A. (1999). ValuJet Flight 592: Crisis communication theory blended and extended. *Communication Quarterly, 47,* 345–375.

Foot, K. A., & Schneider, S. M. (2002). Online action in campaign 2000: An exploratory analysis of the U.S. political Web sphere. *Journal of Broadcasting & Electronic Media, 46,* 222–244.

Goldsborough, R. (2001, November 12). In a crisis, old media trump new media. *Community College Week,* p. 19.

Guglielmo, C. (2001, September 24). Net helps spread information, solace. *Interactive Week,* p. 24.

Hu, J., & Sandoval, G. (2001). *Web acts as hub for info on attacks.* [Online]. Retrieved April 26, 2003, from http://news.com.com/2100-1023-272873.html

Hundt, R. (2002, January). The agenda-telecommunications: Keeping the Net secure: September 11 demonstrated the great strength of the internet; now it's time to address the internet's weaknesses. *Atlantic Monthly,* pp. 26–27.

Johnston, H., & Klandermans, B. (1995). *Social movements and culture.* Minneapolis: University of Minnesota Press.

Klandermans, B., Kriesi, H., & Tarrow, S. (Eds.). (1988). *From structure to action: Comparing social movement across cultures.* Greenwich, CT: JAI.

McAdam, D. (1988). Micromobilization contexts and recruitment to activism. In B. Klandermans, H. Kriesi, & S. Tarrow (Eds.), *From structure to action: Comparing social movement research across cultures* (pp. 125–154). Greenwich, CT: JAI.

McAdam, D., McCarthy, J. D., & Zald, M. N. (Eds.). (1996). *Comparative perspectives on social movements: Political opportunities, mobilizing structures, and cultural framings.* New York: Cambridge University Press.

McCormick, J. (2001, September 17). Extending a hand. *Interactive Week,* p. 8.

Mears, J. (2001). Content delivery networks carry the heavy load. *Network World Fusion.* [Online]. Retrieved April 26, 2003, from www.nwfusion.com/news/2001/0924carrier.html

Mueller, C. M. (1992). Building social movement theory. In A. D. Morris & C. M. Mueller (Eds.), *Frontiers in social movement theory* (pp. 3–25). New Haven, CT: Yale University Press.

Oldenburg, R. (1989). *The great good place: Cafés, coffee shops, community centers, beauty parlors, general stores, bars, hangouts, and how they get you through the day.* New York: Paragon House.

Oldenburg, R. (2001). *Celebrating the third place: Inspiring stories about the "great good places" at the heart of our communities.* New York: Marlowe.

Olsen, S. (2001). *Net offers lifeline amid tragedy.* [Online]. Retrieved April 26, 2003, from http://news.com.com/2100-1023-272893.html?legacy=cnet

Piotrowski, C., & Armstrong, T. R. (1998). Mass media preferences in disaster: A study of Hurricane Danny. *Social Behavior and Personality, 26,* 341–345.

Rainie, L., & Kalsnes, B. (2001). *The commons of the tragedy: How the internet was used by millions after the terror attacks to grieve, console, share news, and debate the country's response.* Washington, DC: Pew Internet and American Life Project. Retrieved April 26, 2003, from www.pewinternet.org/reports/pdfs/pip_tragedy_report.pdf

Schneider, S. M., & Foot, K. A. (2002). Online structure for political action: Exploring presidential Web sites from the 2000 American election. *Javnost* (The Public), 9(2), 43–60.

Schneider, S. M., Foot, K. A., & Harnett, B. H. (2001, May). *Catch and code: A method for mapping and analyzing complex Web spheres.* Paper presented at the meeting of the International Communication Association, Washington, DC. Retrieved April 26, 2003, from www.sunyit.edu/~steve/ica2001

Sood, R., Stockdale, G., & Rogers, E. M. (1987). How the news media operate in natural disasters. *Journal of Communication, 37*(3), 27–41.

Wiggins, R. W. (2001). The effects of September 11 on the leading search engine. *First Monday, 7*(10). [Online]. Retrieved April 26, 2003, from http://firstmonday.org/issues/issue6_10/wiggins/index.html

Part III

Economic Life Online

10

"sHoP onLiNE!"

Advertising Female Teen Cyberculture

David Silver
University of Washington

Philip Garland
University of Washington

I n the advertising section within the final few pages of the November 1999 issue of *Seventeen,* three large ads dwarf the skimpy ones for stronger, thicker, and longer hair; "World Famous Rice Necklaces"; and the Miss Teen of the Nation Pageant. The first, for Delias.com, screams "sHoP onLiNE!" and offers "roam at home" e-commerce, free shipping for online orders, and a free e-mail newsletter that contains "a screenful of news, updates, sales, and other fun bits and bytes." The second, this one for Alloy.com, features a family of labeled icons representing what the site offers: accessories, special deals, glam, roomwares, tunes, magstand, auctions, and videos. Below the retro, paisley-psychedelic font that exclaims "CHECK IT OUT NOW!" is a list of other available activities, including gaming, chat, advice, and horoscopes. The third ad, for gURL.com, asks readers whether they are "feeling creative?" Offering a form of interaction that goes beyond point-and-click online shopping, the ad's copy reads as follows: "Now you can do more than just GET a virtual makeover at gURL.com . . . you can give makeovers, too!" Offering "reader makeovers," the ad invites readers to put "your creative genius (and sense of humor) to work!"

At first glance, it may seem strange that advertising agencies are already identifying niche markets for a communication medium most commonly referred to as "new." Indeed, although the origins of the Web can be traced to Tim Berners-Lee's experiments at CERN in 1990 (Abbate, 1999; Berners-Lee, 1999), the massive mainstreaming and subsequent commercialization of the Web began in 1994 with the introduction of the popular Netscape browser and its user-friendly, point-and-click software. Throughout the mid- to late 1990s, advertisements for dot-coms, Web sites, and the suite of technologies that make them possible have employed broad rhetorical strategies, appealing to the "common user" with promises of instant access to utopian-like communities where democratic principles reign and a Benetton-like multiculturalism awaits (Howard, 2001; Nakamura, 2000).

However, as the century has turned, so have the ads—as well as their placement. Recently, advertising firms, perhaps all too aware of and made nervous by the decentered nature of the Web, have begun to fortify more general audience advertising campaigns in mainstream magazines, such as *Time* and *Newsweek*, and in technology magazines, such as *Wired* and *Business 2.0*, with niche market pitches. One of the most coveted niche markets is American teens—today's Web users and tomorrow's Web consumers. Indeed, as a research paper sponsored by the Pew Internet and American Life Project suggests, teen cyberculture gives new meaning to the cliché that teens "live in a world all their own." Parents and pundits have remarked anecdotally that American teens are turning increasingly to the internet, and Lenhart, Rainie, and Lewis's (2001) *Teenage Life Online* confirmed these observations with extensive and telling data.

Based on telephone interview surveys of 754 children and one of their parents or guardians conducted between November 2 and December 15, 2000, Lenhart and colleagues' (2001) study reported that approximately 73% of American teens ages 12 to 17 years, or some 17 million kids, use the internet in some capacity—be it e-mail, the Web, chat rooms, or (increasingly) instant messaging (IM). Moreover, American teens' internet use involves multiple segments of their lives, including their social, academic, and familial spheres. Among the most popular applications are sending and reading e-mail (92%), surfing the Web for fun (84%), visiting entertainment Web sites (83%), and IM (74%). Somewhat less popular are retrieving information, playing games, and accessing music. For example, 69% of teens reported looking for information on hobbies, 68% reported using the internet to obtain news, and 66% admitted to researching a product or service before buying or seeking it. In addition, 66% indicated that they use the internet to play or download games, 59% use it to listen to music online, and 53% use it to download music files. And uses generally associated

Table 10.1   What Teens Have Done Online: Percentages of Youth With Internet Access, Ages 12 to 17 Years, Who Have Engaged In Various Activities Online (percentage)

Send or read e-mail	92
Surf the Web for fun	84
Visit an entertainment site	83
Send an instant message	74
Look for information on hobbies	69
Get news	68
Play or download games	66
Research a product or service before buying or seeking it	66
Listen to music online	59
Visit a chat room	55
Download music files	53
Check sports scores	47
Visit a site for a club or team of which they are members	39
Go to a Web site where they can express opinions about something	38
Buy something online	31
Visit sites for trading or selling things	31
Look for health-related information	26
Create a Web page	24
Look for information on a topic that is hard to talk about	18
N	754

SOURCE: Pew Internet and American Life Project, *Teens and Parents Survey*, 2000.

with some form of individual empowerment were of even less interest to teens, with only 24% reporting experience in Web page development and 18% using the internet to look for information that is difficult to talk about (Table 10.1).

Echoing the findings of recent scholarship (Cassell & Jenkins, 1998; Evard, 1996; Kafai, 1996, 1999) on gendered practices among teen and adolescent computer and internet users, *Teenage Life Online* provided additional data on such differences. Isolating teen girls, we find an interesting set of popular uses and priorities (Lenhart et al., 2001). Fully 78% of girls online reported using IM compared with 71% of online boys who did so. In addition to using IM more than do boys, girls send or receive e-mail more than do boys, with 95% of girls reporting such use compared with 89% of boys. Older female teens, ages 15 to 17 years, are the most likely to visit sites about movies, television shows, music groups, or sports stars, with 87% of them reporting that they have done this compared with 80% of boys the same age. In addition, 40% of girls ages 15 to 17 years have looked for dieting, health, or fitness information, whereas only 26% of boys the same age have done so (Table 10.2).

Table 10.2   Differences and Similarities Between Girls and Boys Online: Percentages of Teens Who Engage in Various Activities Online, by Gender (percentage)

	Girls	Boys
What more girls do online	95	89
Send or receive e-mail	78	71
Use instant messaging	30	22
Look for dieting, health, or fitness information		
What more boys do online	55	77
Research items that they might like to buy	62	76
Look for hobby information	57	75
Play or download games	32	62
Look for sports scores	47	60
Download music	20	42
Go to a Web site where people trade or sell things	19	29
Create their own Web sites		
What boys and girls do at about the same level	85	83
Go online for fun		
Visit Web sites about movies, television shows, music groups,		
or sports stars	85	81
Look for news	70	66
Listen to music online	59	59
Visit a chat room	56	55
Visit Web sites for clubs, activities, or sports teams of which they are		
members	38	41
Visit Web sites where they can express their opinions about things	38	38
Go online to find information that is hard to talk about with other people	17	19
n	377	377

SOURCE: Pew Internet and American Life Project, *Teens and Parents Survey,* 2000.

Finally, in terms of online consumer behaviors, the findings are telling (Lenhart et al., 2001). Fully 64% of girls ages 12 to 14 years reported that the internet helps them to find fashion and music, yet only 50% of all female teens believe that the internet is helpful in researching prices for items they would like to purchase. Just over half (55%) of female teens reported having researched product information compared with 77% of male teenagers who did so. Furthermore, only 47% of female teens reported having clicked on internet ads or billboards compared with 60% of their male counterparts who did so.

Although this Pew Internet and American Life Project report (Lenhart et al., 2001) taught us much about the ways in which American teens use the internet, it did so within a rather limited media ecology. Unlike subsequent Pew reports on, for example, American sentiment regarding dot-coms that explore not only Americans' opinions on the matter but also the ways in which popular media help to inform and influence such beliefs, *Teenage Life Online* restricted American teens' experiences with the internet to solely "within the wires."

Considering the widespread adoption and use of the internet by American teenagers, we became interested in the ways in which advertising agencies rhetorically present the internet to teen audiences in general and to female teen audiences in particular. Intrigued by recent scholarship arguing that particular nodes of the internet, as well as discourses regarding those nodes, are "coded" as male at best and as sexist at worst, we explored the *social construction of female teen cyberculture* vis-à-vis popular teen magazines for girls and young women as our site of inquiry. Furthermore, we compared such constructions of female teen cyberculture with actual female teen cyberculture as reported in the Pew report. This chapter examines a series of print advertisements that appeared between December 1998 and December 1999 in the three most popular magazines for female teens: *Seventeen, Teen,* and *Teen People.* We argue that although certain rhetorical elements of individual and collective empowerment can be found within some of the ads, the majority of them rhetorically construct the internet as a sphere of idle chatter and online consumption, thereby reinforcing gendered stereotypes of girls and young women being technologically inept, socially frail, and domestic consumers—characteristics that stand in stark contrast to the findings of the Pew study.

Discourse of Cyberspace

Although the majority of early internet studies scholars examined cyberspace as an already existing environment, recent scholars approach the site of study as a culture in its own right as well as a cultural artifact (Bell, 2001; Hine, 2000; Silver, 2000; Sterne, 1999). As a cultural artifact, the internet is constructed by technology, policy, social practices, and its users, among other factors, but also through discourse. Indeed, like other forms of culture, internet culture is, in part, a product of the stories we tell and hear about it. Such discourses, whether found in magazine features in *Wired,* within panels of cartoon strips such as *Doonesbury* and *The Boondocks,* in films such as *The Net* and *You've Got Mail,* or in television commercials during the Super Bowl, encapsulate and reify particular ideologies that, in turn, influence and inform the ways in which we engage with and within the internet. Furthermore, these stories—or the lack of these stories—can potentially discourage and dissuade would-be cybernauts from going online.

From this perspective, cyberspace is not only a site for communication and community but also a site of discourse, at once a real and imagined place where a variety of interests stake their claims on cyberspace's origins, its future directions, and its very meaning. As a number of scholars (Borsook, 1996; Miller, 1995; Sobchack, 1993) have noted, politicians, pundits, and publishers often rhetorically construct the internet as a *digital frontier,* one that "conjures up traditional American images of the individual lighting out from the territories, independent and hopeful, to make a life" (Doheny-Farina, 1996, p. 16) and that performs a historical erasure, as if cyberspace exists as an accidental, undesigned digital domain (Turner, 1999). A second and somewhat related discourse is *cyberlibertarianism,* produced when the "information wants to be free" cult meets the "free market capitalism" camp, resulting in technozines such as *Wired* and *Mondo 2000* (Borsook, 2000; Millar, 1998; Sobchack, 1993; Warnick, 2001). For example, Sobchack's (1996) incisive analysis of the now defunct *Mondo 2000* revealed a contradictory stance between cyberutopianism and cybermarketeerism where "the dream of democratic enfranchisement is grounded not only in the desire for free access to information and free interactive communication and social participation, but also in the desire for the freedom to buy and the freedom to sell, for a freely interactive and capitalist commerce" (p. 86).

Another commonly used cyberdiscourse is what we call *virtual multiculturalism.* Exemplified most dramatically in MCI's television commercial "Anthem" (Gómez-Peña, 1996; Lockard, 2000; Nakamura, 2000), the rhetorical strategy pitches the internet as a space free of traditional cultural and geographic barriers, thereby erasing racial, ethnic, and gender prejudices. Such a vision is problematic, of course, especially for feminist scholars who argue that computer culture in general and cyberculture in particular are wrapped in gendered and sexist discourse (Balsamo, 1996; Coyle, 1996; Dietrich, 1997; Millar, 1998; Ross, 1991; Weinstein, 1998).[1] As we began our research, we asked the question: Which of these discourses, if any, are used to engage American female teens?

Methods and Analysis

With female American teens going online in increasing numbers, we can expect a discursive battlefield of e-brand loyalties played out within media environments frequented by female teens. To explore this terrain, we examined three of the four most popular female teen magazines—*Seventeen, Teen,* and *Teen People*—to investigate what kinds of rhetorical strategies advertisers use to attract teens to dot-com companies and their Web sites.[2] Interested in exploring the possible correlations between the kinds of online activities the advertisements promote and the kinds reported in *Teenage Life Online* (Lenhart et al., 2001), we analyzed all issues between December 1998 and December 1999, a year's worth of advertising appearing directly before the data collection for the Pew study. It is important to note that it was not our intention to separate advertising and editorial content; indeed, as a number of scholars have noted, such a division is problematic (Solomon & Greenberg, 1993; Steinem, 1990; Yi, 1993). However, because we found only one feature devoted to the internet, we decided to focus our attention on the advertisements.[3]

Analyzing a year's worth of issues of three magazines generated a healthy number of internet-related advertisements, yet ads for three dot-coms appeared with a significantly higher frequency than did those for others: Alloy.com, Delias.com, and gURL.com. To examine these ads, we assessed quantitatively the relationship, if any, between the activities presented rhetorically in the advertisements and those reported in *Teenage Life Online* (Lenhart et al., 2001). In total, we coded for 11 key activities.

We hypothesize that the frequency of words used in girls' magazine ads is related to the uses reported in the Pew study. It is plausible that some relationship exists between activities that were promoted during 1998–1999 and those that teens actually engaged in during 2000. Again, *frequency* is strictly the number of times a word appeared in the top three girls' magazines.

Using the Pew survey's topics as our key words, we coded for the following (with percentage use, as reported in the *Teenage Life Online* report [Lenhart et al., 2001], reflected in parentheses). Key words are those words that reflect the following online activities researched in the Pew study. We think that girl-dominated activities—e-mail (95%), IM (78%), and dieting, health, and fitness information (30%)—are the most crucial, so an analysis was run isolating these key words. Activities equally used by boys and girls were also analyzed, including fun (84%), entertainment (e.g., movies, television, music groups, sports stars) (83%), news (68%), listening to music (59%), visiting chat rooms (55%), sites for visiting member clubs or teams (39%), opinion expression sites (38%), and sites about information that is hard to talk about (18%). Ultimately, we believe that the complexity of ads—that is, the degree of mixture of frequency and depth of key words—will reflect the most widely used internet activities by girls (e.g., e-mail, IM, health information).

Influenced by advertising historians' (Goodrum & Dalrymple, 1990; Jackson Lears, 1983; Marchand, 1985) arguments that modern advertising practices are linked intricately with anxiety and desire, on the one hand, and by relatively recent work in cultural studies (Ang, 1985; Fiske, 1989; Lipsitz, 1990; Radway, 1987) that suggest polysemic readings between cultural texts and their audiences, on the other hand, our content analyses focused on the ways in which female teens become identified with particular online practices, and our discussion includes ideas regarding how female teens resist such identifications.

Results

This study began with the expectation that, given the relative infancy of the internet as a widely used medium by teens during 1998–1999, there would be occurrence and style differences in advertising among the three sites. The analysis focuses on the frequency differences in the magazines because the magazine (rather than the site) as the unit of analysis helps to drive teen cyberculture discourse. We found 34 instances of at least one advertisement in the 39 possible issues in our sample. Thus, frequency percentages are calculated controlling for issues with ads (i.e., the actual sample size is 34). gURL.com and Delias.com appeared 13 times each, whereas Alloy.com appeared just 8 times. gURL.com appeared in *Seventeen* 6 times and in *Teen* 7 times. Alloy.com appeared in *Seventeen* 3 times and in *Teen* 5 times. Delias.com appeared in *Seventeen* 5 times and in *Teen* 7 times. Delias.com placed the only ad in *Teen People*.

There were, in fact, significant frequency differences of key word use in the magazines and within the series of advertisements for the sites. In accordance with our hypothesis, two of the top three uses by teenage girls reported in the Pew study—e-mail and health information seeking—appeared the most in the ads; the top two uses promoted during 1998–1999 appeared as the second and third highest actual uses in 2000 (Table 10.3). Specifically, e-mail, the most widely reported online teen use in 2000, appeared at least once in 19 of the 34 ads (56%) and appeared twice in one magazine six times (17%). Furthermore, e-mail appearing twice in one magazine means that nearly one third (31%) of all instances of e-mail ads were twofold in one issue (Table 10.4). Thus, e-mail ads yielded a higher use rate than the invested space to promote such activity. Moreover, advertisers got more back than they put out for e-mail. This finding is especially significant considering the highly valuable and sought after e-mail lists that remain a positive income source for both brick-and-mortar and online companies.

Table 10.3   Internet Activities Promoted by Girls' Magazine Ads Between 1998 and
Reported Activities in 2000

	Promoted Use, 1998–1999			Actual Use, 2000	
What Girls Do Online	Percentage	n	Rank	Percentage	Rank
Send or receive e-mail	56	19	2	95	1
Use instant messaging	6	2	13	78	2
Look for dieting, health, or fitness information	53	18	3	30	3
Shop	70	24	1	30	15

SOURCE: Pew Internet and American Life Project, *Teens and Parents Survey,* 2000; advertisements
taken from *Seventeen, Teen,* and *Teen People,* December 1998 to December 1999.

Table 10.4   The Internet and Parents (percentages)

	Parents	Teens
Experience		
Not online	13	0
1 year or less	25	27
2 to 3 years	34	52
More than 3 years	28	21
Internet use		
Go online for fun	63	84
Look for information about movies or other leisure activities	65	83
Use instant messaging	44	74
Play or download games	34	66
Listen to music online	40	59
Visit a chat room	26	55
Download music	29	53
Check sports scores online	38	47
Negligible difference between teens and parents		
Send or receive e-mail	93	92
Get news	66	68
Activities favored by parents		
Research or purchase a new product	73	66
Buy a product	53	31
Look for health information	57	26
n	754	754

SOURCE: Pew Internet and American Life Project, *Teens and Parents Survey,* 2000.

Shopping was the most frequently used key word, appearing in 24 issues (70%) and appearing twice seven times (30%). Again, in an attempt to remain viable in a consumer economy with millions in venture capital on the line, companies demonstrated urgency for consumerism in the ads. The Pew report did not offer statistics by gender regarding shopping; however, 31% of boys and girls reported using the internet to shop. But it is likely that boys drive this percentage considering that they heavily outpace girls for product research (77% vs. 55%); in fact, product research was male teens' number one reported use in 2000. In sum, a negative relationship exists between shopping ads and reported use, meaning that advertisers failed to tap the teen market significantly.

Health-related information, the third highest reported online activity for girls, appeared 18 times (53%), 3 of which included two occurrences, and in one instance health was coded three times in one magazine. Interestingly, health information was the only item that experienced a use rate exactly comparable to its promotion rate in the ads. In other words, health information was the third highest advertised and reported use word. Arguably, this is the one area where advertisers seem to have the most consistent user response. Contrary to our hypothesis, the second highest reported activity, IM, appeared just twice (6%). In other words, with only 2 appearances in ads, IM yielded the strongest response with 78% of girls using IM in 2000 (the second highest use).

Discussion

As noted previously, internet studies scholars have identified three major discourses—the internet as a digital frontier, cyberlibertarianism, and virtual multiculturalism—used by various interests to introduce, explain, and sell cyberspace. As a result of our analysis, we introduce a fourth major discourse: community as commerce or Community.com. Here, the internet is rhetorically constructed as a virtual space for users to come together, share ideas, and shop. Although it is a cultural product of the (temporarily?) defunct dot-com daze of the late 1990s, the rhetoric remains the same, as seen in our findings.

Our findings suggest that advertising at the onset of the "internet rush" of the 1990s is currently making a difference in online activity in the new millennium. Future research following this model of analysis and using a larger sample by including an increased number of magazine issues is needed to strengthen the causal relationship between cyberspace discourse in ads and online activity.

Comparing magazine advertisements for female teen cyberculture with Pew survey data regarding what female teens do online yields interesting results. With respect to select elements, there is a positive correlation. On the one hand, two activities in particular—using e-mail and seeking health information—appeared frequently in the magazine advertisements and in the Pew report. With respect to two others—shopping and IM—there was a negative correlation. Although further research is required, we believe that one factor behind the high use of e-mail and health information seeking among female teens is the frequency with which such activities appear in female teen-oriented magazines.

On the other hand, our hypothesis was significantly misguided, especially with respect to IM and e-commerce. Magazine advertisements seldom feature IM (only twice, or 6%, in the issues studied), a strange phenomenon considering that the Pew study found IM to be the second highest reported internet activity among American teens. To explain this, we offer two possible answers. First, although IM gained popularity during the mid- to late 1990s, it remained relatively new during the time period spanning our analysis. Second, it is possible that during 1998–1999, internet companies failed to recognize the commercial potentials of IM, a point to which we return shortly.

There was also a negative correlation between the magazine advertisements and reported female teen internet activity with respect to e-commerce. In the magazine ads, shopping was by far the most common key word, appearing in 70% of the issues. As noted in the Pew report, however, shopping online represented a relatively small portion of reported internet activity among American teens (30%). This reflects a larger trend, of course, with online shopping failing to meet the expectations set during the late 1990s and the subsequent crash of dot-coms.

Although we are quick to acknowledge that we have not seen the last of e-commerce, dot-coms, and the commercialization of the internet, we suggest that such a finding reveals a local and important development in internet culture. Although further research is necessary, it is possible to interpret the finding as a legitimate sign of resistance on the part of American teens, especially female teens, to read against the grain of the commercially driven discourse found in magazine advertisements. Stated simply, American female teens approach and use the internet as a communication tool rather than as a consumer medium. It appears to us that although American female teens are eager to use and explore various activities on the internet, e-commerce is not one of the major ones. As internet payment systems expand to include non-credit card transactions, this may change. But for the moment, we believe that teens represent a strong and important site of resistance to the commercialization of the online sphere.

Perhaps as a reaction to similar findings, internet companies are beginning to explore new strategies. For example, one application that we believe merits future research is "IM bots," an instant messaging tool developed by ActiveBuddy. Launched in June 2001, an early demo called SmarterChild was downloaded by more than 8 million users by July 2002 (*Corporate Profile,* 2002; Frey, 2002). Although ActiveBuddy promotes their software as a means to improve customer service and business operations, the potential for direct marketing, especially among teens, has not been lost on companies. For example, in February 2002, teen site Ellegirl.com introduced ELLEgirlBuddy, an IM bot ready and willing to chit-chat, offer fashion news and trends, and suggest relevant Web sites to visit. Interspersed between idle chat about boys and lip gloss are promos for subscriptions to *ELLEgirl* magazine as well as strategic product placement (Frey, 2002). We believe that IM bots such as ELLEgirlBuddy reveal an industry interested in exploring consumer-driven IM applications for teens, perhaps because of the widespread use of IM and the industry's failure to advertise this use in 1999.

Conclusion

Ultimately, this study is most significant in light of two crucial findings: how adult power holders portray American girls and young women's internet use vis-à-vis magazine advertisements and how American female teens resist such identity constructions. Consequently, future survey research to monitor uses based on longitudinal analysis of advertising changes will expand the implications herein. In addition, similar analysis in other demographics, such as ads in popular urban/hip-hop magazines to help answer questions about race, youth, and the digital divide, will be innovative and insightful.

Furthermore, we suggest ethnographic work to explore the ways in which American teens use, interact with, and think about digital technologies. Although the Pew study is helpful in gaining a broad understanding of American teen internet use, this understanding will be made richer with ethnographic approaches similar to those used by Baym (2000) and Clark (1998).

Although advertisements portray American female teen cyberculture as an activity firmly focused on consumption, their actual use is quite diverse and favors communication, entertainment, and information seeking over commerce. As teens become even more techno-savvy, it will be interesting to see whether their activities shift from information consumption to information production. At the same time, as companies continue to court the teen market and test market new technologies, it will be interesting to see how communication technologies are cast as consumer technologies.

Notes

1. The same can be said for the internet's literary counterpart, cyberpunk. As noted by many of the contributors to *Cybersexualities* (Wolmark, 1999), canonical works such as Gibson's (1984) *Neuromancer* recapitulate traditional gendered discourses and patriarchal roles.

2. We determined popularity from the 24th edition of the *Standard Periodical Directory* (2001). This edition of the directory lists the following circulation numbers for our three magazines: *Seventeen*, 2,415,727; *Teen*, 2,126,567; and *Teen People*, 1,665,974. We decided not to examine another popular teen magazine, *YM*, due to lack of availability.

3. The feature, titled "What Do Guys Think About Meeting Girls Over the Internet?," appeared on page 36 of the February 1999 issue of *Teen*.

References

Abbate, J. (1999). *Inventing the internet.* Cambridge, MA: MIT Press.

Ang, I. (1985). *Watching Dallas.* London: Methuen.

Balsamo, A. (1996). *Technologies of the gendered body: Reading cyborg women.* Durham, NC: Duke University Press.

Baym, N. K. (2000). *Tune in, log on: Soaps, fandom, and online community.* Thousand Oaks, CA: Sage.

Bell, D. (2001). *An introduction to cybercultures.* London: Routledge.

Berners-Lee, T., with Fischetti, M. (1999). *Weaving the Web: The original design and ultimate destiny of the World Wide Web by its inventor.* New York: HarperCollins.

Borsook, P. (1996). The memoirs of a token: An aging Berkeley feminist examines *Wired*. In L. Cherny & E. R. Weise (Eds.), *Wired women: Gender and new realities in cyberspace* (pp. 24–41). Seattle, WA: Seal Press.

Borsook, P. (2000). *Cyberselfish: A critical romp through the terribly libertarian culture of high tech.* New York: Public Affairs.

Cassell, J., & Jenkins, H. (Eds.). (1998). *From Barbie to Mortal Kombat: Gender and computer games.* Cambridge, MA: MIT Press.

Clark, L. S. (1998). Dating on the Net: Teens and the rise of "pure" relationships. In S. G. Jones (Ed.), *Cybersociety 2.0: Revisiting computer-mediated communication and community* (pp. 159–183). Thousand Oaks, CA: Sage.

Corporate Profile. (2002). [Online]. Retrieved April 26, 2003, from www.activebuddy.com/about_us

Coyle, K. (1996). How hard can it be? In L. Cherny & E. R. Weise (Eds.), *Wired women: Gender and new realities in cyberspace* (pp. 42–55). Seattle, WA: Seal Press.

Dietrich, D. (1997). (Re)-Fashioning the techno-erotic woman: Gender and textuality in the cybercultural matrix. In S. G. Jones (Ed.), *Virtual culture: Identity and communication in cybersociety* (pp. 169–184). Thousand Oaks, CA: Sage.

Doheny-Farina, S. (1996). *The wired neighborhood.* New Haven, CT: Yale University Press.

Evard, M. (1996). "So please stop, thank you": Girls online. In L. Cherny & E. R. Weise (Eds.), *Wired women: Gender and new realities in cyberspace* (pp. 188–204). Seattle, WA: Seal Press.

Fiske, J. (1989). *Reading the popular.* Boston: Unwin Hyman.

Frey, C. (2002, July 18). Web friend or faux? *Los Angeles Times,* p. A1.

Gibson, W. (1984). *Neuromancer.* New York: Ace Books.

Goodrum, C., & Dalrymple, H. (1990). *Advertising in America: The first 200 years.* New York: Harry N. Abrams.

Gómez-Peña, G. (1996). The virtual barrio @ the other frontier (or the Chicano interneta). In L. H. Leeson (Ed.), *Clicking in: Hot links to a digital culture* (pp. 173–179). Seattle, WA: Bay Press.

Hine, C. (2000). *Virtual ethnography.* London: Sage.

Howard, P. (2001, October). *Privatizing the citizen: Technology elites and the reconstruction of democracy.* Paper presented at the Second International Conference of the Association of internet Researchers, Minneapolis, MN.

Jackson Lears, T. J. (1983). From salvation to self-realization: Advertising and the therapeutic roots of the consumer culture, 1880–1930. In R. Wightman Fox & T. J. Jackson Lears (Eds.), *The culture of consumption: Critical essays in American history, 1880–1980* (pp. 1–38). New York: Pantheon.

Kafai, Y. B. (1996). Gender differences in children's constructions of video games. In P. M. Greenfield & R. R. Cocking (Eds.), *Interacting with video* (pp. 39–66). Norwood, NJ: Ablex.

Kafai, Y. B. (1999). Video game designs by girls and boys: Variability and consistency of gender differences. In M. Kinder (Ed.), *Kids' media culture* (pp. 293–315). Durham, NC: Duke University Press.

Lenhart, A., Rainie, L., & Lewis, O. (2001). *Teenage life online: The rise of the instant message generation and the internet's impact on friendships and family relationships.* Washington, DC: Pew Internet and American Life Project. Retrieved April 27, 2003, from www.pewinternet.org/reports/toc.asp?report=36

Lipsitz, G. (1990). *Time passages: Collective memory and American popular culture.* Minneapolis: University of Minnesota Press.

Lockard, J. (2000). Babel machines and electronic universalism. In B. Kolko, L. Nakamura, & G. Rodman (Eds.), *Race in cyberspace* (pp. 171–189). New York: Routledge.

Marchand, R. (1985). *Advertising the American dream: Making way for modernity, 1920–1940.* Berkeley: University of California Press.

Millar, M. S. (1998). *Cracking the gender code: Who rules the wired world?* Toronto: Second Story Press.

Miller, L. (1995). Women and children first: Gender and the settling of the electronic frontier. In J. Brook & I. A. Boal (Eds.), *Resisting the virtual life: The culture and politics of information* (pp. 49–57). San Francisco: City Lights.

Nakamura, L. (2000). "Where do you want to go today?": Cybernetic tourism, the internet, and transnationality. In B. Kolko, L. Nakamura, & G. Rodamn (Eds.), *Race in cyberspace* (pp. 15–26). New York: Routledge.

Radway, J. (1987). *Reading the romance.* London: Verso.

Ross, A. (1991). *Strange weather: Culture, science, and technology in the age of limits.* London: Verso.

Silver, D. (2000). Looking backwards, looking forward: Cyberculture studies 1990–2000. In D. Gauntlett (Ed.), *Web.studies: Rewiring media studies for the digital age* (pp. 19–30). London: Arnold.

Sobchack, V. (1993). New Age mutant ninja hackers: Reading *Mondo 2000*. *South Atlantic Quarterly,* *92*, 569–584.

Sobchack, V. (1996). Democratic franchise and the electronic frontier. In Z. Sardar & J. R. Ravetz (Eds.), *Cyberfutures: Culture and politics on the information superhighway* (pp. 77–89). New York: New York University Press.

Solomon, M., & Greenberg, L. (1993). Setting the stage: Collective selection in the stylistic context of commercials. *Journal of Advertising, 22*, 11–23.

Standard Periodical Directory (24th ed.). (2001). New York: Oxbridge Communications.

Steinem, G. (1990, July–August). Sex, lies, and advertising. *Ms.,* pp. 18–28.

Sterne, J. (1999). Thinking the internet: Cultural studies vs. the millennium. In S. Jones (Ed.), *Doing internet research* (pp. 257–288). Thousand Oaks, CA: Sage.

Turner, F. (1999, May). *Cyberspace as the new frontier? Mapping the shifting boundaries of the network society.* Paper presented at the meeting of the International Communication Association, San Francisco. Retrieved April 27, 2003, from http://commons.somewhere.com/rre/1999/rre.cyberspace.as.the.ne.html

Warnick, B. (2001). *Critical literacy in a digital era: Technology, rhetoric, and the public interest.* Mahwah, NJ: Lawrence Erlbaum.

Weinstein, M. (1998). Computer advertising and the construction of gender. In H. Bromley & M. W. Apple (Eds.), *Education/Technology/Power: Educational computing as a social practice* (pp. 85–100). Albany: State University of New York Press.

Wolmark, J. (Ed.). (1999). *Cybersexualities: A reader on feminist theory, cyborgs, and cyberspace.* Edinburgh, UK: Edinburgh University Press.

Yi, Y. (1993). Contextual priming effects in print advertisements: The moderating role of prior knowledge. *Journal of Advertising, 22*, 1–10.

11

Permanently Beta

Responsive Organization in the Internet Era

Gina Neff
University of California, San Diego

David Stark
Columbia University and Santa Fe Institute

How has the internet influenced economic organization? Rather than approach this question by examining the productivity gains produced by internet technologies or the roles that dot-coms play in the economy, this chapter examines how the *process* of technological change influences the organization of economic life. The social effects of the internet include emerging organizational innovations in addition to technological innovations. Although skeptics may point to failed dot-coms or the internet's broken promises of productivity gains, the values embedded in widely used information technologies have become encoded into the routines of the market and into organizational forms. Thus, the internet has already transformed economic life not just through direct influence on the marketplace but also through encoding these new routines and new ways of doing things into daily practice.

AUTHORS' NOTE: The authors thank the volume editors for their insightful comments as well as Pablo Boczkowski, Danyel Fisher, Gernot Grabher, Rajiv Shah, and the participants in the National Science Foundation's Internet Scholars Program at the University of Maryland for comments on an earlier draft. This chapter is adapted from a longer article that is available online (www.coi.columbia.edu/workingpapers.html).

Many economic and organizational processes have been *informationalized* since the diffusion of internet technologies (Castells, 2000), but informationalization alone could not create a *new* economy. Information during this era may indeed "yearn to be free," but it has yet to figure out how to break the boundaries of existing economic forms considering that the economy is still organized around information having a price. During the internet stock market frenzy, the conflict between information's openness and profitable business models symbolized the differences between these technological and economic values. Technological advances and the values of the people involved in creating them may have promoted information's openness, but social and economic organization has yet to catch up. In those realms driven by a sense of public or collective ownership, such as in e-government initiatives, nonprofit and social movement organizations, and community-developed projects (e.g., Linux), interactivity has meant somewhat freer access to information. But openness in general, it seems, is not yet a market value.

However, organizational forms and technology are influencing one another in unexpected ways, coevolving toward more open structures in both that may present the opportunity for broader participation in the design of both products and organizations. The coding of software and information technologies has the potential to extend beyond the economic implications for particular products to the rewriting of social codes and patterns of behavior, influencing not only what activities happen online but also the ways in which things are done offline.[1] The push toward more open structures is no exception, even as tensions remain between openness and control, between market and community, and between conflicting values. Computer protocols, as Galloway (2001) wrote, are "how control exists after decentralization"[2] and are deeply influenced by the values of the designers, organizations, and societies that create those protocols. The heyday of the new economy is over, but left remaining are the tensions between the market values of technological innovation and the community values of openness enabled by the internet.

One of these values of the contemporary economy embedded into the internet and computer technologies is what Manovich (2001) characterized as "variability." Unlike mass-produced objects, programmed products are never stable, can have a potentially infinite number of versions, and can be customized for a particular user almost immediately (p. 36). Software is "patchy"; versions change, systems evolve, and applications die.[3] This cycle shapes the organizational and economic forms around it, so that adaptability, flexibility, and responsiveness become the norms within the technology industry and, increasingly, throughout the economy as a whole. Adaptation to variability emerges partly due to the pervasiveness of information technologies but also due to the values of a postindustrial economy that favors just-in-time and customizable production over mass production. The internet or any technology, of course, does not exist outside of society; the variability of the internet both embodies and magnifies the ongoing effects of the shift away from industrial production.

Variability produces organizational flux. Organizations' bureaucratic structures are destabilized because the challenges of responsiveness are too great for institutional routinization. "Heterarchies"—flatter organizational structures with distributed accountability, decentralized decision making, and multiple (often competing) evaluative principles—emerge (Stark, 1999). This chapter argues that the internet, in addition to magnifying the variability of production, enables a closer connection between products' design and their use—a connection that, in turn, transforms organizational processes. Continual change necessitates responsiveness in the design of both products and organizations. The influence of design—whether the design of products, technology, or services—and organizational form on each other emerges partly due to the process of continual technological change in which the cycle of testing, feedback, and innovation facilitates ongoing negotiations around what is made and how to organize making it. We call the organizational state of flux that emerges from this negotiation "permanently beta." *Permanently beta is a fluid organizational form resulting from the process of negotiation among users, employees, and organizations over the design of goods and services.* The instability associated with being permanently beta is not without social costs, but it may present opportunities for organizing broader participation in the design of products and organizations.

Countering the social costs of instability depends on the level of organization of participants—users and employees alike. Within permanently beta organizations, as products and the structures around them are being tested, individual users and employees bear a greater responsibility for adaptation to change. The "changing scripts" of workplaces, as Kunda and Van Mannen (1999) argued, force adaptation by those who work in permanently beta organizations. Continual reconfiguration in heterarchial organizations can be exhausting, especially in work environments organized around projects that exert extraordinary time pressures and demand a fast pace of action, as Grabher (2002) found in his study of British advertising agencies. The responsiveness required for the flexibility and adaptability of work puts new pressures on employees, thrusting a "large number [of people] into a condition of permanent survival-oriented tension" in "unfettered" organizations within an information-intensive economy (Child & McGrath, 2001).

But this permanently beta ethic of continual change can be thought of, borrowing from Max Weber, as a key influence on the spirit of the information economy. Consider the following "manifesto" written by a Web design company during the spring of 1997:

> For better or worse, we have decided to enter into an industry that does not make things that enjoy a spatial or temporal existence. . . . *Since the world is in constant flux, any work that is truly integrated into its environment can never be viewed as a finished entity,* but rather a point in an ongoing dialectical process. . . . Our approach is not about design in any traditional sense. Instead, we make work that may be adapted to people's differing needs and contexts. *Internally, we must practice what we preach.* . . . Through the open design of both our physical and electronic environments, we will foster the exchange of information between our employees and allow them to share ideas and engage in critical dialogue.[4] (emphasis added)

Besides the fact that a company—especially one that has produced major Web sites for blue-chip clients such as Motorola and Sony—would even issue a manifesto, there are three aspects of change and adaptability that are well worth noting. First, this manifesto assumes ongoing instability both in internet design and in the larger environment around that design. Second, the manifesto challenges a traditional sense of design that believes in a final product that is neither responsive to its users nor adaptable in its use. Finally, this particular dot-com wants to "practice" internally what it preaches by encouraging the openness of organizational forms within the company. Just as Weber understood the rise of Protestantism linked inexorably to the rise of capitalism, this manifesto proclaims an almost religious belief in "constant flux" that is occurring alongside a digital reformation of capitalism.[5]

Three aspects of applications design—beta testing, encoded responsiveness, and community development—illustrate how permanently beta organizational structures emerge alongside older organizational forms.

Never Leaving the Beta Phase

Permanently beta encompasses the social implications of continual technological change and is, of course, a play on the term for software testing. Software and internet sites that are being tested are called *beta versions,* and strictly speaking, permanently beta would be a product that never leaves the test phase. The internet makes it possible to distribute products that are continually updateable and almost infinitely customizable—products that, in effect, never leave a type of beta phase.

According to Techweb's *TechEncyclopedia,* a beta version is "a pre-shipping release of hardware or software that has gone through [an] alpha test." It is "supposed to be very close to the final product, but in practice, it is more a way of getting users to test the software . . . under real conditions." Rather than duplicate "the myriad of configurations that exist in the real world," beta tests expose software to those conditions and users.[6] According to CambridgeSoft, a company that makes software for life sciences research, the benefits to beta testers include getting a look at the new features before anyone else does, the "pleasure" of finding unsuspected bugs, making the software better as a result of detecting those bugs, and perhaps affecting the company's future direction of development through beta testers' suggestions.[7]

Beta testing is not without risks: CambridgeSoft states that it "pretty much guarantee[s] that you will receive buggy software" that "may crash your computer (or worse)." Being one of the first to have a new application, experiencing the "pleasure" of debugging, and becoming involved in "your!" software development, as well as the possibility of free or cheaper software, outweigh these risks for many. More than 2 million people volunteered to be one of the 20,000 beta testers for the new version of Napster (Ross, 2002). Although Apple's "public beta" release of OS X, its first completely new operating system since 1984, cost $29.95, thousands downloaded it despite reports that it was still quite "buggy" and the fact that little compatible software was available. Beta users saw the long-awaited new operating system 6 months before its first commercial release, and Steve Jobs, Apple's chief executive officer, thanked them in advance by saying, "We're excited to have our users test drive this public beta version and provide us with their valuable feedback."[8] Apple fans and the press provided invaluable buzz about OS X as they tested it. Beta may still have bugs, but beta testers are among the first outside of a company to have the new product.

A typical nomenclature denotes beta versions. Dyson (1997) explained the numbering of beta versions and continually updated versions in her book, *Release 2.0:*

The very title of this book embodies the concept of flexibility and learning from errors: In the software business, "Release 1.0" is the first commercial version of a new product, following test versions called 0.5, 0.8, 0.9, 0.91, 0.92. It's fresh and new, the realization of the hopes and dreams of its developers. It embodies new ideas, and it is supposed to be perfect. Usually the vender comes out with Release 1.1 a few months later, fixing unexpected bugs and tidying up loose ends. . . . Release 2.0 is a total rewrite, hammered out by older, wiser programmers with feedback from thousands of tough-minded, skeptical users. Release 2.0 is supposed to be perfect, but usually Release 2.1 comes out a few months later. (p. 5, emphasis added)[9]

Commercial products do eventually leave the beta stage in "shrink-wrap" or as purchasable products for consumers. The quote from Dyson, however, points to software development's never-ending cycles of innovation, real-world testing, feedback, and revision, a cycle that is much shorter than that in manufacturing design but longer than that in Web site development. The internet is compressing this cycle to the extent that, as suggested by Garud, Jain, and Phelps (n.d.), "it is difficult to distinguish between one product generation and the next" (p. 3). They examined the releases of Netscape, which had 39 beta versions between the beta stage of Navigator 1.0 and the release of Communicator 4.0. In the words of Marc Andreesen, the founder of Netscape, the philosophy behind so many beta releases was to "kick it out the door. It may not even work reliably. . . . [but] go out and get feedback. . . . [Customers] will tell you, often in no uncertain terms, what's wrong with it and what needs to be improved" (quoted in Garud et al., n.d., p. 14). Andreesen's attitude toward building software that could rapidly integrate user response into the design—not simply the number of beta versions—made the early days of Netscape permanently beta.

Netscape risked the reliability of its product for increased responsiveness to its users. However, beta testing does not always incorporate users into the design process or treat users as a community with a stake in the outcome of the product. In fact, several large software makers are known for their hierarchical organization and rigid divisions between product design and product testing. Although users' participation in design and redesign of products may be limited in practice, beta testing as a process provides a model for how to involve users more fully in products' design cycles. *Permanently beta* as a phrase highlights this aspect of product variability during the internet era and the impact of that variability on the line between users and producers.

Encoded Responsiveness

Permanently beta forms also emerge where responsiveness is designed into products and organizations. Continual testing is one way in which to incorporate user response, but responsiveness can be encoded into products and organizations in other ways.

Open source projects are one such example where the line between users and producers of a product is blurred. Open source projects are a hodgepodge of formal and informal organization; for-profit and volunteer organizational goals, processes, and values; and hierarchical and heterarchial modes of organizing. In a now classic essay on open source, *The Cathedral and the Bazaar,* Raymond (1999) described Linus Torvald's management of the development of the operating system Linux. Raymond pointed to two key aspects of open source philosophy that challenge traditional models of software engineering: "release early and often" (p. 38) and "all bugs are shallow with enough eyes" (p. 41). At one point in the evolution of Linux, a new kernel (the most fundamental part of an operating system) was released *daily.* So long as the volunteers examining the code could see that their input mattered, they would keep testing it, pushing the project to its limits and ensuring that the code was sound. Bugs, the inevitable glitches in any programming project, could best be eliminated not through the attempts of a few people to release flawless software but rather through the efforts of many to examine software in use, identify problems, propose fixes, and watch carefully to ensure that good ideas are implemented. Treat the users of a program as codevelopers, Raymond argued, and they will act like codevelopers. Raymond's cathedrals and bazaars describe more than an approach to debugging software. Responsiveness to users in the design of products has the power to influence organizational form.

When a user downloads a version of Mozilla, an open source and community-developed[10] internet browser, the user is greeted with the following friendly message:

> Congratulations! You've downloaded a Mozilla build. This means that you've volunteered to become part of the Mozilla testing community. Great! Welcome aboard. Helping out won't take much of your time, doesn't require special skills, and will help improve Mozilla.[11]

Mozilla was the original code name for the product that became known as Netscape Navigator.[12] Mozilla.org, the main coordinating group of Mozilla source code, is a nonprofit organization that began under the aegis of Netscape to develop the source code on which its products were based. Mozilla has now grown into its own open source program, quasi-autonomously of Netscape, and at the time of this writing it was releasing beta versions of an internet browser.[13] According to its mission statement, the Mozilla organization provides the technical and architectural direction for the Mozilla project, synchronization of the releases of the browser and code, coordination of the discussion forums, and "roadmaps" to help organize projects based on the code. However, "We are *not* the primary coders. Most of the code that goes into the distribution will be written elsewhere, both within the Netscape Client Engineering group, and increasingly, *out there* on the net, at other companies and other development organizations" (emphasis added).[14] Just as those testing Mozilla are part of a community, so too are those who actually do the work of developing the code for a new browser, and the organization exists primarily to coordinate these independent programmers. To that end, Mozilla.org promises that it will, above all, "be flexible and responsive. We realize that if we are not perceived as providing a useful service, we will become irrelevant, and someone else will take our place."[15] Without responsiveness, the organization would become irrelevant to the community of volunteers organized around developing the code, but without some form of coordination, the project would not have developed into a fully usable Web browser.

Thus, a key aspect of permanently beta is the practice of *design-in-use*, in which products are formed by their use, not simply in their design. Open source projects, for example, display a responsiveness that has allowed users of products to be more directly involved in the design-in-use of these products. Open source models also challenge the traditional notion of boundaries between organizational forms in that they often have more in common with social movements than with traditional formal organizations. O'Mahony (2002) argued that the processes of conflict and compromise in open source projects explain the synthesis of old and new institutional elements into emergent new organizational forms (p. viii). Open source projects combine these elements of organization from community and commerce into a new hybrid organizational form.

Open source projects are not necessarily permanently beta, but they often provide a good example of what von Hippel (2001) called "user innovation communities" (p. 82). These communities are not just in software and hardware production. Von Hippel described the user innovations in high-performance windsurfing, where windsurfers testing out innovations on the open beach share them with each other and ultimately with equipment manufacturers (p. 85). The internet can be an open beach of sorts, with users able to "see" one another online and share innovations. Permanently beta organizational forms arise when user innovation communities overcome the "stickiness" of innovation transfer back into the manufacturing or production process. This occurs in user-produced projects where there is "product development without manufacturers" (p. 82), but it also can occur in settings where user feedback is more fully integrated into the design process. By shortening the cycle of feedback and reengineering, creating reputational benefits for users who innovate, and fostering communities around innovation, the internet strengthens these feedback loops and reinforces the process of continual updating.[16] Responsiveness becomes encoded into software products.

Just as the internet lowers the costs of cooperation in user innovation communities, it can also help to overcome the difficulties of transferring those innovations back to the manufacturer in industries other than software. Users "consume, modify, domesticate, design, reconfigure, and resist technologies," and through this process they shape and are shaped by those technologies (Oudshoorn & Pinch, in press). The "working relations of production," as Suchman (2002) termed it, is an "increasingly dense and differentiated layering of people, activities, and things, each operating within a limited sphere of knowing and acting that includes variously crude or sophisticated conceptualizations of the others." However, the interactions between users and technology occur most often in private settings where users are separated from the producers, unlike the more open, visible, and public interactions with technology that can occur online (Boczkowski, 2001). Permanently beta organizations emerge when the institutional barriers to user involvement in the design process are overcome, and the internet and other interactive tools can facilitate this involvement. Open source communities provide such examples of users becoming producers, but other kinds of community building online can bring users into the production process.

Community Development

Increasingly, commercial internet sites interested in creating "community" are learning that design-in-use instead of top-down design is the best way in which to recruit and maintain users. For a project on work in Manhattan's "Silicon Alley," one of us (David Stark) conducted field research at a company that developed an internet community and e-commerce site.[17] BetaTeen.com (a pseudonym) began as a content-driven online magazine trying to become "America's online high school newspaper."[18] In its original business model, BetaTeen created a youth community for commercial access. As young people came onto the site for the news and entertainment that editors and writers considered relevant, the teens would provide a targeted demographic group for marketing and focus research.

The teen users staged a minor revolt, getting involved in the design-in-use in several ways. First, by tracking how teens used the site, the editors found that teens were more likely to read essays by other teens, and a user-as-producer model of content emerged. As more teens participated in creating the content on the site, traffic increased. BetaTeen's executive vice president explained, "We don't have people sitting around thinking, 'What do teens want?' It doesn't work. Even if you could figure it out, it wouldn't last. You can try to write for them, but it doesn't work. Now, 95% of our content is written by teens themselves." The teens "want to give their opinions" and "want to be in the spotlight," and BetaTeen tries to give them a sense of both. Referring to the teens, the executive vice president said, "*They* own BetaTeen. We just put up the framework." Second, the teens themselves began making demands of the editors to be allowed greater interactivity on the site, more control over the commercial use of information about themselves, and the ability to refuse to be "marketing guinea pigs" for the company. The original intent, according to BetaTeen's executive vice president, was as follows: "We know best. We create the stuff; you use it." But interactivity demanded a responsiveness on the part of BetaTeen to its users' demands and the integration of users into the process of content production. The design of the "product"—from long essays to short, chat-driven, user-written opinions—incorporated the demands of those who used it.

Boczkowski (2001) identified this new form of media production as "distributed construction," which emerges from an information architecture that inscribes users as "co-constructors" of content, a network of multidirectional flows of messages across the medium, and content production characterized by "relationships of interdependence, distributed authority, and multiple rationalities" (p. 30). The interactivity of online communication can create communities that can exist quasi-independently and transparently from manufacturer or producer control. As on BetaTeen, a company can build a framework in which users find each other but then can ultimately communicate independently of it. Once BetaTeen users see one another online, they no longer necessarily need BetaTeen to connect them. Users of nearly any product can find each other to share ideas, talk about product use, or organize to make demands of the manufacturer (such demands are more easily communicated back to the producer through the current structure of the medium). This openness in communication design creates the possibility for permanently beta structures.

Creating community in commercial settings does not guarantee permanently beta organizations. Community values and commercial values are often at odds, but as Epstein (1995, 1997) wrote about the community of AIDS activists and their clashes with pharmaceutical companies, these differences in values can sometimes produce negotiations toward a mutual goal. AIDS activists wanted wider access to health care, including experimental new drug treatments, whereas companies wanted to design and market new for-profit drug treatments. Although two sides' negotiations did not make drug companies community oriented, changes in the approval process did incorporate many of the users' demands. In many traditional settings, users might not have the same goals as those who design the products, and beta testers might not consider themselves part of the same community as software engineers (and vice versa). We call these "practicing communities," which link organized users with professional expertise so as to inform the design process. In a practicing community, an organized group of users become acknowledged as experts in how products are used and can sometimes realize this power to influence design.[19] From product design to organizational design, permanently beta settings have this potential to be participatory.

Architecture in Code

These permanently beta examples point to a process that might be called *collaborative engineering*. Although typically referring to the relationship among producers and not between producers and users, collaborative engineering is "a discursive pragmatics" that allows for the organization of rivalrous logics, values, and organizational principles (Girard & Stark, 2002, p. 1929). Sabel and Dorf (1998) referred to the process of *simultaneous engineering*, a concurrent design process by which separate teams develop different proposals for the final design. Permanently beta is, in part, a form of simultaneous and collaborative design and engineering that brings users into the process. Software beta testers want a first look at new versions of software, whereas software companies need their experience to help determine, with little or no pay (and in the case of Apple, at a *cost* to the testers themselves), the quality of the software. The BetaTeen users want the spotlight on their stories, whereas the BetaTeen editors need teens to visit the site to support e-commerce and marketing functions that make money. Each of these examples points to different sets of values along a divide, and in each of the examples, those who use the software, read the content, or test for bugs gain some voice in the design process. These are not examples of competing companies vying for a contract through simultaneous engineering codes or of subcontractors working under collaborative organizational principles. The various actors in permanently beta settings, however, hold disparate values and principles that must be negotiated in a similar manner.

Through these testing forms, experimentation, and negotiation, values are incorporated into the design of the products themselves. Permanently beta forms produce products that are negotiations in themselves, like the multiple versions of software with its subsequent multiple betas, release versions, and patches. The design process is considered as ongoing rather than as having a final end point in that each of those releases offers an opportunity to go back and incorporate options or fixes left out previously. Bringing users into the design and testing involves a genuine interaction with the users, not an attitude of "we know best," to recall the words of BetaTeen's executive vice president. Table 11.1 summarizes the differences between permanently beta and traditional approaches to design. Permanently beta forms necessarily leave things out to be completed by the users and are like architected designs that are left partially open to the interpretation of the engineered execution. Practicing communities are enabled in permanently beta situations to link lay knowledge to expertise, constant change to responsiveness, users to producers, and buyers to manufacturers.

The internet allows us to see permanently beta in action and to become accustomed to its rhythms. The Web, at least at this juncture in its history, is quite an unstable place; Web sites die, disappear, and are modified in a flash. More important, the internet facilitates users being a part of that continual updating. Web sites such as Plastic.com and Slashdot.com recycle "the Web in real time" (as Plastic says on its site), manifesting a permanently beta approach to news. Users of these services continually update the news, not with new reporting but rather by catching the "bugs" in published media reports, drawing connections between stories, and appending their own commentaries and analyses onto circulating stories. Digital media allow this bricolage to be formed out of the pieces found online, forming a permanently beta news that is constantly updated, analyzed, reconfigured, and tested by nonreporters.

Table 11.1   Permanently Beta Design Versus Traditional Design

	Permanently Beta Design Process	Traditional Design Process
Product	Multiple versions	End product
Design process	Design-in-process	Design with a user in mind
Use	Interactive; flexible and adaptable	User-friendly; easy to use but inflexible
Conception of user	User as designer	User as consumer
Communication of user	Consciously voiced preferences	Revealed preferences
Community metaphor	Practicing communities	Professional expertise; isolated users
Model of use	Participation	Consumption
Computer metaphor	Adaptability	Usability

Users of permanently beta products may also find the experience to be frustrating. Products are not final, clean end versions but rather are destabilized, constantly changing products. Users of computer software understand the continuous updating of applications; those who have experienced the "bugginess" of new versions understand all too well the downside of continual change. Having to reconfigure ever-changing products is part of what Terranova (2000) termed "extraction of value out of continuous, updateable work" that exploits the "free labor" of users in a digital economy (p. 48).

The "new economy," too, has shown us how quickly economic experimentation can end. Real jobs were lost just as quickly as stock option millionaires were created. Digital landscapes are much faster than our physical ones, as Girard and Stark (2002) pointed out about sites that have closed: "An abandoned warehouse is a boarded-up blight on the landscape until it is destroyed or gentrified into luxury apartments. An abandoned Web site is a Code 404, 'File Not Found'" (p. 1947). Although many innovative start-ups of Silicon Alley and Silicon Valley pushed organizational logics to their brink, those involved felt just that—*involved.* One veteran of Silicon Alley felt that he was creating "the freest medium around" (Neff, 2003).[20] For many of these start-ups, the new economy boom meant that they were involved in the design of their companies—creating new kinds of work, new ways of collaborating, and new ways of relating their jobs to their lives—as much as they were involved in creating new products. Not everyone was so lucky. Income inequality grew in the United States as the internet revolution was taking place, and during the latest economic boom more jobs were created in low-end service work—where employees often have no autonomy or voice in how their work is organized—than in high-end knowledge work. As silicon mavericks were testing their sites, their organizations, and themselves, other people were forced to adapt to an economy where the rules were rapidly becoming less favorable to them.[21]

If, as has been said, architecture is politics set in stone, then information architecture is politics in code. Code is not set in stone as buildings literally are, but is it as mutable as we would like to think? Code's rigidities, including path dependencies and legacies in both technological and social systems, shape what can come next. The values embedded in code at one point become the structuring factors of future development. These values are not mutable simply because of continual technical change, nor are the values in code necessarily good or bad because they have a political valence. Technological artifacts such as codes have values, and as a society we can either actively engage in the negotiations around these values or choose imprudently to ignore them.

There are no guarantees, however, that this process of negotiation over encoded values will lead to a settlement on a single value or strategy. Several scholars have outlined how multiple rationalities of production can exist simultaneously, often without mutual comprehension between those with coexisting values (Boczkowski, 2001; Galison, 1997; Star & Griesemer, 1989; Stark, 1999). Nor are innovation and creativity in "practice" necessarily integrated into the organizational process (Brown & Duguid, 2001, p. 93). Permanently beta structures show how users and producers can actively shape the technology around them. These new economic and organizational structures can be tested and negotiated, and they may prove ultimately to be more inclusive. The lack of settlement on a single path in permanently beta settings can be confusing, frustrating, or worse. Permanently beta affords the possibility of influencing which values are encoded into organizations and technologies—and for users to incorporate *their* values into the structures around them.

Notes

1. See Thrift (2001b) for more on software code's passion for inscription.
2. Galloway's (2001) dissertation is one of the first we know of that used computer protocols as its literary texts.
3. Indeed, the name of one program, *Apache,* is a play on the patches that programmers use to smooth out software. For more on *Apache* and other open source projects, see Kogut and Metiu (2001).
4. See www.plumbdesign.com/manifesto.

5. We are not the first to borrow from Weber to make a point about a new spirit of capitalism. Our analogy owes much to the theory laid out in both Castells's (2000) trilogy, *The Rise of the Network Society,* and Boltanski Chiapello's (1999) book, *Le Nouvel Esprit du Capitalisme.*

6. See www.techweb.com/encyclopedia.

7. See www.cambridgesoft.com/about/betatesting.cfm.

8. A press release is available at www.apple.com/pr/library/2000/sep/13macosx.html.

9. Dyson's *Release 2.1,* the paperback version of the book, came out in October 1998.

10. O'Mahony (2002) pointed out the difference between source code being open and community development of software. Several, but not all, open source projects are community developed, and Mozilla and Linux are two examples of community-developed open source projects.

11. See www.mozilla.org/start.

12. Mozilla stands for the "Mosaic Killer" or the application that would replace Mosaic, the first graphical interface application for the internet.

13. Mozilla can be downloaded for use at www.mozilla.org. Mozilla's first "release" was in June 2002.

14. See the Mozilla.org mission statement at www.mozilla.org/mission.html.

15. Again, see the Mozilla.org mission statement at www.mozilla.org/mission.html.

16. Kollock (1999), in his now classic essay on online cooperation, identified these mechanisms as supporting exchange online.

17. For more on this research project area in general, see Girard and Stark (2002).

18. All quotes about BetaTeen are cited directly from field notes and from interviews with BetaTeen management.

19. Changes in product design can influence organizational structure, as Epstein (1995, 1997) noted in the case of the AIDS drug approval process changing the organization of the Food and Drug Administration.

20. This quote is taken from an interview transcript for Neff's research on uncertainty in Silicon Alley with the editor of an online division of a major publishing house in 1997.

21. See Smith (2001) for more on worker adaptation within the new economy. See Thrift (2001a) for more on the rhetorical strategies of finance that enabled the technological boom of the late 1990s to even occur.

References

Boczkowski, P. (2001). *Affording flexibility: Transforming information practices in online newspapers.* Unpublished doctoral dissertation, Cornell University.

Boltanski, L., & Chiapello, E. (1999). *Le Nouvel Esprit du Capitalisme.* Paris: Éditions Gallimard.

Brown, J. S., & Duguid, P. (2001). Creativity versus structure: A useful tension. *MIT Sloan Management Review, 42*(4), 93–95.

Castells, M. (2000). *The rise of the network society* (2nd ed.). Oxford, UK: Blackwell.

Child, J., & McGrath, R. G. (2001). Organizations unfettered: Organizational form in an information-intensive economy. *Academy of Management Journal, 44,* 1135–1148.

Dyson, E. (1997). *Release 2.0: A design for living in the digital age.* New York: Broadway Books.

Epstein, S. (1995). The construction of lay expertise: AIDS activism and the forging of credibility in the reform of clinical trials. *Science, Technology, & Human Values, 20,* 408–437.

Epstein, S. (1997). Activism, drug regulation, and the politics of therapeutic evaluation in the AIDS era. *Social Studies of Science, 27,* 691–726.

Galison, P. (1997). *Image and logic: A material culture of microphysics.* Chicago: University of Chicago Press.

Galloway, A. (2001). *Protocol: Or, how control exists after decentralization.* Ph.D. dissertation, Duke University.

Garud, R., Jain, S., & Phelps, C. (n.d.). *Unpacking internet time innovation.* Unpublished manuscript, New York University.

Girard, M., & Stark, D. (2002). Distributing intelligence and organizing diversity in new media projects. *Environment and Planning A, 34,* 1927–1949.

Grabher, G. (2002). The project ecology of advertising: Tasks, talents, and teams. *Regional Studies, 36,* 245–262.

Kogut, B., & Metiu, A. (2001). Open source software development and distributed innovation. *Oxford Review of Economic Policy, 17,* 248–264.

Kollock, P. (1999). The economies of online cooperation: Gifts and public goods in cyberspace. In M. A. Smith & P. Kollock (Eds.), *Communities in cyberspace* (pp. 220–242). London: Routledge.

Kunda, G., & Van Mannen, J. (1999). Changing scripts at work: Managers and professionals. *Annals of the American Academy of Political and Social Science, 561,* 64–80.

Manovich, L. (2001). *The language of new media.* Cambridge, MA: MIT Press.

Neff, G. (2003). *Organizing uncertainty in Silicon Alley: Work and entrepreneurialism in New York's internet industry, 1995–2000.* Unpublished manuscript, Columbia University.

O'Mahony, S. (2002). *The emergence of a new commercial actor: Community managed software projects.* Unpublished doctoral dissertation, Stanford University.

Oudshoorn, N., & Pinch, T. (in press). Introduction. In N. Oudshoorn & T. Pinch (Eds.), *How users matter: The co-construction of users and technologies.* Cambridge, MA: MIT Press.

Raymond, E. (1999). *The cathedral and the bazaar: Musings on Linux and open source from an accidental revolutionary.* Sebastapol, CA: O'Reilly & Associates.

Ross, R. (2002, January 11). Born-again Napster takes baby steps. *Toronto Star,* p. E-4.

Sabel, C. F., & Dorf, M. C. (1998). A constitution of democratic experimentalism. *Columbia Law Review, 98*(2), 267–529.

Smith, V. (2001). *Crossing the great divide.* Ithaca, NY: Cornell University Press.

Star, S. L., & Griesemer, J. R. (1989). Institutional ecology, "translations," and boundary objects: Amateurs and professionals in Berkeley's Museum of Vertebrate Zoology, 1907–39. *Social Studies of Science, 19,* 387–420.

Stark, D. (1999). Heterarchy: Distributing intelligence and organizing diversity. In J. Clippinger (Ed.), *The biology of business: Decoding the natural laws of enterprise* (pp. 153–179). San Francisco: Jossey-Bass.

Suchman, L. (2002). *Located accountabilities in technology production.* Unpublished manuscript, Lancaster University. Retrieved April 27, 2003, from www.comp.lancs.ac.uk/sociology/soc039ls.html

Terranova, T. (2000). Free labor: Producing culture for the digital economy. *Social Text, 18*(2), 33–58.

Thrift, N. (2001a). "It's the romance not the finance that makes the business worth pursuing": Disclosing a new market culture. *Economy & Society, 30,* 412–432.

Thrift, N. (2001b, February). *Software writing cities.* Address given at the Taub Urban Research Center, New York University.

von Hippel, E. (2001). Innovation by user communities: Learning from open-source software. *Sloan Management Review, 42*(4), 82–86.

12

Art Versus Code

The Gendered
Evolution of Web Design Skills

Nalini P. Kotamraju
University of California, Berkeley

Productopia was one of the first highly visible dot-com companies in the San Francisco Bay Area to close its doors. Soon after, others came toppling down like dominoes. (The tribulations of many of these dot-com companies were chronicled by former employees on Fuckedcompany.com.) Web design power-houses and boutiques announced layoffs. As unemployment rose, San Francisco Bay Area newspapers ran articles about the high number of former dot-com employees who were cluttering neighborhood cafés and nursing single lattes for hours while working on their resumés. As what Americans saw as the "irrational exuberance" of the dot-com boom sputtered out, many Bay Area internet work-ers, with advanced degrees and salaries upward of $50,000 per year, found them-selves with worthless stock options issued by defunct companies and, more shockingly, without what they—and the market—saw as profitable skills. Among the hardest hit, as the *San Francisco Chronicle* noted, were those who called themselves Web designers.

This chapter traces how Web site design skills developed before, during, and after the heyday of dot-com companies in the San Francisco Bay Area. According to previous sociological research, as occupations evolve, they often specialize, making a more narrowly defined range of tasks their exclusive territory (Abbott, 1988). Tasks that are too complex or time-consuming for one person to perform efficiently become smaller tasks. However, we do not know nearly enough about how specialization actually happens, that is, how a skill gets broken up into smaller units and who gets assigned to each of the units. Although the technological logic of a task, of course, influences some of these decisions, we also know from science and technology studies that technological logics are inseparable from social structures. Therefore, I argue that the case of Web design skills illustrates how preexisting social cleavages may also dictate, to a degree that has been underestimated previously, the path of specialization. Examining the evolution of Web design skills before, during, and after the dot-com boom reveals just how convoluted and contested the specialization process turns out to be.

Sociologists who study professions and occupations have fairly established narratives about the process of specialization, usually following Weber's emphasis on rationalization as a key feature of modern capitalist society. Licensing boards and membership associations are just some of the professional institutions that may arise to regulate skills, designating which kind of people with which kind of backgrounds can be said, with any legitimacy, to possess a given expertise. In other instances, formal educational requirements may be introduced, ensuring that all members of a profession will have had the same pedagogical experience and acquired expertise.

The processes of rationalization are so closely tied with our understanding of modern capitalism that we often take it for granted that specialization is an inevitable, if sometimes regrettable, feature of work life. Adam Smith described this process, in *An Inquiry Into the Nature and Causes of the Wealth of Nations*, with his famous description of a pin maker's labor: "One man draws out the wire, another straights it, a third cuts it, a fourth points it, a fifth grinds it at the top" (Smith, 1776/1976, p. 15). Subdividing one task and codifying the skills needed for each subdivided portion is a powerful way in which to rationalize a work process. However, skill's tendency to specialize is not nearly as straightforward and inexorable as sociological accounts since Smith's may imply. Accounts of specialization processes, particularly those based in manufacturing, tend to present the process of specialization as self-evident—not only that skills will specialize but also that the decision that one person should straighten the wire and another person should cut it, not to mention who gets assigned to each task, seems so logical. What my research suggests is that we need to know more about the separation between the task of straightening and the task of cutting, not to mention how people get assigned to and compensated for each one of those tasks.

The data for this research come from a systematic ethnography and an analysis of historical-archival material. As part of the ethnographic endeavor, I spent 5 years working in various capacities (but never as a Web designer) at various dot-com companies: Productopia (an online consumer product magazine), Phoenix Pop (a multimedia design firm), and Liquid Thinking (an e-services firm). My main historical-archival data source is a sample of newspaper classified job advertisements that I assembled as well as other industry resources such as magazines and listservs. Expanding on my earlier findings (Kotamraju, 2002), I identify three distinct phases of Web design skills evolution: a fusion of art and code, a bifurcation of art and code, and the dominance of code over art. Conceptualizing Web design skills in terms of stages permits an analysis of a Web design skill set that integrates historical and technological context, taking into account, for example, that the Web design skill set of the internet boom looked very different from the Web design skill set of the internet crash and that the popularity of particular programming languages (e.g., Java) influenced the skill set.

Stage 1: Art and Code Fusion, 1993–1996: Pre-Boom Internet Economy

The early years of the Web were a heady time, and the skill set mirrored this sensibility. During this era, with the exception of a few visionaries, no one imagined how revolutionary the Web (and the internet) would be and with what speed and power it would transform so many aspects of our lives. This sense of opportunity, what some insiders think of as "the internet before the MBAs took over," characterized the Web design skill set. During these years, the Web design skill set was not an established domain of knowledge, largely because the technology on which it was based was new and turbulent. Consequently, both employers and skill practitioners experimented with what constituted Web design skills, much as they experimented with the Web and the internet (see Table 12.1).

The Web design skill set, during these formative years, was a largely amorphous set of proficiencies to which many college-educated people could lay claim. The pioneers of Web design, the very first people who created the World Wide Web, were a small elite group of people, largely engineers, academics, and some social activists. However, as the Web diffused, more and more institutions and companies began to look for people who could build Web sites. Because the technology was new, both employers and employees fumbled with the idea of what it took to create a Web site. For example, my first exposure to creating a Web site took place at the not-for-profit organization at which I worked just before graduate school. My supervisor tasked me with figuring out how the organization

Table 12.1   Web Design Skills

Phase	Years	Internet Economy
Phase 1: Art and code fusion	1993–1996	Pre-boom
Phase 2: Art and code bifurcation	1997–1999	Boom
Phase 3: Domination of code over art	2000 onward	Post-boom

could use the internet to spread its message, largely because I was comfortable with several computer software programs. The first experience of creating Web sites for many of the people I interviewed had similar contours. Some, of course, had been heavily involved with computer programming before turning their attention to the Web. Others, such as the founder of a successful Web design company who had created a new font as his undergraduate senior honors thesis, had been working in graphic design. For still many others, at least in their own words, a high comfort level with computers and an ability to learn new skills are what allowed them to create their first Web sites. Some familiarity with computers was essential, but what is striking about my observations of this early period is the number of people who were building their skill sets as they went. As a Web producer at Hotwired.com told me, they were "just winging it."

The advertisements for job positions during this period suggested the skills necessary to "wing it" as a Web site designer. Positions for Web expertise ran in sections as diverse as "computer," "graphic," "programming," "multimedia," "publishing," and "art." During these years, an employer seeking someone with Web design skills could reasonably ask for expertise in areas as diverse as UNIX, proofreading, SQL, HTML, graphic design, and Photoshop. At that time, simply putting the word "Web" or "internet" in the job title or description was enough to attract people who saw themselves as having something akin to Web design skills or who were interested enough to get them. Similarly, a September 1995 job advertisement in the *San Francisco Chronicle* sought graphic designers with experience in "worldwide web pages etc." The advertisement did not specify what skills such a graphic designer should have. Would the ideal skill set include knowledge of HTML, understanding the principles of visual design, the ability to run scripts on a Web server, or a combination of all of these?

Defining Web design skills so ambiguously was an excellent, and maybe the best, strategy for responding to the burgeoning demand for Web designers. In 1995 and 1996, when major companies were exploring whether they needed to "get a Web site" (Girard & Stark, 2002), the prospect for Web design work seemed limitless and experienced while skilled workers were remarkably few in number. In part, the lack of skilled workers prompted many Web design companies to hire the first generation of workers who had grown up with computers on which they played games and wrote term papers but who might not have known much else about the world of computers, much less about the internet. Coupled with this intense demand was the perception that this kind of position was a "'cool job' in a 'hot' industry" (Neff, Wissinger, & Zukin, 2001).

It makes no sense to think of art and code as separate areas within the Web design skill set during this early period. The distinction has very little relevance because Web site deign, as we experience it now, did not exist at that time. The Web sites of the pre-boom era—drab affairs involving black text on gray backgrounds with perhaps one digital image and a few graphic elements—bore little resemblance to the sophisticated, elaborately designed Web sites of today. Similarly, the Web design skill set of the pre-boom era, a polyglot of proficiencies, bore little resemblance to the Web design skill set that would flourish during the dot-com boom.

Stage 2: Art and Code Bifurcation, 1997–1999: Boom Internet Economy

Whereas during the early to mid-1990s employers looked for workers who knew something—anything—about the Web, by the end of the 1990s, both employers and employees had reached more of a consensus about what constituted the Web design skill set. As Web design continued to evolve, the "art" aspects of the skill set (e.g., relying on visual design techniques, emphasizing user interface, using graphic software programs such as Photoshop) began to separate from the "code" aspects of the skill set (e.g., building back end databases, writing JavaScript code and scripts).

Advertisements for job positions clearly began to ask for experience in one of these two camps, either Web design or Web development, marking the first strong signs of specialization. Web developer positions typically appeared under the heading of "computer" or "programming" in *San Francisco Chronicle* classifieds in 1997 and asked for skills such as "CGI, PERL, HTML" or "Oracle, C++". Web designer positions, on the other hand, tended to run under the heading of "graphic design" and called for skills such as "to review materials, generate concepts and designs, and control the quality of Web art" or "the ability to communicate design concepts to clients and technical team."

The case of Web design makes it very clear that this split follows the line of preexisting concepts of a division between serious and frivolous as well as assumptions about what kinds of people perform which kinds of tasks. The graphic designers ("design/layout"), with the exception of the stars in the field, were largely women and more lowly paid in the hierarchy, with an average salary of $46,734 in 1999. Programmers, generally men, earned average yearly salaries of $72,503 ("software development") and $56,931 ("Web interface systems") in 1999 (Association of Internet Professionals, 1999). This bifurcation of art and code is significant because it dispels the prevailing idea that specialization is somehow a neutral process, subject to a logic of either the impartial free market or objective technological requirements.

In the case of Web design, the perception that visual design is about "making things look pretty" and that code is about "making things work" prevails in the industry to some degree or another, according to my research. During a stint as a user experience researcher in an e-services firm, I attended a typical production meeting about the "refresh" of a Web site of a client that wanted to be able to process orders by credit card on its site. Six people attended this internal meeting: the male project manager, a female Web designer, a male graphic designer, a male lead software engineer, a male software engineer, and a female user researcher (me). Like employees at many new media firms, everyone at this meeting was juggling several projects. Still, the client wanted the new features in an impossibly short amount of time. The engineers and designers engaged in the rather typical tug-of-war between how much project time should be spent on the user interface design and how much time should be spent on the credit card–related database and encryption technology. Toward the end of the skirmish, the exasperated male software engineer blurted out, "If I don't get the time to make it work, it doesn't matter what it looks like." The engineer's statement argued for the primacy of what he saw as making the site work over what he saw as window dressing, that is, the visual design of the site. I regularly saw manifestations of this privileging of code over art, but never as cogently expressed as in this meeting.

The specialization of the murkily defined Web design skill set into art expertise and code expertise is a story in which technology and social cleavages are inextricably linked. What became very apparent in the team meeting was that the engineering and design teams saw different technological objects. The engineer, from his position "close to the machine" (Ullman, 1997), viewed the back end of the site—the database and the code for encryption—as the technology that needed to "work." The designers, on the other hand, thought the technological object was the Web site. As I quipped later with the design team, however, if the users could not easily find the box on the screen to input their credit card numbers, the site would not really "work" either.

This relegation of work performed by women as superficial or as concerned only with appearances is familiar territory. We know that "jobs have 'gender' labels and are part of a broader gender system which is both structural and symbolic" (Webster, 1996, p. 180). For example, Cockburn and Ormrod (1993), in their investigation of microwave design and manufacture during the mid-1990s in Britain, found that in the mostly male microwave manufacturing company, "it was suggested that any difference home economists were permitted to make to microwave oven design was cosmetic" (p. 92). We see a familiar pattern in which the devaluation of skills is reinforced by the fact that it is women who tend to possess the skills.

The narratives of specialization often suggest that as tasks become more complex or take more time, breaking them into smaller components is the rational process to remain effective and competitive with other companies. For example, Abbott (1988) wrote that "specialization most commonly arises because the skills applicable to a given task area develop beyond the ability of single practitioners" (p. 106). The technology of Web design did indeed require this kind of task subdivision. Constructing and maintaining a commercially viable Web site expanded beyond the expertise and ability of single practitioners, those who years before would have responded to any job description with the word "Web" in it. However, the fact that the technology evolved and specialized along gender lines reflected assumptions about what kinds of people do which kinds of work, as well as the economic and cultural value of that work, and serves as a warning that specialization is not necessarily the technically neutral process that is often implied.

Stage 3: Post-Boom, 2000–2001: Domination of Code Over Art

On the morning of Monday, October 2, 2002, the chief executive officer of Productopia gathered the 40 or so survivors of two previous rounds of layoffs into a room and announced that the company would be closing for business. By early afternoon, as people reeled from the not entirely unexpected shock, and as the doors were barred against both curious *cNet* reporters and any disgruntled former employees inclined to abscond with company property, the telephones began to ring. One phone would ring and go unanswered, and finally the caller would give up and the phone on the next desk would begin to ring. Recruiters from employment companies who had heard of the dot-com's demise were attempting to scavenge available staff. They were calling for system administrators and software engineers, promising immediate positions as well as bonuses for referrals. They were not calling for Web designers.

Web designers were particularly dependent on the success of the Web; therefore, the disappearance of so many dot-com companies in the Bay Area, starting in late 1999 and peaking in 2000, affected them in particular. Some work remained as Web design companies that previously scorned work that they saw as mainstream, such as simple e-commerce solutions, competed vigorously for the few remaining clients. Overall, Web design jobs became very scarce in the Bay Area.

As company after company closed, the salience of code—and the negligibility of art—within the Web design skill set became very apparent in my formal interviews, in offline and online water cooler discussions, and in classified advertisements for technology jobs. It is during this period that we saw the complexity of skill's evolution and the murkiness of the specialization process. First, the ability to program, sometimes embedded within a broader Web design skill set, became the most salient and marketable single aspect of the skill set. Consequently, the coding elements of the skill set, usually practiced by male software engineers, maintained their economic and cultural value in a way that the artistic elements of the skill set, usually practiced by female Web designers, did not. Second, code colonized the arena of art to an unprecedented degree, rendering visual design almost invisible in favor of programming code.

Programming experience remained a valuable part of the larger Web design skill set. Software engineers expressed much less anxiety about finding new jobs after being laid off. Even software engineers from overseas who were dependent on their employers to maintain their visa status expressed confidence that their skill set would stand them in good stead. Prasad, a Punjabi software engineer at one of the e-services firms, told me in an interview that "something new will come down the road." And he felt that his skill set, formally obtained in one of India's technical powerhouse institutions and honed at several Silicon Valley start-ups, would prepare him for that something new. And until something new came along, Prasad, like many other software engineers, could apply his skills to non-Web spheres. In my field sites, all laid-off software engineers, the majority of whom were men, were able to find new positions as engineers in other companies or in several companies in a row as the collapse continued.

During the post-boom of the dot-com industry, Web design skills that were seen as coding remained unscathed, if slightly less in demand, while Web design skills that were seen as closer to art emerged as devalued and suspect. The back-to-basics attitude that characterized Americans' attitude toward the dot-com fallout (Horrigan, 2001) also affected the perception of Web design skills. The idea that "anyone can design a Web site," which people exclaimed joyfully in 1996, became a condemnation in 2001. Most of the Web designers who had worked in my three field sites, all but one of whom were women, found employment after their companies closed, although most of them took jobs that did not have "Web design" anywhere in the titles. For example, a junior designer at one site turned her skills to becoming an artist and paid her bills as a waitress. Another Web designer decided to pursue a master's degree in computer science. And another more senior Web designer went to work in the marketing department of a branding agency.

Some Web designers, of course, stayed within the broad field of technology design. The Web designers who were most successful at obtaining design jobs after the dot-com boom were those who were able to represent their skill set as code heavy. For example, at a Web design firm, a junior Web designer had spent the past 8 months working on a fairly complex site for an educational software company and, in the process, had to learn quite a bit of JavaScript. When the Web design firm laid her off, she was able to secure a position at the educational software company, more on the basis of her familiarity with the project and the critical knowledge of the code involved and less on the basis of her impressive formal training from the renowned Rhode Island School of Design.

Code also dominated art in the sense that even art-focused solicitations demanded technological skills in a way that they did not in the past. Kaiser Permanente, the nation's largest integrated health care organization, posted a position on Monster.com in March 2002. Its "Web designer" position required "a strong knowledge of HTML," expertise in 10 different software tools, and "knowledge of CGI scripting languages, extensive knowledge of client/server-side scripting, familiarity with database applications, knowledge of Java, PERL, XML." Although the position posting welcomed people with graphic design degrees or experience, not one of the required competencies directly engaged visual design. Similarly, a position for a "Web designer" advertised by a clothing manufacturing

Table 12.2   Evolution of Web Design Skills

Period	Phase of Skill Set	Classified Advertisements		
		Section	Job Title	Job Description
Pre-boom internet economy, 1993–1996	Fusion of art and code Web design skills	Programming	Web expert	"Internet exp[erience]"[a]
Boom internet economy, 1997–1999	Bifurcation of art and code Web design skills	Programming	Web page developer	"C/C++, html, ColdFusion, CGI"[b]
		Graphic	Senior visual interface designer (for Web sites)	"Typography, spatial layout, conceptual design, & design methodology"[c]
Post-boom internet economy, 2000–2002	Domination of code over art Web design skills	Web/ Information design	UI designer (for Web development company)	"Good eye for visual design and typography. Familiarity with back-end scripting technologies (ASP, PHP, JSP, ColdFusion, PERL) desirable."[d]

a. *San Francisco Chronicle,* September 8, 1996.

b. *San Francisco Chronicle,* April 13, 1997. C/C++ are programming languages. ColdFusion is a software product to build database-driven Web applications. CGI stands for Common Gateway Interface, an interface that can be written in many languages that defines how data are passed and serves to connect the Web with other software and databases. See http://about.webdesign. com.

c. *San Francisco Chronicle,* July 13, 2002.

d. Craigslist.com (www.craigslist.com), posted April 6, 2002. ASP stands for Active Server Pages, a method (developed by Microsoft) of dynamically generating Web pages. PHP is a scripting language. JSP stands for Java Server Pages, is promoted by Sun Microsystems, and is an extension of server technology for creating dynamic content in Web pages. PERL is a programming language. See http://about.webdesign.com.

company on Salary.com in February 2001 required a "B.S./B.A. in computer science."

Table 12.2 illustrates just how general an advertisement for Web design expertise could be during the first period, the distinction that emerged between Web developers and Web designers during the second period, and the degree to which code, or programming knowledge, became essential to the very definition of Web design during the third period.

In part because code is seen as more legitimate and more directly tied to revenue, Web designers who could cast their skill set as being closer to code enjoyed more success. One Web designer, who was working at one of the nation's largest software companies at the time of our interview, told me that she sent out two versions of her resumé: one with the title of "Web designer" and one with the title of "Web developer." Without fail, she said, she received more responses to her Web developer version, even though the skill sets she described in both resumés were identical. One might think that in a competitive environment, the ideal employee is someone who can design broadly with a solid understanding of how to communicate ideas effectively. However, what Web designers found is that the ideal employee is someone who can design broadly for many different technologies. Companies recruited people to design for new digital technologies such as personal digital assistants (PDAs), mobile phones, and instant messaging software. And knowing how to make these technologies work—"code" in the sense of the frustrated engineer in the client meeting discussed earlier—became the most important component of design skill for companies.

Conclusion

The evolution of skills is not a neutral process. As I have argued in this chapter, skills are neither defined nor valued in a vacuum. Rather, like all social phenomena, they are both the creation and the creators of structural and social considerations. Tasks may specialize because they become too technically complex for one practitioner, but this entire process happens within a social context. During the early years of the Web, the Web design skill set was an amorphous one that, as one informant described, was "up for grabs." As the demand for Web expertise grew during the 1997–1999 period, the skill set bifurcated into two different specialties: art and code. This split, rather than being dictated solely by either market efficiency or technological efficiency, overlaid preexisting occupational segregation and the accompanying symbolic and financial valuation of skills. As the internet economy continued to decline, the Web design skill set adapted to this economically fraught period. Employers began to concentrate on the elements of the skill set that they saw as most directly tied to revenue and profitability. As a result, the ability to write code quickly became the most crucial element of the skill set, forcing art and design to take a back seat to what was portrayed and understood as the real work of Web site creation.

We, as a society or as academics, are not used to thinking of skills, particularly technology-related skills, as such socially fraught entities. We tend to think of skills as objective objects, things that we need to get and then use in our paid work, often measured simply by educational level or years of work experience. Tracing the evolution of Web design skills before, during, and after the internet economy demonstrates just how contested the very nature of skills can be. Furthermore, this research suggests that we need to learn a great deal more about how skills change over time. Our model of skill, as well as its evolution and specialization, is one born when manufacturing was the main mode of production. What would a model of skill based on information technology look like? The internet has certainly wrought substantial transformations in the ways in which we live, but the categories we use and the values we attribute to them are also powerful and remarkably durable.

References

Abbott, A. (1988). *System of professions: An essay on the division of expert labor.* Chicago: University of Chicago Press.

Association of Internet Professionals. (1999). *Compensation and benefits survey report* (Vol. 1.0). [Online]. Retrieved April 28, 2003, from www.association.org

Cockburn, C., & Ormrod, J. (1993). *Gender in the making.* London: Sage.

Girard, M., & Stark, D. (2002). Distributing intelligence and organizing diversity in new media projects. *Environment and Planning A, 34,* 1929–1949.

Horrigan, J. (2001). *Risky business: Americans see greed, cluelessness behind dot.com's comeuppance.* [Online]. Retrieved May 10, 2003, from www.pewinternet.org/reports/toc.asp?report=31

Kotamraju, N. (2002). Keeping up: Web design skill and the reinvented worker. *Information, Communication, and Society, 5*(1), 1–26.

Neff, G., Wissinger, E., & Zukin, S. (2001). *"Cool" jobs in "hot" industries: Fashion models and new media workers as entrepreneurial labor.* Unpublished manuscript, City University of New York.

Smith, A. (1976). *An inquiry into the nature and causes of the wealth of nations.* Indianapolis, IN: Liberty Classics. (Original work published 1776)

Ullman, E. (1997). *Close to the machine: Technophilia and its discontents.* San Francisco: City Lights.

Webster, J. (1996). *Shaping women's work: Gender, employment, and information technology.* New York: Longman.

Part IV

Culture and
Socialization Online

13

Wired and Well Read

Wendy Griswold
Northwestern University

Nathan Wright
Northwestern University

A s technology and as a cultural phenomenon, the internet moved from "high" to "popular" to "mass" with extraordinary speed during the 1990s. The sudden flood of e-everything produced giddiness but also alarm. Observers have worried about the internet's uncontrollable broadcast of images and sounds, its penetration of privacy, and its impact on how people live their lives, including how they read. The comparison with television is unavoidable. For some 50 years, people have feared—justly, it turned out—that television would overwhelm other leisure activities, including reading. Now the worry is that the internet will wipe out what little reading remains.

This chapter examines the relationship between internet use and reading. "Reading" here refers to nonwork reading, that is, the sustained reading of printed materials that people do for pleasure and information in their leisure time.[1] Some leisure activities are highly valued, with their possible atrophy being a cause for concern, and reading is one of these.[2] So, questions such as the following arise. What is the relationship between reading and using the internet? Do the two activities compete? Is one dominant, soaking up people's time and attention? Or, is the competition image wrong? Do reading and internet use support each other? How do people who do both think about the relationship between reading and internet use? Can people be both wired and well read?

Zero-Sum and More-More

Two perceptions of the relationship between reading and internet use are common. One holds that because there is a limit to people's time and energy, time spent on one activity is taken away from the other. This *zero-sum* view supports several hypotheses. First, if someone spends more time on the internet, he or she will have less time to spend reading and vice versa. Second, if the amount of time spent on one of these activities increases, the amount of time spent on the other activity will decrease. Third, if someone is a heavy internet user, he or she will have different social characteristics than will heavy readers. In contrast, an alternative is that time spent on one activity enhances time spent on another activity. This *more-more* view predicts that people who spend a lot of time on the internet will also spend a lot of time reading. Thus, if someone spends more time on one activity, he or she will also spend more time on the other activity, and heavy internet users will have the same social characteristics as will heavy readers. They will be, to a considerable extent, the same people.

Survey data—still scanty and hard to compare—seem to offer support for both viewpoints. Nie and Erbring (2000) suggested that heavy internet use is associated with reduced use of other media, including television and newspapers. On the other hand, a 1999 survey suggested that early internet users were also inclined to be heavy readers (Griswold & Wright, 2002). The current study builds on what this survey hinted.

There are some reasons to have confidence in the more-more assumption. The internet's impact on books and reading may turn out to be less revolutionary than was the impact of previous new media. Svedjedal (2000) reminded us of what he calls the "Gutenberg capacity," that is, the ability of book culture to appropriate technological advances and benefit from them. Moreover, highly educated people do not just take in highbrow culture; they also participate in a wider range of activities than do less educated people (Peterson & Kern, 1996). Cultural variety is socially useful, and it tends to increase with education (Erickson, 1996). As for time pressures, despite all of their talk to the contrary, Americans may actually have more leisure time than ever before (Robinson & Godbey, 1999). So, they may have the time to surf and to read.

On the other hand, some activities are "greedy" in that they demand a great deal in terms of time and attention. Greedy activities do not lend themselves to multitasking; for example, it is hard to do much else when one is swimming laps. Reading, especially reading books or challenging material, is quite greedy.

Television is at the nongreedy extreme in that people routinely do other things while they are watching television. Internet use seems to fall in between these two extremes. In most cases, it requires a fixed position and some continuous attention, yet it is very conducive to multitasking; high school kids download music, chat with their friends, do research, and write papers—all at the same time. So, one can easily imagine "doing something else" while using the internet, but it is harder to imagine doing something else while reading.

Our questions address the relationship between time spent reading and time spent online, looking for confirmation of the zero-sum or more-more assumption. We also examine the types of connections that may link the two activities. Questions such as "Do you use the internet to purchase books?" and "Do you read *Wired* magazine?" allow us to assess the ways in which reading and internet use may be mutually supportive as well as the ways in which they may compete.

Readers and Internet Users

What do we know about readers? The basic demographic picture is both clear and stable: Education is the strongest predictor of how much a person reads (Zill & Winglee, 1990). Although this is obvious at the divide between illiterate and literate people, research shows a finely graded difference among the fully literate: People with graduate degrees read more than do people with undergraduate degrees, people with undergraduate degrees read more than do people with high school degrees, and so forth. Other characteristics associated with reading include being female, being affluent, being neither elderly nor living in a rural area, and (in the United States) being white, but none of these effects is nearly as powerful as sheer years of schooling.[3]

Two questions bear on reading's relation to the internet. First, what is the relationship between reading and other media? Second, is reading in general decline? The answer to the first question seems clearer than the answer to the second one. Television came to most Western countries during the 1950s and 1960s, at the very time when leisure time was increasing. The fascination of the then new medium was such that it seemed to absorb the newly available leisure time and to draw time away from other activities, including reading. The Netherlands, which has unusually good data over time, shows this trend very clearly (Knulst & Kraaykamp, 1997). From 1955 to 1995, evening and weekend reading declined from 5.0 hours to 2.9 hours while television viewing rose from 0.2 hours to 10.9 hours. The big drop in reading came during the early years of television, although there seems to have been a slow decline even since 1975. Other surveys support this pattern of television displacing reading during leisure hours (Cushman, Veal, & Zuzanek, 1996).

A sharp drop in leisure time reading accompanied the advent of television, but what since? Does reading continue to decline? Here the evidence is mixed. The Netherlands study suggests continuing decline, with younger cohorts reading less than older ones. Other research suggests more stability among core readers; educated people may even be reading more. A New Zealand survey suggested that although more people were watching television during the 1990s than during the 1970s, more people claimed to prefer reading during the later decade. Furthermore, reading's rank as the most common leisure activity remained unchanged (Laidler & Cushman, 1996).

What do we know about internet users? Academic research on the internet has exploded during recent years, and some signs of consensus are emerging. Early work was heavily theoretical, tending to forecast either a utopia of greater community and political action unbounded by physical space (Mitchell, 1995; Rheingold, 1993) or a dystopia of atomized anomic individuals dwelling in a blurring of fantasy and reality (Slouka, 1995; Stoll, 1995). Both of these visions ignored the social contexts embedding the internet and suffered from a lack of good data (Wellman, 1997). More recent research, as DiMaggio, Hargittai, Neuman, and Robinson (2001) highlighted, has focused on five main areas: inequality (the "digital divide"), community and social capital, political participation, economic and other organizations and institutions, and cultural participation and diversity. (The current study falls within the latter area.) Research exploring how the internet fits into preexisting activities generally conclude that that the internet complements and supports offline practices rather than displacing, undermining, or competing with them (DiMaggio et al., 2001; Haythornthwaite, 2001; Howard, Rainie, & Jones, 2001).[4]

Most of the research that has been done to date has been on the "early adopters" of internet use, who may differ from their successors (Haythornthwaite, 2001). Nie (2001), in particular, was concerned that celebrations of the internet's alleged positive effects on community involvement and social capital overlooked the fact that most of the internet users studied to date were already well advantaged in terms of their levels of social integration and social capital. Furthermore, he argued that heavy internet users were spending increasingly longer periods of time online, and given that time is a finite resource, other offline activities were likely to be displaced eventually. Data from the Stanford Internet and Society survey suggest that users who are online more than 5 hours per week (36% of all users) are displacing local face-to-face interactions, time spent talking on the phone, and time spent engaging other media such as television and newspapers (Nie & Erbring, 2000).

This time or "greediness" question is the second main thrust of the chapter. How does time spent online affect time spent offline, including time potentially spent reading? Nie's (2001) argument relies on the notion that the internet is greedy and so prevents people from engaging in other activities at the same time. He argued explicitly that the internet is potentially more isolating than television, for instance, because the internet requires more direct user interface, cannot easily fade into the background, and cannot easily be experienced collectively. In contrast, Robinson, Kestnbaum, Neustadtl, and Alvarez (2000) argued that the internet should be seen as a "time-enhancing home appliance" like telephones rather than as a "time-displacing device" like television; whereas television eats away time that could be spent on other activities, the internet saves time in communication and information gathering, thereby freeing up time for other activities.

Perhaps the best data come from the University of California, Los Angeles (UCLA) Center for Communication Policy, which is conducting annual surveys of internet use. The two that had been conducted as of this writing found that internet users use other media—including books, magazines, and newspapers—more than do internet nonusers (UCLA Center for Communication Policy, 2000, p. 18, 2001, p. 30). This supports the more-more assumption, as does the intriguing finding that users have "slightly higher levels of life satisfaction" (UCLA Center for Communication Policy, 2001, p. 73). Internet users seem to spend a little less time reading than do nonusers, however (p. 32). We suspect that the contradictory results of reading—internet users are more likely to read for pleasure but spend less time doing it—may be due to life course. College students (virtually all of whom use the internet) generally report a sharp decline in their reading for pleasure, and this pattern seems to persist into young adulthood. Hours on the internet increase until people's mid-30s (mostly due to work) and then tail off, whereas most surveys suggest that reading remains steady through late middle age (UCLA Center for Communication Policy, 2000, p. 14; Cushman et al., 1996, pp. 27, 42, 46, 137).

The UCLA reports show that the big effect of the internet is not on reading but rather on television: Internet users have equal access to television but spend much less time watching it (16.8 hours per week for internet nonusers vs. 12.3 hours per week for internet users). When asked how the internet had changed their non-computer activities at home, a third of respondents reported that they watched less television. As for reading, 19% reported that they read less since going online, 5% said that they now read more, and 75% said that there was no change in their reading (UCLA Center for Communication Policy, 2001, p. 79). So, the zero-sum assumption seems to be true for television but not for reading. If young adults read less than they did in high school and less than they will when they reach their 30s and beyond, this is due more to time pressures than to competition with the internet.[5] In addition, Griswold and Wright (2002) found that early internet users (i.e., those who used the internet regularly before internet service providers supplied widespread services) recognized various authors more than did recent internet users, and this finding was independent of other factors such as age, gender, education, region, and self-reported interest in and knowledge of literature. Once again, this seems to be a case of more-more.

Survey2001

Survey2001 was an internet survey, the second of its kind (the first was Survey2000), that the National Geographic Society, with James Witte as principal investigator, conducted during late 2001 and early 2002. As with the earlier survey, it offers large numbers of respondents allowing for good internal comparisons, but because it is not representative of a larger population, one must be cautious about extrapolating to the society at large. Slightly more than half of the Survey2001 respondents were men. They were a well-educated group, with well over half having graduated from college and nearly a quarter having graduate degrees.[6] It was an international survey; more than two thirds of the respondents were born in the United States, and most of these lived there as well.[7]

Each of the 23,299 survey respondents saw at least one randomly assigned module with questions on the environment, the internet, music, or reading, and some chose to fill out more than one of these modules. The reading questions, answered by 5,379 respondents, covered both reading practices and specific authors and works. The three types covered were (a) general authors, both popular (e.g., Stephen King) and literary (e.g., Joyce Carol Oates); (b) authors and works dealing with the environment (e.g., Rachel Carson's *Silent Spring*); and (c) authors and works dealing with the internet, computing, and technology (e.g., *Wired* magazine).

When asked how much time they spend reading books for pleasure, about one third of the respondents indicated that they read less than 2 hours per week, another third read from 2 to 5 hours per week, and a third read more than 5 hours per week. Most (61.8%) reported that they usually read fiction for pleasure. Note that it is this type of reading that corresponds to "reading" in most surveys. (Survey2001 also asked about work-related reading, but we are not analyzing those data here.) Although it is difficult to compare across studies, the respondents appeared to be above average in terms of the time they spend reading during their leisure time.

Although they read quite a bit, the survey respondents indicated that they were not especially knowledgeable about literature. Their average response to "general authors" was 1.37, somewhere between having heard of the authors and having actually read them. Given that one of the authors was Ernest Hemingway, this suggests that they were not exactly bookworms. The overwhelming majority never (79.6%) or rarely (12.5%) participated in book discussion groups. On the other hand, close to half read book reviews occasionally (34.1%) or often (11.9%).

Internal comparisons revealed some of the respondents' interests, including what they might like to read. For example, the recognition of environmental authors (.74) was higher than that of technological authors (.51). The noteworthy point here is that despite the fact that this was a survey both taken on and focusing on the internet, the respondents did not seem to be especially interested in reading about technology.

Combined responses to a series of questions on how much time respondents spent using the internet created a single measure. We compared this with the combined score for reading recognition questions and with different types of reading: environmental authors, technical authors, general authors, and internet magazines. Simple correlations, shown in Table 13.1, support the more-more hypothesis: *Using the internet is positively correlated with reading, as indicated by knowledge of various authors.* This is the case for the combined reading recognition score and for each specific area: general fiction, technology, and the environment. The correlations for combined reading, and for general fiction and technology, hold true net of education.[8] (For example, Table 13.1 shows the correlations for respondents with bachelor's degrees or higher.) Although the correlations between internet use and technological or internet reading are perhaps to be expected, the correlation between internet use and general authors gives unambiguous support to the more-more hypothesis.

Table 13.1   Simple Correlations With Average Score for Internet Use

	Correlations With Internet Use: All Respondents	Correlations With Internet Use: Respondents With at Least a College Degree
All reading recognitions	.197*	.163*
	(n = 4,920)	(n = 1,954)
Internet magazines	.322*	.326*
	(n = 4,889)	(n = 1,944)
Technological authors	.272*	.265*
	(n = 4,917)	(n = 1,954)
Environmental authors	.085*	.005
	(n = 4,911)	(n = 1,953)
General fiction authors	.107*	.113*
	(n = 4,915)	(n = 1,952)

NOTE: Internet use is an average score compiled from respondents' answers to questions asking how frequently they engaged in several online activities: sending e-mail, accessing e-mail listservs, browsing digital libraries, participating in online education, making online purchases, accessing Web sites for information or pleasure, chatting online, participating in online multi-user dimensions (MUDS), and playing online games.

*$p < 0.001$.

Making finer distinctions between internet users leads to similar conclusions. Comparing the top quartile of internet users with less frequent users, and comparing users who first accessed the internet from home more than 5 years prior to the survey (when internet service providers were not readily available) with those who first accessed the internet more recently reveals that the heaviest internet users are more likely to be heavier readers as well, even controlling for education.

Internet use is negatively related to general environmental concerns, but this is not the case for readers given that there is a strong correlation between reading about technology and reading about the environment. This offers further support for the more-more idea; although environmentalists and internet buffs are not the same, people who are internet buffs are also readers and read everything.

No difference appears between heavy readers—those who read 5 hours per week or more for pleasure—and light readers in their relationship to the internet. If the zero-sum hypothesis were correct, one might expect heavier readers to be lighter internet users, but this does not appear to be the case. Nor are heavier readers heavier internet users, as the more-more hypothesis would predict. This suggests that heavy readers may or may not be attracted to the internet but that the internet does not crowd out reading from their leisure time.

A few other findings were intriguing. Not surprisingly, heavier readers tended to be more knowledgeable about all three types of books and authors. Surprisingly, readers who preferred fiction had nearly the identical score on internet use as did those who preferred nonfiction. One might have expected nonfiction readers to be more interested in the internet, but this did not seem to be the case. We also note that respondents who claimed to be very interested in the environment and conservation were somewhat more knowledgeable about books and authors than were those who were less interested. Not surprisingly, the difference was greatest for environmental authors.

If reading and internet use appear to have a more-more relationship, is it just a case of some people doing more of everything or is there an interaction between the two activities? If there is a positive interaction, it would take one of two forms:

Reading facilitates internet use. People who read specifically internet material (e.g., *Wired* magazine, "Circuits" section in *The New York Times*) will be heavier internet users than will people who do not. We have already seen support for this in Table 13.1, which shows a correlation between internet use and the recognition scores for these two. Using the internet and reading about the internet go hand in hand.

Internet use facilitates reading. People read on the internet and use the internet to obtain books. Survey results provide multiple indicators of the relationship between using the internet and getting books (and talking about them as well). First, 14.5% of respondents get at least half of their leisure-related reading material from the internet, and 68.2% sometimes get leisure reading materials online. (For work-related reading material, the percentage is even higher.) The wording of the questions—"How often to you get leisure-related reading online?" and "How often do you get work-related reading online?"—might mean that respondents simply read the text on Web sites rather than, for example, downloading newspapers or articles. Although hard to interpret, the high percentage of people who get reading online at least sometimes suggests that the two activities are not regarded as opposed or occupying separate spheres.

Furthermore, many respondents reported that they actively use the internet to obtain of reading materials. A third of them buy books online occasionally (25.9%) or often (6.5%). Two fifths check library catalogs online occasionally or often, although only half as many actually order library books this way. Most do not run down rare, used, or out-of-print books online, but more than 10% do so occasionally or often. Much more common is looking up author information online, with 30.8% of respondents doing so occasionally and 10.4% doing so often. And nearly half of the respondents read book reviews online often or occasionally.

Finally, Survey2001 produced a cluster of findings that suggest the robust nature of the relationship between reading and internet use. First, people who like to use the internet are even more likely to want to "curl up with a set of books" than are people who do not like to use the internet (88.0% vs. 83.7%). But second, as noted earlier, heavy readers are no different from light readers in terms of frequency of internet use. And third, of those people who participate in book discussion groups, many participate either only online or only offline. However, there is a significant relationship between the two: People who talk about books offline are more likely to participate in online discussion groups than are people who do not and vice versa. Taking these together gives a general picture of mutual support (more-more), with the commitment to reading being the stronger of the two.

Focus Group

To flesh out the survey results, we met with a focus group of 10 college freshmen to talk about their reading, their internet use, and the impact of one on the other. These students are quite conscious of themselves as being the first generation to "grow up with" the internet, and their practices may indicate what will become the norm. On the other hand, they also recognize that college life is different from both their previous lives and what they imagine their post-college lives to be and that this difference affects their reading and their time online.

Asked about their reading habits, most students reported that they read newspapers early in the day, especially the college newspaper, "to know what's going on." Ryan said that she starts her morning with her hometown Minnesota newspaper and also likes the *Chicago Sun-Times*.[9] Several of the students reported that they read magazines before going to sleep. In between the morning newspaper and perhaps a bedtime glance at a magazine, their days are filled with reading for their classes. Most said that they do the bulk of their reading in their rooms, although this can be a problem with people constantly dropping by. Stephanie admitted that she hides out in a friend's room where no one comes looking for her. Callie said that she likes to go to the library to study—"it's a mental thing." Several focus group members commented that they enjoy reading outdoors whenever possible. Ryan said that she reads in her sorority's television room. Kate noted that she reads anywhere except at the computer (she gets distracted) or on the bed (she falls asleep). Several students mentioned reading newspapers at meals or (for one student) at a local bakery. Surprisingly, most students indicated that they find it hard to listen to music while reading because it is too distracting. Victoria talked about matching the place, the time, and the nature of the reading, and the other students agreed.

Beyond newspapers and an occasional magazine, the members of this focus group were unanimous in saying that although they read constantly for their courses, they have little time for pleasure reading. All except Elizabeth, who said she is burned out from studying, they all would like to read more. Chelsea mentioned that she would like to delve into more classic American fiction such as *Grapes of Wrath*, and the others chimed in agreement. Floyd said that he reads the *New York Times Book Review*, although he rarely has time to follow up and read the books themselves. Several mentioned wanting to read Oprah Winfrey's recommended books.

When asked about their online activities, the students reported using the internet primarily from their rooms, with a few occasionally checking e-mail during long stints at the library. Roy talked about how he has "little pockets of time" that are suitable for using the internet and how he goes online for a break during those times. Stephanie said that the internet is always on when she is in her room. Ryan chimed that she is online all of the time and is always hooked up to Instant Messenger so that she can talk with family and friends. Most students said that they read newspapers online. Many classes use the university's online course management system, so students need to check this frequently. All of the focus group members reported multitasking, with many windows open and Instant Messenger constantly running. Most internet use is very local, involving campus friends and activities or connecting with hometown news and friends. The group members reported making little use of the internet's potential for global contacts. And surprisingly, these students claimed to use the internet relatively little for research, saying that they do this less than in high school; they believe that college professors expect them to master the books. In another change from high school, the students reported doing less casual surfing.

These freshmen reported using computers more at college than they did at home. Thomas remarked that at home he relaxed by plopping down in front of the television, whereas at college he goes online, again bringing up the idea of little bits of time being best filled by the internet. Floyd agreed that he generally used the computer less at home but that he needs to keep on top of school and community news while at college. Several remarked that the access to the internet is much better at college than at home; Chelsea added that the ease of access tempts her to be "compulsive" about checking Instant Messenger and e-mail at college. Callie and Thomas agreed that Instant Messenger is "academic death" but hard to resist.

When asked to consider whether the internet and reading competed for their time, the students firmly rejected this idea. Most said that their pleasure reading is not affected by being online, reiterating that they do less reading for pleasure in college because of the workload, not because of the internet. Stephanie and Thomas said that they probably read more overall at college and use the internet more as well. Several students said that there is more driving around and more television watching at home. No one said that they could read books online, but they use the internet to keep up with current events and news from home. Thomas said that he reads *The Wall Street Journal* editorials online each day, offering this as an example of how the internet enables him to read more than he would otherwise. Callie pointed out that the internet can be a relief from so much reading, just as pleasure reading offers a relief from sitting at the computer.

Nor do these students see any competition between reading and internet use in people they know. Thomas reported that his mother is both a high internet user and a great reader. Victoria said that her mom is the same and also reported having a lawyer uncle who reads a great deal and uses the internet constantly. Elizabeth noted that her mom is a big reader and uses the internet to support her reading. Floyd told of a friend at another college who is online all of the time and who is also a voracious reader. Not everyone does both, of course. Chelsea reported that her mom is a heavy reader but spends little time on the internet. Roy agreed that his family members who read a lot do not use the internet much. Victoria commented that this is a generational difference; heavy readers may be either older or younger, but older people are less likely to be heavy internet users than are younger people.

Most of these freshmen expect to read much more for pleasure, but possibly less overall, once they are finished with college. They found it harder to predict their future internet use, believing that it would depend on their jobs, although they believed that with less "broken time" there would be less going online for brief periods. Several expected to be online less often than they are now. The group members agreed that college life involves a lot of short stretches of time that are conducive to checking e-mail or Instant Messenger but not to reading.

Most believed that reading requires relatively large blocks of time, which they expect to have when they are finished with their college years.

More-More, But for How Long?

Piecing together information from Survey2001, from previous surveys, and from our focus group, one might hazard several conclusions. First, reading and the internet do not compete for time. The internet is less greedy than television, so heavy internet use does not displace reading in the same way in which it replaces television. Second, reading is greedy. Whereas the internet can be woven into the fabric of everyday life, reading requires some time clearly demarcated as leisure time. Therefore, there are certain periods in the life course—college, new parenthood, and/or unusually intense times at work—when reading declines. Once leisure time opens up again, the reading habit reasserts itself. Third, the internet offers some support for reading in terms of reviews, author information, book orders, and the ability to pursue particular topics. Reading supports internet use as well.

Although this compatibility offers a sunny future, there are at least two clouds. The first is the possibility of cohort replacement. It may be that the baby boomers are carrying the reading habit and that they are the only generation whose members will participate enthusiastically in both reading and internet use. The students in our focus group certainly did not expect this to be the case; they were convinced that they would return to reading for pleasure when they had the time, but this remains to be seen. The second cloud is gender. Reading is tilted toward women, whereas internet use is tilted toward men. This division may be exacerbated over time, for example, with the internet's propensity for disseminating pornography and facilitating sexual harassment. Either cohort replacement or gendering could eventually mean that the current tendency for some people to be both wired and well read might not last.

Sociologists have long remarked on the tendency for initial advantages to accumulate, what Robert K. Merton called the "Matthew effect"—the rich get richer. The more-more relationship between reading and internet use seems to be another case of this. People who exhibit the more-more pattern, reading a lot and using the internet a lot, are doubly advantaged. They possess information, social connections, and cultural capital, and they know how to get more when they need them. They can adapt to circumstances—satisfying professors who require books, staying in touch with distant friends, chatting about the latest novels, filling pockets of time—with the flexibility of those comfortable with two powerful media. The world of the more-more is rich with possibilities. Because the logical alternative to more-more is less-less, on the other hand, the digital divide and the persistence of pockets of literary disadvantage go together. The internet is not going to displace reading, but it is going to give readers yet one more advantage. This is what everyone should be worrying about.

Appendix

Reading Questions From Survey2001

111. Over the course of a typical week, how much time do you spend reading books for pleasure? [used the following options for 113, 115, and 116 as well]

Less than 2 hours

2 to 5 hours

5 hours or more

112. What types of books do you read most for pleasure?

Fiction and literature (e.g., novels, mysteries, short stories, poetry, romances)

Nonfiction (e.g., bibliographies, history, science, politics)

113. Over the course of a typical week, how much time do you spend reading materials other than books (e.g., newspapers, magazines) for pleasure?

114. How often do you get your leisure-related reading online? [used the following options for 117 as well]

Frequently: I get half or more of my reading from the internet

Occasionally: I've gotten some reading material online but usually use traditional print media such as books, newspapers, and magazines

Rarely

Never

115. Over the course of a typical week, how much time do you spend reading books for your work or studies?

116. Over the course of a typical week, how much time do you spend reading materials other than books (e.g., newspapers, magazines) for pleasure, work, or study?

117. How often do you get your work-related reading online?

For each of the following activities, please indicate whether you do them often (once a week or more), occasionally (once a month or more), or rarely (less than once a month):

118. Purchase a new book online (e.g., Amazon.com, Barnes&Noble.com)

119. Check a library catalog online

120. Order a book from a library online (e.g., recalling a book from another patron, ordering a book through interlibrary loan)

121. Participate in a book discussion group

122. Read book reviews

123. Purchase a rare, used, or out-of-print book online (e.g., eBay, 21 North Main)

124. Look up author information (e.g., an author's Web site)

Now we are going to ask you about some authors, books, and reading materials. Some are about technology and the internet, some are about environmental concerns, and some are just general reading. Please indicate whether you recognize any of the following:

125. Thomas Friedman, *The Lexus and the Olive Tree* [used the following options for all remaining items]

> Never heard of it/this author/this publication
>
> Heard of this book but never read it

Read this book

Read this book and recommend it

126. Edward Abbey

127. Agatha Christie

128. Aldo Leopold, *A Sand Country Almanac*

129. Ernest Hemingway

130. *Wired* magazine

131. Ursula Le Guin

132. Henry David Thoreau, *Walden*

133. The "Circuits" section of *The New York Times*

134. Stephen King

135. Rachel Carson, *Silent Spring*

136. Tracy Kidder, *The Soul of a New Machine*

137. Joyce Carol Oates

138. Sherry Turkle, *Life On the Screen*

139. Rosamunde Pilcher

Notes

1.   Virtually all surveys of reading use this definition, which also accords with common use of the word. If a woman married to an attorney refers to her husband as "a great reader" or "not much of a reader," everyone understands that this describes his leisure pursuits, not what he does

in his profession. Our definition excludes online reading. Although virtually every online activity involves some reading, people seldom read a single text for any length of time online; they print out papers or book chapters, and they even buy newspapers if they are available. This may change, but so far e-books to be read online have not caught on.

2.   Other leisure activities include participating in organized religious and community activities; going to museums, theaters, and concerts; and playing sports. Some leisure activities are neither esteemed nor scorned (e.g., spectator sports), and others are disparaged even by those who engage in them a lot (e.g., watching television). The status of a leisure activity determines whether something that competes with it is considered to be a threat or not.

3.   The association between reading and gender is stable in advanced industrial countries. Some suggest that this is because women have more empty pockets of time, whereas others point to the early associations of physical outdoor activities with masculinity and of passive indoor activities with femininity (Alloway & Gilbert, 1997; Cherland, 1994). The picture is quite different in developing countries, where literacy itself tends to be much higher for males, the same pattern that was seen in the West during the early years of the literacy revolution (Griswold, 2000).

4.   Studies using a variety of methods (including in-depth qualitative interviews, focus groups, national random telephone surveys, convenience and snowball sample Web surveys, time use diaries, internet activity tracking, and ethnographic fieldwork) have repeatedly demonstrated that the internet strengthens and expands social networks and corresponds with both greater political, community, and voluntary association participation and greater involvement in physical outdoor activities offline (Franzen, 2000; Ho & Lee, 2001; Katz, Rice, & Aspden, 2001; Matei & Ball-Rokeach, 2001; Robinson et al., 2000; Wellman, Quan Haase, Witte, & Hampton, 2001). Howard and colleagues (2001) tracked internet activities and found that most online activity involves either communication with friends, family, and coworkers or information gathering. Some observers are cautiously optimistic, however, due to the persistent "digital divide" that exists between those with regular access to the internet and the skills to use it effectively and those without such access and skills. Research has consistently identified regular internet users as more likely to be male, young, of majority racial status, native English speakers, well educated, financially well off, and urban or suburban. All signs point to the ever-increasing bridging of the digital divide on all of these dimensions, with some evidence that the gender gap has already been closed, at least in terms of access if not in internet use patterns (Bimber, 2000; Dietrichson, 2001; Ervin & Gilmore, 1999; Howard et al., 2001; Jackson, Ervin, Gardner, & Schmitt, 2001; Korgen, Odell, & Schumacher, 2001).

5.   Korgen and colleagues (2001) found in their survey of college students at internet-accessible campuses that heavy internet use was positively correlated with heavy offline studying among all racial and ethnic groups. And Anderson and Tracey (2001) found from in-depth interviews and extensive longitudinal time use diaries that persons with internet access at home who used it regularly did not spend any less time reading books, magazines, or newspapers than did persons who did not use the internet at home.

6.   Bachelor's degree only = 33.7%; graduate degree = 23.3%.

7.   For more information on Survey2001, see Witte's prologue in this volume.

8.   Knowledge of environmental authors is not correlated with internet use once we control for education.

9.   The names used in this section are not the students' real names. The 10 Northwestern University students participated in the focus group in late April of their freshman year.

References

Alloway, N., & Gilbert, P. (1997). Boys and literacy: Lessons from Australia. *Gender and Education,* *9,* 49–58.

Anderson, B., & Tracey, K. (2001). Digital living: The impact (or otherwise) of the internet on everyday life. *American Behavioral Scientist, 45,* 456–475.

Bimber, B. (2000). Measuring the gender gap on the internet. *Social Science Quarterly, 81,* 868–876.

Cherland, M. R. (1994). *Private practices: Girls reading fiction and constructing identity.* London: Taylor & Francis.

Cushman, G., Veal, A. J., & Zuzanek, J. (Eds.). (1996). *World leisure participation: Free time in the* *global village.* Wallingford, UK: CAP International.

Dietrichson, A. (2001). *Digital literacy: How to measure browsing behavior.* Unpublished dissertation, Columbia University.

DiMaggio, P., Hargittai, E., Neuman, W. R., & Robinson, J. P. (2001). Social implications of the internet. *Annual Review of Sociology, 27,* 307–336.

Erickson, B. H. (1996). Culture, class, and connections. *American Journal of Sociology, 102,* 217–251.

Ervin, K. S., & Gilmore, G. (1999). Traveling the superinformation highway: African Americans' perceptions and use of cyberspace technology. *Journal of Black Studies, 29,* 398–407.

Franzen, A. (2000). Does the internet make us lonely? *European Sociological Review, 16,* 427–438.

Griswold, W. (2000). *Bearing witness: Readers, writers, and the novel in Nigeria.* Princeton, NJ: Princeton University Press.

Griswold, W., & Wright, N. (2002). *Cowbirds, locals, and the dynamic endurance of regionalism.* Unpublished manuscript, Northwestern University.

Haythornthwaite, C. (2001). The internet in everyday life. *American Behavioral Scientist, 45,* 363–382.

Ho, S. M., & Lee, T. M. C. (2001). Computer usage and its relationship with adolescent lifestyle in Hong Kong. *Journal of Adolescent Health, 29,* 258–266.

Howard, P. E. N., Rainie, L., & Jones, S. (2001). Days and nights on the internet: The impact of a diffusing technology. *American Behavioral Scientist, 45,* 383–404.

Jackson, L. A., Ervin, K. S., Gardner, P. D., & Schmitt, N. (2001). Gender and the internet: Women communicating and men searching. *Sex Roles, 44,* 363–379.

Katz, J. E., Rice, R. E., & Aspden, P. (2001). The internet, 1995–2000: Access, civic involvement, and social interaction. *American Behavioral Scientist, 45,* 405–419.

Knulst, W., & Kraaykamp, G. (1997). The decline of reading: Leisure reading trends in the Netherlands (1955–1995). *Netherlands Journal of Social Sciences, 33,* 130–150.

Korgen, K., Odell, P., & Schumacher, P. (2001). Internet use among college students: Are there differences by race/ethnicity? *Electronic Journal of Sociology, 5*(3).

Laidler, A., & Cushman, G. (1996). New Zealand. In G. Cushman, A. J. Veal, & J. Zuzanek (Eds.), *World* *leisure participation: Free time in the global village* (pp. 165–181). Wallingford, UK: CAP International.

Matei, S., & Ball-Rokeach, S. J. (2001). Real and virtual social ties: Connections in the everyday lives of seven ethnic neighborhoods. *American Behavioral Scientist, 45,* 550–564.

Mitchell, W. J. (1995). *City of bits: Space, place, and the Infobahn.* Cambridge, MA: MIT Press.

Nie, N. H. (2001). Sociability, interpersonal relations, and the internet: Reconciling conflicting findings. *American Behavioral Scientist, 45,* 420–435.

Nie, N, H., & Erbring, L. (2000). *Internet and society: A preliminary report* (Stanford Institute for the Quantitative Study of Society, Stanford University, and Intersurvey Inc.). [Online]. Retrieved April 29, 2003, from www.stanford.edu/group/siqss

Peterson, R. A., & Kern, R. (1996). Changing highbrow taste: From snob to omnivore. *American Sociological Review, 61,* 900–907.

Rheingold, H. (1993). *The virtual community: Homesteading on the electronic frontier.* Reading, MA: Addison-Wesley.

Robinson, J., & Godbey, G. (1999). *Time for life* (2nd ed.). University Park: Pennsylvania State University Press.

Robinson, J. P., Kestnbaum, M., Neustadtl, A., & Alvarez, A. (2000). Mass media use and social life among internet users. *Social Science Computer Review, 18,* 490–501.

Slouka, M. (1995). *War of the worlds: Cyberspace and the high-tech assault on reality.* New York: Basic Books.

Stoll, C. (1995). *Silicon snake oil: Second thoughts on the information superhighway.* New York: Doubleday.

Svedjedal, J. (2000). *The literary Web: Literature and publishing in the age of digital production.* Stockholm, Sweden: Kungl. Biblioteket.

UCLA Center for Communication Policy. (2000). *The UCLA internet Report: Surveying the digital future.* [Online]. Retrieved April 29, 2003, from www.ccp.ucla.edu

UCLA Center for Communication Policy. (2001). *The UCLA internet Report 2001: Surveying the digital future: Year Two.* [Online]. Retrieved April 29, 2003, from www.ccp.ucla.edu

Wellman, B. (1997). The road to utopia and dystopia on the information superhighway. *Contemporary Sociology, 26,* 445–449.

Wellman, B., Quan Haase, A., Witte, J., & Hampton, K. (2001). Does the internet increase, decrease, or supplement social capital? Social networks, participation, and community commitment. *American Behavioral Scientist, 45,* 436–455.

Zill, N., & Winglee, M. (1990). *Who reads literature: The future of the United States as a nation of readers.* Cabin John, MD: Seven Locks Press.

14

The Disembodied Muse

Music in the Internet Age

Richard A. Peterson
Vanderbilt University

John Ryan
Virginia Tech

Like every major technological change, the internet is having a profound effect on virtually all aspects of our society. Some of these changes are only dimly apparent, and most are not fully actualized yet. In the area of popular music, the widespread sharing of music files is now the most widely commented-on effect of internet technology. Some view the practice as a great boon to music appreciation, whereas others see it simply as an act of stealing private property and as a threat to the popular music industry as we have known it (Garrity, 2002). The terms of this debate change almost monthly, yet questions of property rights really do not speak to the impacts on music per se.

As recently as two centuries ago, all popular music was embodied. The medium of transmission was the human voice as well as the breath or hand on the instrument. Transmission and reception were face-to-face and full of potential for intimacy and interactivity. Music was "live" and disappeared as soon as it was performed. The only way in which to hear music was to attend when and where a performance was taking place, and so most people knew practically nothing about other people's music. In effect, either audiences had to travel to where performances were taking place or performers had to move physically to find their audiences. Although differing in their particular character, all musical art worlds (Becker, 1982) were built on this particular medium—moving audiences to musicians or moving musicians to audiences.

A shift of great historical importance has taken place with accelerating speed over the past several centuries, a shift from embodied music to disembodied music as most people move from playing instruments to playing records and hearing music television. Increasingly, musical performances can be faithfully recorded; frozen on a sheet of paper, in a phonograph record, as a digital file, or the like; stored indefinitely; transferred electronically; and then reactualized at the pleasure of the listener. Thus, increasingly, it is the music that moves, and people do not need to move to hear whatever music they please whenever they choose to hear it.

To better understand the range of possible impacts of the internet on music, we examine four earlier technological innovations and the impacts they had on music. In the light of these examples, we explore the potential effects of the internet and related technologies on popular music. We conclude the chapter with the results of a small pilot study that may be a harbinger of changes to come.

The Invention of Music Notation

Although it may now seem trivial, the invention of musical notation, culminating in the work of Guido of Arezzo in the early 11th century AD, began the shift from embodied music to disembodied music. As Goodall (2000) noted,

> In the 3,000 years from Moses to Charlemagne, music basically consisted of a tune and some rhythmic accompaniment. From the arrival of notation, the speed of change and development of music up to our own century was in comparison dazzlingly fast. (p. 41)

As important at this point in time, Western music diverged from the musics of the rest of the world.

Why did it happen? During the seventh century, Pope Gregory the Great, shocked at the wide variety of liturgical music across Christendom, ordered a compilation and standardization of the whole chant repertoire. The resulting Gregorian chants became the official liturgical music of the Roman Church, and all variants from these were branded heretical. But at the time, there was no such thing as written music. In consequence, every chorister had to learn by heart the full cycle of religious songs, an arduous process that was said to take at least 10 years (Goodall, 2000, p. 15). There were a number of efforts to develop a system of notation to reduce the training time for novice choristers, but none was very successful until Guido of Arezzo devised the system that is still in use today. Although this invention satisfied its intended purpose, it had unanticipated consequences that slowly unfolded over the next several centuries.

First, a specific piece of music could now transcend the moment of its performance, and it could be taken from place to place by people with no knowledge of music. More important for the development of music, notation made possible the separation of performance and composition and so began the process of disembodying music. In Gregorian chant, singers all sang the same note, but with musical notation it was now possible to work out ever more elaborate patterns of counterpoint in which several melody lines are woven together. It also became possible to experiment with harmonies and chords, but this was a very slow process because many labeled harmony and chords as devilish noise. As Goodall (2000) noted, "Even *three* simultaneous notes took the finest brains of Europe centuries to handle with ease" (p. 40, emphasis in original).

A number of lessons about the impact of new technology can be drawn from this early example. First, the beginning of the disembodiment of music is associated with that critical juncture when Western music split off from music of the rest of the world. Second, the innovation not only achieved its intended purpose but had much more important and wide-ranging unintended consequences that were impossible to foretell at the time. Third, the consequences took hundreds of years to work out.

Industrialization, the Movement of People, and the Parlor Piano

The massive technological transformation that took place during the 19th century influenced music both through the mixing of people and through the development of the piano, the first music-making machine to be invented for centuries. These two very different kinds of influences need to be looked at in turn.

The new factory system of production drew millions of European peasants displaced from the land by the mechanization of agriculture to work in the factories of the industrializing cities of Europe and North America, flows of populations made possible by the development of the ocean-going steamship and the continent-spanning railroads. These changes entailed an unprecedented mixing of people who brought with them the diverse musical traditions of their homelands. Until then, the popular music of America had been primarily based in British and West African traditions. During the 19th century, German, Irish, Scottish, Italian, Jewish, Scandinavian, Spanish, Eastern European, Caribbean, and Asian musics were swirled into the increasingly rich mix of American urban popular music. Many nuances of the older folk music were lost, but at the same time popular music was greatly enriched by the admixture of all the styles carried by immigrants to the cities of Europe and the Americas. In its earliest days, the Industrial Revolution brought much privation, but as levels of productivity rose during the second half of the 19th century, urban working people earned enough money and had enough leisure time to seek out cheap public entertainment where the musics of various traditions mixed freely in cabarets, dance halls, concert halls, and minstrel and vaudeville shows.

At the same time, the rising middle class, wishing to distance itself from all of these licentious goings-on, worked to firmly locate entertainment in the home, where it could be supervised by the elders (Levine, 1988). The middle class found the perfect way in which to enhance family entertainment—the newly developed home parlor piano, a large expensive piece of furniture that connoted cultivated tastes and moral refinement. In musical terms, the piano had distinct advantages over all other available instruments. One could play melody as well as the accompanying harmonies, so it sounded good if played without the accompaniment of other instruments. At the same time, it was the perfect accompaniment for the human voice. The piano was easy to play with only the most rudimentary instruction, yet it would reward the most prodigious talent. Another asset commented on at the time was the fact that a young woman could play the instrument sitting up in a ladylike fashion (McCleary, 1991). Thus, as the 19th century progressed, the parlor piano became a prime symbol of middle class rectitude, and the ability to play the instrument became the leading sign of middlebrow taste (Goffman, 1951; Goodall, 2000, pp. 160–185).

Of course, to be on the leading edge of fashion, the thousands of parlor pianists had to be able to play the latest tunes featured in the leading shows of New York and Boston and performed by the leading touring soloists of the day. Young women led the way in this fashion trend (McCleary, 1991). This created a huge demand for the sheet music of the newly composed songs that were quickly printed and distributed around the country via the national system of railroads that was then being established. These sheet music publishers became the center of a rapidly developing and highly profitable popular music industry.

The staple of the industry was sentimental songs that told of lost love and expressed nostalgia for family and the rural ways that were being lost. Stephen Foster was the foremost of these early songwriters, and his works included nostalgic weepers such as *Swanee River* and *Old Folks at Home*. He is widely credited with founding the role of the professional songwriter, and royalties from his songs are seen as the most important contribution to the founding of the music publishing industry (Emerson, 1997). The jarring separation, homesickness, and dangers of the Civil War were a further stimulant to the production of sentimental songs of separation and loss. A note of levity and ethnic satire was added to the mix of sheet music by the minstrel and vaudeville tunes that lampooned the newly free African Americans and the recently arrived Irish, German, Italian, Jewish, and Eastern European immigrants drawn to America by the industrial expansion of the 19th century (Snyder, 1989). In the process, the fledgling popular music industry was nurtured by all of these sources.

In this example, we have seen the importance that the 19th-century movement of diverse people engendered by the Industrial Revolution had on the cross-fertilization of diverse musical traditions. We have also shown the effect that the spread of the parlor piano had on the establishment of the commercial music industry based on sheet music production, a new manufacturing and distribution system that made possible the widespread rapid transportation of disembodied music across vast distances. This case also illustrates the importance of unanticipated consequences, both because the forces of the Industrial Revolution were not intended to make for the mixing of diverse musical forms and, more concretely, because the developers and promoters of the parlor piano did not intend to found the commercial music industry. In this example, we also see how the development of a new hardware (the parlor piano) can stimulate the development of complementary software (the sheet music industry).

Records Versus Radio in the Early 20th Century

Popular music was further disembodied by the widespread acceptance of phonograph records and radio during the first three decades of the 20th century. The phonograph record captured on disk the fleeting musical performance so that it could be mass produced, widely distributed, and played back at will. During the same period, the perfection of radio broadcasting made possible the instantaneous diffusion of a musical performance to millions of listeners who (in the United States) received the music without cost. In the early days, these two technologies were in direct competition with each other—strange as that might seem now.

Thomas Alva Edison, one of the inventors of the phonograph, predicted in 1878 that the device would be used in offices for recording dictation but that it could not be used as an entertainment device in the home because of the low fidelity and fragility of the early cylinders. Yet by 1910, disk record players were in wide use throughout the land, even being carried in great numbers into rural areas, where there was no electricity, because the early players ran by being wound up like a clock. Although many of the early records were drawn from classical music and the opera, the manufacturers found that to sell ever more phonographs, they had to offer records that would be of interest to diverse tastes. This merchandising desire led to the development of separate lines of records aimed at African Americans, urban ethnics, religious communities, and rural whites—in effect, partitioning the common heritage of American folk music. At the very outset of the recording era, many of the recordings by southern white performers were in what became labeled the African American blues tradition, and numerous African Americans played fiddle-based "country music." But with the coming of record merchandising, the lines between these genres became more rigid and fixed (Peterson, 1997, pp. 194–196), with the common stock of American folk music eventually becoming segregated into seven distinct marketing categories—or, as Ennis (1992) called them, "streams of music."

Perhaps the most important consequence of this general niche market strategy was that songwriters and record producers could focus on the tastes of specific kinds of people. Consequently, innovation in each form of music occurred quite rapidly as new songs were produced and distributed nationally in a matter of weeks. The rapid development of jazz during the 1920s is an excellent case in point (Lopes, 2002; Shipton, 2001, pp. 72–162), but the same can be said for country music (Peterson, 1997). Thus, although the advent of the phonograph record narrowed and sharpened the genres of music, it also made for more rapid changes in music within genres. And it facilitated innovation in music in yet another way. Some adventurous musicians raised in one musical tradition listened to records of another genre and, after repeated listenings, were able to incorporate the other genre into their own style. The fruits of this cross-fertilization can be seen in the groundbreaking works of musicians from Bix Beiderbeck and Chet Atkins to Eric Clapton, Paul Simon, and Peter Rowan, whose most recent work is a blend of bluegrass and reggae (Schuller, 1968, pp. 177–193; Waksman, 1999, pp. 75–79).

After phonograph records became the predominant new way in which music was propagated between 1910 and 1920, radio burst onto the scene between 1922 and 1926, quickly surpassing the phonograph record player in popularity and as a force in shaping popular music. The sales of phonograph records, which had grown steadily until 1921, then fell precipitously and did not reach the same levels again until the late 1930s (Sanjek, 1988). The explanation most commonly given was that whereas one had to pay for phonograph records, radio music was delivered directly to the radio owner's home free of charge. There was great pressure from the record industry not to play phonograph records on the air, so much so that during the 1930s some records had "not licensed for radio airplay" explicitly printed on their labels.

Although records were made for a number of different niche markets, radio of the 1920–1940 period was dominated by four networks, each targeting the mass audience. To ensure popularity, radio programming had to be bland and unobjectionable to the mass audience. In consequence, songs that contained even a hint of political commentary, religious fervor, sexual innuendo, or anything but the most sentimental ethnic flavor were kept off the air. Federal Communications Commission regulations were often cited, but in practice the censorship was actually carried out by advertisers who wanted nothing aired that might offend any potential buyer's ears. Even programming targeted to niche markets such as country music was "cleaned up" and carefully monitored (Peterson, 1997, pp. 119–125).

Again we see how new technologies changed popular music by further disembodying it. The phonograph record was profoundly important in preserving musical sounds so that they could be mechanically replayed on demand at any place and time. And although radio transmission did not preserve music, it made possible the instantaneous and effortless transport of disembodied music across thousands of miles and the recapture of such music in an easily operated home radio. However, radio was interactive, and ease of transmission and consumption had come at the expense of choice. At the same time, this case study shows that two new technologies that facilitate the disembodiment of music do not necessarily have the same effects on music.

Records and Radio: The Rock Revolution of the Mid-1950s

Our final pre-internet example deals not so much with new technologies as with the realignment of two established ones: radio and records. The decade was again a time of massive geographical movement in America. As millions of young

Americans in uniform were shipped overseas, as workers moved to where war plants were located, and as African Americans migrated from the rural South to the urban North, each group brought their music with them and mixed it with other forms in the new environment.

Following World War II, there was an explosion in the number of small independent radio stations. Because they could not afford to pay live bands, most were dependent on recorded music for their programming. And because many of the smaller stations drew audiences from niche markets, there was a huge new demand for records appealing to these niches. Thus, the two media came together in a mutually beneficial alliance; records provided radio with a cheap form of programming, whereas radio air play proved to be an excellent tool for merchandising phonograph records. This new arrangement linking radio and record companies was a great boon to artists in the niche music markets such as polka, gospel, classical, children's, and ethnic, but the two genres that benefited the most from the cooperation between radio and records were rhythm-and-blues music and country music. Most important for the future of music was rock and roll, a hybrid of these targeted at the newly affluent teens that coalesced during the mid-1950s (Ennis, 1992; Peterson, 1990).

A more refined analysis would show that a number of other innovations in technology and law combined together at this time, bolstering the marriage of radio and records. To note but one example, the newly developed small, cheap, and extremely portable transistor radio was crucial to these developments. Before this time, radios were large expensive pieces of furniture placed in the living room and largely under the control of parents. With the advent of the portable transistor radio, individuals could easily take radios with them to work, to the beach, to school, and into their own private rooms, greatly facilitating the appreciation of prerecorded music as isolated individuals abstracted from the crowd of others around them.

This final example has reinforced the importance of a number of the forces we have seen before, including the mixing of populations, technological developments in facilitating the disembodiment of music, and a number of influences working in concert with each other. In addition, this case brings to the fore two additional considerations. The first is that the meaning of an innovation is not fixed. As we have seen, the antagonistic competition between radio and records that characterized the 1920s and 1930s gave way during the 1950s to a solid partnership that forged a whole new kind of popular music.

This review of four case studies clearly shows the progressive disembodiment of popular music beginning during the Middle Ages and progressing with ever greater speed to the current time. These cases sensitize us to the range of considerations that should be kept in perspective when exploring the impact of the internet on popular music. At the very least, the examples should caution humility because none of the prime movers in the innovations predicted the most important changes that would result from their innovations.

The Internet and the Digital Revolution

The internet is a crucial part of a revolutionary set of new technologies, all of which are based on having information—in this case music—in digital form. Digital music can be stored, manipulated, and moved with no measurable loss of fidelity, a promise that was unheard of 20 years ago. These changes make the disembodiment of music from the musician virtually complete (Ryan & Peterson, 1994).

The consequences for music are wide-ranging. Here we focus briefly on four. First, digital technology has democratized the recording process, allowing many more musicians to get into the business of recording their own music. For a few hundred dollars and a short period of do-it-yourself training, a musician today can buy and set up, in a corner of a room at home, recording equipment that in many ways is superior to equipment that a generation ago cost tens of thousands of dollars, had to be housed in a large dedicated studio, and required a cadre of professionals to operate.

Second, digital technology makes it possible to manipulate sound in ways that were undreamed of previously. Musical performances can be captured, broken into numerous parts, and played back in new combinations weeks or years later so that a person with no ability to play a violin or an electric guitar can digitally create sounds that may rival those of the finest masters. In addition, the recorded performance of a piece can be tweaked so that an off-pitch vocal performance can be made perfect and ham-handed instrumental work can be made to sound good. In consequence, although digital engineers are in great demand, there is much less call for excellent musicianship.

Third, digital technology has made it easy for an amateur to manufacture his or her own records at home, and the cost of manufacturing small runs of records has gone down precipitously from the days of vinyl LP (long-play) records. Thus, digital technology has led to a democratization of music production not seen since the only medium of expression was live performance more than a century ago.

Fourth, unlike previous physical media such as human performance, records, and cassettes, digital content can be distributed via the internet across the country, or across the globe, in seconds. This is similar to radio and television, but with the crucial difference that the technology to share files is in the hands of the independent producer and the average consumer. A 2001 national sample survey of respondents between 16 and 40 years of age (Edison Media Research, 2001) asked respondents "How did you first find out that the last CD you bought was available?," and 6% of the sample replied "the internet." When asked "Have you ever used your computer to burn your own CD with songs you select?," 24% replied "yes." In addition, respondents were asked "Have you downloaded music files from the internet for playback at any time in the past few months?," and 35% replied "yes." More specifically, 29% reported that they had both downloaded music and purchased CDs during the past few months, whereas the other 6% of active downloaders reported that they had not purchased any CDs during the past few months.

For the short run at least, the digital production and dissemination of culture greatly enlarges the menu of available choices for listening or acquisition, with an unprecedented array of music choices available to internet-savvy consumers (Marshall, 2001; Towse, 2001). But this is seen as a major threat by the established music industry (Garrity, 2002), and the role of the internet may well change in the foreseeable future. Using its ownership of intellectual property rights to music and considerable political and legal influence, the industry has worked diligently to close off the explosion of alternative access to music via the internet (Kretschmer, Klimis, & Wallis, 2001). In addition, provisions of the U.S. Copyright Law and recent federal legislation have served to increasingly narrow the definition of "fair use" of copyrighted material (Vaidhyanathan, 2002). And most recently, the U.S. Copyright Office has enacted a royalty-fee plan that has effectively silenced independent Web radio broadcasters, most of whom are unable to pay the fees. So, the future of the internet as a medium is still contested ground, but so far the menu of musical offerings is unprecedented.

The Internet and Musical Taste: First Findings

These developments suggest that there should be a link between internet use and cultural tastes, but the Web has many countervailing tendencies. Relative to the older broadcast media, the internet allows consumer to choose instantly from a large and diverse menu of available information, and so internet use should greatly increase the range of individual music tastes. That is, it should make consumers' tastes more omnivorous (Peterson & Kern, 1996; van Eijck, 2000). At the same time, the internet can be used by individuals to filter out information about all but those kinds of music in which they are interested. If this tendency predominates, the internet could have the effect of narrowing the tastes of people as they are able to focus with ever greater precision on those kinds of music they like best. This would make music tastes more nearly "univorous." To get a first suggestion about the direction of the influence, we explore the relationship between internet use and musical taste using data from Survey2001, a large Web-based survey of internet use, cultural taste, lifestyles, and values. For further information on the formulation and content of the study, see Witte's prologue to this volume. A total of 3,135 U.S. respondents received the form containing the questions on music.

In Survey2001, respondents were asked to indicate how much they liked various musical genres on a 5-point scale ranging from *like very much* to *dislike very much*. "Omnivorousness" was operationalized as the number of genres an individual reported liking or liking very much. Detailed information on the study can be found in Peterson and Ryan (2002). Survey2001 also asked a number of questions about internet use, but unfortunately, there was no direct measure of listening to, learning about, discussing, or downloading music from the internet. Instead, the survey asked respondents about their use of the internet for 11 different purposes, and these items were used in constructing the internet Use Index. Finally, based on previous research on cultural taste, four demographic control variables were used in the study: age, gender, education, and race/ethnic identity.

To estimate the relationship between music taste and internet use, we performed an ordinary least squares regression analysis on our index of omnivorous music taste while taking into account the effects of the four control variables. The results of the regression analysis show that omnivorous musical taste is not significantly related to age, ethnicity, or education among these relatively affluent and well-educated internet-using respondents. Gender proves to be significantly related to omnivorous musical taste, with women on average being significantly more omnivorous than men. Although this finding is not unexpected, it is unusual for it to have the strongest association with omnivorousness when education and other factors are included in the analysis. When men, particularly young men, like a particular kind of music very much, they seem to identify with it more deeply. They tend to download more songs, buy more records, go to more concerts, wear the distinctive "uniform" of the particular genre more often, and talk derogatively about other kinds of music. Most genres of music are seen as a male domain. Women, particularly young women, are more likely to identify with particular artists and be agreeable with others about music choices.

Finally, we come to our prime measure of interest, that is, internet use. The study shows that there is a significant relationship between greater internet use and greater omnivorousness. Although the variance explained is modest, it is remarkable that there is a significant relationship at all between musical taste and internet use as measured here. First, all of the respondents were internet users to some degree, so people who do not use the Web at all (approximately half of the population) are not represented among the respondents. Second, although some individuals may use the internet largely to find out about and download music, most uses of the internet have nothing to do with listening to, talking about, or exchanging music, so many wide-ranging internet users might not be engaging with music at all on the internet. Insofar as this is the case, the significant association between omnivorousness and internet use may be part of an unmeasured active inquisitiveness, as suggested by DiMaggio (1996). These initial results strongly suggest that greater internet use increases the range of musical tastes, but the data are crude and the relationship between internet use and musical taste deserves further study.

Conclusion

This chapter has shown that the advent of the internet can be seen as a stage in the historical shift from embodied music to disembodied music. If the historical examples have taught us anything, it is that the consequences of technological innovations are not anticipated at the time of their implementation but rather unfold over decades. With this caution in mind, we have suggested two alternative consequences that the internet might have on musical tastes. Relative to the older broadcast media, the internet makes information on a vast array of subjects instantly available, so Web use may facilitate exploration of a diverse range of cultural opportunities on offer, facilitating the already well-developed trend toward omnivorous music tastes. At the same time, the various filtering devices built into the internet technology, as well as the rapid development of ever more circumscribed niche media, make it possible to filter out all but those topics in which an individual is interested. The preliminary data presented here suggest that the internet is a new tool available for those seeking to enrich and broaden their tastes, furthering the historic drive toward disembodied music.

References

Becker, H. S. (1982). *Art worlds*. Berkeley: University of California Press.

DiMaggio, P. (1996). Are art-museum visitors different from other people? The relationship between attendance and social and political attitudes in the United States. *Poetics, 24*(2–4), 161–180.

Edison Media Research. (2001). *The National Record Buyers Survey*. [Online]. Retrieved April 30, 2003, from www.edisonresearch.com/r&rrecordbuyers.htm

Emerson, K. (1997). *Stephen Foster and the rise of American popular culture*. New York: Simon & Schuster.

Ennis, P. H. (1992). *The seventh stream*. Hanover, NH: Wesleyan University Press.

Garrity, B. (2002, September 7). Sales, shipments drop in first half. *Billboard*, p. 3.

Goffman, E. (1951). Symbols of class status. *British Journal of Sociology, 2*, 294–304.

Goodall, H. (2000). *Big bangs: The story of five discoveries that changed musical history*. New York: Random House.

Kretschmer, M., Klimis, G. M., & Wallis, R. (2001). The global music industry in the digital environment: A study of strategic intent and policy responses, 1996–2000. In S. Janssen, M. Halbertsma, & K. Ernst (Eds.), *Trends and strategies in the arts and culture industries* (pp. 419–440). Rotterdam, Netherlands: Barjesteh Press.

Levine, L. W. (1988). *Highbrow/Lowbrow: The emergence of cultural hierarchy in America*. Cambridge, MA: Harvard University Press.

Lopes, P. D. (2002). *The rise of a jazz art world*. New York: Cambridge University Press.

Marshall, L. (2001). The future of bootlegging: Current legal and technological pressures. In S. Janssen, M. Halbertsma, & K. Ernst (Eds.), *Trends and strategies in the arts and culture industries* (pp. 441–453). Rotterdam, Netherlands: Barjesteh Press.

McCleary, S. (1991). *Feminine endings: Music, gender, and sexuality*. Minneapolis: University of Minnesota Press.

Peterson, R. A. (1990). Why 1955? Explaining the advent of rock music. *Popular Music, 9*, 97–116.

Peterson, R. A. (1997). *Creating country music: Fabricating authenticity*. Chicago: University of Chicago Press.

Peterson, R. A., & Kern, R. M. (1996). Changing highbrow taste: From snob to omnivore. *American Sociological Review, 61*, 900–907.

Peterson, R. A., & Ryan, J. (2002). *Internet use and broadening musical taste: A first look*. Unpublished manuscript, Vanderbilt University.

Ryan, J., & Peterson, R. A. (1994). Occupational and organizational consequences of the digital revolution in music making. In M. Cantor & S. Zollars (Eds.), *Creators of culture* (pp. 173–201). Greenwich, CT: JAI.

Sanjek, R. (1988). *American popular music and its business: The first four hundred years*, Vol. 3: *From 1900 to 1988*. New York: Oxford University Press.

Schuller, G. (1968). *Early jazz*. New York: Oxford University Press.

Shipton, A. (2001). *A new history of jazz*. London: Continuum.

Snyder, R. W. (1989). *The voice of the city: Vaudeville and popular culture in New York*. New York: Oxford University Press.

Towse, R. (2001). Cultural economics, copyright, and cultural industries. In S. Janssen, M. Halbertsma, & K. Ernst (Eds.), *Trends and strategies in the arts and culture industries* (pp. 85–103). Rotterdam, Netherlands: Barjesteh Press.

Vaidhyanathan, S. (2002, August 2). Copyright as cudgel. *Chronicle of Higher Education*, p. B7.

van Eijck, K. (2000). Richard A. Peterson and the culture of consumption. *Poetics, 28,* 207–224.

Waksman, S. (1999). *Instruments of desire: The electric guitar and the shaping of musical experience.* Cambridge, MA: Harvard University Press.

15

Technology and Tolerance

Public Opinion Differences
Among Internet Users and Nonusers

John P. Robinson
University of Maryland

Alan Neustadtl
University of Maryland

Meyer Kestnbaum
University of Maryland

Speculations about the impact of the internet often focus on social life, personal communication, and mass communication. Two widely publicized studies of early internet impact reported results consistent with the hypothesis of Kraut and colleagues (1998) and Nie and Erbring (2000) about declines in certain aspects of social life brought about by internet use. However, studies that have used a less ambitious set of questions and research designs have produced somewhat different results (Robinson, Barth, & Kohut, 1997; Robinson & Kestnbaum, 1999; Robinson, Kestnbaum, Neustadtl, & Alvarez, 2000). Based on 1995 Pew Internet and American Life Project data, for example, Robinson and colleagues (1997) found that 1995 internet and information technology users were significantly *more* likely to use print media, radio newscasts, and movies than were nonusers and that the former were not less likely to be television viewers of either entertainment or news content. These results are robust, remaining after statistical controls for gender, age, education, income, race, and marital status were introduced to the analyses.

Nonetheless, the results from the early Kraut and colleagues (1998) and Nie and Erbring (2000) studies do raise questions about the constrained nature of social life conducted through the internet and suggest that it may restrict the kinds of information that people use to form their opinions. Opposite to that are the demographic characteristics of early internet users, in particular, their greater years of education and higher incomes. Indeed, well-publicized studies of the "digital divide" in government reports have made it clear that education and income are the main ways in which internet users differ from nonusers (McConnaughey, Everette, Reynolds, & Lader, 1999; McConnaughey, Lader, Chin, & Everette, 1998; McConnaughey, Levy, & Lader, 2002; McConnaughey, Nika, & Stein, 1995). But outside of these factors, can we expect the opinions of internet users to differ significantly from those of nonusers?

Internet Use and Social Norms

Early studies of the digital divide have identified other social correlates of internet use that were not economic or status related in character such as the greater use by men and younger adult age groups. More recent studies, however, have shown that many of the gaps across these groups have disappeared or closed significantly (DiMaggio, Hargittai, Neuman, & Robinson, 2001).

These features are clearly to be expected from the literature on the diffusion of innovations, as summarized in Rogers's (1995) classic work on the topic. According to Rogers, early adopters of innovations are notably distinguished by their higher levels of education (this is associated with greater awareness of social changes, mainly via their greater attention to news media) and higher levels of income (being able to afford purchasing the innovation).

The same patterns were found for extent of internet use as measured in the General Social Survey (GSS). As described in more detail later, GSS respondents were asked to estimate the weekly hours they spent using e-mails and the weekly hours they spent using the World Wide Web, with the figures then added together to give an estimate of the total amount of time spent on the internet. Again, weekly use was far more related to respondents' education than to their household income, both when including people who do not use the internet at all and when examining only internet users.

PUBLIC OPINION

In addition to education and income (and often younger age), Rogers (1995) noted the greater "cosmopolitanism" of earlier adopters that prompted them to adopt innovations. Rogers also hypothesized that earlier adopters would be less dogmatic, better able to deal with abstractions, more change oriented, more favorable toward science, and more intelligent. He further described them as having more social connections, more empathy, more opinion leadership, and exposure to both mass and interpersonal communication channels. According to this view, then, we would expect that earlier internet users would be more open to and tolerant of deviant or nonconforming individuals in society as well as more positive on other social characteristics.

In contrast, and in particular reference to the internet and its potentially isolating features, Sunstein (2001) raised concerns about its ability to constrain political dialogue. In particular, he raised concerns over the potential of creating "Daily Me" productions of internet content that isolate users from opposite points of view. He sees this as completely antithetical to the wish of America's Founding Fathers to use such public forums to provoke and promote political dialogue in which opposing views could be fully and fairly aired and deliberated. The internet in this model promotes more "group polarization" in which like-minded people in isolated groups reinforce each other's opinions, thereby leading to extremist and less tolerant views. As the role of traditional media diminishes, "the customization of our communications universe increases, society is in danger of fragmenting, [and] shared communities [are] in danger of dissolving" (p. 18). This pessimistic assessment stands in marked contrast to earlier upbeat speculations about how the internet could provide national "town meetings," at which everyone gets to speak, and to Rogers's (1995) positive depiction of new technology users being more open and cosmopolitan. It also stands in contrast to Borsook's (2000) contention that the "libertarian" character of internet content would rub off on the attitudes of its users.

We now turn our attention to describing a national public opinion data set that allows these contrasting points of view to be examined. The GSS has been used to collect national public opinion data about social issues regularly since 1972. The 2000 GSS was a personal in-home interview that usually took about 90 minutes to complete with a national probability sample of 2,817 respondents age 18 years or over. At each selected household, one adult person was interviewed at random using sampling procedures.[1] Interviewing took place between February and mid-June 2000.

GSS INTERNET USE QUESTIONS

The main internet questions used in the current analysis are the internet use questions asked of all respondents at the outset of most versions. Respondents were first asked whether they used a computer at all at home, at work, or at another location. If not, they were asked whether they had access to the internet via WebTV. If they said "no" to both questions, they were coded as having zero hours or minutes of both e-mail use and World Wide Web use per week; that is, they were categorized as nonusers in the analyses that follow. Just over half of the 2,353 GSS respondents fell into this category.

Those who said "yes" to either the general use or WebTV question were asked to estimate how many hours or minutes a week they used their computer/WebTV to send or receive e-mail. To estimate the total time spent per week for both e-mail and Web use, their hour figures were added to their minute figures (divided by 60) to arrive at a total hourly amount of use of both features. To arrive at a total amount of internet use, the e-mail figures were added to the Web figures. Thus, if a respondent estimated 2.0 hours of e-mail use and 2.5 hours of Web use, his or her hourly internet time figure would be 4.5 hours; if the respondent used e-mail for 6.0 hours but had no Web use, the figure would be 6.0 hours.

The general plan in the following analyses, then, is to see how the various GSS questions dealing with openness, tolerance, and diversity differ by extent of internet use. Do internet users report more open and tolerant attitudes, as expected under Rogers's (1995) diffusion model, or are they less open and more intolerant, as suggested by Sunstein's (2001) arguments?

GSS ATTITUDE QUESTIONS

Of particular interest in the GSS data set is the set of questions on tolerance. These are questions that provided a main impetus for conducting the GSS during its first years. They involved the questions developed by Stouffer (1956) in his classic study of political tolerance conducted during the 1950s "McCarthy era." Stouffer found that levels of public tolerance at that time were disturbingly low (e.g., about 90% of respondents felt that Communist teachers should be fired and about 66% felt that Communists should not be allowed to make speeches or have their books in public libraries).

However, Stouffer (1956) also found that tolerance was strongly related to respondents' level of education. Because increasing numbers of young Americans were now attending college, Stouffer hypothesized that tolerance in the United

States would likely increase in the future. This hypothesis of an increasingly politically tolerant America by the process of "generation replacement" was subsequently confirmed by Davis (1975). Additional GSS items related to tolerance include attitudes toward African Americans and other minorities as well as toward immigration of new ethnic and racial groups to the United States. GSS respondents were also asked about attitudes toward traditional roles for women, especially in relation to work, child rearing, and family expectations. Other GSS questions inquired into attitudes toward sexual relations, such as premarital sex and pornography, another area involving tolerance of what might be considered deviant behavior.

Further tolerance-related items more directly addressed legal and justice-related issues such as capital punishment and drug use. Included here are questions about support for various police actions, gun ownership, and general court lenience. Broader questions were raised about whether the government should legislate help to disadvantaged and less affluent segments of society. Related questions examined what respondents thought was equitable pay for various professions in society. New GSS questions in 2000 asked about government clearances and punishments for government and military employees who are involved in breaking government regulations on these matters. New questions also were asked about respondents' perceptions of various freedoms in the United States; presumably, people on the internet may feel more "free" because they have such new and open channels of communication.

The GSS also asked questions about how people felt about the government agenda and about spending public funds on programs to support education, the military, or crime reduction. To the extent that these issues connect to the "libertarian" outlook presumably embodied in the internet (Borsook, 2000), internet-connected respondents should be more supportive of reduced government spending in most areas. Similarly, they may have lower confidence in government than in private institutions. Finally, we might find them to have more trust in their fellow citizens. In Table 15.1, each of these sets of questions was correlated with not using the internet and with four categories of internet users, from the lightest users to the heaviest users.[2]

In the analyses that follow, one can see that some internet differences are "monotonic" in that the amount of tolerance for different social attitudes keeps steady pace with the amount of internet use. If the relationship between internet use and tolerance were monotonic, there should be a straightforward linear relationship between the amount of time spent online and the amount of tolerance a

Table 15.1   Differences Between Internet Users and Nonusers on Scales of Public Opinion and Tolerance (percentages except scale scores)

| Social Attitude | Nonuser | Internet User | | | | User-Nonuser Difference |
		Light User (0.1–1.9 hours/week)	Moderate User (2.0–4.9 hours/week)	Heavy (5.0–9.9 hours/week)	Heaviest (10 + hours/week)	
Tolerance Scale	9.7	10.1	11.3+	10.7	10.9	+1.2
Racial attitudes						
Minority assertiveness tolerable	46	65	69+	69+	64	+21
Minorities have abilities	84	91	91	89	90	+6
Minorities have willpower	47	53	54	54	58+	+7
Gender and family						
Support women working outside home	55	63	65	63	68+	+10
Support women in politics	77	74	84+	83	82	+7
Support women's right to abortion	36	38	43	48+	50+	+9
Child obedience unimportant	75	75	87+	79	82	+7
Important that child thinks for self	42	51	53	55+	52	+11
Sex attitudes						
Premarital sex tolerable	69	69	70	79+	79+	+5
Homosexuality tolerable	35	40	53+	44	52+	+10
Pornography laws tolerable	59	60	66	69+	71+	+8
Sex education tolerable	82	89	89	91	91	+8
Confidence in institutions						
Companies	23	36+	27	32	31	+9
Supreme Court	29	31	33	36	39+	+6
Science	38	44	49	53+	53+	+12

Social Attitude	Nonuser	Internet User				User-Nonuser Difference
		Light User (0.1–1.9 hours/week)	Moderate User (2.0–4.9 hours/week)	Heavy (5.0–9.9 hours/week)	Heaviest (10+ hours/week)	
Personal Trust Scale	2.6	3.3	3.3	3.3	3.0	+0.6
People can be trusted	30	40	41	47+	36	+11
People are fair	49	58	67+	58	59	+12
People are helpful	43	54+	51	50	48	+8
Verbal Skills Scale	5.6	6.4	6.3	6.7+	6.4	+0.8
Comprehension of questions	76	90	94	92	92	+17
Health and outlook						
Health is excellent	27	38+	34	31	30	+6
Life is exciting	41	52	55+	56+	44	+11
Finances are above average	20	25	30+	27	28	+8
Total number of plusses	0	3	8	6	7	+10
n	658	174	155	141	194	

SOURCE: Data from 2000 General Social Survey.

NOTE: These are after MCA adjustment for age, education, gender, race, income, and marital status. A plus sign (+) indicates a value above what would be expected if there were a steadily increasing monotonic relationship between the social attitude and the amount of time spent using the internet.

person has. We should be able to predict how tolerant a person is by the amount of time he or she spends online, and every additional period of time spent online should be matched with an additional unit of tolerance on our scale. For example, if a person who spends 1 hour online each week has a tolerance score of 2 out of 10 and a person who spends 2 hours online each week has a tolerance score of 4 out of 10, we might anticipate that someone who spends 3 hours online each week will have a tolerance score of 6 out of 10. If we sample the population and find that people who spend 3 hours online each week actually have a tolerance score of 7 out of 10, we would mark this jump with a plus sign (+) because the value is above what we would expect if the relationship between internet use and tolerance were straightforwardly monotonic. Some groups of internet users have surprisingly high or surprisingly low tolerance levels on particular questions, and such differences, noted with (+) signs in the final column of heaviest users in Table 15.1, suggest that internet use itself could underlie the relation. On the other hand, many of the patterns are found to be nonmonotonic, that is, with the highest (+) values found among moderate or light users. This indicates that the amount of internet use is less important than the differences between internet users and nonusers.

Technology and Tolerance

For the 2000 GSS, questions on tolerance basically involved three types of toler-ance situations—making a public speech, teaching in a college, and having a book in a public library—crossed by five types of spokespersons for various causes (atheists, racists, Communists, militarists, and homosexuals) that cover both the political "right" and "left" in content. All questions were asked in simple dichotomous terms, for example, whether an atheist should be allowed (a) to speak, (b) to teach, or (c) to have a book in the library. Each response option was recoded to a score of 1 for a tolerant response or 0 for a nontolerant, uncertain, or qualified response.

As in previous GSS studies of these items, they are found to tap essentially a single dimension of tolerance when the items are factor analyzed. That is, responses to each item correlate at about the same level (from about .30 to .50) with each other. That means that GSS respondents who are tolerant of atheists speaking in public are also significantly more tolerant of having racist books in a public library.

Thus, responses were added into a single additive index, with 1 point given for each tolerant response. The resulting scale had an average score of 10.2 posi-tive responses, higher than the 7.5 score that would have resulted if respondents had given tolerant responses to half of the items. Scores on that scale were then entered into a multiple classification analysis (MCA) as the dependent variable, with five major predictor variables of tolerance included as predictors. Male, white, and higher income respondents generally gave more tolerant responses. However, the major two predictors of tolerance, namely education and age, were the same as for internet use. Are the tolerance differences, then, simply a function of internet users being younger and more highly educated?

When the average scores on the 15-item index are statistically adjusted by MCA for the respondent's age, education, income, gender, and race, the original average 3-point difference in tolerance scores is cut to just over a 1-point difference, as shown in the first row of Table 15.1. The original correlation of .29 between tolerance and internet use was reduced to .13. Thus, it is the case that most of the difference in tolerance scores can be accounted for by common background predictors of internet use. Nonetheless, the internet difference is still statistically significant after this adjustment, although it can be seen that the relation is not monotonic; heaviest users (10.0+ hours per week) are above average in tolerance after adjustment, but their tolerance scores are not as high as those of moderate internet users (2.0–4.9 hours per week). At the same time, both user types show up as being notably more tolerant than the lightest internet users and the nonusers. Clearly, then, internet users give more tolerant responses, even though their tolerance levels increase as a simple function of more internet exposure. These differences, moreover, are not a simple function of a common correlation with the basic demographic predictors of internet use. Internet users tend to be more tolerant on these GSS items independent of their demographic background.

RACIAL/ETHNIC ATTITUDES

The GSS has also regularly examined the public's attitudes toward racial and ethnic minorities, particularly attitudes toward African Americans. These questions were largely developed during the 1960s and involve opposition to mixed-race marriages, "pushing" for equal rights, open housing, and perceived reasons for African American inequality with whites. The 2000 GSS included more than 100 new questions on ethnic and race relations, including the contributions of various ethnic/racial groups to the country, opposition to increased immigration of various groups, and extent/degree of contact with various groups.

Turning first to the GSS questions asked in previous surveys, increased internet use is correlated with more positive orientations toward African Americans such as support for interracial marriage and opposition to pushiness as well as explanations for African American inequality in terms of less inborn ability or lack of willpower (but not discrimination or educational opportunity). Heavier internet use is also correlated with perceptions that African Americans' condition has not improved over the years, with the feeling that African Americans can work their way out of poverty in the same way white immigrant groups can, and with living in an integrated neighborhood. At the same time, no differences in internet use can be found in support for affirmative action or for generally feeling closer to whites or African Americans as a group.

However, after MCA adjustment for race, education, age, and gender, about half of these correlations no longer hold significantly. In particular, the relations with attitudes toward interracial marriage, African Americans' lives not improving, living in a nonintegrated neighborhood, and feeling that African Americans cannot work their way up in the same way white immigrant groups can are explained by correlation with demographic factors. Table 15.1 shows that the only relations that remain significant after MCA adjustment are for opposition to racial pushiness and for rejecting explanations for African Americans' poorer position in terms of inborn inability to learn and lack of motivation or willpower. These are the only three racial questions for which a response can be significantly predicted by internet use, indicating attitudes that are distinctively held by internet users.

Of the large number of new questions about race, minorities, and immigrants in the 2000 GSS survey, about a quarter of the responses to these questions are correlated with internet use. These are mainly clustered in three areas of GSS questioning: contributions of various groups to American life, opposition to immigration, and personally knowing members of various minorities. In general, nearly all of these correlations are explained by the demographic predictors after control. The main exception among internet users is their lower suspicion that immigration causes Americans to lose jobs. At the same time, there is still clearly and consistently (if not significantly) lower opposition to immigration among internet users, particularly among heaviest users.

It is more important to note all of the attitudes in this series for which no significant correlations with racial/ethnic perceptions are found among internet users: perceptions of intelligence, proneness to violence, commitment to family life, and fairness to other minorities. Nor do internet users differ significantly in their ability to speak other languages, have different attitudes toward various language policies, or estimate different proportions of minorities in the country (or in their communities, workplaces, schools, and other locations).

In brief, internet users express more tolerant attitudes toward African Americans and immigrants on a few selected issues. On most such minority/immigrant questions, however, differences are either nonexistent or explained by basic demographic variables. In other words, the rather strong and consistent pattern of more tolerant responses to civil liberties situations does not carry over consistently or as well to minority/ethnic/racial issues.

GENDER AND FAMILY

Traditional GSS questions regarding gender and family cover three general areas: working wives and mothers, abortion, and child rearing values and physical discipline. All of the items related to women's employment are significantly correlated with internet use (except for special hiring practices) in that users are more likely to espouse more "liberated" attitudes so far as women's employment is concerned. Users are more likely to say that working mothers have just as close a relation with their children, that preschool children do not suffer, that the benefits to the family are not better if the wife simply stays at home, and that women are not less suited to politics than are men.

However, Table 15.1 shows that only two of these correlations remain significant after adjustment by MCA: those for disagreeing that it is best for the family if the wife stays at home and for women being suited for politics. The items related to abortion all show internet users as being more supportive, with generally increasing support the greater their internet use. Only two of the six bivariate correlations with child-rearing values and practices are significant, but both remain significant after MCA adjustment. Internet users place notably lower value on obedience in child rearing and place higher value on independent "thinking for oneself." Internet use is unrelated to wanting children to be popular, to work hard, or to help others—and to approving of the use of spanking as a means of controlling children. As with race issues, then, internet users tend toward more tolerant or liberal views on certain gender and family issues.

SEX ATTITUDES

The GSS has asked seven questions on sex attitudes over the years. Four of them concern the acceptability of sexual relations under various conditions (premarital, extramarital, teenage, and homosexual), and the other three ask about sex education, divorce laws, and pornography laws. In addition, there is a question about attending X-rated movies. On all of these questions, internet users are more tolerant or supportive of various sexual practices—more accepting of various sexual practices not being "wrong" and more liberal on pornography, divorce laws, and sex education. However, after MCA adjustment, four of these eight correlations (for extramarital sex, teen sex, divorce laws, and attending X-rated movies) no longer hold. As shown in Table 15.1, the strongest of these is for acceptability of homosexual relations, although again the relation is not monotonic across extent of internet use, with the 5.0- to 9.9-hour group being below a plus sign (+) for the 2.0- to 4.9-hour group in support. The differences for the items on premarital sex, pornography laws, and sex education are monotonic but are smaller between nonusers and heaviest internet users.

CONFIDENCE IN INSTITUTIONS

The GSS regularly asks questions about public confidence in 13 institutions using a 3-point response scale. It can be seen that internet use correlates significantly with higher trust in four of them—major companies, science, television, and the Supreme Court. Internet use is not significantly correlated with confidence in religion, education, labor, Congress, or the military.

Of the four correlations that are significant, only the three shown in Table 15.1 remain significant after MCA adjustment. Of the three, the strongest relation is with confidence in science, perhaps reflecting in some way the role that science played in constructing the internet. After MCA adjustment, 53% of heaviest internet users reported a great deal of confidence in science compared with 38% of nonusers. Smaller, but still incrementally increasing, confidence was found for the Supreme Court, but the plus sign denoting highest confidence in companies was found among least active internet users (less than 2 hours per week).

GENERAL TRUST IN PEOPLE

In contrast to the scattered pattern of internet correlations with institutions, users reported significantly more trust in people in the three items used to tap that construct. This was true after MCA adjustment as well. The overall pattern is somewhat curvilinear, however, with the plus sign for highest overall trust (3.3) found among those who use the internet from 0.1 to 10.0 hours per week, that for intermediate trust (3.0) found among those who use it 10.0+ hours per week, and that for lowest trust (2.6) found among nonusers after adjustment. This means that heavier internet users are less trustful than intermediate users.

In examining the individual three trust items in Table 15.1, it can be seen that this pattern is evident in each of them. The overall differences are greatest for the "fair" item and are less so for the "trust" and "helpful" items. In all three items, however, lowest general trust is found among the heaviest group of internet users.

GOVERNMENT SPENDING PRIORITIES

To test whether internet users take a more antigovernment libertarian stand on government spending, one can examine 16 areas of government spending in the GSS questionnaire. None of these correlations remains significant after MCA adjustment, however. In other words, internet use is generally unrelated to feelings about government spending in any area—either positively or negatively.

Moreover, internet use is also unrelated to feelings that one is paying too much taxes or that the government should do more to reduce the income gap between the rich and the poor. This would seem to be counter to Borsook's (2000) hypothesis that internet use is associated with libertarian points of view.

FREEDOM

The 2000 GSS included 14 new questions about attitudes toward freedom, beginning with respondent definitions of what the word "freedom" meant to them and then moving on to estimates of how much freedom they felt Americans and they had today, whether it was more or less than that during previous years, and their satisfaction with that freedom. Respondents were then asked about six definitional statements about freedom (e.g., "Freedom is being left alone to do what I want to do") and how important those statements were to them. Finally, they were asked about freedom of the press, about a few people having a great deal of wealth in a free society, and how much freedom and control they had over their own lives.

Only one of these questions is significantly correlated with internet use: the amount of freedom that respondents felt they had now. However, after MCA adjustment, even this relation does not hold.

GENERAL VERBAL SKILLS

The GSS interviews routinely end by asking respondents about their awareness of the meaning of 10 vocabulary words, similar to multiple-choice questions asked on college entrance exams. The task is for respondents to find suitable synonyms for words such as "belief" and "solitude" among a list of five words presented to them. In addition, interviewers are asked to rate the general ability of respondents to comprehend the meaning of the questions asked of them. Both measures are significantly related to extent of internet use.

Both of these relations are reduced but continue to hold after MCA adjustment for age, education, income, and gender in Table 15.1. In the case of vocabulary scores, nonusers scored 5.4 words, or 0.6 words below the overall average of 6.0 words correct. Lightest internet users, in contrast, scored a full word higher, at 6.5 words, the same as the next heaviest group. In the second highest and highest groups, word scores averaged more than 6.8. After MCA adjustment, the overall user versus nonuser difference drops below 1 point and varies little by extent of use. Much the same conclusion emerges from analyses of interviewer ratings of comprehension (with lower scores reflecting higher perceived understanding).

HEALTH AND OUTLOOK

Finally, there are differences by the GSS questions dealing with health and outlook. In particular are the repeated GSS single items asking respondents to rate their health, their happiness, their happiness with their marriage (if married), their life as exciting or dull, and their satisfaction with their financial situation. Only the bivariate correlations with health and financial satisfaction are statistically significant.

Table 15.1 shows the pattern of responses after MCA adjustment. In the case of physical health, it can be seen that the major difference after MCA adjustment is between users and nonusers, with the highest proportion rating their health as "excellent" among the lightest internet-using group (38%) and then declining the more the internet is used, with the heaviest internet-using group (30%) only slightly higher than the nonusers (27%).

A similar nonmonotonic pattern is found for rating one's life as exciting, with the highest level found among moderate internet users (55%) and the 44% rating of heaviest users barely higher than the 41% rating of nonusers.

The latter pattern emerges as well for rating one's financial situation as "above average," with the highest ratings found for moderate, heavy, and very heavy internet users (30%, 27%, and 28%, respectively) compared with lightest users and nonusers (25% and 20%, respectively). It is important to note that annual income has been added to the MCA as a crucial control variable. In other words, internet users rate their financial situation as above average no matter what their income level; both poor and rich internet users rate their financial situations as above average more than do comparably poor and rich nonusers.

Overall, then, Table 15.1 indicates that internet users do appear to feel healthier and more upbeat about their lives than do nonusers, although moderate users feel healthier and more upbeat than do heaviest users. The same is not true, however, for marital happiness—or for several other mental health indicators added to the 2000 GSS dealing with feelings of depression, inactivity, and nonsociability.

To recapitulate, Table 15.1 summarizes the major GSS attitude items on which significant differences were found between internet users and nonusers, arranged into six rough categories. As with the tolerance questions, internet users generally emerge as more open on most of these issues. They are more open to "pro-minority" views and to the idea that African Americans' poor position in society is not biologically determined. They are more open to married women working, being in politics, and having abortions as well as to children thinking for themselves rather than simply obeying. They are more open to premarital sex and homosexuality as well as to supporting current pornography laws and sex education in the schools. They have more confidence in "independent" institutions—companies, the Supreme Court, and science. They are more trusting of others in general, viewing them as mainly fair and trying to be helpful. Finally, they report feeling healthier and having exciting lives and above average financial situations.

The overall relations in Table 15.1 are summarized by the number of plus signs for each of the five groups of internet users in the table. It is important to note three factors about these differences:

1. The average difference of 10 percentage points between internet users and nonusers in general (including heavier and lighter users) holds after MCA adjustment for other demographic predictors of these opinions.

2. The differences are not monotonic; that is, they do not increase with increasing internet use. As shown by the placement of plus signs in Table 15.1, there are actually more among moderate users (eight) than among heaviest users (seven), although light users show the fewest plus signs (three) at the bottom of the table.

3. These are the only significant differences after MCA adjustment among the hundreds of attitude questions in the GSS. On other GSS questions, there are either no differences or the differences can be explained by internet users being younger, better educated, or different on other demographic background factors.

Thus, internet users are clearly more open or tolerant on these items. Internet users are only selectively more tolerant in ways that defy description in simple terms such as liberal, libertarian, and progressive.

Conclusion

In this chapter, the 2000 GSS data and 2001 National Telecommunications and Information Administration data were used to gain insight into the attitude and demographic differences between internet users and nonusers, with particular attention to questions about whether internet use is associated with tolerant social attitudes. The analysis is limited because GSS respondents were interviewed at a single point in time, precluding causal inferences. Nonetheless, it seems likely that these are preexisting differences that made the internet an attractive new medium for these users.

In general, the analysis shows that where differences are found, they are in the direction of internet users being more open and tolerant than nonusers. However, the differences are often nonmonotonic; that is, tolerance does not always increase the more one uses the internet. Moreover, the differences occur for some on some specific race, family, sex, or politics items but not on others.

The differences are often subtle and do not hold for all issues. They do not fit easily under standard labels such as liberal, conservative, and libertarian. But independent of internet users' higher education, lower age, and other demographic factors, we can say a number of things about their attitudes. Internet users support the view that minority and controversial (atheist, Communist, racist, and militarist) writings should be available in public libraries and that spokespersons for those ideas should be allowed to speak or teach. Internet users agree that children should be taught to think for themselves and not simply be expected to be obedient. Internet users oppose the view that African Americans are pushing too hard for equality and reject attributing African Americans' lower social status to genetic factors or lack of motivation. Finally, internet users express greater tolerance for premarital and homosexual sex (but not extramarital or teenage sex), support sex education in public schools (but not birth control for teenagers), and express greater confidence in science, the courts, and business.

Internet users also tend to express a more optimistic view of life, describing themselves as healthier, happier, and having above average financial situations. They are more trusting of their fellow citizens. Because these data are from one snapshot at the turn of the 21st century, it remains to be seen how much these patterns of tolerance change in the years to come.

Notes

1. Like its predecessors, the 2000 GSS national probability sample was selected in two major stages, with primary sampling units (PSUs) consisting of one or more counties selected at the first stage and segments consisting of one or more blocks selected at the second stage. The sample

consisted of 100 first-stage selections, PSUs consisting of metropolitan areas or nonmetropolitan counties. Prior to the PSU selection, the United States was divided into 2,489 PSUs, and the PSUs were then sorted into strata. The major strata again grouped metropolitan and nonmetropolitan PSUs within each of the four census regions. A total of 19 PSUs (e.g., Chicago, Boston) were so large that they had to be included in the sample with certainty. For the 2000 GSS, approximately five housing units per segment were selected. Professional interviewers hired and trained by NORC conducted the interviews. In addition to a 2- or 3-day general training session before hiring, these NORC interviewers went through a mailed training session focusing on the various goals and modules of the 2000 GSS. Interviewers made repeat visits to households where no one was home or where the designated household respondent was not available. Enough repeat callbacks were made to such households that the main form of nonresponse was respondent refusal to participate. Interviewers were able to complete interviews with 70% of designated respondents. The total of 2,817 GSS respondents completed one of the six versions or ballots described in this chapter and shown in their entirety at the following Web site: www.webuse.umd.edu. Five of the six ballots in the 2000 GSS, except Ballot 3 ($n = 454$), contained some internet questions. That left 2,363 respondents eligible for the internet module questions on the remaining five ballots, with each ballot representing a separate (and minimally clustered) random sample of the country. All questions about basic or core e-mail and World Wide Web use were asked of all 2,363 respondents across each of the five ballots.

    2. Because these bivariate correlations could be due simply to common correlations with internet use, in Table 15.1, the extent to which these common correlations are changed is adjusted by multiple classification analysis (MCA) for age, education, gender, race, income, and marital status. MCA was developed by survey statisticians (Andrews, Morgan, & Sonquist, 1973) to perform the function of adjusting differences in bivariate analysis for one predictor variable (e.g., age) for other predictors (e.g., education, income) in that model. MCA adjustments allow us to make parts of the sample comparable to one another.

References

Andrews, F., Morgan, J., & Sonquist, J. (1973). *Multiple classification analysis.* Ann Arbor, MI: Institute for Social Research.

Borsook, P. (2000). *Cyberselfish: A critical romp through the terribly libertarian culture of high tech.* New York: Public Affairs.

Davis, J. A. (1975). Communism, conformity, cohorts, and categories: American tolerance in 1954 and 1972–73. *American Journal of Sociology, 81,* 491–513.

DiMaggio, P., Hargittai, E., Neuman, W. R., & Robinson, J. P. (2001). Social implications of the internet. *Annual Review of Sociology, 27,* 307–336.

Kraut, R., Patterson, M., Lundmark, V., Kiesler, S., Mukophadhyay, T., & Scherlis, W. (1998). Internet paradox. *American Psychologist, 53,* 1017–1031.

McConnaughey, J., Everette, D. W., Reynolds, T., & Lader, W. (1999). *Falling through the net: Defining the digital divide.* Washington, DC: U.S. Department of Commerce.

McConnaughey, J., Lader, W., Chin, R., & Everette, C. (1998). *Falling through the net II: New data on the digital divide.* Washington, DC: U.S. Department of Commerce.

McConnaughey, J., Levy, K., & Lader, W. (2002). *A nation online: How Americans are expanding their use of the internet.* Washington, DC: U.S. Department of Commerce.

McConnaughey, J., Nika, C. A., & Stein, T. (1995). *Falling through the net: A survey of the "have nots" in rural and urban America.* Washington, DC: U.S. Department of Commerce.

Nie, N. H., & Erbring, L. (2000). *Internet and society: A preliminary report—Feb. 17 report.* Stanford, CA: Stanford Institute for the Quantitative Study of Society.

Robinson, J. P., Barth, K., & Kohut, A. (1997). Personal computers, mass media, and use of time. *Social Science Computer Review, 15*, 65–82.

Robinson, J. P., & Kestnbaum, M. (1999). The personal computer, culture, and other uses of free time. *Social Science Computer, 17*, 209–216.

Robinson, J. P., Kestnbaum, M., Neustadtl, A., & Alvarez, A. (2000). Mass media and social life among internet users. *Social Science Computer Review, 18*, 490–501.

Rogers, E. M. (1995). *Diffusion of innovations* (4th ed.). New York: Free Press.

Stouffer, S. A. (1956). *Communism, conformity, and civil liberties.* Garden City, NY: Doubleday.

Sunstein, C. R. (2001). *Republic.com.* Princeton, NJ: Princeton University Press.

Part V

Personal and Global
Contexts of Life Online

16

Informed Web Surfing

The Social Context
of User Sophistication

Eszter Hargittai
Northwestern University

There are many studies that look at how people use the internet (for a review, see DiMaggio, Hargittai, Neuman, & Robinson, 2001) and, in particular, what types of content they view online (e.g., Howard, Rainie, & Jones, 2001). There is a separate body of literature that looks at how people use information retrieval systems and, in particular, how people search for information on the Web (for a review of this literature, see Jansen & Pooch, 2001). However, these two areas of inquiry rarely intersect, leaving the discussion of what people do online in isolation from studies of what people are *able* to do online.

In this chapter, I report findings from a project that explores people's skills in locating content on the Web. Documenting differences in people's Web use

AUTHOR'S NOTE: I thank Paul DiMaggio for his insightful comments throughout this project, Stan Katz for his ongoing support, and Erica Field and Hank Farber for helpful discussions. I am also grateful to Inna Barmash, James Chu, Jeremy Davis-Turak, Edward Freeland, Anne Healy, Veronica McRipley, Carolyn Mordas, and Katy Niner for their assistance with various components of the project. I also express my gratitude to the many people who took time from their busy schedules to participate in the study. Generous support from the Markle Foundation is kindly acknowledged. The project has also been supported in part by National Science Foundation Grants SES9819907 and ITR0086143, a grant from the Russell Sage Foundation, and a grant from the Pew Charitable Trusts to the Center for Arts and Cultural Policy Studies at Princeton University. I am also grateful to the Fellowship of Woodrow Wilson Scholars at Princeton.

skills allows us to distinguish between how various kinds of people take advantage of the medium in different ways resulting not merely from their particular interests but also from their abilities in using the medium in ways that they prefer. This chapter focuses on internet users' skills and how people's online skills are embedded in a web of social relations. Skill, in this context, is defined as *the ability to find information on the Web effectively and efficiently.* Social relations refers both to people's immediate living partners (e.g., family and roommates) and to their wider networks of family, friends, and colleagues both physically close and distant.

First, I review literature on various people's use of the Web and the relationship between technology uses and people's social ties. Next, I outline the methods used in the project for studying how people locate content online, the sampling methodology, and how the data were analyzed. Then, I describe the findings from 66 interviews and in-person observations conducted during the summer and fall of 2001 in a New Jersey county. I present evidence to show that there is considerable variation in people's ability to find information online, and I explore what explains these differences. I pay particular attention to the relationship between people's online ability and their social relationships because these seem to play an important role in how people navigate the contents of the Web.

Web Use in Social Context

Many social factors may influence one's level of Web use sophistication. Although there is little literature on the social predictors of Web use skills, I draw on analogous work from the literature about how people use the medium to hypothesize about the role of social factors in people's online skills. Age, gender, education, and income all are factors that have been associated with the extent of people's connectivity and Web use patterns during the period of mass internet diffusion in the United States (National Telecommunications and Information Administration [NTIA], 1995, 1998, 1999, 2000, 2002) and are likely to be associated with people's online skills as well.[1] Younger generations have grown up with computers—if not in their homes, then often in their schools—leading to wider exposure to the technology among the young. Loges and Jung (2001) also found that older users engage in fewer activities online than do their younger counterparts.

Although the most recent figures show that men and women are network connected in about equal numbers (NTIA, 2002), Howard and colleagues (2001) did find differences in the types of activities in which female and male users engage while online. Men spend more time browsing for fun, looking up financial and product information, and consuming news online, whereas women spend more time looking up health information. Gender differences in online skills may be due to women having less leisure time at home (Kelsey, 2002; Lally, 2002). Insofar as home use is the most autonomous use in that it allows for the most freedom in exploring sites of interest to users, having less free time in the home to browse the Web may have a negative influence on women's Web use skills.

People's levels of education and income have been consistently related to their level of internet access and use and are likely to affect their level of Web use skills as well. Universities were the first to embrace the technology; thus, those who attended college during the past decade would have had exposure to the medium during their schooling. Moreover, people with higher levels of education are likely to have had more exposure to computer technology in general, and familiarity with the technology is an important first step in gaining access to the internet. Similarly, more affluent households are likely to have better resources, allowing them to purchase more up-to-date computers and high-speed internet access. With the spread of high-volume graphics and video technology, the need for various plug-ins and additional software to view many sites and documents (e.g., portable file documents [pdf]), high-capacity machines and high-speed connections are increasingly necessary to benefit from all the Web has to offer.

Of particular interest here is how people's social relationships also may be associated with users' online abilities. The literature on the diffusion of innovations emphasizes the importance of social support networks in the spread of new technologies (Rogers, 1995). Those with exposure to innovations in their surroundings are more likely to adopt new technologies such as personal computers (Dutton, Rogers, & Jun, 1987; Rogers, 1985). The availability of friends and family who are also internet users provides support for problems encountered while using the medium and is also a source of new knowledge via advice and recommendations.

For online skills in particular, this implies that people who are able to draw on their networks for information on how to use the medium will learn more quickly and will be exposed to a broader repertoire of online services than will those who have few people to whom they can turn for advice with their Web use. A study of home computer diffusion found that people were more likely to give up using the technology when they had no neighbors or friends to call on for support (Murdock, Hartmann, & Gray, 1992). By contrast, people whose social circles include users knowledgeable about the Web can draw on their networks for site recommendations and suggestions when they run into problems.

The presence of children in the household may have particular effects on people's Web use skills. Controlling for time spent online (a factor likely influenced by the time spent on caring for children), presence of offspring may improve one's level of Web use sophistication due to knowledge passed on to parents by their children. A study of requests for help with internet use in 93 families found that children were significantly more likely to help adults in their home internet use than vice versa (Kiesler, Zdaniuk, Lundmark, & Kraut, 2000). This suggests that adults who have children whom they can ask for advice about internet use will be better skilled due to the knowledge passed on from their kids.

Studies of Web Searching

Scholars from many fields have explored how people use the Web for information retrieval. Advertising and marketing specialists usually analyze users' behavior on one particular site instead of exploring users' overall online behavior, and they focus solely on users' commercial activities online (Bell & Tang, 1998; Jarvenpaa & Todd, 1996). Researchers in the human-computer interaction field have used large-scale aggregate logs about people's Web use to analyze Web activity over a specified period (Catledge & Pitkow, 1995; Huberman, Pirolli, Pitkow, & Lukose, 1998; Spink, Jansen, Wolfram, & Saracevic, 2002). In cases where data are derived from larger segments of the online population (e.g., Hoelscher, 1998; Huberman et al., 1998; Jansen, Spink, & Saracevic, 2000; Silverstein, Henzinger, Marais, & Moricz, 1999), there is no information about specific users; thus, it is impossible to make any claims about how attributes of users may be related to their online behavior. Although some have tried to develop more general models from data on what sites people visit (Goldfarb, 2002; Sinai & Waldfogel, 2001), these studies are based on assumptions about users' behaviors that cannot be verified. They offer interesting information on users' aggregate search patterns (Spink et al., 2002), but search activities are discussed in isolation of people's social attributes.

Some researchers in the library and information science community have explored how people search for information on the Web. However, these projects limit their scope to people in particular academic communities, such as graduate students in information science programs (Wang, Hawk, & Tenopir, 2000) or, at best, college students in general (Cothey, 2002; Dennis, Bruza, & McArthur, 2002;

Kim & Allen, 2002), making their findings impossible to generalize to the broader internet user population. To gain a better understanding of how the general population is using the internet, it is important to include people from beyond the academic community in such studies. Moreover, the just-cited studies rarely connect questions of Web usability with social factors; rather, they are interested in the technical specifics of search queries and users' experiences with online interfaces and tools (Spink, 2002).

These studies provide important information for a baseline understanding of how certain people navigate particular parts of the Web. However, they either limit their scope to specific user populations (e.g., information technology professionals, college students), do not collect background information about user attributes, or look at use patterns on an aggregate level without collecting data about the specific goals of a Web session. Moreover, these projects consider only people's use of search engines, ignoring the fact that the use of a search engine is only one of many ways in which to find content on the Web. In contrast, the project on which this chapter draws collects information about both user attributes and online actions. The next section describes the methodology in detail.

Methodology

The study is based on in-person observations and interviews with a random sample of internet users.[2] Respondents were given the choice of using a PC or a Mac, both of which had the three most popular browsing software applications (Internet Explorer, Netscape Communicator, and America Online) to allow respondents to replicate their usual online experience.[3] The computers connected to the internet on a high-speed university network line. In addition, a program called Don't Panic from Panicware was used to erase the browser and URL histories on each browser program so that each respondent started out with a clean slate and was not influenced by previous users' actions. The search sessions were recorded with a screen capture program that generated audio-visual files of the entire search session.[4]

Participants were given a list of tasks to perform online to see how they would find various types of information on the Web. The particular tasks were chosen to explore people's ability to find information on the Web in various topical domains. They explore whether users can find locally relevant content (specifically, information about local cultural events), the multimedia nature of the Web (e.g., music that users can listen to online), and whether users can use the Web for political purposes (e.g., finding a site that compares various presidential candidates' views), for government information (e.g., locating tax forms), and for less common tasks (e.g., finding children's art online).

The researcher sat behind and to the left of respondents and refrained from influencing their strategies (e.g., never suggesting any particular online actions, not answering questions about spelling or whether a certain click would be useful). Respondents were encouraged to look for the information until they found it. No one was cut off from pursuing a search. In some cases where respondents looked frustrated or agitated, they were given the option of moving on. However, when respondents simply stated that they were unable to perform a certain task, they were encouraged to try several times before moving on to the next task. When respondents suggested multiple times that they would not be able to complete a search, they were presented with the next task.

Information about respondents' usual internet use and histories, as well as data on their demographic backgrounds and social support networks, was collected via surveys, one that was orally administered at the beginning of the study session and one that was filled out online at the end of the study session. Administering the questionnaire right before the observation session proved to be very useful. Because the questions explore many facets of Web use, respondents were prompted to think about numerous details of their Web experiences before sitting down at the computer and embarking on the tasks presented by the researcher.

Data

The findings reported here are based on 66 interviews conducted during the summer and fall of 2001 in the suburban towns and boroughs of a New Jersey county.[5] Respondents ranged in age from 18 to 81 years (for details, see Table 16.1). Just under half (45%) of the sample was male. More than half (58%) of the respondents worked full-time, and an additional 14% worked part-time. Their occupations included real estate agents, environmental policy analysts, blue-collar workers, office assistants, teachers, service employees, and medical professionals as well as students, unemployed persons, and retired persons.

Fully 91% of the respondents were white; there were four African American respondents and one Asian American respondent, and one respondent chose the "other" category for race and self-identified as Hispanic. In addition, 29% reported living alone, half lived with their spouses, and the rest lived with

Table 16.1   Descriptive Statistics for Independent Variables

	Mean	Standard Deviation	Median	Minimum	Maximum
Age (years)	44.26	15.65	42.5	18	81
Education[a]	N/A	N/A	College	Less than high school	Ph.D.
Family income[a]	N/A	N/A	$90,000–$99,000	$17,500–$19,000	> $250,000
Number of years since first use of the internet	6.10	3.38	6.0	0	16[b]
Amount of time spent browsing the Web weekly	9.02 hours	10.51 hours	5.5 hours	8 minutes	70 hours[c]

a. Education and family income have no means because those variables were collected categorically.

b. Number of years since first internet use was top coded at 8 for the analyses.

c. Number of hours on the Web was top coded at 56 (8 hours per day) for the analyses. Excluding this top value, the mean time spent browsing the Web per week was 7.63 hours, with a standard deviation of 6.75 hours and a median of 5.0 hours.

roommates or others (in most cases, parents). More than half (55%) of the respondents had children. Of these 36 people, 20 had children currently living with them.

On average, participants in this study were more educated than the general internet user population. This suggests that findings from the study will be conservative with respect to effects of various educational levels on people's ability to use the Web effectively. The average family income of respondents was greater than the national average, although it is important to note that this New Jersey county is one of the highest income counties in the United States; thus, despite the high median income, the sample is not out of the ordinary for the local population.[6]

Regarding Web use frequency and history, the group was diverse. Participants' Web use ranged from just a few minutes per week to more than 30 hours per week. The group was similarly diverse in respondents' overall experience with the medium. One person had gone online the year of the study, and an additional 17% had been online for 2 years or less. However, many of the respondents (42%) had been users for 5 to 7 years. There were also several long-term users among the respondents, with 14% having had their first exposure to the internet more than 10 years ago.

Table 16.2   Number of Successfully Completed Tasks

Number of Tasks Completed Successfully	Number of Respondents	Percentage
1	2	3
2	9	14
3	9	14
4	19	29
5	27	40
Total	66	100

DIFFERENCES IN PEOPLE'S ABILITY TO FIND CONTENT ONLINE

I measured people's online skills in two ways. First, the binary success/failure rate showed what portion of the respondents was able to complete each of five tasks analyzed in this study. Second, the time to completion of each task was measured in seconds to show the gradual differences in how long people take to find information on the Web. The exact time spent on each task was recorded for every respondent so that information is available on both when respondents successfully completed a task and when they decided to give up on a task.

There is some variance in people's success rates in performing tasks and large variance in the amounts of time they took to complete tasks. Of the 66 respondents, 27 (41%) were able to successfully complete all tasks, and an additional 19 (29%) succeeded in locating four of the five types of information sought (for details, see Table 16.2). However, the remaining 20 people were able to successfully complete only one to three tasks. This is a considerable proportion given that people were encouraged to pursue tasks without any time constraint.

Overall, people spent anywhere from 2½ minutes to 33 minutes on the five tasks. There was a gradual increase in the amount of time people spent on all of the tasks. Four respondents spent less than a total of 5 minutes on all five tasks, making them the expert searchers. A 26-year-old woman whizzed through the tasks by using Google in an informed manner with multiple-term queries (e.g., *Al Gore views on abortion* for the political comparison task). An 18-year-old college woman also used elaborate queries in some cases (e.g., *Bush and Gore and abortion* for the same comparison question) but turned to directory listings on Yahoo for other tasks such as finding local movie listings. People who are good searchers and who rely mostly on one search engine can get quite affectionate about their favorite online service. A 42-year-old woman who was in between jobs and who got through the five tasks very quickly commented at the start of one task, "I go back to Google, my old friend."

Four respondents spent more than a total of 30 minutes on the five tasks, exhibiting very limited Web user skills. Simply using Google is not enough. One 56-year-old man who worked in business development clicked on the Advanced Search feature of Google and then typed *abortion comparison Bush and Gore* in the search field labeled "with the exact phrase"; this proved to be too nuanced and yielded no results. Confused by this, he clicked on the search button a few more times—without changing anything in the search field—and continued to get no results. After some additional attempts at using that feature of the search engine, he moved on to CNN's site and found the information via its search engine.

An action typical of those who understand little about the Web and searching is to continuously click on "related search" items after a search result. This leads to yet more search results. If the user simply keeps clicking on these links, he or she never gets to an actual site. A 44-year-old woman who worked in retail repeatedly used this method to find sites and took many iterations of searches to finally arrive at a page with content of interest. There are also those who never use search engines. These users rely on site recommendations from their internet service providers.

EXPLAINING DIFFERENCES IN PEOPLE'S ONLINE SKILLS

To look at what accounts for the differences in whether people are able to find certain types of content online, I estimated probit models of task completion.[7] I have valid completion data for 317 tasks of the total 330 tasks performed by the 66 individuals (data are missing for 13 tasks). Table 16.3 presents the estimates of the probit models normalized to represent the marginal effect at the average of the explanatory variables on the probability of completion of tasks. Model 1 includes demographic variables only. Results suggest that age was negatively associated with people's ability to complete tasks successfully. In contrast, having a graduate degree was significantly associated with people's ability to find various types of content online. Model 2 adds information about people's prior experience with the internet by including data about the amount of time people spend surfing the Web each week and the number of years since the respondents first used the internet.[8] The results suggest that the latter was positively associated with users' ability to find information on the Web.

Table 16.3   Probabilities of Successful Completion of Tasks (probit analysis)

	Model 1: Demographics	Standard Error	Model 2: Demographics and Online Experience	Standard Error
Demographics				
Age	−.006**	.002	−.005***	.002
Gender (female)	.058	.147	−.032	.051
Age × Gender interaction	−.001	.003		
Family income (logged)	.063	.041	.057	.037
Less than college education	−.007	.069	−.021	.067
Graduate degree	.126**	.052	.084	.055
Recently in school	.024	.086	.021	.080
Children in household	−.090	.082	−.101	.080
Children × Gender interaction	−.012	.101	−.040	.100
Internet experience				
Amount of time spent browsing the Web per week			−.001	.002
Number of internet use years			.022**	.010
Chi-square	0.0000		0.0000	
Log likelihood	−132.061		−129.932	
N	300		300	

$**p \leq 0.05$, $***p \leq 0.01$.

To examine what explains differences in how long people take to complete tasks, I specified a linear regression model of the log time to completion. I used a normal-censored data model for estimation due to the fact that we cannot observe the actual time to completion for those who gave up (i.e., right-censored data).[9] Table 16.4 presents the results of the censored normal regression models.[10] First, I looked at the predictive power of the demographic variables on their own.[11] The older people were, the longer they took to complete tasks. Education was also related to people's ability to find information online quickly; those with graduate degrees were considerably faster than those without graduate degrees. The payoffs of higher education were especially relevant for those who obtained their college and graduate degrees during the years since the Web has been widely available on university campuses. However, the kind of task presented had significant effects on the time to completion. Music-related tasks were completed more quickly, whereas people needed more time to complete the political search task.

In Model 2, I added information about previous experience with the technology to control for amount of time spent online and number of years of experience with the medium. Those who spent more time online each week were quicker at finding content on the Web. Moreover, each additional year of experience with the internet led to a few seconds of improvement in searches. The findings from the previous model were robust. Having a graduate degree helped a respondent's ability to quickly find content online by resulting in searches that were, on average, 49 seconds quicker, and this payoff was especially strong for those who attended school during recent years (resulting in searches that were more than a full minute quicker). Older people were slower, and the presence of children in the household was also associated with less efficient searching behavior, even when controlling for the amount of time spent online each week. In Model 1, the interaction of children in the household with gender was significant, suggesting that the presence of children especially takes a toll on women's online performance. However, after controlling for time online each week, the interaction term lost significance.

The presence of children in the household added an average of 39 seconds to each search task. This effect is the opposite of the predicted outcome; the expected relationship suggested that the presence of children would be beneficial to people's internet skills due to knowledge passed on from kids to parents. Rather, it seems that parents may simply hand over tasks to their offspring when in need of help. Kraut, Scherlis, Mukophadhyay, Manning, and Kiesler (1996) found that in households with children, teenagers tend to dominate use of the network-connected machines. The data presented in this chapter suggest that young users tend to be much more skilled than older users. Because of the presence of other experts in the household, parents might not develop certain online skills, preferring to delegate the tasks of looking up certain information to their children.

Table 16.4   Linear Regression Model of the Log Time to Completion of Tasks (standard errors in parentheses)

	Model 1:		Model 2:	
	Demographics	Standard Error	Demographics and Online Experience	Standard Error
Constant	4.823***	.478	5.155***	.484
Demographics				
Age	.011*	.006	0.012**	.005
Gender (female)	−.248	.323	.080	.123
Age × Gender interaction	.006	.007		
Less than college education	−.227	.143	−.195	.142
Graduate degree	−.529***	.120	−.395***	.127
Recently in school	−.469***	.179	−.410**	.180
Children in household	.307*	.161	.329**	.159
Children × Gender interaction	.364*	.217	.217	.220
Internet experience				
Amount of time spent browsing the Web per week			−.003	.005
Number of internet use years			−.073***	.025
Tasks				
Music task	−.480***	.153	−.486***	.151
Political task	1.110***	.189	1.120***	.157
Tax task	.144	.150	.144	.149
Children's art task	.110	.150	.113	.148
Uncensored	242		242	
Right censored	56		56	
Pseudo-R^2	0.1951		0.2058	
N	298		298	

NOTE: The task variables are dichotomous.

*$p \leq 0.10$, **$p \leq 0.05$, ***$p \leq 0.01$.

This finding suggests the importance of a more in-depth look at the influence of people's social relationships on online behavior. Here, I turn to the qualitative data derived from the conversations with participants during the observation sessions to tease out the role of social ties and the influence of people's social surroundings on their Web use. As suggested earlier, child rearing may cut into people's Web use by limiting the amount of time people have to explore the Web freely (Kelsey, 2002; Lally, 2002). A 39-year-old, stay-at-home mother successfully completed the five tasks analyzed in this study but was one of the slowest to do so (she took 25 minutes, meaning that she was slower than 90% of the respondents). She lived with her husband and three children and noted the following about how her family situation may influence her online behavior:

I think having children definitely affects my Web use in that I just don't have the time to sit at the computer and spend the time that is takes to figure out how to get around. It is extremely frustrating to try and concentrate with kids around.

Another related and seemingly important factor is how new media resources are allocated within the household. Some parents commented on how their children's time spent online influences their own ability to access the Web. A 48-year-old widow, a social worker who lived with her 15-year-old daughter, described her access to the computer in the context of her daughter's internet use: "My internet usage is affected by the amount of time [my daughter] is on the internet. I have to ask her to get off so I can just check my e-mail a couple of times each week." Although this participant successfully completed all of the tasks, she was among the slowest 25%.

In contrast, a 39-year-old man, the information systems director of a small business, has created an environment at home that allows all members of his family full access to the Web at their leisure:

We have four computers in the house: one PC for my wife and I, one PC for my 16-year-old, one PC for my 8-year-old, and a fourth PC on the network with 2 LPT ports on it that acts as a print server; we have a laser printer and a color ink jet. It also acts as a shared drive for exchanging files on the network. It also has access to the internet, so even if my wife and both kids are on the Web, I can do a quick search or surf for whatever I need on the print server PC.

In addition to these resources at home, this participant also said he had access to two computers at work. It is not surprising that he succeeded with all five tasks and finished among the top 25% of users in speed.

Admittedly, few have access to such an abundance of technical resources. Instead, others rely on their social ties to improve their online techniques. They turn to family and friends for site recommendations and specific advice with particular queries. A 47-year-old public school teacher who succeeded with four of the five tasks and placed in the slower half of the group explicitly stated that her children are the "primary source of my knowledge. And my husband, too. They certainly know more than I do." In the study setting, her family members were not with her, so she had to rely on memory of what more general strategies she may have picked up from them.

A 39-year-old man who assembles air conditioners for a living relied on public transportation to come to the study location. Several times when he was unable to perform a task, he referred to his nephews:

> I don't know how to do that. I've seen my nephews and them do it and my daughter. They on the computer all the time. . . . I even have a nephew that's, boy, 6 years old. . . . He will get up out of bed and get on the computer.

This man attempted online shopping once and completely relied on his nephew's help to place a book order. However, the order was not successful; the book never arrived despite the fact that he had a money order made out for it. This participant was unable to complete three of the five tasks in the absence of his support network.

A younger respondent, a 20-year-old college student who successfully completed all five tasks and was the second quickest of all respondents, was asked about her use of a particularly powerful search engine. She noted, "One of my friends told me about it, and so I've been using it a lot." A 40-year-old professor who quickly found the Web site of a radio station for music commented that he had first heard about it from a friend.

From the preceding quotes, it seems that people's Web use is significantly influenced by their social surroundings. Users turn to their social support networks for advice on use of the internet. Although constrained by how much autonomy they have otherwise—the available time to explore the medium and access to a machine whenever convenient—they rely on recommendations and advice from their family and friends for more efficient use of the Web. Consequently, those who do not have such support networks to draw on miss out on important ways in which they could improve their online abilities.

Conclusion

In general, young people (those in their late teens or 20s) have a much easier time in getting around online than do their older counterparts (whether in their 40s or their 70s). Education is also significantly associated with online skills. Some of these relationships are clearly based on comfort with the technology and are not necessarily based on elaborate techniques that people have mastered specifically with respect to the Web. Given that the amount of time people have been internet users also affects how well they are able to navigate the contents of the Web, it is possible that those who are currently less skilled will learn over time and improve their ability to find content online. However, people may be discouraged by the difficulties of finding information on the Web and so may end up spending less time with the medium, resulting in continued lower level skills. Moreover, those who can draw on family and friends for advice have continuing support to help improve their online skills or, at least, to alleviate some of the frustrations caused by confused Web searching.

Using a mix of quantitative and qualitative methods to analyze the online actions of a random sample of internet users allows us to uncover generalizable trends in people's online use while also understanding the more intricate reasons for their particular online actions. People rely on their social support networks for suggestions of site recommendations and for answers to particular questions that come up as they look to the Web for answers to questions or for mere entertainment. By using a mix of methods for data collection, it is possible to give voice to users without having to make unfounded assumptions about their online behavior based on aggregate data. The quasi-experimental methods used in this study can be replicated to look at other aspects of people's use of the internet and other new communication technologies, resulting in rich data allowing nuanced analyses of processes underlying how these new media are being incorporated into people's everyday lives.

Notes

1. Because of the small number of minority participants in this study, it is not possible to explore the relationship between race/ethnicity and people's online skills based on the data in this study.

2. This approach has both advantages and shortcomings. Requesting users to come to a location will affect response rates. It also places people in an unfamiliar location and requires them to use a computer that is configured differently from the machines they usually use for browsing. This may influence the results because certain settings (e.g., the default homepage, bookmarks) are

not equivalent to their own. However, this approach controls for quality of internet connection and hardware/software differences. It also allows the researcher to concentrate on Web use knowledge in a setting that is equally different and new for all. Moreover, using one computer allows for the setup of particular software applications that are required for data recording. To be able to generalize from the findings, respondents were recruited through a random sample of residential addresses obtained for a suburban county in New Jersey from Survey Sampling Inc. This list was then checked against the National Change of Address Database maintained by the U.S. Postal Service to minimize the number of nonresidential and out-of-service numbers. Potential respondents were first mailed a letter and brochure explaining the project and requesting participation. They were directed to the study's Web site (www.webuse.org) for more information and were given the option of calling or writing the researcher to schedule an appointment. A few days after the letters had been sent, the households were contacted by telephone. In each household, the eligible English-speaking internet adult over 18 years of age with the next nearest birthday was selected to randomly sample from within households. If this person was not willing to participate, the household was coded as a refusal even if another member of the household would have been willing to take part in the study. Such strict standards help to achieve a representative sample of the internet user population. Web users were defined as people who go online at least once every month for more than just using e-mail. This is a low threshold for including people in the study and is used to maximize variance in experience (for the distribution of participants' weekly Web use, see the final row in Table 16.1). For their participation, respondents were offered $40, which they received after the observation session. Respondents were asked to come to the research site on the university campus and were offered assistance with transportation if they could not provide their own. One person took advantage of this option and was reimbursed for bus fare. The response rate was 48%, considerably high given the time cost involved in participation.

3. No default page was set on browsers so as not to influence respondents' initial actions once online. The sessions were started off by the researcher asking respondents to recall, if possible, the default homepages on the computers they use most often. The respondents were also asked whether they had personalized anything on their browsers and whether they had set any bookmarks or favorites.

4. The Hypercam program from Hyperionics was used on the PC, and the SnapZPro e program from Ambrosia Software was used on the Mac. The whole screen was captured, as was every action (e.g., click of the mouse, scrolling) and every verbal comment respondents made during their searches. These files were then analyzed to measure whether people successfully completed a task and how long they took to do so.

5. I conducted 55 of the interviews, and a research assistant conducted 11.

6. The average median per capita income in this county was nearly $40,000 in 2000 (based on census data). Here, I look at household income, which is likely to be considerably higher on average. Moreover, because this sample excludes the inner-city population of the county's biggest town due to logistical purposes of the study, the poorest neighborhoods are not in the sample, suggesting that the median per capita income in the county is considerably higher than $40,000.

7. I used the "cluster" command in the Stata statistical software package due to repeated observations on individuals. Without clustering, error terms would not be independent across tasks due to individual characteristics of respondents not accounted for in the model.

8. I removed the interaction of age and gender from the second model because it did not prove to be significant in the initial model.

9. This model was estimated by maximum likelihood using the command "cnreg" in the Stata statistical software program.

10. A dummy variable was included in four of the five tasks to control for task-specific effects.

11. It is important to note that times-to-task within one person will be correlated based on the person's individual characteristics not accounted for in the model. This results in error terms that are not independent across tasks within a person.

References

Bell, H., & Tang, N. K. H. (1998). The effectiveness of commercial internet Web sites: A user's perspective. *Internet Research, 8,* 219–228.

Catledge, L. D., & Pitkow, J. E. (1995). *Characterizing browsing strategies in the World Wide Web.* Paper presented at the Third International World Wide Web Conference, Darmstadt, Germany.

Cothey, V. (2002). A longitudinal study of World Wide Web users' information-searching behavior. *Journal of the American Society for Information Science and Technology, 53*(2), 67–78.

Dennis, S., Bruza, P., & McArthur, R. (2002). Web searching: A process-oriented experimental study of three interactive search paradigms. *Journal of the American Society for Information Science and Technology, 53*(2), 120–133.

DiMaggio, P., Hargittai, E., Neuman, R., & Robinson, J. (2001). Social implications of the internet. *Annual Review of Sociology, 27,* 307–336.

Dutton, W. H., Rogers, E. M., & Jun, S-H. (1987). Diffusion and social impacts of personal computers. *Communication Research, 14,* 219–250.

Goldfarb, A. (2002). Analyzing Website choice using clickstream data. In M. R. Baye (Ed.), *Advances in applied microeconomics,* Vol. 11: *The economics of the internet and e-commerce* (pp. 209–230). Amsterdam: Elsevier Science.

Hoelscher, C. (1998). *How internet experts search for information on the Web.* Paper presented at the Conference of the World Wide Web, Internet, and Intranet, Orlando, FL.

Howard, P. E. N., Rainie, L., & Jones, S. (2001). Days and nights on the internet: The impact of a diffusing technology. *American Behavioral Scientist, 45,* 383–404.

Huberman, B. A., Pirolli, P. L., Pitkow, J. E., & Lukose, R. M. (1998). Strong regularities in World Wide Web surfing. *Science, 280,* 94–97.

Jansen, B. J., & Pooch, U. (2001). A review of Web searching studies and a framework for future research. *Journal of the American Society for Information Science and Technology, 52,* 235–246.

Jansen, B. J., Spink, A., & Saracevic, T. (2000). Real life, real users, and real needs: A study and analysis of user queries on the Web. *Information Processing and Management, 36,* 207–227.

Jarvenpaa, S. L., & Todd, P. A. (1996). Consumer reactions to electronic shopping on the World Wide Web. *International Journal of Electronic Commerce, 1*(2), 59–88.

Kelsey, D. (2002, January 18). U.S. women's net use grows at triple the rate of men's. *NewsBytes.* Retrieved May 10, 2003, from www.washingtonpost.com

Kiesler, S., Zdaniuk, B., Lundmark, V., & Kraut, R. (2000). Troubles with the internet: The dynamics of help at home. *Human-Computer Interaction, 15,* 323–351.

Kim, K-S., & Allen, B. (2002). Cognitive and task influences on Web searching behavior. *Journal of the American Society for Information Science and Technology, 53*(2), 109–119.

Kraut, R., Scherlis, W., Mukophadhyay, T., Manning, J., & Kiesler, S. (1996). The HomeNet Field Trial of Residential Internet Services. *Communications of the ACM, 39*(12), 55–63.

Lally, E. (2002). *At home with computers.* Oxford, UK: Berg.

Loges, W. E., & Jung, J-Y. (2001). Exploring the digital divide: internet connectedness and age. *Communication Research, 28,* 536–562.

Murdock, G., Hartmann, P. & Gray, P. (1992). Contextualizing home computing: Resources and practices. In R. Silverstone & E. Hirsch (Eds.), *Consuming technologies* (pp. 146–160). New York: Routledge.

National Telecommunications and Information Administration. (1995). *Falling through the net: A survey of the "have-nots" in rural and urban America.* Washington, DC: Author.

National Telecommunications and Information Administration. (1998). *Falling through the net II: New data on the digital divide.* Washington, DC: Author.

National Telecommunications and Information Administration. (1999). *Falling through the net: Defining the digital divide.* Washington, DC: Author.

National Telecommunications and Information Administration. (2000). *Falling through the net: Toward digital inclusion.* Washington, DC: Author.

National Telecommunications and Information Administration. (2002). *A nation online.* Washington, DC: Author.

Rogers, E. M. (1985). The diffusion of home computers among households in Silicon Valley. *Marriage and Family Review, 8,* 89–101.

Rogers, E. (1995). *Diffusion of innovations.* New York: Free Press.

Silverstein, C., Henzinger, M., Marais, H., & Moricz, M. (1999). Analysis of a very large Web search engine query log. *SIGIR Forum, 33*(1), 6–12.

Sinai, T., & Waldfogel, J. (2001). *Geography and the internet: Is the internet a substitute or a complement for cities?* Paper presented at the 29th Annual Telecommunications Policy Research Conference, Alexandria, VA.

Spink, A. (2002). Introduction to the special issue on Web research. *Journal of the American Society for Information Science and Technology, 53*(2), 65–66.

Spink, A., Jansen, B. J., Wolfram, D., & Saracevic, T. (2002). From e-sex to e-commerce: Web search changes. *Computer 35*(3), 107–109.

Wang, P., Hawk, W. B., & Tenopir, C. (2000). Users' interactions with World Wide Web resources: An exploratory study using a holistic approach. *Information Processing and Management, 36,* 229–251.

17

American Internet Users and Privacy

A Safe Harbor of Their Own?

Doreen Starke-Meyerring
University of Minnesota

Dan L. Burk
University of Minnesota

Laura J. Gurak
University of Minnesota

The rise of popular internet use has been accompanied by a parallel rise in concern over personal and data privacy. According to a 1999 *Wall Street Journal* poll, for example, privacy violations rank among the top concern of Americans. Similarly, a Lou Harris poll found that the percentage of respondents concerned about their privacy rights surged from 34% in 1970 to 90% in 1998 (Identity Theft Resource Center, 2002). The Pew Internet and American Life Project (2000) report, *Trust and Privacy Online: Why Americans Want to Rewrite the Rules,* underscored this new intensity of privacy concerns. According to the report, 84% of respondents would be "very concerned" or "somewhat concerned" about their personal information possibly falling into the wrong hands (p. 22).

The Pew report also provided valuable insights into the online privacy practices and wishes of American internet users such as their expectations about the privacy of their personal information, their knowledge about privacy or privacy-invading technologies, their perceptions of corporate privacy practices, their strategies for protecting their personal information online, and their view of who should assume responsibility for managing online privacy protection in a way that respects and balances the rights of all stakeholders—governments, corporations, and individuals—involved in this public problem.

Using the Pew study, this chapter examines how American internet users may relate to the two currently predominant models of balancing privacy interests: the European Union (EU) model of comprehensive government regulation embodied in the EU Data Protection Directive, which guarantees control over personal information as a governmentally enforced right, and the U.S. model of corporate self-regulation, which views personal information as a private sector concern. The chapter first provides an overview of the stakes involved in online privacy, then discusses each model and its approach to balancing stakeholder interests, and finally discusses what, based on the Pew report, may emerge as a possible alternative model—one of direct citizen control.

Indeed, although American internet users seem to prefer the stipulations of the EU directive to the current U.S. approach of corporate self-regulation, they may ultimately prefer an alternative approach that rejects both government oversight and corporate self-regulation. Instead of these two dominant approaches, they may be looking for more direct citizen involvement. From the Pew report, however, it is difficult to tell exactly the type of alternative with which Americans may be comfortable. Therefore, the chapter concludes with a set of questions and directions for future research to help chart the path toward exploring an alternative model of online privacy regulation.

The Stakeholders in the Online Privacy Debate

Although privacy issues themselves are not new, the rise of the internet has increased the ability to compile, store, search, mix, match, copy, distribute, or otherwise manipulate, change, or exchange personal information in increasingly large networks of databases. As Moor (2000) put it, electronic information is "greased" (p. 200); it "moves like lightning and will have applications and reapplications that are impossible to imagine when initially entered into a computer" (p. 211). Once personal information is submitted to a recipient that turns out to be untrustworthy, individuals have no way of tracking, let alone knowing, what happens to their information.

In addition, the stakes are high because most interactions between people, including those related to public services and commerce, require the exchange of personal information. Governments, for example, need such information to fulfill their missions of providing public services such as law enforcement, traffic regulation, and public safety. Operation TIPS (Terrorism Information and Prevention System) is an example of such an effort. As part of the Citizen Corps, the program is designed for workers who "will use their common sense and knowledge of their work" to identify and report on "potentially unusual or suspicious activity in public places" (Citizen Corps, 2002). Although intended to prevent terrorist attacks—high stakes indeed—the stakes for individuals are high in another way. Rachel King, legislative counsel for the American Civil Liberties Union, provided the following scenario: "Suppose you're looking for a job and you can't get security clearance because one of these volunteers thought you were a little strange and wrote down your name; this could impact your life in ways you don't know" (quoted in Scheeres, 2002).[1]

Businesses also need personal information for marketing, human resources, identification, and other purposes. Large collections of aggregated personal data prove to be highly valuable because they can be traded quite profitably in electronic networks. Typically, the individuals providing data need not be compensated for sharing their information or for taking the risk of having their information fall into the wrong hands. If it does, the stakes for individuals are high again. The consequences range from receipt of annoying "spam" to perpetration of a more serious crime, identity theft, which in turn may trigger a cascade of potential consequences such as the loss of a job and the the loss of credit. In fact, identity theft is the fastest growing crime in the United States. In 2001 alone, up to 1.1 million people became victims of identity theft, with the average victim spending 175 hours and $1,000 in out-of-pocket expenses to regain his or her identity (Identity Theft Center, 2002).

Even without such dramatic crimes, an environment that does not protect the personal information of individuals can cost them several hundred dollars per year for tools and services such as Credit Watch, anonymization services, and opting-out initiatives (Gellman, 2002). For telephone privacy alone, U.S. consumers spend more than $400 million per year (Gellman, 2002). From the perspective of businesses, however, privacy technologies generate revenue. Yet as industry research shows, even for corporations, the picture is more complex. Concerned about their privacy, many online consumers might not complete their online purchases. In fact, citing industry research, the Federal Trade Commission

(FTC, 2000) estimated a loss of $18 billion in online sales by 2002 due to privacy concerns.

The stakes are not only high but also global. The global reach of the internet, however, does not mean that countries negotiate the various stakes involved in online data sharing and privacy problems in the same way. So far, two major types of approaches to electronic privacy have emerged: the comprehensive government approach in the EU and the corporate self-regulation approach in the United States.

COMPREHENSIVE GOVERNMENT APPROACH:
THE EU DATA PROTECTION DIRECTIVE

Implemented by the EU in 1998, the EU Data Protection Directive is a comprehensive legislative template that conceives of privacy as a fundamental human right, guaranteeing individuals the right to their personal information and control over its use.

Stipulations of the Directive

The stipulations of the EU Data Protection Directive reflect the consensus of the 15 EU member nations and provide the framework for data protection legislation in each member state. The goal of the directive is to protect the personal information of EU citizens from privacy violations in both the private and public sectors. According to Article 18[1] of the directive, for example, any entity collecting personally identifiable information about an individual is required to obtain full and unambiguous consent from that person before the information can be collected.

Data collectors must also reveal their identity, the purpose of the data collection process, any possible recipients of the collected data, and the possible consequences for failing to provide the requested information. This principle of informed and unambiguous consent is a cornerstone of the directive; it requires data collectors to obtain consent of the individual for each new use of the personal data collected. Personal data can be used and processed only for the purposes agreed to by the individual.

Furthermore, individuals must be provided with unrestricted access to their collected personal information so that they can erase, block, or correct their personal information. According to the directive, EU citizens have the right to stop the data collection or processing procedure at any time and also have the right to withdraw their information at any time. To ensure these rights, the directive mandates that EU citizens be provided with appropriate redress mechanisms against violations of these rights. Only a public independent authority is acceptable as a guarantor of redress.

Even this brief overview shows that European data protection officials regard an individual's rights regarding personal information as fundamental human rights. As noted by Ulf Brühann, a senior official in the European Commission responsible for implementing the directive, "Nobody should underestimate the problem by doubting the political will of the European Union to protect the fundamental human rights of citizens" (quoted in Swire & Litan, 1998, p. 46). Because privacy is conceptualized as a human right in the EU model, the stakes of individuals outweigh those of other stakeholders.

Implications for Non-EU Countries

Realizing that data flows are global, the EU Data Protection Directive stipulates in Article 25[1] that "the Member States shall provide that the transfer to a third country of personal data . . . may take place only if . . . the third country in question ensures an adequate level of protection." Although the directive does not define adequacy, it likely reflects the principles laid out in the directive: no data collection without the unambiguous informed consent of the individual, no data processing for purposes not revealed to the individual at the time of data collection, guarantee of redress, and so forth.

This stipulation affects non-EU countries that lack comprehensive data protection laws. Under the directive, any personal information except data collected "by a natural person in the course of a purely personal or household activity" (Article 3[2]) could not be transferred into a third country with inadequate data protection. Swire and Litan (1998) illustrated these consequences in the example of a business traveler who compiles information about a business meeting, including files listing names, addresses, and other personal information about business contacts (p. 71). Theoretically, the directive does not allow the transfer of these data to noncompliant third countries.

Although some European non-EU countries, such as Hungary and the Czech Republic, have adopted similar legislation to that of the EU directive, other countries have different data protection traditions. Countries such as the United States, Canada, Australia, and Japan, for example, have traditionally "rejected the 'omnibus' approach, preferring to regulate only the public sector's practices and to leave the private sector governed by a few sectoral laws and voluntary codes of practice" (Bennett, 1998, p. 100). Given the consequences of the EU directive, however, Canada, Australia, and Japan have implemented data protection laws that now apply to both the private and public sectors, providing an "adequate level of data protection." This leaves the United States as the only industrialized nation without such a comprehensive law that would provide adequate data protection under the EU directive.

CORPORATE SELF-REGULATION: THE U.S. APPROACH

The United States instead espouses what has been called a "sectoral" approach (Rotenberg, 1998). This approach includes a mix of limited government oversight and corporate self-regulation. But this patchwork does not provide a comprehensive legislative guarantee of ownership of personal information as a human right. Instead, it views personal information as a free commodity subject to contractual negotiation. Hence, under this approach, corporate stakes in online privacy far outweigh individuals' stakes in online privacy. Corporations, for example, are not required to obtain the explicit consent from individuals before taking and using their personal information for business, marketing, and other purposes. The onus is on individual consumers to negotiate some different arrangement if they object.

This stance does not necessarily reflect trust of corporations; the American history of antitrust law, securities regulation, and new accounting regulations in the wake of recent financial scandals demonstrate a healthy mistrust of large business entities. Rather, Americans take as an article of faith the idea that markets are better at ordering society than is what they would perceive as constituting "command and control" by government. Indeed, much of the deregulatory fervor in the United States during the final years of the 20th century was an attempt to introduce private market mechanisms into areas, such as electromagnetic spectrum allocation and pollution control, that had previously been the sole provenance of regulatory oversight.

In contrast, Europeans generally have much less faith in market ordering and are more likely to expect government to provide services or order resources in ways that Americans supposedly would prefer to have the market provide. Indeed, as Reidenberg (1997) showed, Europeans may see the intervention of elected officials as more constitutive of democratic values than is ceding control of important societal decisions to unelected private actors. This is particularly true where protection of personal rights is concerned; ironically, Americans may tend to perceive the government as the greatest threat to such rights (Reidenberg, 2000; Schwartz, 1995).

Consequently, to shield U.S. companies doing business in Europe from possible prosecution under European law for privacy violations, the U.S. government worked with the European Commission to create a set of voluntary privacy principles called Safe Harbor Privacy Principles. By adhering to these principles, companies can demonstrate to European citizens and government authorities that they meet EU standards for adequate data protection when doing business with European citizens. In addition, companies that purport to follow the principles but that fail to follow them are subject to prosecution by U.S. authorities for fraudulent representation. Thus, the Safe Harbor principles shield American corporations from European enforcement of the EU's privacy laws while at the same time maintaining the principle of voluntary corporate self-regulation.

With corporate self-regulation at the core of the U.S. approach, voluntary private sector initiatives, such as the Platform for Privacy Preferences (P3P) project, TRUSTe, and BBBOnline, have emerged. The P3P platform, for example, is an industry-funded project of the World Wide Web Consortium intended as a standardized privacy protocol. As the consortium explained, "P3P is a standardized set of multiple-choice questions, covering all the major aspects of a Web site's privacy policies" (World Wide Web Consortium, 2002). The standard allows users to compare their privacy preferences with the machine-readable standards of a Web site to determine whether the Web site meets their privacy needs.

The principle here is similar to that of browser "cookie" files. If users want to engage a site that uses cookies, they are forced to accept cookies to use the Web service. If users do not activate their browsers' cookie function, they will be excluded from the service. Given that the vast majority of Web sites now use cookies, individuals would be excluded from much of the Web if they refused to accept cookies. Moreover, as the Electronic Privacy Information Center points out, studies have shown that users find changing the default cookie setting to be "burdensome and confusing" (Electronic Privacy Information Center and Junkbusters, 2000) and so simply give up, keeping the cookie function enabled.

Similarly, if internet users need to adjust their privacy preferences each time a P3P-enabled Web site reports that their preferences are too high, they may lower their privacy standards in cases where they do not want to be excluded from the service. Consequently, what at first sight appears to be a set of privacy choices may prove to be a mechanism for forcing internet users to either lower their privacy standards or forgo Web services. The underlying assumption is to *forgo either your privacy or your Web functionality.* Moreover, the P3P protocol does not provide individuals with functions to access, correct, or erase their data, nor does it provide redress in the case of privacy violations.

The TRUSTe program, perhaps the most popular self-regulation initiative, does provide oversight and a resolution process in addition to guidelines for privacy policy development. However, these mechanisms provide only limited privacy enforcement through auditing practices of participating Web sites and allowing users to notify TRUSTe of any apparent misuses of the TRUSTe mark. For resolution mechanisms, the program offers investigations that may result in "revocation of the TRUSTe trustmark, termination from the program, or in extreme cases, referral to the appropriate government agency" (TRUSTe, 2002a).

Yet considering that TRUSTe is funded by some of the corporations it serves, conflicts of interest may hamper these redress mechanisms. For example, the Federal Trade Commission charged Microsoft, a sponsor of TRUSTe and a TRUSTe seal holder, with false security and privacy promises in the privacy statement for its Passport services (FTC, 2002), but TRUSTe never mentioned the problems in its list of investigations or problem sites. TRUSTe merely provided a statement lauding that "Microsoft worked with TRUSTe to adopt privacy best practices and respond to the FTC's investigation" (TRUSTe, 2002b). Such examples call into question TRUSTe's reliability for investigating its corporate sponsors.

BBBOnline is an industry-sponsored self-regulation initiative that is similar to TRUSTe but that adds the well-known independent redress mechanism of the Better Business Bureau. In addition, the program features monitoring services, consumer dispute resolution, and a compliance seal. Consequences for noncompliance include seal withdrawal, publicity, and referral to government enforcement agencies. The program is very thorough; a 90-item questionnaire helps to clarify all aspects of a Web site's privacy practices, including mechanisms for allowing customers to verify and correct their information. However, the program does not provide legal redress mechanisms.

Finally, as self-regulation initiatives, these programs are by definition voluntary, meaning that internet users have this protection only at participating Web sites. At the time of this writing, 707 Web sites subscribed to the BBBOnline privacy program and approximately 2,000 subscribed to the TRUSTe program— hardly comprehensive protection of privacy considering that there are hundreds of millions of Web sites. In addition, although the BBBOnline program costs roughly 20% less than the TRUSTe program, it attracts less than half of the subscribers enlisted by TRUSTe. BBBOnline seems to be the less popular program for industry because of its independent mechanisms for redress and publicity for violations; for example, although Microsoft is a sponsor of BBBOnline, it does not subscribe to the program.

Ultimately, then, industry self-regulation always allows industry to draw up a "self-regulation program" that meets the needs of industry but not necessarily those of individuals. Moreover, internet users need to determine which of these programs really offers independent monitoring of a Web site's privacy practices. It is hard to imagine that most users would have the time and resources to determine the level of independent monitoring they could expect of each program.

CITIZENS' SELF-MANAGEMENT AS AN ALTERNATIVE: A SAFE HARBOR OF THEIR OWN?

Arguably, for Europeans, the EU Data Protection Directive largely settles the corporate privacy debate. Problems are referred to the appropriate data protection commissioner in each country for resolution. Concerns over the balance between governmental intrusion and public safety may arise, as in recent proposals requiring internet service providers in the EU to archive user content for 2 years to facilitate law enforcement. But these concerns are relatively muted compared with American apprehensions. In the United States, the debate continues at full volume. It is difficult to open a newspaper without encountering stories about privacy (or the lack thereof) on the Web. This raises the question: What do American internet users make of the situation, and how do they relate to the main approaches?

From the Pew Internet and American Life Project (2000) report, it appears that protection of personal information is important to U.S. Internet users. More than half (59%) of respondents indicated that they were "very concerned," and 25% said that they were "somewhat concerned" (p. 22), that unknown entities might obtain their personal information. U.S. Internet users also seem to feel strongly about key privacy principles such as consent prior to collection of personal information and enforcement of privacy rights. With regard to openness and permission, Americans seem to prefer an "opt-in" approach and feel that the rules should be in their favor. According the Pew report, "86% of internet users are in favor of 'opt-in' privacy policies that require internet companies to ask people for permission to use their personal information" (p. 2). This finding is, in fact, predictive of recent election results in the state of North Dakota, where

87% of voters supported a new state law requiring an opt-in policy for personal data.

On this point, then, Americans seem to agree with the EU Data Protection Directive principle of requiring unambiguous consent prior to data processing, including transfers of data to third parties—clearly, an opt-in policy as American internet users seem to prefer it. Yet this concept "makes U.S. companies reel in horror" (Oakes, 2000), and current U.S. self-regulation approach does not provide individuals with the right to be asked before their personal information is taken from them. Interestingly, the Safe Harbor principles do not include this requirement either except in cases involving sensitive information such as personal medical, racial, ethnic, political, religious, or other information (U.S. Department of Commerce, 2000).

With regard to another important fair information principle, the question of redress in case of privacy violations, the Pew Internet and American Life Project (2000) report indicated that Americans do want effective enforcement mechanisms, although the report did not clarify the kind of mechanisms that Americans might want to see or what they might consider to be an appropriately independent mechanism. Nevertheless, according to the report, "94% of internet users want privacy violators to be disciplined" (p. 3), choosing these options from the list of possible answers:

- [The] company's owners [should] be put in jail. (11%)
- [The] company's owners [should] be fined. (27%)
- The internet site [should] be shut down. (26%)
- The internet site [should] be placed on a list of fraudulent Web sites. (30%) (p. 29)

The first three options seem to favor legal enforcement mechanisms, whereas the fourth option—placing the Web site on a list of fraudulent Web sites—could be achieved through a self-regulation mechanism. Perhaps if the answer choices had included more self-regulation options, the results might have been different. Nevertheless, American internet users clearly desire protection and enforcement of privacy rights.

With regard to redress and enforcement of privacy rights, American internet users also seem to agree with the EU directive. According to the directive, "Each Member State shall provide that one or more public authorities are responsible for monitoring the application within its territory of . . . this Directive. These authorities shall act with complete independence" (Article 28[1]). As a consequence, European countries and states within those countries have established offices of data protection commissioners who handle, investigate, and seek penalties for privacy violations. The current U.S. approach provides some independent redress (e.g., in the form of the BBBOnline program), but only in the case of the few Web sites that participate in the program. There is little legal enforcement unless the privacy violation falls under the category of fraudulent consumer information.

Despite their apparent agreement with such key privacy principles of the EU directive, American internet users might not embrace the directive's comprehensive government regulation approach. When asked, "Who do you think should have the MOST say over how internet companies track people's activities online and use personal information?" (Pew Internet and American Life Project, 2000, p. 28, emphasis in original), survey participants responded as follows:

- Federal government (19%)
- Internet companies (6%)
- People who use Web sites (62%)
- Don't know/Refused (13%)

This is the point where Americans clearly diverge from the European approach. Although Americans want their personal information clearly protected and want the protections enforced, they do not seem to endorse the governmental oversight mandated by the EU directive. Neither do they seem to want to entrust internet companies with the protection of their privacy rights, rejecting the much-touted corporate self-regulatory approach as well.

The rejection of, or ambivalence about, government regulation of privacy issues suggested by the Pew report is consistent with findings of other surveys conducted at the time. For example, Bellman, Johnson, Kobrin, and Lohse (2000), in their online privacy study of internet users in the United States, Canada, New Zealand, Australia, and Western Europe, found that "people from the U.S. were the only ones in our sample to disagree that governments should regulate data collection practices" (p. 29). The Electronic Privacy Information Center (2002), however, cited two polls—a February 2002 Harris Poll and a March 2000 *Business Week*/Harris Poll—showing that 63% and 57% of respondents, respectively, favored federal legislation to protect their personal information. Polls might not arrive at clear conclusions due to their designs and the specific answer options from which respondents must choose. In any case, neither poll indicated an overwhelming agreement on the question of who should be responsible for managing this public issue. The Pew report and the Bellman and colleagues (2000) study also indicated more ambivalence than agreement on this question.

It appears that American internet users, instead of strongly supporting one of the predominant approaches, are looking for an alternative approach to creating a "safe harbor" for themselves. However, this raises the question: What might that alternative be? The usual U.S. approach to "letting people make their own rules" is to create markets. Americans typically believe that by assigning ownership to something and then letting people trade or sell it freely, or even letting people refuse to trade or sell it, opportunities for people to make their own decisions about that particular issue will be maximized.

The trouble with privacy, of course, is that under anyone's theory it is subject to massive market failure. First, as Gurak (2001) pointed out in *Cyberliteracy,* personal information typically becomes valuable only when assembled into large data sets. The value of any one person's information is negligible, and the transaction costs in trading the information are probably much larger than the value of the information itself, at least from the consumer's perspective. So, we would not expect markets for information to arise spontaneously. To the extent that a market does arise, there will be network effects; that is, the value accruing to the holder of the database from adding each increment of data will be much larger than the value of the data to the individual surrendering control of it.

When markets fail, Americans sometimes simply declare the market to be off-limits such as with organ donations, babies, and other inalienable properties (Radin, 1987; Rose-Ackerman, 1985). Because inalienability frequently attaches to items with a strong moral or human rights component for which monetary value is incommensurable, this approach to privacy closely resembles the rights-based approach of the EU. Occasionally, Americans may expect government to undertake to provide functions that the failed market might have provided, as in the case of public utilities or certain other public services. Alternatively, Americans may sometimes expect governments to intervene to create or optimize a failed market, as in the case of securities or intellectual property. This latter approach, commodifying personal information to allow it to be traded, has been suggested by some privacy theorists (Bartow, 2000; Samuelson, 2000) but has also been criticized as subject to the same policy problems experienced from reifying other forms of intellectual property (Lemley, 2000; Samuelson, 2000).

The stakes in online privacy are high for everyone involved (Table 17.1).

Table 17.1 Benefits and Risks to Governments, Firms, and Citizens in Three Privacy Regulation Strategies

Stakeholders	Government Regulation: European Data Protection Directive	Corporate Self-Regulation: The U.S. Approach	Citizen Self-Management: The Third Way?
Benefits and risks for governments	*Benefits:* legal coherence (especially for e-commerce); consumer confidence; ownership of public problem with elected representatives *Risks:* costs of monitoring and enforcement mechanisms (e.g., data protection authorities)	*Benefits:* no costs for enforcement mechanisms *Risks:* legal ambiguity; lower consumer confidence and reduced economic activity; costs of negotiating and monitoring special international agreements for U.S. corporations	*Benefits:* consumer confidence; possibly balanced needs of all stakeholders (if multiple stakeholder model); no need for privacy law enforcement mechanisms *Risks:* legal ambiguity; unelected groups in control of public problem; possibly less flexibility for government to change laws as needed for government missions (e.g., increased data collection for fighting terrorism)
Benefits and risks for firms	*Benefits:* stable legal framework (especially for e-commerce); consumer confidence; cost savings from more targeted advertising (only to those customers who opted in or are interested in the product rather than to all customers)	*Benefits:* growing industry for privacy technologies; profits from sale of data to marketing and human resources firms; profits from better products based on consumer data and optimally screened employees (especially if firms do not have to compensate customers for data, manage customer requests to opt out or access personal data, or comply with privacy legislation)	*Benefits:* participation in management of privacy (if multiple stakeholder model); consumer confidence *Risks:* subject to management of public problem by unelected groups; legal ambiguity; costs of compliance with citizen self-management program; similar risks to those of government regulation if citizen self-management stipulations are similar to those of EU (e.g., opt-in)

(Continued)

287

Table 17.1 Continued

Stakeholders	Government Regulation: European Data Protection Directive	Corporate Self-Regulation: The U.S. Approach	Citizen Self-Management: The Third Way?
Benefits and risks for firms	Risks: costs of compliance; costs of managing customer consent to data collection (opt-in) and customer access to personal data; loss of profits from customers refusing to provide data; restrictions on aggregation of and trade with customer data and therefore loss of profits; restrictions on screening potential employees; costs of legal consequences of privacy violations	Risks: costs of maintaining different data protection practices for U.S. customers and customers from the EU and other parts of the world; reduction in profits from low consumer confidence; costs of substitute but potentially less effective mechanisms designed to instill consumer confidence (e.g., online privacy programs); legal ambiguity	Benefits: More balanced representation of the needs of individuals compared with corporate self-regulation; possibly alternative and less costly models of privacy protection (vs. legal enforcement mechanisms) Risks: no legal enforcement options; legal ambiguity
Benefits and risks for citizens	Benefits: choice to refuse participation in data collection or to be compensated; better control over personal information and therefore lower risk of identity theft and its consequences (e.g., loss of credit or employment); legal enforcement mechanisms against violations; less spam; one well-known standard Risks: potential risks to be blacklisted in government law enforcement initiatives (depending on the government regulation)	Benefits: improved products from unfettered access to all customer data (vs. only the data of those who agree to data collection in the government or citizen self-management models) Risks: reduced control over personal data; higher risk of identity theft and other consequences (e.g., loss of employment or credit, cost of clearing personal record or credit, cost of dealing personal record or privacy protection technologies); cost of dealing with spam; no legal recourse against violations of privacy; confusion over various standards and technologies; exclusion from services when refusing to provide data	

Future Questions and Directions for Research

As with any survey, the responses in the Pew Internet and American Life Project (2000) data are limited to the options provided and, in that respect, reflect the perspectives of the survey designers to at least some extent. In assessing who should have control over privacy regulation, for example, it would have been interesting to know how respondents might have reacted to combinations of the answer choices, for example, a citizen-driven approach that would include all stakeholders. In addition, it is difficult to tell what respondents meant when they responded that decisions about privacy should be left to individual Web users; whether such control would mean wider deployment of technologies such as P3P, governmentally enabled redress through private lawsuits, commodification of personal information to allow for its sale, or some other option is not clear. Indeed, it is unclear what options the survey designers may have had in mind and to what extent the responses may have reflected those assumptions. In any case, research on alternative untried models will be an important direction for privacy research to pursue (Schwartz, 2000).

Surveys, by nature, are also limited in another way. They usually do not provide insights into the kinds of opinions that respondents provide. Are these opinions based on an informed debate? In what discursive spaces did respondents participate? Were the respondents drawing on public debates of some sort? On what kinds of grounding did they base their opinions? These questions are important because, as Fishkin (1995) showed, people often revise their survey responses after participating in informed debates and being exposed to the views of various stakeholders. Surveys, then, shed little light on the kind of public sphere of debates and deliberation that form around a public problem and that could influence public policy. Future surveys may be designed to include questions such as where respondents received their information on the issue and what debates (if any) they are aware of or participate in.

In some sense, the Pew report pointed in this direction. For example, one of its findings, that less than half of the respondents (43%) knew what a cookie was, indicated that respondents might not participate much in public discussion of the issue or perhaps that there is little public discussion of the issue. Possibly, the kind of public sphere that forms around a public issue may be influenced by cultural factors. Specifically, with regard to the knowledge that individuals have about privacy technologies, Bellman and colleagues (2000) found that Americans know less about "putting a cookie on a machine" than do their European counterparts. Whereas only 54% of Americans felt "pretty knowledgeable" about this topic, 72% of continental Europeans did, as did 59% of Britons. Similarly, only 16% of Americans knew about "clickstreams and log files," compared with 33% of continental Europeans and 22% of Britons. However, more Americans (63%) than continental Europeans (57%) or Britons (50%) knew about privacy policies—perhaps because in the United States, privacy policies rather than federal laws provide the key stipulations for the privacy practices of a Web site. Also interesting for Americans, the situation has not changed much; the Consumer WebWatch (2002) survey reported that about half of the respondents knew what a cookie was. Although the reasons for these cross-cultural differences could be in the survey design such as the sampling procedure, a research direction that examines the formation of public knowledge and public debate about online privacy may be particularly fruitful in building the kind of public sphere the privacy problem might need to be resolved.

Furthermore, a comparative cultural approach may enhance our understanding of how Americans use the internet and of how they feel about an important issue such as online privacy, compared with other stakeholders in their own and other cultural environments. For example, from the lens of a comparative European and American approach, it would be interesting to know how Americans regard other important privacy concerns such as issues of access to their data and the security and accuracy of their data. Although surveys that include respondents from various national backgrounds exist (e.g., Bellman et al., 2000), data from different surveys are often difficult to compare.

A comparative cultural approach may also reveal possible cultural biases in the Pew report such as assessments of users who refused to provide their personal information to Web companies as "hardcore privacy protectionists" who use "guerrilla tactics." From a different cultural perspective, these same practices may appear merely sensible, especially in an environment where anyone can grab a person's information, distribute it to anyone for any purpose, profit from it, or even potentially turn it against the person (intentionally or unintentionally)—all without that person's knowledge, let alone consent.

Conclusion

Although privacy problems occur globally, various countries have developed different approaches to solving privacy problems and negotiating the stakes involved. Yet as the Pew Internet and American Life Project (2000) report on online privacy showed, the perspectives of individuals can differ considerably from those of their governments, providing important information for policy-makers struggling with these issues. However, more research on privacy policy alternatives is needed to find a path that meets the specific needs of American internet users for privacy. Future research on privacy and the internet needs to move from generic questions to ones with a specific focus—medical privacy, privacy when shopping online, privacy when Web surfing, and so forth. The answers to such questions may provide a better basis for making an argument to policy-makers for privacy alternatives in the United States. Similarly, as an important part of such an alternative privacy policy project, research on the public sphere emerging around the privacy problem may help to determine how the public opinion process on online privacy may best be advanced. There may be education campaigns and the like that could be introduced, educating U.S. citizens on the various privacy alternatives and getting feedback on these ideas. Advocacy groups such as the Electronic Privacy Information Center already exist; perhaps what is needed are partnerships among such groups and academic researchers, industry representatives, and government representatives. Finally, when viewed through the lens of culturally different approaches, the Pew report on online privacy raises interesting questions for future research as well, including questions about other privacy practices and cultural bias—questions that may help to shape the path to a safe harbor from privacy violations and concerns for American internet users.

Note

1. In December 2002, the TIPS proposal was made irrelevant by the passage of the Homeland Security Act, but other law enforcement or anti-terrorism initiatives, such as the Pentagon's Total Information Awareness (TIA) system, collect information about private individuals as well. Therefore, our point remains the same.

References

Bartow, A. (2000). Our data, ourselves: Privacy, propertization, and gender. *University of San Francisco Law Review, 34*, 633–704.

Bellman, S., Johnson, E. J., Kobrin, S. J., & Lohse, G. L. (2000). *Cultural and regional influences on concerns about internet privacy and security.* [Online]. Retrieved August 5, 2002, from www.cebiz.org/downloads/privacy_concerns.pdf

Bennett, C. J. (1998). Convergence revisited: Toward a global policy for the protection of personal data? In P. Agre & M. Rotenberg (Eds.), *Technology and privacy: The new landscape* (pp. 99–124). Cambridge, MA: MIT Press.

Citizen Corps. (2002). *Operation TIPS: Terrorism Information and Prevention System.* [Online]. Retrieved August 13, 2002, from www.citizencorps.gov/tips.html

Consumer WebWatch. (2002). *A matter of trust: What users want from Web sites—Results of a national survey of internet users.* [Online]. Retrieved August 13, 2002, from www.consumer webwatch.org/news/1

Electronic Privacy Information Center. (2002). *Public opinion on privacy.* [Online]. Retrieved August 14, 2002, from www.epic.org/privacy/survey

Electronic Privacy Information Center and Junkbusters. (2000). *Pretty poor privacy: An assessment of P3P and internet privacy.* [Online]. Retrieved August 14, 2002, from www.epic. org/reports/prettypoorprivacy.html

Federal Trade Commission. (2000). *Privacy online: Fair information practices in the electronic marketplace.* [Online]. Retrieved July 14, 2002, from www.ftc.gov/reports/privacy2000/ privacy2000.pdf

Federal Trade Commission. (2002). *Microsoft settles FTC charges alleging false security and privacy promises.* [Online]. Retrieved August 13, 2002, from www.ftc.gov/opa/2002/08/microsoft.htm

Fishkin, J. (1995). *The voice of the people.* New Haven, CT: Yale University Press.

Gellman, R. (2002). *Privacy, consumers, and costs: How the lack of privacy costs consumers and why business studies of privacy costs are biased and incomplete.* [Online]. Retrieved August 13, 2002, from www.epic.org/reports/dmfprivacy.pdf

Gurak, L. (2001). *Cyberliteracy: Navigating the internet with awareness.* New Haven, CT: Yale University Press.

Identity Theft Resource Center. (2002). *Facts and statistics.* [Online]. Retrieved July 17, 2002, from www.idtheftcenter.org/html/facts_and_statistics.htm

Lemley, M. (2000). Private property. *Stanford Law Review, 52,* 1545–1557.

Moor, J. H. (2000). Toward a theory of privacy in the information age. In R. M. Baird, R. M. Ramsower, & S. E. Rosenbaum (Eds.), *Cyberethics: Social and moral issues in the computer age* (pp. 200–212). Buffalo, NY: Prometheus Books.

Oakes, C. (2000, November 2). Web enters privacy "safe harbor." *Wired News.* [Online]. Retrieved July 18, 2002, from www.wired.com/news/politics/0,1283,39909,00.html

Pew Internet and American Life Project. (2000). *Trust and privacy online: Why Americans want to rewrite the rules.* [Online]. Retrieved July 17, 2002, from www.pewinternet.org/reports/ toc.asp?report=19

Radin, M. (1987). Market inalienability. *Harvard Law Review, 100,* 1849–1937.

Reidenberg, J. (1997). *Lex informatica:* The formulation of policy rules through technology. *Texas Law Review, 76,* 553–593.

Reidenberg, J. (2000). Resolving conflicting international data privacy rules in cyberspace. *Stanford Law Review, 52,* 1315–1371.

Rose-Ackerman, S. (1985). Inalienability and the theory of property rights. *Columbia Law Review, 85,* 931–969.

Rotenberg, M. (1998, May 7). *Testimony and statement for the record of Marc Rotenberg, director, Electronic Privacy Information Center, adjunct professor, Georgetown University Law Center, on the European Union Data Directive and Privacy, before the Committee on International Relations, U.S. House of Representatives.* [Online]. Retrieved October 15, 1999, from www.epic.org

Samuelson, P. (2000). Privacy as intellectual property. *Stanford Law Review, 52,* 1125–1173.

Scheeres, J. (2002, August 13). A site to despise untrained spies. *Wired News.* [Online]. Retrieved August 13, 2002, from www.wired.com/news/print/0,1294,54492,00.html

Schwartz, P. (1995). Privacy and participation: Personal information and public sector regulation in the United States. *Iowa Law Review, 80,* 613–618.

Schwartz, P. (2000). Internet privacy and the state. *Connecticut Law Review, 32,* 815–859.

Swire, P., & Litan, R. (1998). *None of your business: World data flows, electronic commerce, and the European Privacy Directive.* Washington, DC: Brookings Institution.

TRUSTe. (2002a). *Privacy Seal Program.* [Online]. Retrieved August 13, 2002, from www.truste.org

TRUSTe. (2002b). *Viewpoint on FTC's recent action.* [Online]. Retrieved August 13, 2002, from www.truste.org/about/truste_ftc_response.html

U.S. Department of Commerce. (2000). *Safe Harbor Privacy Principles.* [Online]. Retrieved July 14, 2002, from www.export.gov/safeharbor/shprinciplesfinal.htm

World Wide Web Consortium. (2002). *Platform for Privacy Preferences (P3P) project.* [Online]. Retrieved August 15, 2002, from www.w3.org/p3p

18

Sited Materialities
With Global Span

Saskia Sassen
University of Chicago

The difficulty that analysts and commentators have had in specifying or understanding the impact of digitization on complex social settings essentially results from two analytic flaws. One of these (especially evident in the United States) confines interpretation to a technological reading of the technical capabilities of digital technology. This is crucial for the engineering side but is problematic for the social sciences.[1] A purely technological reading of technical capabilities inevitably neutralizes or renders invisible the material conditions and practices, place-boundedness, and thick social environments within and through which these technologies operate. A second tendency is the continuing reliance on analytic categorizations that were developed under other spatial and historical conditions, that is, conditions preceding the current digital era. Thus, the tendency is to conceive of the digital as simply and exclusively digital and to conceive of the nondigital (whether represented in terms of the physical/material or the actual, both of which are problematic but common conceptions) as simply and exclusively that—nondigital. These "either/or" categorizations filter out alternative conceptualizations, thereby precluding a more complex reading of the impact of digitization on material and place-bound conditions.

The challenge for social science is not so much to deny the weight of technology as to develop analytic categories that allow us to capture the complex imbrications of technology and society that cannot be confined to applications and impacts. Here I develop two particular aspects of this challenge. One concerns the variable outcomes of these technologies for different social orders. They can be constitutive of new social dynamics, but they can also be derivative or merely reproduce older conditions. Second, such an effort will, in turn, call for categories that capture what are now often conceived of as contradictory, or mutually exclusive, attributes.

Digital networks are embedded in the technical features and standards of the hardware and software as well as in actual societal structures and power dynamics (Latour, 1991; Lovink & Riemens, 2002; Mackenzie & Wajcman, 1985/1999).[2] For instance, there is no purely digital economy and no completely virtual corporation or community. This means that power, contestation, inequality, and hierarchy inscribe electronic space and shape the production of software.

The fact that electronic space is embedded and cannot be read as a purely technological condition, or merely in terms of its technical features, is illuminated by the nature of segmentations evident inside electronic space. One instance is captured in the differences between private and public access digital networks.[3] The so-called internet is a different type of space from the private networks of the financial industry, and the firewalled corporate sites on the Web are different from the public access portion of the Web. The financial markets, operating largely through private dedicated digital networks, are a good instance of private electronic space. The three properties of digital networks—decentralized access, simultaneity, and interconnectivity—have produced strikingly different outcomes in the private digital space of global finance from the distributed power of the public access portion of the internet. Although the power of these financial electronic networks rests on a kind of distributed power (i.e., millions of investors and their millions of decisions), it ends up as concentrated power. The trajectory followed by what begins as the distributed power we associate with the public access internet may assume many forms—in this case, one radically different from that of the internet.

This difference points to the possibility that network power is not inherently distributive. Intervening mechanisms that may have little to do with the technology per se can reshape its organization. To keep it as a form of distributed power requires that it be embedded in a particular kind of structure. We cannot take the distributed power, and hence the democratizing potential, of digital networks as an inevitable feature of this technology, as is so often the case in utopian readings, perhaps most prominently exemplified by John Perry Barlow's now famous *Declaration of Independence of Cyberspace*.

Beyond these issues of intentionality and use lies the question of infrastructure and access (e.g., National Telecommunications and Information Administration, 1998; Petrazzini & Kibati, 1999; Sassen, 1998, chap. 9; Shade, 1998; Thomas, 1995). Electronic space is going to be far more present in highly industrialized countries than in the less developed world, and it is going to be far more present for middle clazss households in developed countries than for poor households in those same countries (Harvey & Macnab, 2000; Hoffman & Novak, 1998; Jensen, 2000). However, what needs to be emphasized here is that there are very cheap ways in which to deliver access to the internet—far cheaper than the standard telephone system. Hence, once such access is secured, the opportunities for low-income households and communities, especially in the less developed world, can increase enormously (e.g., International Telecommunications Union, 1998; Mele, 1999; Nadeau, Lointier, Morin, & Descoteaux, 1998).

Recognizing the embeddedness of electronic space, in my research I have come to regard the internet as a space produced and marked through the software that shapes its use and the particular aspects of the hardware mobilized by the software (Sassen, 1999). These features can also function as an indicator of transformations in the articulations between electronic space and larger institutional orders. There are significant implications attached to the fact that one of the leading internet software design focuses during the past few years has been on firewalled intranets for firms and encrypted tunnels for firm-to-firm transactions.[4] Both of these represent, in some sense, private appropriations of a "public access" space.[5] Furthermore, the growing interest in e-commerce has stimulated the development of software linked to identity verification, trademark protection, and billing. The rapid growth of this type of software and its use on the internet does not necessarily strengthen the "publicness" of electronic space (e.g., Elkin-Koren, 1996; Lovink & Riemens, 2002). This is especially significant if there is less production of software aimed at strengthening the "openness" and decentralization of the internet, as was the case during the earlier phases of the internet. Far from strengthening the internet's democratic potential as many liberal and neo-liberal commentators maintain, this type of commercialization can threaten it. It also carries major implications for the impact of democratizing initiatives.

However, electronic space remains a crucial force for new forms of civic participation, especially in its public access portion. Noncommercial uses still dominate the internet, even though the race is on to invent ways in which to expand electronic commerce and ensure safety of payment transactions. But at the same time, there has been a proliferation of noncommercial uses and users. Civil society, whether in the form of individuals or nongovernmental organizations (NGOs), is an energetic presence in electronic space. From struggles around human rights, the environment, and worker strikes around the world to genuinely trivial pursuits, the internet has emerged as a powerful medium for nonelites to communicate, support each other's struggles, and create the equivalent of insider groups on scales ranging from the local to the global (e.g., Frederick, 1993; Kobrin, 1998; Perritt, 1999; Ronfeldt, Arquilla, Fuller, & Fuller, 1998).

Looking at electronic space as embedded allows us to go beyond the common duality between utopian and dystopian understandings of the internet and electronic space generally. For instance, even as it reproduces masculine cultures and hierarchies of power, electronic space also enables women to engage in new forms of contestation and in proactive endeavors in multiple realms, from political to economic. Furthermore, in the context of globalization, these initiatives can go global and bypass national states and major national economic actors, thereby opening a whole new terrain for initiatives of historically disadvantaged peoples and groups (e.g., Cleaver, 1998; Correll, 1995; Mele, 1999; Ronfeldt et al., 1998).

Three analytic issues that capture various features of the embeddedness are the complex imbrications between the digital and material conditions, the destabilizing of existing hierarchies of scale made possible by the new technologies, and the mediating cultures between these technologies and their users. The next three sections develop these issues.

Digital and Material Imbrications

Hypermobility and dematerialization are usually seen as mere functions of the new technologies. This understanding erases the fact that it takes multiple material conditions to achieve this outcome. Once we recognize that the hypermobility of the instrument, or the dematerialization of the actual piece of real estate, had to be *produced,* we introduce nondigital variables into our analysis of the digital. Obversely, much of what happens in electronic space is deeply inflected by the cultures, the material practices, and the imaginaries that take place outside electronic space. Much of what we think of when it comes to cyberspace would lack any meaning or referents if we were to exclude the world outside cyberspace (e.g., Garcia, 2002). In brief, digital space and digitization are not exclusive conditions that stand outside the nondigital. Digital space is embedded in the larger societal, cultural, subjective, economic, and imaginary structurations of lived experience and the systems within which we exist and operate.

For instance, producing capital mobility takes capital fixity: state-of-the-art built environments, well-housed talent, and conventional infrastructure—from highways, to airports, to railways. These are all partly place-bound conditions, even when the nature of their place-boundedness differs from what it may have been 100 years ago when place-boundedness was far more likely to be a form of immobility. Today it is a place-boundednesss that is inflected or inscribed by the hypermobility of some of its components, products, and outcomes. Both capital fixity and capital mobility are located in a temporal frame where speed is ascendant and consequential. This type of capital fixity cannot be fully captured through a description confined to its material and locational features, that is, through a topographical description (Sassen, 2001, chaps. 2 and 5).

Conceptualizing digitization along these lines allows us to recognize the ongoing importance of the material world, even in the case of some of the most dematerialized digitized activities. This can be illustrated by the case of finance, one of the most digitized activities and one that involves a dematerialized instrument. Yet it cannot simply be thought of as exclusively digital. To have electronic financial markets and digitized financial instruments requires enormous amounts of matériel, not to mention human talent (which has its own type of physicality). This matériel includes conventional infrastructure, buildings, airports, and so forth. Much of this matériel is inflected by the digital insofar as it is a function of financial markets. Also, much of the digital composition of financial markets is inflected by the agendas that drive global finance, and these are to be distinguished from the engineering side of technology development.

Digitization brings with it an amplification of those capacities that make possible the liquefying of what is not liquid. Therefore, digitization raises the mobility of what we have customarily thought of as not mobile or barely mobile. At its most extreme, this liquefying dematerializes its object. Once dematerialized, it gains hypermobility—instantaneous circulation through digital networks with global span. It is important, in my reading, to underline that the hypermobility gained by an object through dematerialization is but one moment of a more complex condition. Representing such an object as hypermobile is, then, a partial representation because it includes only some of the components of that object, that is, those that can be dematerialized. Much of what is liquefied and circulates in digital networks, and is marked by hypermobility, remains physical in some of its components.[6] The real estate industry further illustrates some of these issues. Financial services firms have invented instruments that liquefy real estate, thereby facilitating investment and circulation of these instruments in global markets. Yet part of what constitutes real estate remains very physical. At the same time, however, that which remains physical has been transformed by the fact that it is represented by highly liquid instruments that can circulate in global markets. It may look the same, it may involve the same bricks and mortar, and it may be new or old, but it is a transformed entity.

We have difficulty in capturing this multivalence through our conventional categories (if it is physical, it *is physical;* if it is liquid, it *is* liquid). In fact, the partial representation of real estate through liquid financial instruments produces a complex imbrication of the material and the dematerialized moments of that which we continue to call real estate. And so does the partial endogeneity of physical infrastructure in electronic financial markets.

Destabilizing Hierarchies of Scale

The complex imbrications between the digital (as well as the global) and the nondigital bring with them a destabilizing of older hierarchies of scale and often dramatic rescalings (Sassen, 2003). As the national scale loses significance along with the loss of key components of the state's formal authority, other scales gain strategic importance. Most especially among these are subnational scales (e.g., global cities) and supranational scales (e.g., global markets). Older hierarchies of scale, dating from the period that saw the ascendance of the nation-state, continue to operate; they are typically organized in terms of institutional size and territorial scope—from the international to the national, to the regional, to the urban, to the local. But today's rescaling dynamics cut across institutional size and across the institutional encasements of territory produced by the formation of nation-states (Sassen, 2003). This does not mean that the old hierarchies disappear; rather, it means that the rescalings that emerge alongside the old ones can often trump the latter.

For instance, through the internet, local initiatives can become part of a global network of activism without losing the focus on specific local struggles (e.g., Cleaver, 1998; Espinoza, 1999; Mele, 1999; Ronfeldt et al., 1998). It enables a new type of cross-border political activism, one centered in multiple localities yet intensely connected digitally and with simultaneous access worldwide. Not only can activists develop networks for circulating information (e.g., about environmental, housing, or political issues), but they can also engage in actual political work.

There are many examples of such a new type of cross-border political work. For instance, the Society for the Promotion of Area Resource Centers (SPARC), started by and centered on women, began as an effort to organize slum dwellers in Bombay to get housing. Now SPARC has a network of such groups throughout Asia and in some cities in Latin America and Africa. This is one of the key forms of critical politics that the internet can make possible—a politics of the local with a big difference; these are localities that are connected with each other across a region, a country, or the world. Just because the network is global does not necessarily mean that participation has to occur on the global scale.

Existing theory is not enough to map today's multiplication of nonstate actors and forms of cross-border cooperation and conflict such as global business networks, NGOs, diasporas, global cities, transboundary public spheres, networks for open source software development, and the new cosmopolitanism. International relations theory is the field that, to date, has had the most to say about cross-border relations. But current developments associated with various mixes of globalization and the new information and communications technologies point to the limits of international relations theory and data. Its models and theory remain focused on the logic of relations between states and the scale of the state at a time when we see a proliferation of nonstate actors, cross-border processes, and associated changes in the scope, exclusivity, and competence of a state's authority over its territory, all partly enabled by these new technologies. Theoretical developments in other disciplines may prove to be important; especially relevant in the case of sociology's contribution is the type of network theory that is developed in economic sociology.

These transformations in the components of international relations and the destabilization of older hierarchies of scale can be captured in the notion that the local today is increasingly a multiscalar condition. Much of what we might still experience as the "local" (e.g., an office building, a house, or an institution right there in our neighborhood or downtown) actually is something I would rather think of as a microenvironment with global span insofar as it is deeply internetworked. Such a microenvironment is, in many senses, a localized entity, but it is also part of global digital networks that give it immediate far-flung span. To continue to think of this as simply local is not very useful. More important, the juxtaposition between the condition of being a sited materiality and that of having global span captures the imbrication of the digital and the nondigital and illustrates the inadequacy of a purely technological reading of the technical properties of digitization that would lead us to posit the neutralization of the place-boundedness of that which precisely makes possible the condition of being an entity with global span.

An example of how this might operate at a complex systemic level is the bundle of conditions and dynamics that marks the model of the global city. Just to single out one key dynamic: The more globalized and digitized the operations of firms and markets, the more their central management and coordination functions (and the requisite material structures) become strategic. It is precisely because of digitization that simultaneous worldwide dispersal of operations (whether factories, offices, or service outlets) and system integration can be achieved. And it is precisely this combination that raises the importance of central functions. Global cities are, among other components, strategic sites for the combination of resources necessary for the production of these central functions. The cross-border network of global cities emerges as one of the key components in the architecture of international relations.

Mediating Practices

There are multiple ways in which to examine the interactions between the new digital technologies and their users. There is a strong tendency in the literature to conceptualize the matter of use as an unmediated event, that is, as unproblematized activity.

In contrast, a long-standing concern with what I have called "analytic borderlands" has led me to try to detect the mediations in the act of using the technologies. In my research, I have found that use is constructed or constituted in terms of specific cultures and practices through and within which users articulate the experience or utility of electronic space. Thus, my concern here is not with the purely technical features of digital networks and what these might mean for users, nor is it simply with the impact of digital networks on users. My concern is, rather, with this in-between zone that constructs the articulations of cyberspace and users.

This conceptualization clearly rests on the earlier proposition that electronic space is embedded and not a purely technological event. Thus, electronic space is inflected by the values, cultures, power systems, and institutional orders within which it is embedded. For instance, if we were to explore these issues in terms of gendering, or specifically the condition of the female individual, we would posit that insofar as these various realms are marked by gendering, this embeddedness of cyberspace is also gendered in at least some of its components and, furthermore, that so is cyberspace itself.[7] This is so even though there is enormous variability in this gendering by place, age, class, race, nationality, and issue orientation; at the same time, there are likely to be various situations, sites, and individuals not marked by gendering or marked by hybrid or queered genderings.[8]

The second consequence of this embeddedness is that the articulations between cyberspace and individuals—whether as social, political, or economic actors—are constituted in terms of mediating cultures; it is not simply a question of access and understanding how to use the hardware and software. To some extent, these mediating cultures are likely to be shaped by a variety of marking conditions.

Conclusion

There is a strong tendency in the social sciences to understand and conceptualize the new information technologies in terms of their technical properties and to construct the relation to the sociological world as one of applications and impacts. Less work has gone into developing analytic categories that allow us to capture the complex imbrications of technology and society. This chapter has addressed two particular aspects of this challenge through two organizing efforts. First, understanding the place of these new technologies from a sociological perspective requires avoiding a purely technological interpretation and recognizing the embeddedness and variable outcomes of these technologies for different social orders. These technologies can indeed be constitutive of new social dynamics, but they can also be derivative or merely reproduce older conditions. Second, such an effort in turn calls for categories that capture what are now often conceived of as contradictory, or mutually exclusive, attributes. The chapter examined these two aspects by focusing on three analytic issues for sociology: the embeddedness of the new technologies, the destabilizing of older hierarchies of scale when these technologies come into play, and the mediating cultures that organize the relation between these technologies and users. The chapter briefly examined these analytic issues as they get instantiated in substantive sociological arenas, including the interactions between capital fixity and capital mobility, the emergence of a new politics of places on global networks, and the gendering of access to and use of electronic space.

Notes

1. For critical examinations that reveal particular shortcomings of technology-driven explanations, see Loader (1998) and Wajcman (2002) and, more generally, Latour (1991), Lovink and Riemens (2002), Mackenzie (1999), Mackenzie and Wajcman (1985/1999), and Munker and Roesler (1997).

2. Although using a different vocabulary, we can see Latour (1991) making a radical statement in this direction. Lovink and Riemens (2002) gave us a detailed account of the multiple nondigital conditions (including neighborhood subcultures) that had to come together to create what was for several years an enormously successful, citywide digital internetwork called Digital City Amsterdam.

3. Elsewhere, I have examined the extent to which our thinking about electronic space and network power has been shaped by the properties of the internet, disregarding the crucial differences between the public access digital networks of the internet and private digital networks to which there is no access no matter what one is willing to pay, for example, private dedicated networks of financial services firms and wholesale financial markets (Sassen, 1999).

4. This saves companies the cost of private computer networks, the cost of the associated staffing and servicing, and the cost of frame relay connections or of using intermediaries for firm-to-firm transactions.

5. An additional issue, one not examined here, is the privatization of infrastructure that has also taken place since the mid-1990s. The backbone has been privatized where before it was financed by the U.S. government, that is, taxpayers. This, in turn, changes the normative issues about private appropriations of internet space as a public space. But it does so only partly because it does not override the new distinction between privatized internet space and public access space, even if for a fee (for a resource to be public, it need not necessarily be free). Internet space can remain public even if there is a fee to be paid for access, but privatized internet space is not accessible no matter what the fee.

6. Much of my work on global cities (Sassen, 2001) has been an effort to conceptualize and document the fact that the global digital economy requires massive concentrations of material conditions to be what it is. Finance is an important intermediary in this regard; it represents a capability for liquefying various forms of nonliquid wealth and for raising the mobility (i.e., hypermobility) of that which is already liquid.

7. Much of what has been described for cyberspace in the specialized and general literature is explicitly or implicitly far more likely to be about particular groups of men because these have so far dominated use and produced many of the cybercultures. Thus, we also need more information about men who do not fit into those particular groups.

8. The concept of gendering has increasingly become problematic and is used here as shorthand for a complex bundle of issues. There is a vast critical literature on various aspects relating to gendering and feminist categories generally. For how this relates to the subject of digital technology, see Featherstone and Burrows (1995) and Wajcman (1991). The notion of queering gender is, in this context, a powerful repositioning.

References

Cleaver, H. (1998). The Zapatista effect: The internet and the rise of an alternative political fabric. *Journal of International Affairs, 51,* 621–640.

Correll, S. (1995). The ethnography of an electronic bar: The lesbian cafe. *Journal of Contemporary Ethnography, 24,* 270–298.

Elkin-Koren, N. (1996). Public/Private and copyright reform in cyberspace. *Journal of Computer-Mediated Communication, 2*(2). [Online]. Retrieved May 11, 2003, from www.ascusc.org/jcmc/vol2/issue2

Espinoza, V. (1999). Social networks among the poor: Inequality and integration in a Latin American city. In B. Wellman (Ed.), *Networks in the global village* (pp. 147–184). Boulder, CO: Westview.

Featherstone, M., & Burrows, R. (1995). *Cyberspace/Cyberbodies/Cyberpunk: Cultures of technological embodiment.* London: Sage.

Frederick, H. (1993). Computer networks and the emergence of global civil society. In L. M. Harasim (Ed.), *Global networks: Computers and international communications* (pp. 283–295). Cambridge, MA: MIT Press.

Garcia, L. (2002). The architecture of global networking technologies. In S. Sassen (Ed.), *Global networks/Linked cities.* London: Routledge.

Harvey, A. S., & Macnab, P. A. (2000). Who's up? Global interpersonal temporal accessibility. In D. Janelle & D. Hodge (Eds.), *Information, place, and cyberspace: Issues in accessibility* (pp. 147–170). Amsterdam: Elsevier.

Hoffman, D. L., & Novak, T. P. (1998). Bridging the racial divide on the internet. *Science, 280,* 390–391.

International Telecommunications Union. (1998). *Challenges to the network: Internet for development.* Geneva, Switzerland: Author.

Jensen, M. (2000). *Internet connectivity in Africa* [report]. [Online]. Retrieved May 11, 2003, from www3.sn.apc.org/africa/afstat.htm

Kobrin, S. J. (1998). The MAI and the clash of globalizations. *Foreign Policy, 112,* 97–109.

Latour, B. (1991). Technology is society made durable. In J. Law (Ed.), *A sociology of monsters* (pp. 103–131). London: Routledge.

Loader, B. (Ed.). (1998). *Cyberspace divide: Equality, agency, and policy in the information age.* London: Routledge.

Lovink, G., & Riemens, P. (2002). Digital City Amsterdam: Local uses of global networks. In S. Sassen (Ed.), *Global networks/Linked cities* (pp. 327–345). New York: Routledge.

Mackenzie, D. (1999). Technological determinism. In W. H. Dutton (Ed.), *Society on the line: Information politics in the digital age* (pp. 41–46). Oxford, UK: Oxford University Press.

Mackenzie, D., & Wajcman, J. (1999). *The social shaping of technology.* Milton Keynes, UK: Open University Press. (Original work published 1985)

Mele, C. (1999). Cyberspace and disadvantaged communities: The internet as a tool for collective action. In M. A. Smith & P. Kollock (Eds.), *Communities in cyberspace* (pp. 264–289). London: Routledge.

Munker, S., & Roesler, A. (Eds.). (1997). *Mythosinternet.* Frankfurt, Germany: Suhrkamp.

Nadeau, J., Lointier, C., Morin, R., & Descoteaux, M. A. (1998, July). *Information highways and the Francophone world: Current situation and strategies for the future.* Paper presented at INET '98 Conference: The Internet Summit, Geneva, Switzerland. Retrieved May 5, 2003, from www.isoc.org/inet98/proceedings/5f/5f_3.htm

National Telecommunications and Information Administration. (1998). *Falling through the net II: New data on the digital divide.* Washington, DC: Author. Retrieved May 5, 2003, from www.ntia.doc.gov/ntiahome/net2/falling.html

Perritt, H. H., Jr. (1999). International administrative law for the internet: Mechanisms of accountability. *Administrative Law Review, 51,* 871–900.

Petrazzini, B., & Kibati, M. (1999). The internet in developing countries. *Communications of the ACM, 42*(6), 31–36.

Ronfeldt, D., Arquilla, J., Fuller, G., & Fuller, M. (1998). *The Zapatista "social Netwar" in Mexico.* Santa Monica, CA: RAND.

Sassen, S. (1998). *Globalization and its discontents.* New York: New Press.

Sassen, S. (1999). Digital networks and power. In M. Featherstone & S. Lash (Eds.), *Spaces of culture: City, nation, world* (pp. 49–63). London: Sage.

Sassen, S. (2001). *The global city: New York, London, Tokyo* (rev. ed.). Princeton, NJ: Princeton University Press.

Sassen, S. (2003). Globalization and denationalization? *Review of International Political Economy, 10*(1), 1–22.

Shade, L. R. (1998). A gendered perspective on access to the information infrastructure. *The Information Society, 14,* 33–44.

Thomas, R. (1995). Access and inequality. In N. Heap, R. Thomas, G. Einon, R. Mason, & H. MacKay (Eds.), *Information technology and society: A reader* (pp. 90–99). Milton Keynes, UK: Open University Press.

Wajcman, J. (1991). *Feminism confronts technology.* Cambridge, UK: Polity.

Wajcman, J. (2002). The social world in the 21st century: Ambivalent legacies and rising challenges of technologies [special issue]. *Current Sociology, 50*(3).

19

The Future of the Internet

Cultural and Individual Conceptions

William Sims Bainbridge

National Science Foundation

O ur culture's conception of the future of the internet will illustrate how
novel surveys can archive aspects of an individual's personality—a new
application that has begun to appear on the internet and may have much greater
significance in the future. The research reported in this chapter is based in the
tradition of computer-administered surveys (Bainbridge, 1989, 1992), but it
reverses the conventional relationship between social scientist and research participant. Instead of having one person compose a questionnaire to be answered
by a thousand respondents, thousands of people provided input over the internet
to create a questionnaire for a single respondent.

Surviving in Cyberspace

Throughout history, a few individuals have been immortalized in art and literature. More than 2,000 years after the death of Julius Caesar, we can see his face in
sculptures and read his thoughts in the books he wrote. Philosophers may debate
how much of a human personality can be preserved in artifacts, but clearly a few
historical individuals continue to influence life through their works, from Moses
and Aristotle to Jefferson and Einstein.

Today, anyone can be memorialized in computer data files burned onto CDs
or distributed via the internet. The Library of Congress offers searchable texts of

2,900 life history interviews from the 1930s on its American Memory Web site. A vastly larger such project is the 180-terabyte digital library of the Survivors of the Shoah Visual History Foundation, which contains videotaped interviews with more than 50,000 survivors of the European Holocaust of the early 1940s.

Many ordinary citizens have found ways of storing aspects of personality on the World Wide Web. For example, a man who calls himself Meathead offers a three-dimensional image of himself that can be downloaded onto an avatar in the popular computer virtual environment, *The Sims,* where he can cavort with avatars of the music group Nine Inch Nails. Many people have created memorial Web sites for deceased relatives, and an average of 24 Web sites are linked into each of 92 Web rings concerning the loss of children as of February 14, 2002.

Anyone who has ever responded to a major questionnaire may have contributed fragments of his or her personality to an online survey archives such as the Inter-university Consortium for Political and Social Research (ICPSR) at the University of Michigan, the Roper Center at the University of Connecticut, and the Virtual Data Center at Harvard University. For example, more than 38,000 people have answered the questions of the General Social Survey (GSS), and their personal facts and opinions are currently available anonymously on the Web. Information about another 62,000 anonymous individuals are posted on the Web by the Panel Study of Income Dynamics (PSID), a longitudinal survey that repeatedly contacted them for as long as 34 years.

However, such surveys collect only a very small fraction of the information that defines an individual's uniqueness. Traditional surveys are extremely expensive activities, and the data in the GSS cost more than a dollar per byte to collect. Administration of surveys over the internet makes a great variety of new kinds of research possible. In particular, the Web facilitates a fresh approach to the development of questionnaire instruments to capture aspects of a person's opinions, attitudes, beliefs, and preferences.

In May 1997, I launched an experimental Web site called The Question Factory, with the goal of creating 20,000 new questionnaire items that could be used to archive aspects of a personality. To be sure, a vast number of sociological and psychological questionnaire scales already exist (Goldman et al., 1995–1997), but they were typically created to measure a particular variable of theoretical interest, rather than to chart the ornate contours of an individual human mind. The aim of The Question Factory was to collect a very large number of thoughts that were influential in the culture, without any theoretical preconceptions whatsoever, which then could be used to document the mental characteristics of a member of that culture.

For example, The Question Factory obtained responses from 131 people to an online survey consisting of open-ended questions about death and the afterlife (Bainbridge, 2000), for example, "What do you BELIEVE will happen to you personally after you die?" Some respondents were recruited from a sociology class, a Bible college, and a Buddhist Web ring, and they wrote a very wide range of opinions in response to such inquiries. Their responses were collated into groups expressing similar ideas, and then summary statements were written using the verbiage practically verbatim, resulting in 100 "afterlife" fixed-choice items and 100 "death" items.

The following illustrates a fairly conventional, if pessimistic, afterlife belief: "After death, you will writhe in the pit and the lake of fire, seeing distant Heaven and knowing you can never have the happiness of the souls who are there." In contrast, the following is an unconventional technologically oriented item: "After death, you will be restored to life by scientists of the future, using samples of your DNA and data about how you thought and acted in this life." The Question Factory produced many topical modules, some of which were calibrated through online surveys of fixed-choice items. A total of 2,000 items became the material for the first of 10 software modules, called *Beliefs*, assessing a person's view of many aspects of life. The modules were placed on The Question Factory Web site for anyone to download for personal use.

Another Question Factory questionnaire pretested open-ended questions about the future. The following worked very well: "Imagine the future and try to predict how the world will change over the next century. Think about everyday life as well as major changes in society, culture, and technology." On the basis of the pilot studies with The Question Factory, I was invited to participate in a massive online questionnaire study, sponsored by the National Geographic Society, called Survey2000 (Witte, Amoroso, & Howard, 2000). Questions contributed by other researchers included food preferences and, incidentally, provided me with the material for another 2,000-item module, *Taste*. About half of the 46,000 adults who responded to Survey2000 wrote something in response to my future item, providing material I collated and edited to make a set of 2,000 items for the software module, *The Year 2100*.

The Year 2100

Data from one actual but anonymous respondent illustrates the process here. These data have been placed on the internet and recently published on a CD-ROM included with a book on social science computing (Bainbridge, 2002b; Burton, 2002) as the "test data" in *The Year 2100*. The module administers 2,000 statements about the future to the respondent, asking him or her to rate each item on two 8-point scales: how good it would be if the particular statement came true (from 1 = *bad* to 8 = *good*) and how likely it is that the statement will come true (from 1 = *unlikely* to 8 = *likely*).

One of several analysis modes extracts statements rated in a selected manner. For example, the respondent gave just 2 of the 2,000 statements the maximum 8 rating on both the "bad-good" and "unlikely-likely" scales:

Human consciousness will be transmitted to advanced computers.

For the first time in human history, human-computer interfaces will permit development of technologies of the soul.

The respondent rated 2 proposals as very bad (1 on the bad-good scale) but rather likely (7 on the unlikely-likely scale):

Humanity will not leave the Earth in meaningful numbers because the technology required will be beyond its grasp.

Space exploration will stall, symbolizing the failed promises of technology.

The respondent's *utopia* is the set of predictions judged to be very good but very unlikely (a bad-good rating of 7 or 8 and an unlikely-likely rating of 1 or 2). For this respondent, there were 16 utopian statements, all concerning space flight:

Humanity will become a spacefaring species.

Arrays of solar panels on the Moon will provide much of the Earth's electric power.

Colonization of nearby moons and planets will lead to rapid gains in space transportation.

The other planets will be colonized, creating a united solar system.

There will be a federation of planets to organize colonization of uninhabited worlds.

Outer space pioneers will no longer be Earthlings but [will] form autonomous communities that leave the solar system in the hope that their descendents will inhabit distant worlds.

Colonies on the Moon and on Mars will become independent nations.

Humanity will have colonized this solar system and begin to look beyond.

Scientists will learn to master gravity and how to repel it in order to hover any object.

Anti-gravity or levitation will be developed to permit space travel to distant galaxies.

Scientists will prove that it is possible to exceed the speed of light.

How to achieve space travel at light speed will be understood completely.

Faster than light speed travel will have been perfected.

A manned spaceship will have reached the closest star.

Spaceships will leave this solar system, bound for moons around some of the larger gas giant planets discovered in other solar systems.

First direct contact with another intelligent species will be achieved through interstellar travel.

In contrast, the respondent's *dystopia,* or statements rated as 1 or 2 on both scales, consists of statements about nuclear doom plus the following five about millenarian religion:

People will seek God once again as science comes full circle and realizes that Darwin was wrong about evolution.

God will rule over the Earth, destroy wickedness, and bring perfection to mankind.

God will bring an end to war, famine, and disease.

Those who do not accept Jesus as their savior will perish in a time of terrible tribulation.

Government will be by divine intervention since human government has not achieved good for all mankind, and only God can do that.

To make the task of rating predictions manageable for the respondent, the software arranged the 2,000 items into 20 groups of 100 each and gave them descriptive labels: art, business, conflict, domestic, education, family, government, health, international, justice, knowledge, labor, miscellaneous, nature, outer space, population, quality of life, religion, society, and technology. These labels are very rough, as illustrated by the domestic label, which refers to 100 items about home life, the physical attributes of houses, foods, and urban and rural communities. Table 19.1 shows the average ratings from the 100 items in each of these categories.

The 100 items about space flight were rated highest on the bad-good scale by the same respondent, with an average of 6.13 in the range of 1 to 8, but were rated lowest on the unlikely-likely scale, with an average of just 4.25. Within each set of items, the software calculates the respondent's *optimism*, which is the correlation between the two scales. The respondent is optimistic to the extent that he or she thinks the best predictions are most likely. But here we see that the coefficient for outer space items is –.36, reflecting the pessimism we have already seen in this respondent. Note that the items themselves came from the surrounding culture, contributed by thousands of respondents to Survey2000, but this measure of optimism or pessimism is normed to the particular values of the individual respondent.

Once someone has rated all 2,000 predictions along both scales, we have 4,000 measurements of the individual's values and expectations about the future that logically should be reflections of his or her essential view of life and so central to personal identity. The 20 categories are very rough, so for the purposes of this study, I went one step further and asked the respondent to categorize the items afresh. We transferred the items and the respondent's ratings to a spreadsheet and then asked the respondent to mark each item that concerned technology. The respondent organized them in the following groups: internet, electronic, space, biotechnology, nuclear, other technology, and nontechnology.

Individuals will vary in their categorizations, and with 2,000 statements there are many opportunities to draw fine distinctions. Understandably, the respondent placed the following in the internet category: "Books will be purchased online as packages of text documents." But the following one went there as well, even though it does not explicitly refer to the internet: "Instead of borrowing books from libraries, people will read them over their computers." However, the following very similar statement wound up in the electronic category rather than the internet category: "Textbooks and hardcover books will no

Table 19.1   Respondent's Ratings of 2,000 General Predictions

Category	Examples of Predictions in the Group	Mean Good	Mean Likely	Optimism (r)
Outer space	There will be permanent colonies on several of the major moons of Jupiter, Saturn, Neptune, and Uranus. First direct contact with another intelligent species will be achieved through interstellar travel. Hybrid engines will be developed for space exploration, working like jets in the atmosphere and like rockets outside it.	6.13	4.25	–0.36
Domestic	Houses and furniture will be made from recyclable plastics. Many people will have returned to a traditional town setting, where they need to travel only short distances on a daily basis to fulfill their needs. Cities will have networks of delivery tunnels for trucks.	4.83	5.15	0.54
Knowledge	Answers will be found to many of the vexing fundamental questions about who we are and the universe we live in. Human consciousness will be transmitted to advanced computers. Increasing numbers of people will spend their lives seeking truth.	4.82	5.29	0.08
Health	People will be able to locate and read any medical publication online. Repair of damaged heart tissue will be a common medical practice. Medicines will be created to suit the patient's personal genetic makeup.	4.73	4.97	0.30
Technology	Society will become so dependent on computer technology that normal daily functions will collapse if that technology fails. Magnetic levitation trains running in vacuum tunnels will provide cheap long distance transportation at more than five hundred miles [per] hour. There will be artificial intelligence systems that are able to respond to the full experience of the real world.	4.72	4.82	0.52
Labor	Workers will revolt against supporting the many nonworkers such as the aged and those on welfare. Manufacturing of many kinds will be done at home, using computer-assisted design and fabrication techniques. Manual labor will be a thing of the past, as robots and computers will do the undesirable jobs.	4.55	5.30	0.08
Miscellaneous	People will more and more choose their cultural group [and] not be born into it. Cameras will be entirely digital, and photographic film will be manufactured only in small quantities for special purposes. The [U.S.] Marine Corps will be alive and well as it nears its 325th birthday.	4.51	5.07	0.51
Religion	Science will become the official state religion, with scientists as high priests. The spiritual deadness affecting prosperous societies will lead to a proliferation of strange cults and fanatic religious movements. Christian monastic activity will bring the church back to harmony with nature.	4.51	4.53	0.61

(Continued)

Table 19.1 Continued

Category	Examples of Predictions in the Group	Mean Good	Mean Likely	Optimism (r)
Art	The media will no longer be programmed by large corporations, but people will be free to program their own entertainment. People will have easy access to foreign books, movies, and music over the Internet. There will be a resurgence of high culture such as classical music, nonabstract paintings, and classical ballet.	4.48	5.20	0.40
Education	Astronomy will be taught in the early grades of school. English will be the official global language. A college degree will have only modest significance because there will be other options of respected higher education.	4.48	4.98	0.26
Government	Governments will be heavily burdened by debt, preventing them from providing necessary services. Democratic governments will vacillate between liberalism and conservatism. Political power will be decentralized, with most public decision making occurring at the local level.	4.38	4.82	0.28
Nature	Desalinization of sea water to produce drinking water will become widespread and inexpensive. The rain forests will slowly regain their former health and extent. The hole in the ozone layer of the atmosphere will reach a massive size, causing vast numbers of deaths.	4.32	4.74	0.13
Society	There will be a shift in power from the holders of capital to knowledge workers. There will be agents of change, who enjoy creating chaos, and resisters of change, who fear the loss of their security. Society will evolve into a unified federal world system with a common secondary language, monetary system, and justice system.	4.31	4.46	0.47
Family	A wide variety of alternative family structures will be accepted. The elderly will be revered rather than hidden in nursing homes away from their families. There will be many more intercultural marriages whose offspring are likely to be bilingual.	4.27	4.91	0.10
Business	Small companies and individuals will have a competitive edge over large multinational corporations because of their flexibility and cost-effectiveness. International financial organizations, [such as] the World Bank and International Monetary Fund, will be abolished because they pushed developing countries into debt to protect the developed economies. Consumers will have a vast variety of choices through Internet shopping.	4.23	4.90	0.46
Justice	People will come to realize that morality does not need religious justification. Prison systems will use computers and electronic restraints to control inmates rather than walls or guards. There will be courageous individuals willing and able to counter injustice.	4.23	4.70	0.26

Table 19.1 Continued

Category	Examples of Predictions in the Group	Mean Good	Mean Likely	Optimism (r)
Population	At least 500,000 people will live on the Moon and Mars. Population growth will slow as women become more involved in decision making. There will be frequent minor wars in which nations deliberately try to exterminate their enemies' populations to free up more resources for the victors.	4.20	4.90	−0.14
International	Africans educated in developed nations will return to their homelands, causing rapid development. New York City will no longer be the cultural center of the world. There will be much unrest in Asia as the lower class revolts against the regimes.	4.19	4.54	0.55
Conflict	Weaker cultures will merge into stronger ones. Wars will no longer be fought on the battlefield but [rather] in cyberspace with computer terminals. Society will change from a melting pot to self-segregation in which ethnic groups choose not to assimilate, wishing to retain strong ties to their original culture.	4.17	4.88	0.37
Quality of life	Only a small fraction of the population will smoke tobacco. Groups of like-minded people will band together and set up their own communities, largely ignoring the surrounding world. Improved transportation and storage will allow adequate distribution and stockpiling of food throughout the world.	4.05	4.68	0.23

longer be sold by the millions but will be replaced by laser discs." And the following statement was placed in the nontechnology category: "Reading an actual paper book will be considered a quaint historical affectation." Perhaps the respondent imagined that some nontechnological substitute for books (e.g., storytelling) might be found, but other respondents might place this item in one of the technological categories.

As indicated in Table 19.2, the respondent placed only 17 items in the nuclear category. Of these items, 7 concern atomic war, so it is not surprising that the respondent rated this as the worst of any category. However, this category also contains some potentially very good items such as "Once the infrastructure of nuclear fusion power generation and distribution is installed, there will be unlimited wealth." This illustrates the potentially irrational impact of cultural categories. The technologies from which fusion may be developed are quite remote from the technologies of nuclear weaponry, yet by being placed in the same category, they may share the stigma.

Table 19.2 Respondent's Categorization of Technology and New Media Predictions

Category	Examples of Predictions in the Category	Number of Items	Mean Good	Mean Likely	Optimism (r)
Internet	The art of letter writing will revive through use of e-mail. E-commerce will provide consumers around the world with the best products and services at the cheapest prices. The Internet will allow gifted individuals to be heard without being controlled by the marketplace and nay-sayers.	99	5.1	5.6	0.44
Electronic	Digitized art will be the most influential approach in fields as diverse as painting, movie making, and music. Everyone will be required to have some type of microchip implanted under their skin in order to buy and sell. The typical house will be controlled by a main computer that does the basic tasks around the home.	120	4.7	5.3	0.48
Space	Arrays of solar panels on the Moon will provide much of the Earth's electric power. There will be a defense system to protect Earth from asteroids. The meek will inherit the Earth, and the brave will travel to other worlds.	128	6.2	4.3	−0.30
Biotechnology	Genetic engineering will be extremely useful in agriculture. Alzheimer's [disease] and other forms of senility will have been wiped out. A vaccine to prevent AIDS will have unleashed a second sexual revolution.	120	5.1	5.2	0.41
Nuclear	A major nuclear world war will occur between the West and Islamic states. Energy will be chiefly supplied by nuclear fusion facilities that operate on hydrogen derived from water. There will be a political crisis over the disposal of spent fuel from nuclear power plants.	17	3.9	4.4	0.15

Table 19.2 Continued

Category	Examples of Predictions in the Category	Number of Items	Mean Good	Mean Likely	Optimism (r)
Other technology	Terrorists having weapons of mass destruction will force nations to become police states in order to provide security for their people. Engineers will be able to build microscopic machines, assembled molecule by molecule, to do useful work. More and more women will enter the fields of engineering, science, research, computing, and technology.	148	4.9	5.0	0.24
Nontechnology	Natural foods and herbs will be used widely for good health and fitness. The typical person will experience multiple divorces and remarriages. Radical politics will draw strength from the alienation of vast numbers of people who are disconnected from their neighbors.	1,368	4.2	4.8	0.29

As in Table 19.1, the respondent rated the space category best and least likely, but here with 128 items rather than 100. This reveals the particular values and perceptions of the individual respondent, but it also suggests the tragic reality of space flight in contemporary culture. Awareness of potential future accomplishments in space is very widespread, and the respondents to Survey2000 believed that many things are possible beyond the Earth. Yet little of that great potential has been realized during the three decades since the last trip to the moon, and there is no assurance that it ever will be.

In terms of fulfillment of technical promise and public perceptions, the internet is practically the opposite of space flight. Three decades ago, only a few federally funded scientists knew what internet was, and only a few visionaries imagined what it could become. Internet applications continue to proliferate, and there is every reason for optimism that we have seen only the very beginning of its benefit to humanity. The respondent rated the 99 internet statements as very good, tied with biotechnology but well behind the space statements that were so important for this particular respondent. The respondent considered the internet predictions the most likely ones to be fulfilled among all the categories.

The 21st-Century Internet

The respondent also sorted the 99 internet-related statements into subcategories, collecting statements related to the same fundamental idea. I then arranged the statements in each category as a paragraph and wrote an italicized introductory sentence. Naturally, some of the statements in each group contradict each other or give somewhat different perspectives on the same topic. The result that follows is a brief synthetic essay on the future of the internet produced cooperatively by the thousands of Survey2000 online respondents, the individual respondent whose views I am archiving, and the computer software.

The technology for [the] internet will continue to develop for many years. "Wireless digital systems will become standard, so that every house will have a small satellite dish which will provide TV, internet, and mail service. Every person will have a personal communications device that they carry everywhere, performing the functions of phone, fax, pager, laptop, and message service. Interactive holographic imaging, producing lifelike three-dimensional pictures, will change the way people are entertained and the way they communicate. Computer electrodes implanted in the scalp will connect the brain to the world's databases."

Computer-supported cooperative work will be increasingly common. "With improved communication, it will become less necessary to meet in person, and therefore business trips will become less common. Videoconferencing and virtual internet meetings will be everyday occurrences. With [the] internet, people will be able to work in any company in the world without the need to migrate to another country. People will be able to collaborate on projects with anyone anywhere in the world, using videoconferencing and computer technology. Telecommuting will become mandatory in every area where it is feasible, simply to curb excessive traffic on the roads. Many people will work in a general office, where a collection of people from different companies work in the same place using information technology. Workers will be largely self-employed and work by computer from whatever location they happen to be in at the time."

Online business will be a major part of the economy. "E-commerce will provide consumers around the world with the best products and services at the cheapest prices. Consumers will have a vast variety of choices through internet shopping. The local grocery store will post its daily specials on the Web, so customers can think about what recipe they would like to prepare and make a shopping list of needed items. Groceries will be ordered online and delivered to the home. Homes will be completely wired, to the point that a refrigerator will know it is out of milk and will order some. Food will be delivered to the home from online grocery stores. Paper money will become a thing of the past, and all payments will be made electronically. People will use a debit card for all purchases, linked to a master account for each individual. There will be one world stock market in cyberspace."

Electronic commerce will destroy some existing businesses and services. "E-mail will replace the postal system for letters. The telephone companies will be replaced by an expanded bandwidth internet. People will buy products and food online directly from the producer, all but eliminating large physical department stores and supermarkets. Malls will close as entrepreneurs escape the physical overhead and adopt electronic commerce. Movie houses and video rental stores will disappear, replaced by instant download through a phone line onto an in-home computer screen. Electronic commerce on [the] internet will greatly reduce the role of middlemen and retailer distributors in the economy. Small shop owners and middlemen will be under extreme pressure from the intense global competition of electronic commerce. The internet will allow individual entrepreneurs to compete with large corporations through their Web sites."

Publishing and libraries will migrate to [the] internet. "Daily newspapers will disappear, replaced by internet delivery of news. Newspapers and books will no longer be printed because everyone will be able to read them online. Books will be purchased online as packages of text documents. In [an] effort to conserve paper and rare books, and also to reach more patrons with their limited supply, libraries will offer books online to read. Instead of borrowing books from libraries, people will read them over their computers. People will have easy access to foreign books, movies, and music over the internet. The increasing influence of electronic information technology will dramatically reduce the amount of paper used."

The creation and distribution of art and music will evolve. "Entertainment will become compartmentalized as people tailor their entertainment packages to their own desires using [the] internet and rental of multimedia recordings. There will be virtual concerts where no one will actually sit in a concert hall with the musicians, who appear realistically in thousands of homes courtesy of the computer. There will be great demand for writers and illustrators for internet publications."

Culture more generally will undergo radical upheaval. "Information technology will minimize interest in mass culture in favor of smaller cultures that have greater personal relevance. Online news services will use client profiles to tailor the selection of stories to fit the individual user's interests. The art of letter writing will revive through use of e-mail. E-mail and other text-based interpersonal communication will be very popular in the younger generation, improving the quality of their use of written language. A new kind of English language will evolve from the internet. The extensive use of electronic communication will mean that there will be no documents, letters, or even newspapers to preserve the day-to-day knowledge of the era for future historians. Archaeologists will dig through landfills and unearth old disk drives, re-discovering a Pompeii of culture from ancient Web sites."

Education at all ages will change its form and content. "Education will be transformed from institutions based at single sites to networks manifesting themselves from time to time in cyberspace or at various public locations. Children will attend school in their own homes through interactive television. Many children will attend school electronically via their computers. Public schools will decline in importance as it becomes easier to get an education at home using computer technology. Universities will put all but the most intensively physical studies online, with high-level degrees being offered in many subjects via [the] internet. Centuries-old universities will be rendered obsolete by [the] internet. Distance education will be the norm, not the exception, and dynamic professors will share their love of learning with millions of students around the world in virtual classrooms. The average educational level of people will be higher due to the intellectual benefits of computers and [the] internet rather than formal schooling."

Health services will improve. "People will be able to locate and read any medical publication online. Delicate surgeries will be performed through computers, allowing the best surgeons to operate at a distance on patients wherever they are. People with disabilities will be more independent because of the internet. People in nursing homes will have computers hooked up to the internet in order to communicate with those outside the nursing homes and thus not feel so isolated from the rest of the world."

Digital government will become a reality. "The general public will have ready access to government information and services over their computers. The internet will be an agent for democracy, as each community has an electronic town hall. Voting will be done online via personal computer. Internet-based voting will dramatically strengthen democracy. The selection of leaders will be done via electronic media, without paper ballots or voting booths. Citizens will vote from home by computer on daily and weekly issues which are raised by their elected representatives."

People will be liberated from political oppression. "No government will be able to regulate the internet. Electronic media will be disseminating information through many of the current physical barriers placed by governments. Electronic commerce will undermine the effectiveness of government restrictions in the global economy. Politically biased media will no longer be able to control populations since multiple opinions and potentially conflicting facts can be accessed over [the] internet. The internet will allow gifted individuals to be heard without being controlled by the marketplace and nay-sayers. The flow of information on the internet will become one of the primary means to fight large corporate agendas. The internet will completely revolutionize the urban versus rural struggle, ending the advantages of cities. [The] internet will diminish the importance of nations, political factions, and religious groups."

Cybercommunities will grow in importance. "Friendships with those who have moved far away will be common due to the ease of maintaining regular contact by phone calls, e-mail, and video. People will belong to virtual towns made up of all their friends and family members far and wide. People will have moved away from physical communities, toward online communities. Religious services will be conducted on the internet. People will meet as a result of the internet, often marrying someone they first contacted electronically. Many people will have more cyberfriends than real-life friends."

Loss of privacy will be among the dangers of [the] internet. "Economic privacy and anonymous transactions will be increasingly difficult because digital currency will have replaced traditional cash. The government will be able to trace every purchase people make, every phone call they place, and every TV program they watch. Privacy will be a thing of the past as electronic systems of payment and information exchange monitor people's every movement."

[The] significance of the digital divide is a matter of controversy. "The gap between the information rich and information poor will both widen and become more

important, creating a global elite and proletariat. [Or, conversely,] the digital divide will decrease as most people gain access to information technology. Information will be available to all, but only a few will use it effectively. Even the poorest members of the poorest countries will have access to the internet, and they will use it for a variety of purposes, from everyday requirements to education to recreation."

There is great uncertainty about whether people will be able to handle all the information available. "The combination of wireless technology, fast computer processing, and large databases will give anyone the answer to any question anywhere at anytime. More information will be at everyone's disposal, but the accuracy of such information will be uncertain. It will be difficult to sort out what information is really important to the individual. People will be bombarded with too much information to the point of mental information overload. [Or, conversely,] people generally will not suffer from information overload because computer agent programs will automatically collect the information they want."

The result of cybercommunity and information overload could be personal isolation. "People's desire to explore their environments will fade as information is delivered faster, cheaper, and easier to their computers. The continued increase in communication devices such as pagers, cellular phones, and the internet will reduce personal contacts. People will spend more and more time on the computer and less time going out to socialize with friends and neighbors. Electronic communication will increasingly isolate people from direct human contact and bring a coldness and emptiness to life. People will prefer cybersex to the traditional pleasure of two bodies touching. Society will be so fragmented and lacking in support systems that people will rely on the false sense of community provided by communication technology."

[Finally, the] internet could become an arena for many forms of conflict. "Debates over internet privacy, freedom of speech, accuracy of information, and the safety of [the] internet for children will make internet regulation a hot field for lawyers. Crimes against children will be greatly stimulated by pedophile internet newsgroups and pornographic Web sites. Labor unions will be obsolete because individuals will compete for jobs on the internet. Wars will no longer be fought on the battlefield but [rather] in cyberspace with computer terminals."

Conclusion

This chapter has presented the values and expectations of one individual concerning the internet, based on ideas from thousands of people that were collected in an internet-distributed survey.[1] Some of the visionaries who are creating the technology of the future have begun to speculate that it will be possible, over the next century, for people to merge with their computers and achieve a kind of immortality as dynamic patterns of information (Bainbridge, 2002a; Kurzweil, 1999). This study has considered one small step in that direction: the archiving of an individual's opinions on a large number of related issues, notably the future of the internet itself. The approach is based on the realization that the study of any individual person must also take account of the cultural ambience in which he or she exists.

Traditionally, surveys have been used to test social scientific theories and guide public policy. As machines become smarter, surveys will gain the new function of gathering fragments of personality to make computers both more humane and more sociable. In the future, society will consist not merely of individual people and social institutions but also of software agents, robots, and information systems (Roco & Bainbridge, 2003). This methodological exploration is a contribution to the complex system of tools we will need to create personable machine intelligences. More modestly, it suggests how traditional tools of questionnaire survey research can be extended to the new environment of the internet.

References

Bainbridge, W. S. (1989). *Survey research: A computer-assisted introduction*. Belmont, CA: Wadsworth.

Bainbridge, W. S. (1992). *Social research methods and statistics*. Belmont, CA: Wadsworth.

Bainbridge, W. S. (2000). Religious ethnography on the World Wide Web. In J. K. Hadden & D. E. Cowan (Eds.), *Religion and the social order*, Vol. 8: *Religion on the internet* (pp. 55–80). New York: Elsevier.

Bainbridge, W. S. (2002a, May). A question of immortality. *Analog,* pp. 40–49.

Bainbridge, W. S. (2002b). Validity of Web-based surveys. In O. V. Burton (Ed.), *Computing in the social sciences and humanities* (pp. 51–66). Urbana: University of Illinois Press.

Burton, O. V. (Ed.). (2002). *Computing in the social sciences and humanities*. Urbana: University of Illinois Press.

Goldman, B. A., et al. (1995–1997). *Directory of unpublished experimental mental measures* (7 vols.). Washington, DC: American Psychological Association.

Kurzweil, R. (1999). *The age of spiritual machines: When computers exceed human intelligence.* New York: Viking.

Roco, M., & Bainbridge, W. S. (2003). *Converging technologies to improve human performance: Nanotechnology, biotechnology, information technology, and cognitive science.* Dordrecht, Netherlands: Kluwer.

Witte, J. C., Amoroso, L. M., & Howard, P. E. N. (2000). Research methodology: Method and representation in internet-based survey tools. *Social Science Computer Review, 18,* 179–195.

Note

1. Websites referred to in this chapter include:

American Memory: WPA Federal Writers' Project: http://memory.loc.gov/ammem/wpaintro/wpahome.html

General Social Survey: www.icpsr.umich.edu/gss

Inter-university Consortium for Political and Social Research: www.icpsr.umich.edu

Meathead and Nine Inch Nails: www.theninhotline.net/meatpers/sims.html

Panel Study of Income Dynamics: www.isr.umich.edu/src/psid

The Question Factory: www.erols.com/bainbri/qf.htm

Roper Center for Public Opinion Research: www.ropercenter.uconn.edu

Survivors of the Shoah Visual History Foundation: www.vhf.org

Virtual Data Center at Harvard University: thedata.org

20

Conclusion

Contexting the Network

Steve Jones
University of Illinois at Chicago

It was back in high school during the 1970s, in a suburb of Chicago, that I first encountered a computer. In fact, it was via a network, the telephone system, that I actually encountered the computer. My high school had a teletypewriter and an acoustic coupler modem with which I, as a member of the high school computer club, was able to connect to a computer housed at one of our school district's other high schools. It was some months later, after my nerdish tendencies fully expressed themselves, that I visited the other high school with fellow members of the computer club to see the machine itself. It was about the size of a breadbox, housed in an equipment rack about the size of a refrigerator, and it was the strangest and most mysterious device I had ever seen.

Just down the road from that high school were the offices of A. B. Dick Company (founded with the invention of the mimeograph and with Thomas Edison's financial support), the company that had donated the computer (a DEC PDP-8/e, for those readers who, like me, maintained their computer club memberships). A little farther down the road in the opposite direction was Northwestern University's Vogelback Computing Center, to which my fellow computer club members and I trooped to see the Space Wars game on a CRT. Accustomed as we were to seeing computer output only on the light brown paper that spooled out of our school's teletypewriter, we could only gape at the rapid movement of dots and lines that the computer generated on a television-like screen.

Not long after those visits, I was enrolled as a freshman biology major at the University of Illinois at Urbana-Champaign and was introduced to the PLATO computer system. I began to use it for my classes (lecture notes, quizzes, and study guides were posted on it), but I quickly came to use it for much more than that (e.g., e-mail, discussion groups, news), and eventually I began to author materials for a number of courses.

I bring up this brief history with only a little interest in nostalgia and a much greater interest in contextualization. The things we do by using the internet today are in need of both radical contextualization and radical historicization. They are obviously new in scale and form, but they are less obviously new in kind—and all center on communication. Indeed, if there is any kind of truth to the notion of "convergence," it is not to be found in the packing together of technologies into single devices; rather, it is to be found in the ongoing proliferation of communication media and tools.

What, then, might we learn about the future of communication, and the future of communication research and theory, from contextualizing the internet as has been done in this book? One important lesson is that although the internet has, for some years now, been a means of providing audio and video, most of the human communication that traverses it is text based. Another important lesson is that the internet increasingly is used for human-to-machine and machine-to-machine communication. But perhaps the most important point to be gleaned from the contextualization of the internet is that it is time to abandon the notion of an "Internet" and think about an "internet." The "uppercase I" version refers to an enormous process, begun during the 1960s with U.S. government funding, of connecting computers and standardizing communication among them. The "lowercase i" version refers to the networking of computers that may or (more important) may not rely on that process. In this latter category are included any types of networking projects, from home networking to wireless network, to cellular networks, to Internet2, and so forth. Use of the uppercase "I" also signifies the internet's novelty, which has faded quickly. Internetworks have become part of the background of everyday life. For these reasons, we use the lowercase "internet" throughout this book.

The Network Metaphor for Linked Places

The use of a network is itself important and is a critical element in the internet's contextualization. Whether one is discussing the actual, as in hardware and software, or discussing the symbolic, as in the relatively recent popular use of networks as metaphors for everything from stock markets to relationships to biology, the growth of "network" as a central metaphor and paradigm mirrors the growth of similar concepts throughout history such as steam, electricity, and light. The longest lasting impact of the internet may well be that it makes clear to us that we can connect anything to anything, a postmodern triumph (if only technical) if ever there was one.

The network metaphor is inherently mind-boggling; if everything connects, then whatever we may think about we must consider everything, and in so doing we will achieve a unified field theory of—well, everything. In the first few pages of his book *Linked: The New Science of Networks*, Barabási (2002) somewhat breathlessly wrote,

Very few people realize . . . that the rapidly unfolding science of networks is uncovering phenomena that are far more exciting and revealing than the casual use of the word *network* could ever convey. Some of these discoveries are so fresh that many of the key results still circulate as unpublished papers within the scientific community. They open up a novel perspective on the interconnected world around us, indicating that networks will dominate the new century to a much greater degree than most people are yet ready to acknowledge. They will drive the fundamental questions that form our view of the world in the coming era. (p. 7, emphasis in original)

According to Barabási, not only computers but also religion, science, politics, and medicine—indeed, the gamut of human and natural behaviors—can be viewed from a network perspective.

Particularly given the discussion of terrorist cells and networks after the September 11, 2001, terrorist attacks in the United States, a network perspective seems to have become popular and taken on greater urgency. Other publications, such as Buchanan's (2002) *Nexus: Small Worlds and the Groundbreaking Science of Networks*, Johnson's (2001) *Emergence: The Connected Lives of Ants, Brains, Cities, and Software*, Watts's (2003) *Six Degrees: The Science of a Connected Age*, and Wolfram's (2002) *A New Kind of Science* (2002), focused attention on the notion of networks as a means of understanding complex behaviors.

Among this crop of books, one that stands out, in part for its reading of social behavior as networked and in part for its author's understanding of the social uses of communication technology, is Rheingold's (2002) *Smart Mobs: The Next Social*

Revolution. The reason it stands out is that instead of trying to connect everything to everything (or at least trying to connect everything to a network metaphor), Rheingold wrote about the ways in which communication networks mesh with people and place. Cell phones, pagers, instant messaging, and other media enable the joining and taking apart of social and political groups and actions, often on a moment's notice. By examining not only the internet but also other communication technologies, Rheingold's book forces us to think about the spatial dimensions of a social world that is *both* wired *and* wireless. In his view, networks are no mere metaphor; rather, they have real consequences.

What we need to understand the type of world that Rheingold describes are new understandings of the internet and networks. Our current concept of the internet's physical structure is still strongly rooted in old media and relies on the assumption that resources are scarce. Bandwidth, although not expensive (relatively speaking), is still considered a resource to be conserved. But what if it were free and limitless? And what if it were concerned less with connection and more with bonding? I tried to make a similar point in "The Internet and Its Social Landscape" (Jones, 1997) when I wrote about the prevalence of the metaphor of community as connection in contrast to the definition of community as place. The network metaphor emphasizes connection but deemphasizes everything else, including the consequences of connection and the role of space, both of which are critical to understanding the internet as a social space.

At its root, our concept of the internet as a social space is fixed in what Robins and Webster (1999) wrote about as "the network spaces that have been created in and through new information and communications technologies" (p. 238). But there is an opportunity to expand our notion of network space if we acknowledge that the primacy of the network metaphor derives from the convergence of numerous networks. The networks that we create and invoke every day when we are online are created by the binding together, not simply the connecting (which implies a disconnecting), of the computer grid, the electrical grid, and the telephone network. It is important that these grids and networks are firmly (and virtually permanently) bound, both in regard to their hardwiring and in regard to their scientific, technical, and historical development.

The Network Metaphor for Linked Times

To go a step further, what if the primacy of space as the central metaphor for the experience of networked communication were challenged by an increase in the use of metaphors of time? In 1998, Swatch introduced "internet time" by dividing the 24-hour day into 1,000 "beats." Swatch (n.d.) did it "so that we do not have to think about time zones." Whereas the Swatch effort uses a new meridian (the company's headquarters in Switzerland), another effort by a group of artists in New Zealand, New Earth Time ("NET"), uses the Greenwich meridian but divides the day by 360 degrees rather than by 24 hours. Efforts at manipulating time are not only symbolic but also real. Consider the following description of new cell phone technology:

Real-time audio buffering senses when the phone is removed from the ear. When the phone is returned, the missed incoming audio is played back, but at a rate faster than real-time. Very quickly, the phone catches back up to real-time, and the user misses nothing, despite the distraction. (Dietz & Yerazunis, 2001, p. 193)

Speed is a very real part of the development of network technologies, just as it had been in the development of computer processors, and our experience of network time will change as networks become faster, just as our experience of computer time has changed as things such as "instant-on boot-up" came to be.

Much has been written about the standardization of time, the consequences of that standardization on culture (Anderson, 1983; Carey, 1989; Rifkin, 1987), and the important effects that instantaneous electronic communication had on the need to share an understanding of *the* time. What we have not considered much is the effect of the availability of such communication—of contact from any place at any time—on our understanding of time. Anyone who has used videoconferencing to communicate with someone at least six or so time zones apart knows what this means. The coordination involves not only technical matters but also determination of what the other person would normally be doing at that moment—at the time—that they physically inhabit. Whereas space can be transcended (more or less) due to communication, time will prove to be a much greater challenge.

Tom DeFanti, codirector of the Electronic Visualization Lab at the University of Illinois at Chicago and inventor of the CAVE immersive virtual reality device, has on many occasions stated that bandwidth will increase at a rate comparable to that at which computer chips' speed has increased and that network speeds will increase concomitantly. To hear DeFanti and colleagues describe it, we will before long create a technology that "is 'better than being there' because physical travel, especially international travel, is best devoted to vacation, not work"

(Leigh, DeFanti, Johnson, Brown, & Sandin, 1997). One of my favorite questions DeFanti asked is one that I pose to students new to the study of communication technology, and it is one that I suspect has been asked in one way or another during the development of each new medium: "What if travel were free and instantaneous?" (DeFanti, 2000). What if we could use technology to "tele-immerse," as DeFanti put it, and not simply connect and disconnect?

Using DeFanti's ideas, Argonne National Lab's Rick Stevens envisaged additional consequences of tele-immersion and noted that, by using the technology, people could achieve the following (Leigh et al., 1997):

- Live where they wanted to live
- Meet their colleagues in interesting places
- Leave their things where they needed them, with appropriate security
- Schedule meetings at certain places and times
- Have ways in which to find people and things
- Develop habitual places to discuss science and life

These ideas were rooted not in DeFanti's or Stevens's knowledge of the future but rather in their knowledge of the internet:

People . . . meet their colleagues in chat sessions, exchange e-mail, schedule meetings and work, and set up shared file systems. They find each other somehow, often working together without knowing a new collaborator's age or gender. They develop new habits to increase productivity and communicate the deeper aspects of their personalities and skills. Even so, the latency, bandwidth, and flow management of current networks and operating systems, as well as the capabilities of our end-user visualization and perceptualization systems, do not quite evoke the feeling of free and instantaneous travel. To simulate travel over optical fiber, we need to be able to make n-dimensional phone calls where adding extra capabilities of communicating touch- and force-feedback (haptics), smell, and taste increases the dimensionality substantially. (DeFanti, 2000, p. 60)

The important insight from DeFanti is that when we use future communication technologies, our sense of space will be neither in our imagination nor in our networks. Instead, it will be a space bodily (physically) occupied by one or more humans; created by technological means via computers, projectors, and networks; persistent; and articulated to the cultural, artistic, political, and economic structures of its designer(s), experienced by its human inhabitants.

We will also find tele-immersion to be a technology that will, in interesting and important ways, link history to the present. One example of this is the Virtual Harlem project, an effort to build a virtual environment that looks like Harlem, New York, and thereby to recreate in the CAVE the environment within which art and politics developed during the Harlem Renaissance (Johnson, Leigh, Carter, Sosnoski, & Jones, 2002). Difficult as it is to reconstruct a three-dimensional virtual world from a time when aural and visual recording media were in their infancy, it is not so difficult to imagine that recreating contemporary (and future) environments will be much easier given the plethora of high-resolution and high-fidelity materials being recorded in digital form by more and more people. Rather than being linked only in the present, future network technologies will, in an important sense, link us with the past (perhaps in ways prefigured in director Steven Spielberg's film *Minority Report*). Whereas contemporary networks create connections, tele-immersion will enable forms of habitus (Bourdieu, 1990; Bourdieu & Passeron, 1977), with the technology itself providing (infra)structure not only for communication but also for culture and organization.

Conclusion

These developments will, of course, use an internet that is entirely different from the one we now know—as different as the teletypewriter I used in high school is from the Apple Powerbook on which I typed this chapter. We have reached the point where our networks are faster than our computers, rendering computers (like their predecessors) "dumb terminals" but replacing the mainframes' processing power and intelligence with that found on the networks. The speed at which we can move information exceeds the speed at which computers can process it; in short, computers now suffer information overload.

But networks are the new computers, the processors, and the movers of information. In distributed computing (or what is becoming popularly known as "grid computing" or simply "the grid"), every software system has an "information resource broker" (IRB) that operates as both client and server to communicate with other applications, databases, networks, and so forth. The IRB communicates with other IRBs, determining user and system needs in real time, even (likely) ahead of the user. The computer, rather than serving as an information processor, acts as a processor of audio, visual, and textual information and uses its computing power to draw and realize the most compelling images and sounds that its user seeks.

As observed by Jason Leigh, University of Illinois at Chicago Electronic Visualization Lab senior research scientist, the IRB's "symmetry allows distributed applications to treat each other as information resources" (Leigh et al., 1997, p. 16). The IRB is, in a very real sense, the intelligence within the network, and it is also a communicator. Much as we have struggled with theorizing the concepts of space, place, and time online, so too will the rise of networking as the predominant metaphor for computing, communicating, and (I suspect) living cause us to struggle with our sense of the site of intelligence, information, and action. Only by contextualizing and historicizing network technologies will we avoid a free-for-all and intervene in the reconfiguration of our experience.

References

Anderson, B. (1983). *Imagined communities: Reflections on the origin and spread of nationalism.* London: Verso.

Barabási, A-L. (2002). *Linked: The new science of networks.* Cambridge, MA: Perseus.

Bourdieu, P. (1990). *The logic of practice* (R. Nice, Trans.). Cambridge, UK: Polity.

Bourdieu, P., & Passeron, J-C. (1977). *Reproduction in education, society, and culture* (R. Nice, Trans.). Beverly Hills, CA: Sage.

Buchanan, M. (2002). *Nexus: Small worlds and the groundbreaking science of networks.* New York: Norton.

Carey, J. W. (1989). Technology and ideology: The case of the telegraph. In J. W. Carey (Ed.), *Communications as culture* (pp. 201–230). Winchester, MA: Unwin-Hyman.

DeFanti, T. (2000). Better than being there: Next millennium networks. *IEEE Computer Graphics and Applications, 20*(1), 60–61.

Dietz, P. H., & Yerazunis, W. S. (2001). Real-time audio buffering for telephone applications. In *ACM Symposium on User Interface Software and Technology* (pp. 193–194). Vancouver, British Columbia: ACM Press. Retrieved May 5, 2003, from portal.acm.org/citation.cfm?id= 502383&coll=portal&dl=acm&cfid=3078403&cftoken=37958653

Johnson, A., Leigh, J., Carter, B., Sosnoski, J., & Jones, S. (2002). Virtual Harlem. *IEEE Computer Graphics and Applications, 22*(5), 61–67.

Johnson, S. (2001). *Emergence: The connected lives of ants, brains, cities, and software.* New York: Scribner.

Jones, S. G. (1997). The internet and its social landscape. In S. Jones (Ed.), *Virtual culture: Identity and communication in cybersociety* (pp. 7–35). Thousand Oaks, CA: Sage.

Leigh, J., DeFanti, T. A., Johnson, A. E., Brown, M. D., & Sandin, D. J. (1997, December). *Global tele-immersion: Better than being there.* Paper presented at the Seventh International Conference on Artificial Reality and Tele-Existence, Tokyo.

Rheingold, H. (2002). *Smart mobs: The next social revolution.* Cambridge, MA: Perseus.

Rifkin, J. (1987). *Time wars.* New York: Touchstone Books.

Robins, K., & Webster, F. (1999). *Times of the technoculture.* London: Routledge.

Swatch. (n.d.). *Internet time.* [Online]. Retrieved May 15, 2003, from www.swatch.com/fs_index. php?haupt=information&unter=sitemap

Watts, D. (2003). *Six degrees: The science of a connected age.* New York: Norton.

Wolfram, S. (2002). *A new kind of science.* Champaign, IL: Wolfram Media.

Index

About the Editors

Philip N. Howard is Assistant Professor in the Department of Communication at the University of Washington. He has published several articles and chapters on the use of new media in politics and public opinion research, was the first politics research fellow at the Pew Internet and American Life Project, and currently serves on the advisory board of the Survey2001 project. He teaches courses in political communication, organizational behavior, and international media systems and is currently preparing a book-length manuscript titled *Politics In Code: Franchise and Representation in the Age of New Media*.

Steve Jones is Professor and Head of the Department of Communication at the University of Illinois at Chicago. He is the author or editor of numerous books, including *Doing Internet Research, The Encyclopedia of New Media, CyberSociety,* and *Virtual Culture*. He is cofounder and president of the Association of Internet Researchers and is coeditor of *New Media & Society,* an international journal of research on new media, technology, and culture. He also edits *New Media Cultures,* a series of books on culture and technology (Sage), and *Digital Formations,* a series of books on new media.

About the Contributors

William Sims Bainbridge is Deputy Director of the Division of Information and Intelligent Systems at the National Science Foundation, after having directed the division's Human Computer Interaction, Universal Access, and Knowledge and Cognitive Systems programs. He received his Ph.D. from Harvard University. He is the author of 10 books, 4 textbook-software packages, and approximately 150 shorter publications in information science, social science of technology, and sociology of culture. His software employs innovative techniques to teach theory and methodology: Experiments in Psychology, Sociology Laboratory, Survey Research, and Social Research Methods and Statistics. Most recently, he coedited *Converging Technologies to Improve Human Performance*, which explores the combination of nanotechnology, biotechnology, information technology, and cognitive science.

Dan L. Burk is Professor at the University of Minnesota Law School, specializing in the areas of cyberlaw and biotechnology. He holds appointments at both the law school and the Center for Bioethics and has also been closely involved in the development of the new Joint Degree Program in Law, Health, and the Life Sciences and in the creation of the university's new Internet Studies Center. His publications include "Cyberlaw and the Norms of Science" (in *Intellectual Property & Technology Forum*), "Virtual Exit in the Global Information Economy" (in *Chicago-Kent Law Review*), "Trademark Doctrines for Global Electronic Commerce" (in *South Caroline Law Review*), and "Ownership Issues in Online Use of Institutional Materials" (in *Cause/Effect*).

Carin Dessauer is a principal with mc2 and a Senior Fellow with the American Press Institute. She is a former CNN and CNN.com executive and a recent fellowship professor at the George Washington University School of Media and Public Affairs. She has served as a contributing editor to *Campaigns and Elections* and as associate editor for *Congressional Quarterly's 1990 Politics in America*.

Kirsten A. Foot is Assistant Professor in the Department of Communication at the University of Washington. She is interested in the reciprocal relationship between information/communication technologies and society. Her current research projects include a comparative study of mayoral candidate Web sites and analyses of the Web spheres that developed around the events of September 11, 2001, and in anticipation of the 2002 U.S. elections. She is codirector of the WebArchivist.org research group, where she is developing new techniques for studying social and political action on the Web. She is also coeditor of the book series *Acting With Technology*.

Philip Garland is a second-year M.A. student in the Department of Communication at the University of Washington. He is interested in the intersection of American politics, media, and race as well as inconsistencies in new media or the "digital divide" along racial lines. His current work focuses on racial profiling discourse before and after September 11, 2001, and how rap music, as black political speech, is covered in the news media.

Wendy Griswold is Professor of Sociology and Comparative Literary Studies at Northwestern University. She received her Ph.D. from Harvard University and has taught at Harvard and the University of Chicago. Her research and teaching interests center on cultural sociology; sociological approaches to literature, art, and religion; time and place; and comparative studies in Europe and Africa. Her recent books include *Bearing Witness: Readers, Writers, and the Novel in Nigeria* (2000) and *Cultures and Societies in a Changing World* (1994), which has been translated into Japanese and Italian. She is writing a book on cultural regionalism titled *Regionalism and the Reading Class*. She directs the Culture and Society Workshop at Northwestern.

Laura J. Gurak is Associate Professor of Rhetoric at the University of Minnesota. Her research emphasis in on the rhetorics of science and technology, rhetorical criticism, internet studies, online research methods, social aspects of computing, law and technology (intellectual property and privacy), electronic literacies, and technical and professional communication. Her books include *Cyberliteracy: Navigating the Internet With Awareness* and *Persuasion and Privacy in Cyberspace: The Online Protests Over Lotus MarketPlace and the Clipper Chip*.

Eszter Hargittai is Assistant Professor in the Department of Communication at Northwestern University. Her research focuses on the increasing role of commercial interests in channeling information toward users. Her publications include "Open Portals or Closed Gates? Channeling Content on the World Wide Web" (in *Poetics*),, "Radio's Lessons for the Internet" (in *Communications of the ACM*), and "Weaving the Western Web: Explaining Differences in Internet Connectivity Among OECD Countries" (in *Telecommunications Policy*). She is also Associate Director of the International Networks Archive, whose aim is to assemble data sets relevant to empirical research on mapping globalization in a central location and to standardize them so that the various indicators can be combined.

James E. Katz is Professor in the Department of Communication at Rutgers University. His enduring research interest has been to understand how the interplay between technology and social processes affects interpersonal power, organizational structures, and the creation of cultural meaning. He has won postdoctoral fellowships at Harvard University and the Massachusetts Institute of Technology, served on the faculties of the University of Texas at Austin and Clarkson University, and headed the social science research unit at Bell Communication Research (Bellcore). He was granted national and foreign patents on his inventions in telecommunications technology and is the author of several books in the field of technology and society, including *Connections: Social and Cultural Studies of the Telephone in American Life* (1999), which has been cited in *Choice* as a "landmark" study.

Meyer Kestnbaum is Professor in the Department of Sociology at the University of Maryland. He received his Ph.D., A.M., and A.B. from Harvard University. His publications include "War and the Development of Modern National States" with Theda Skocpol (in *Sociological Forum*) and "Mars Unshackled: The French Revolution in World-Historical Perspective" with Theda Skocpol (in *The French Revolution and the Birth of Modernity*). His current research includes work on state building during times of revolution and a new project titled "Bridging the Gap: Assuring Military Effectiveness When Military Culture Diverges From Civilian Society," under the aegis of the Triangle Institute for Security Studies.

Nalini P. Kotamraju is completing the Ph.D. in sociology at the University of California, Berkeley. She is collaborating with Nina Wakeford on the Mobile Devices and the Cultural Worlds of Young People Project, a comparative ethnography of young people and mobile phones in the United Kingdom and the United States, sponsored by the Annenberg Center for Communication. Her publications include "Keeping Up: Web Design Skill and the Reinvented Worker" (in *Information Communication and Society*) and "The Birth of Web Site Design Skills: Making the Present History" (in *American Behavioral Scientist*). She has also done research for Sun Microsystems, Productopia, and Liquid Thinking.

Elena Larsen is Research Fellow at the Pew Internet and American Life Project. She has a master's degree from the Annenberg School for Communication at the University of Pennsylvania, where her major research projects included analysis of wireless broadband technology policy and a study of the 2000 presidential election campaign on the Internet. She filled her time between college and graduate school by working as a program analyst for the Department of the Treasury.

Lisa Nakamura is Assistant Professor of Communication Arts and Visual Culture Studies at the University of Wisconsin–Madison. She is the author of *Cybertypes: Race, Ethnicity, and Identity on the Internet* (2002) and a coeditor of *Race in Cyberspace* (2000). She has published articles on cross-racial role-playing in Internet chat spaces; race, embodiment, and virtuality in the film *The Matrix;* and political economies of race and cyberspace in publications such as the *Women's Review of Books, Unspun: Key Terms for the World Wide*

Web, The Cybercultures Reader, and *The Visual Culture Reader 2.0.* She is working on a new book tentatively titled *Visual Cultures of Race in Cyberspace.*

Gina Neff is Assistant Professor in the Department of Communication at the University of California, San Diego. She received her Ph.D. from the Department of Sociology at Columbia University, where she was a research associate in the Center on Organizational Innovation. Her doctoral research, titled *Organizing Uncertainty in Silicon Alley,* looks at the ways in which risk and uncertainty were experienced in New York City during the early days of the internet. She is also working on a comparative project that examines social networking practices in the internet industry in New York and Berlin, and she is analyzing the emergence of social structure in an online classroom.

Alan Neustadtl is Associate Professor of Sociology at the University of Maryland. He received his Ph.D. from the University of Massachusetts, Amherst. His research is focused on the distribution of political power across interest groups, campaign finance, and the networks of corporate political action. His books include *Money Talks* and *Dollars and Votes.* His current research interests include examining the nature of the growth of internet use by Americans, with special consideration of internet use for political and cultural purposes, and the nature and existence of a "digital divide."

Pippa Norris is McGuire Lecturer in Comparative Politics at the John F. Kennedy School of Government at Harvard University. Her research compares elections and public opinion, political communications, and gender politics. Her books include *Democratic Phoenix: Political Activism Worldwide,* which focuses on how political activism has been reinvented for modern times, and two books scheduled for publication in 2003: *Rising Tide: Gender Equality and Cultural Change Around the World* (with Ron Inglehart) and *Electoral Engineering: Voting Rules and Political Behavior.*

Richard A. Peterson is Professor of Sociology at Vanderbilt University. His research interests are in the music industry, taste and stratification, and production of culture. His current research projects examine the aging of the fine arts audience, scenes where music genres are created, and the spread of omnivorous tastes. His recent articles include "Two Ways Culture Is Produced" (in *Poetics*), "Alternative Country: Origins, Music, World-view, Fans, and Taste in Genre Formation" with Bruce A. Beal (in *Popular Music and Society*), and a chapter titled "The Re-Creation Indicator" with Carrie Y. Lee (in *Quality of Life Indicators: A New Tool for Assessing National Trends*). His recent book is *The Aging of Arts Audiences National Endowment for the Arts* (with Pamela Hull and Roger Kern).

Harrison "Lee" Rainie is Director of the Pew Internet and American Life Project, a research center that examines the social impact of the Internet, specifically focusing on how people's Internet use affects families, communities, health care, education, civic and political life, and workplaces. Prior to receiving the Pew grant, he was managing editor of

U.S. News & World Report. He is a graduate of Harvard University and has a master's degree in political science from Long Island University.

Ronald E. Rice is Professor and Chairperson of the Department of Communication at Rutgers University. He received his Ph.D. from Stanford University and has corporate experience in systems and communication analysis, banking operations, data processing management, publishing, and statistical consulting. He has published widely in communication science, public communication campaigns, computer-mediated communication systems, information systems, information science and bibliometrics, and social networks. His most recent coauthored or coedited books include *Public Communication Campaigns* (2001), *The Internet and Health Communication* (2001), *Accessing and Browsing Information and Communication* (2001), and *Social Consequences of Internet Use: Access, Involvement, and Interaction* (2002).

John P. Robinson is Professor of Sociology at the University of Maryland, where he also directs the Internet Scholars Program and the Americans' Use of Time Project. He received his Ph.D. from the University of Michigan. He is an expert on time use, societal trends and social change, the impact of the mass media and the internet on society, and social science methodology. He is the author of *Time for Life: The Surprising Ways Americans Spend Time* (1997), *Measures of Political Attitudes* (1999), and *Measures of Personality and Social Psychological Attitudes* (1991). He is the cofounder and editor of the journal *IT & Society.* His more recent articles on the internet and time displacement have appeared in *IT & Society* and *Social Science Computer Review.* He has codirected the University of Maryland's summer "Webshop," in which 50 top graduate students from around the country interact with leading internet scholars.

John Ryan is Professor in and Chairperson of the Department of Sociology at Virginia Tech. His research focuses on the sociology of work, organizations, and occupations, with an emphasis on mass media, industries, and emerging technologies. He also has a long-term interest in the digital transformation of culture industries, with a particular focus on copyright law. His most recent book is *Media and Society: The Production of Culture in the Mass Media* (with William Wentworth).

Saskia Sassen is Ralph Lewis Professor of Sociology at the University of Chicago. She is the author of several books, most recently *Guests and Aliens* (1999), and is the editor of *Global Networks/Linked Cities* (2002). She chairs the newly formed Information Technology, International Cooperation, and Global Security Committee of the Social Science Research Council for the United States.

Steven M. Schneider is Associate Professor of Political Science at the State University of New York Institute of Technology and Codirector of WebArchivist.org. His research focuses on the impact of the Internet on political and social life as well as on the development of systems to identify, collect, analyze, and access large-scale archives of born-digital materials for scholarly study. His recent research has examined the emergence of online structures for political action on campaign Web sites in the United States and the potential for expanding the public sphere through Internet-based persistent conversation.

Leslie Regan Shade is Assistant Professor in the Department of Communication at Concordia University in Montreal, where her research and teaching focus on the social, ethical, and policy aspects of information and communication technologies. She is the author of *Gender and Community in the Social Construction of the Internet* (2002) and is the coeditor of *Mediascapes: New Patterns in Canadian Communication* (2002), *Civic Discourse and Cultural Politics in Canada* (2002), and *E-Commerce vs. E-Commons: Communications in the Public Interest* (2001). Her current research focuses on how children and youth are using the Internet in their homes, and she is preparing a book on Internet policy.

David Silver is Assistant Professor in the Department of Communication at the University of Washington. His research interests focus primarily on the intersections among computers, the internet, and contemporary American cultures. Since 1996, he has been building the Resource Center for Cyberculture Studies, an online, not-for-profit organization whose purpose is to research, study, teach, support, and create diverse and dynamic elements of cyberculture.

David Stark is Arnold A. Saltzman Professor of Sociology and International Affairs at Columbia University, where he directs the Center on Organizational Innovation, and is External Faculty Member of the Santa Fe Institute. He is a major contributor to the new economic sociology and examines problems of worth and value in various organizational contexts. He is currently studying the coevolution of collaborative organizational forms and interactive technologies. His current research in Eastern Europe includes a multi-country study of how nongovernmental organizations use new information technologies as well as a longitudinal analysis of the patterns of ownership and organizational change among the largest 1,800 Hungarian enterprises during the past decade of transformation.

Doreen Starke-Meyerring is Assistant Professor in the Department of Communication at McGill University. She received her Ph.D. from the Department of Rhetoric at the University of Minnesota. Her research focuses on the intersections between culture and rhetoric on and about the internet, especially in the context of higher education. She is a coauthor of *Partnering in the Learning Marketspace* (2001).

Jennifer Stromer-Galley is Assistant Professor in the Department of Communication at the University at Albany, State University of New York. She conducted her research on Internet voting as a doctoral candidate at the Annenberg School for Communication at the University of Pennsylvania. Her research interests include the uses of communication technology and implications for democratic practice, and her current work investigates the motives people have for using political chat spaces online. Her recent publications can be found in the *Journal of Communication, Javnost/The Public,* and *Journal of Computer-Mediated Communication.*

James Witte is Associate Professor in the Department of Sociology at Clemson University. His ongoing research focuses on ways in which to use the World Wide Web to collect survey data and on similarities and differences between society online and society offline. His other research area builds on his dissertation, *Labor Force Integration and Marital Choice,* and examines different ways in which labor market forces construct and define individual identity.

Nathan Wright is completing his Ph.D. in sociology at Northwestern University. His main areas of interest include religion, consumption, and popular culture. He is the coauthor of a paper titled "Cowbirds, Locals, and the Dynamic Endurance of Regionalism" (with Wendy Griswold).